ABOUT THIS PUBLICATION

FOR SERVICE ASSISTANCE

Customer Service
1.704.898.0770

North Carolina General Statues is published by The Muliti-Media Group of Greater Charlotte in Charlotte, North Carolina. Copyright 2015 by the Multi-Media Group of Greater Charlotte. This book or parts thereof may not be reproduced in any form, stored in a retrieval system, or transmitted in any form by any means—electronic, mechanical, photocopy, recording or otherwise—without prior written permission of the publisher, except as provided by United States of America copyright law.

The records required by U.S. Code 2257(a) through (c) and the pertinent regulations 28 C.F.R. Cli. 1, Part 75 with respect to this publication and all materials associated with such records are maintained by The Multi-Media Group of Greater Charlotte, Publisher and available for review by Attorney General.

www.visionbooks.org

Copyright © 2015 by MMGGC
All rights reserved!

TID: 5109337
ISBN (10) digit: 1503254844
ISBN (13) digit: 978-1503254848

123-4-56789-01239-Paperback
123-4-56789-01239-Hardback

First Edition

090520140547

Printed in the United States of America

2015 EDITION

North Carolina Criminal Law

And Procedure-Pamphlet # 91

Printed In conjunction with the Administration of the Courts

North Carolina Criminal Law and Procedure
Pamphlet Reference Guide

Chapters	Pamphlet
Chapter 1 Civil Procedure	1
Chapter 1 Civil Procedure (Continue)	2
Chapter 1A Rules of Civil Procedure	2
Chapter 1B Contribution.	2
Chapter 1C Enforcement of Judgments.	2
Chapter 1D Punitive Damages.	2
Chapter 1E Eastern Band of Cherokee Indians.	2
Chapter 1F North Carolina Uniform Interstate Depositions and Discovery Act.	2
Chapter 2 - Clerk of Superior Court [Repealed and Transferred.]	3
Chapter 3 - Commissioners of Affidavits and Deeds [Repealed.]	3
Chapter 4 - Common Law	3
Chapter 5 - Contempt [Repealed.]	3
Chapter 5A - Contempt	3
Chapter 6 - Liability for Court Costs	3
Chapter 7 - Courts [Repealed and Transferred.]	3
Chapter 7A – Judicial Department	3
Chapter 7A – Continuation (Judicial Department)	4
Chapter 7A – Continuation (Judicial Department)	5
Chapter 7B - Juvenile Code	5
Chapter 8 - Evidence	6
Chapter 8A - Interpreters for Deaf Persons [Recodified.]	6
Chapter 8B - Interpreters for Deaf Persons	6
Chapter 8C - Evidence Code	6
Chapter 9 - Jurors	6
Chapter 10 - Notaries [Repealed.]	6
Chapter 10A - Notaries [Recodified.]	6
Chapter 10B - Notaries	6
Chapter 11 - Oaths	6
Chapter 12 - Statutory Construction	6
Chapter 13 - Citizenship Restored	6
Chapter 14 - Criminal Law	7
Chapter 14 –Criminal Law (Continuation)	8
Chapter 15 - Criminal Procedure	9
Chapter 15A - Criminal Procedure Act (Continuation)	10
Chapter 15A - Criminal Procedure Act (Continuation)	11
Chapter 15B - Victims Compensation	11
Chapter 15C - Address Confidentiality Program	11
Chapter 16 - Gaming Contracts and Futures	11
Chapter 17 - Habeas Corpus	11

Chapter 17A - Law-Enforcement Officers [Recodified.]	11
Chapter 17B - North Carolina Criminal Justice Education and Training System [Recodified.] Chapter 17C - North Carolina Criminal Justice Education and Training Standards Commission	11
	11
Chapter 17D - North Carolina Justice Academy	11
Chapter 17E - North Carolina Sheriffs' Education and Training Standards Commission	11
Chapter 18 - Regulation of Intoxicating Liquors [Repealed.]	12
Chapter 18A - Regulation of Intoxicating Liquors [Repealed.]	12
Chapter 18B - Regulation of Alcoholic Beverages	12
Chapter 18C - North Carolina State Lottery	12
Chapter 19 - Offenses against Public Morals	12
Chapter 19A - Protection of Animals	12
Chapter 20 - Motor Vehicles	13
Chapter 20 - Motor Vehicles (Continuation)	14
Chapter 20 - Motor Vehicles (Continuation)	15
Chapter 20 - Motor Vehicles (Continuation)	16
Chapter 21 - Bills of Lading	17
Chapter 22 - Contracts Requiring Writing	17
Chapter 22A - Signatures	17
Chapter 22B - Contracts Against Public Policy	17
Chapter 22C - Payments to Subcontractors	17
Chapter 23 - Debtor and Creditor	17
Chapter 24 – Interest	17
Chapter 25 – Uniform Commercial Code	18
Chapter 25 – Uniform Commercial Code (Continuation)	19
Chapter 25A – Retail Installment Sales Act	20
Chapter 25B - Credit	20
Chapter 25C - Sales of Artwork	20
Chapter 26 - Suretyship	20
Chapter 27 - Warehouse Receipts [Repealed.]	20
Chapter 28 - Administration [Repealed.]	20
Chapter 28A - Administration of Decedents' Estates	20
Chapter 28B - Estates of Absentees in Military Service	20
Chapter 28C - Estates of Missing Persons	20
Chapter 29 - Intestate Succession	21
Chapter 30 - Surviving Spouses	21
Chapter 31 - Wills	21
Chapter 31A - Acts Barring Property Rights	21
Chapter 31B - Renunciation of Property and Renunciation of Fiduciary Powers Act	21
Chapter 31C - Uniform Disposition of Community Property Rights at Death Act	21
Chapter 32 - Fiduciaries	21
Chapter 32A - Powers of Attorney	21
Chapter 33 - Guardian and Ward [Repealed and Recodified.]	21

Chapter 33A - North Carolina Uniform Transfers to Minors Act	21
Chapter 33B - North Carolina Uniform Custodial Trust Act	21
Chapter 34 - Veterans' Guardianship Act	22
Chapter 35 - Sterilization Procedures	22
Chapter 35A - Incompetency and Guardianship	22
Chapter 36 - Trusts and Trustees [Repealed.]	22
Chapter 36A - Trusts and Trustees	22
Chapter 36B - Uniform Management of Institutional Funds Act [Repealed.]	22
Chapter 36C - North Carolina Uniform Trust Code	22
Chapter 36D - North Carolina Community Third Party Trusts, Pooled Trusts	23
Chapter 36E - Uniform Prudent Management of Institutional Funds Act	23
Chapter 37 - Allocation of Principal and Income [Repealed.]	23
Chapter 37A - Uniform Principal and Income Act	23
Chapter 38 - Boundaries	23
Chapter 38A - Landowner Liability	23
Chapter 39 - Conveyances	23
Chapter 39A - Transfer Fee Covenants Prohibited	23
Chapter 40 - Eminent Domain [Repealed.]	23
Chapter 40A - Eminent Domain	23
Chapter 41 - Estates	23
Chapter 41A - State Fair Housing Act	23
Chapter 42 - Landlord and Tenant	23
Chapter 42A - Vacation Rental Act	23
Chapter 43 - Land Registration	23
Chapter 44 - Liens	24
Chapter 44A - Statutory Liens and Charges	24
Chapter 45 - Mortgages and Deeds of Trust	24
Chapter 45A - Good Funds Settlement Act	24
Chapter 46 - Partition	24
Chapter 47 - Probate and Registration	25
Chapter 47A - Unit Ownership	25
Chapter 47B - Real Property Marketable Title Act	25
Chapter 47C - North Carolina Condominium Act	25
Chapter 47D - Notice of Settlement Act [Expired.]	25
Chapter 47E - Residential Property Disclosure Act	25
Chapter 47F - North Carolina Planned Community Act	25
Chapter 47G - Option to Purchase Contracts	25
Chapter 47H - Contracts for Deed	25
Chapter 48 - Adoptions	26
Chapter 48A - Minors	26
Chapter 49 - Bastardy	26
Chapter 49A - Rights of Children	26
Chapter 50 - Divorce and Alimony	26
Chapter 50A - Uniform Child-Custody Jurisdiction and	

Enforcement Act	26
Chapter 50B - Domestic Violence	26
Chapter 50C - Civil No-Contact Orders	26
Chapter 51 - Marriage	26
Chapter 52 - Powers and Liabilities of Married Persons	27
Chapter 52A - Uniform Reciprocal Enforcement of Support Act [Repealed.]	27
Chapter 52B - Uniform Premarital Agreement Act	27
Chapter 52C - Uniform Interstate Family Support Act	27
Chapter 53 - Banks	27
Chapter 53A - Business Development Corporations and North Carolina Capital Resource Corporations	28
Chapter 53B - Financial Privacy Act	28
Chapter 54 - Cooperative Organizations	28
Chapter 54A - Capital Stock Savings and Loan Associations [Repealed.]	28
Chapter 54B - Savings and Loan Associations	29
Chapter 54C - Savings Banks	29
Chapter 55 - North Carolina Business Corporation Act	30
Chapter 55A - North Carolina Nonprofit Corporation Act	31
Chapter 55B - Professional Corporation Act	31
Chapter 55C - Foreign Trade Zones	31
Chapter 55D - Filings, Names, and Registered Agents for Corporations, Nonprofit Corporations, and Partnerships	31
Chapter 56 - Electric, Telegraph and Power Companies [Repealed.]	31
Chapter 57 - Hospital, Medical and Dental Service Corporations [Recodified.]	31
Chapter 57A - Health Maintenance Organization Act [Recodified.]	31
Chapter 57B - Health Maintenance Organization Act [Recodified.]	31
Chapter 57C - North Carolina Limited Liability Company Act	31
Chapter 58 - Insurance.	32
Chapter 58 - Insurance (Continuation)	33
Chapter 58 - Insurance (Continuation)	34
Chapter 58 - Insurance (Continuation)	35
Chapter 58 - Insurance (Continuation)	36
Chapter 58 - Insurance (Continuation)	37
Chapter 58 - Insurance (Continuation)	38
Chapter 58A - North Carolina Health Insurance Trust Commission [Recodified.]	38
Chapter 59 - Partnership.	39
Chapter 59B - Uniform Unincorporated Nonprofit Association Act.	39
Chapter 60 - Railroads and Other Carriers [Repealed and Transferred.]	39
Chapter 61 - Religious Societies	39
Chapter 62 - Public Utilities	39

Chapter 62 - Public Utilities (Continuation)	40
Chapter 62A - Public Safety Telephone Service And Wireless Telephone Service	40
Chapter 63 - Aeronautics	40
Chapter 63A - North Carolina Global TransPark Authority	40
Chapter 64 - Aliens	40
Chapter 65 – Cemeteries	40
Chapter 66 - Commerce and Business	41
Chapter 67 - Dogs	41
Chapter 68 - Fences and Stock Law	41
Chapter 69 - Fire Protection	41
Chapter 70 - Indian Antiquities, Archaeological Resources and Unmarked Human Skeletal Remains Protection	42
Chapter 71 - Indians [Repealed.]	42
Chapter 71A - Indians	42
Chapter 72 - Inns, Hotels and Restaurants	42
Chapter 73 - Mills	42
Chapter 74 - Mines and Quarries	42
Chapter 74A - Company Police [Repealed.]	42
Chapter 74B - Private Protective Services Act [Repealed.]	42
Chapter 74C - Private Protective Services	42
Chapter 74D - Alarm Systems	42
Chapter 74E - Company Police Act	42
Chapter 74F - Locksmith Licensing Act	42
Chapter 74G - Campus Police Act	42
Chapter 75 - Monopolies, Trusts and Consumer Protection	42
Chapter 75A - Boating and Water Safety	43
Chapter 75B - Discrimination in Business	43
Chapter 75C - Motion Picture Fair Competition Act	43
Chapter 75D - Racketeer Influenced and Corrupt Organizations	43
Chapter 75E - Unlawful Activities in Connection With Certain Corporate Transactions	43
Chapter 76 - Navigation	43
Chapter 76A - Navigation and Pilotage Commissions	43
Chapter 77 - Rivers, Creeks, and Coastal Waters	43
Chapter 78 - Securities Law [Repealed.]	43
Chapter 78A - North Carolina Securities Act	43
Chapter 78B - Tender Offer Disclosure Act [Repealed.]	43
Chapter 78C - Investment Advisers	43
Chapter 78D - Commodities Act	43
Chapter 79 - Strays [Repealed.]	43
Chapter 80 - Trademarks, Brands, etc.	44
Chapter 81 - Weights and Measures [Recodified.]	44
Chapter 81A - Weights and Measures Act of 1975.	44
Chapter 82 - Wrecks [Repealed.]	44
Chapter 83 - Architects [Recodified.]	44

Chapter 83A - Architects	44
Chapter 84 - Attorneys-at-Law	44
Chapter 84A - Foreign Legal Consultants	44
Chapter 85 - Auctions and Auctioneers [Repealed.]	44
Chapter 85A - Bail Bondsmen and Runners [Recodified.]	44
Chapter 85B - Auctions and Auctioneers	44
Chapter 85C - Bail Bondsmen and Runners [Recodified.]	44
Chapter 86 - Barbers [Recodified.]	44
Chapter 86A - Barbers	44
Chapter 87 - Contractors	44
Chapter 88 - Cosmetic Art [Repealed.]	44
Chapter 88A - Electrolysis Practice Act	44
Chapter 88B - Cosmetic Art	45
Chapter 89 - Engineering and Land Surveying [Recodified.]	45
Chapter 89A - Landscape Architects	45
Chapter 89B - Foresters	45
Chapter 89C - Engineering and Land Surveying	45
Chapter 89D - Landscape Contractors	45
Chapter 89E - Geologists Licensing Act	45
Chapter 89F - North Carolina Soil Scientist Licensing Act	45
Chapter 89G - Irrigation Contractors	45
Chapter 90 - Medicine and Allied Occupations	45
Chapter 90 - Medicine and Allied Occupations (Continuation)	46
Chapter 90 - Medicine and Allied Occupations (Continuation)	47
Chapter 90 - Medicine and Allied Occupations (Continuation)	48
Chapter 90A - Sanitarians and Water and Wastewater Treatment Facility Operators	48
Chapter 90B - Social Worker Certification and Licensure Act	48
Chapter 90C - North Carolina Recreational Therapy Licensure Act	48
Chapter 90D - Interpreters and Transliterators	48
Chapter 91 - Pawnbrokers [Repealed.]	48
Chapter 91A - Pawnbrokers Modernization Act of 1989	48
Chapter 92 - Photographers [Deleted.]	48
Chapter 93 - Certified Public Accountants	48
Chapter 93A - Real Estate License Law	49
Chapter 93B - Occupational Licensing Boards	49
Chapter 93C - Watchmakers [Repealed.]	49
Chapter 93D - North Carolina State Hearing Aid Dealers and Fitters Board.	49
Chapter 93E - North Carolina Appraisers Act	49
Chapter 94 - Apprenticeship	49
Chapter 95 - Department of Labor and Labor Regulations	49
Chapter 95 - Department of Labor and Labor Regulations (Continuation)	50
Chapter 96 - Employment Security	50
Chapter 97 - Workers' Compensation Act	50
Chapter 97 - Workers' Compensation Act (Continuation)	51

Chapter 98 - Burnt and Lost Records	51
Chapter 99 - Libel and Slander	51
Chapter 99A - Civil Remedies for Criminal Actions	51
Chapter 99B - Products Liability	51
Chapter 99C - Actions Relating to Winter Sports Safety and Accidents	51
Chapter 99D - Civil Rights	51
Chapter 99E - Special Liability Provisions	51
Chapter 100 - Monuments, Memorials and Parks	51
Chapter 101 - Names of Persons	51
Chapter 102 - Official Survey Base	51
Chapter 103 - Sundays, Holidays and Special Days	51
Chapter 104 - United States Lands	51
Chapter 104A - Degrees of Kinship	51
Chapter 104B - Hurricanes or Other Acts of Nature	51
Chapter 104C - Atomic Energy, Radioactivity and Ionizing Radiation [Repealed and Recodified.]	51
Chapter 104D - Southern States Energy Compact	51
Chapter 104E - North Carolina Radiation Protection Act	51
Chapter 104F - Southeast Interstate Low-Level Radioactive Waste Management Compact [Repealed]	51
Chapter 104G - North Carolina Low-Level Radioactive Waste Management Authority Act of 1987 [Repealed]	51
Chapter 105 - Taxation	51
Chapter 105 - Taxation (Continuation)	52
Chapter 105 - Taxation (Continuation)	53
Chapter 105 - Taxation (Continuation)	54
Chapter 105A - Setoff Debt Collection Act	55
Chapter 105B - Defaulted Student Loan Recovery Act	55
Chapter 106 - Agriculture	55
Chapter 106 - Agriculture (Continue)	56
Chapter 106 - Agriculture (Continue)	57
Chapter 107 - Agricultural Development Districts [Repealed.]	57
Chapter 108 - Social Services [Repealed and Recodified.]	57
Chapter 108A - Social Services	57
Chapter 108B - Community Action Programs	58
Chapter 108C Medicaid and Health Choice Provider Requirements.	58
Chapter 108D Medicaid Managed Care for Behavioral Health Services.	58
Chapter 109 - Bonds [Recodified.]	58
Chapter 110 - Child Welfare	58
Chapter 111 - Aid to the Blind	58
Chapter 112 - Confederate Homes and Pensions [Repealed.]	58
Chapter 113 - Conservation and Development	58
Chapter 113 - Conservation and Development (Continuation)	59

Chapter 113A - Pollution Control and Environment	59
Chapter 113A - Pollution Control and Environment (Continuation)	60
Chapter 113B - North Carolina Energy Policy Act of 1975	60
Chapter 114 - Department of Justice	60
Chapter 115 - Elementary and Secondary Education [Repealed.]	60
Chapter 115A - Community Colleges, Technical Institutes, and Industrial Education Centers [Repealed.]	60
Chapter 115B - Tuition and Fee Waivers	60
Chapter 115C - Elementary and Secondary Education	60
Chapter 115C - Elementary and Secondary Education (Continuation)	61
Chapter 115C - Elementary and Secondary Education (Continuation)	62
Chapter 115C - Elementary and Secondary Education (Continuation)	63
Chapter 115D - Community Colleges	63
Chapter 115E - Private Educational Facilities Finance Act [Recodified]	63
Chapter 116 - Higher Education	63
Chapter 116 - Higher Education (Continuation)	63
Chapter 116A - Escheats and Abandoned Property [Repealed.]	64
Chapter 116B - Escheats and Abandoned Property	64
Chapter 116C - Continuum of Education Programs	64
Chapter 116D - Higher Education Bonds	64
Chapter 116E - Education Longitudinal Data System	64
Chapter 117 - Electrification	64
Chapter 118 - Firemen's and Rescue Squad Workers' Relief and Pension Funds [Recodified.]	64
Chapter 118A - Firemen's Death Benefit Act [Repealed.]	64
Chapter 118B - Members of a Rescue Squad Death Benefit Act [Repealed.]	64
Chapter 119 - Gasoline and Oil Inspection and Regulation	64
Chapter 120 - General Assembly	65
Chapter 120 - General Assembly (Continuation)	66
Chapter 120 - General Assembly (Continuation)	67
Chapter 120C - Lobbying	67
Chapter 121 - Archives and History	67
Chapter 122 - Hospitals for the Mentally Disordered [Repealed.]	67
Chapter 122A - North Carolina Housing Finance Agency	67
Chapter 122B - North Carolina Agricultural Facilities Finance Act [Repealed.]	67
Chapter 122C - Mental Health, Developmental Disabilities, and Substance Abuse Act of 1985	67
Chapter 122C - Mental Health, Developmental Disabilities, and Substance Abuse Act of 1985 (Continuation)	68

Chapter 122D - North Carolina Agricultural Finance Act	68
Chapter 122E - North Carolina Housing Trust and Oil Overcharge Act	68
Chapter 123 - Impeachment	69
Chapter 123A - Industrial Development [Repealed.]	69
Chapter 124 - Internal Improvements	69
Chapter 125 - Libraries	69
Chapter 126 - State Personnel System	69
Chapter 127 - Militia [Repealed.]	69
Chapter 127A - Militia	69
Chapter 127B - Military Affairs	69
Chapter 127C - Advisory Commission on Military Affairs	69
Chapter 128 - Offices and Public Officers	69
Chapter 128 - Offices and Public Officers (Continuation)	70
Chapter 129 - Public Buildings and Grounds	70
Chapter 130 - Public Health [Repealed.]	70
Chapter 130A - Public Health	70
Chapter 130A - Public Health (Continuation)	71
Chapter 130A - Public Health (Continuation)	72
Chapter 130B - Hazardous Waste Management Commission [Repealed.]	72
Chapter 131 - Public Hospitals [Repealed.]	72
Chapter 131A - Health Care Facilities Finance Act	72
Chapter 131B - Licensing of Ambulatory Surgical Facilities [Repealed.]	72
Chapter 131C - Charitable Solicitation Licensure Act [Repealed.]	72
Chapter 131D - Inspection and Licensing of Facilities	72
Chapter 131E - Health Care Facilities and Services	72
Chapter 131E - Health Care Facilities and Services (Continuation)	73
Chapter 131F - Solicitation of Contributions	73
Chapter 132 - Public Records	73
Chapter 133 - Public Works	74
Chapter 134 - Youth Development [Recodified.]	74
Chapter 134A - Youth Services [Repealed.]	74
Chapter 135 - Retirement System for Teachers and State Employees; Social Security; Health Insurance Program for Children	74
Chapter 135 - Retirement System for Teachers and State Employees; Social Security; Health Insurance Program for Children	75
Chapter 136 - Transportation	75
Chapter 136 - Transportation (Continuation)	76
Chapter 137 - Rural Rehabilitation [Repealed.]	76
Chapter 138 - Salaries, Fees and Allowances	76
Chapter 138A - State Government Ethics Act	76

Chapter 139 - Soil and Water Conservation Districts	76
Chapter 140 - State Art Museum; Symphony and Art Societies	76
Chapter 140A - State Awards System	76
Chapter 141 - State Boundaries	76
Chapter 142 - State Debt	76
Chapter 143 - State Departments, Institutions, and Commissions	77
Chapter 143 - State Departments, Institutions, and Commissions (Continuation)	78
Chapter 143 - State Departments, Institutions, and Commissions (Continuation)	79
Chapter 143 - State Departments, Institutions, and Commissions (Continuation)	80
Chapter 143A - State Government Reorganization	80
Chapter 143B - Executive Organization Act of 1973	80
Chapter 143B - Executive Organization Act of 1973 (Continuation)	81
Chapter 143B - Executive Organization Act of 1973 (Continuation)	82
Chapter 143C - State Budget Act	83
Chapter 143D - The State Governmental Accountability and Internal Control Act	83
Chapter 144 - State Flag, Official Governmental Flags, Motto, and Colors	83
Chapter 145 - State Symbols and Other Official Adoptions.	83
Chapter 146 - State Lands	83
Chapter 147 - State Officers	83
Chapter 148 - State Prison System	84
Chapter 149 - State Song and Toast	84
Chapter 150 - Uniform Revocation of Licenses [Repealed.]	84
Chapter 150A - Administrative Procedure Act [Recodified.]	84
Chapter 150B - Administrative Procedure Act	84
Chapter 151 - Constables [Repealed.]	84
Chapter 152 - Coroners	84
Chapter 152A - County Medical Examiner [Repealed.]	84
Chapter 152A - County Medical Examiner [Repealed.] (Continuation)	84
Chapter 153 - Counties and County Commissioners [Repealed.]	84
Chapter 153A - Counties	84
Chapter 153A - Counties (Continue)	85
Chapter 153B - Mountain Resources Planning Act	85
Chapter 153C - Uwharrie Regional Resources Act	85
Chapter 154 - County Surveyor [Repealed.]	85
Chapter 155 - County Treasurer [Repealed.]	85

Chapter 156 - Drainage	85
Chapter 156 – Drainage (Continuation)	86
Chapter 157 - Housing Authorities and Projects	86
Chapter 157A - Historic Properties Commissions [Transferred.]	86
Chapter 158 - Local Development	86
Chapter 159 - Local Government Finance	86
Chapter 159 - Local Government Finance (Continuation)	87
Chapter 159A - Pollution Abatement and Industrial Facilities Financing Act [Unconstitutional.]	87
Chapter 159B - Joint Municipal Electric Power and Energy Act	87
Chapter 159C - Industrial and Pollution Control Facilities Financing Act	87
Chapter 159D - The North Carolina Capital Facilities Financing Act	87
Chapter 159E - Registered Public Obligations Act	87
Chapter 159F - North Carolina Energy Development Authority [Repealed.]	87
Chapter 159G - Water Infrastructure	87
Chapter 159H - [Reserved.]	87
Chapter 159I - Solid Waste Management Loan Program and Local Government Special Obligation Bonds	87
Chapter 160 - Municipal Corporations [Repealed And Transferred.]	87
Chapter 160A - Cities and Towns	88
Chapter 160A - Cities and Towns (Continuation)	89
Chapter 160B - Consolidated City-County Act	89
Chapter 160C - Baseball Park Districts [Repealed.]	90
Chapter 161 - Register of Deeds	90
Chapter 162 - Sheriff	90
Chapter 162A - Water and Sewer Systems	90
Chapter 162B Continuity of Local Government in Emergency.	90
Chapter 163 Elections and Election Laws.	90
Chapter 163 Elections and Election Laws. (Continuation)	91
Chapter 164 Concerning the General Statutes of North Carolina.	92
Chapter 165 Veterans.	92
Chapter 166 Civil Preparedness Agencies [Repealed.]	92
Chapter 166A North Carolina Emergency Management Act.	92
Chapter 167 State Civil Air Patrol [Repealed.]	92
Chapter 168 Persons with Disabilities.	92
Chapter 168A Persons with Disabilities Protection Act.	92

§ 163-122. Unaffiliated candidates nominated by petition.

(a) Procedure for Having Name Printed on Ballot as Unaffiliated Candidate. - Any qualified voter who seeks to have his name printed on the general election ballot as an unaffiliated candidate shall:

(1) If the office is a statewide office, file written petitions with the State Board of Elections supporting his candidacy for a specified office. These petitions must be filed with the State Board of Elections on or before 12:00 noon on the last Friday in June preceding the general election and must be signed by qualified voters of the State equal in number to two percent (2%) of the total number of voters who voted in the most recent general election for Governor. Also, the petition must be signed by at least 200 registered voters from each of four congressional districts in North Carolina. No later than 5:00 p.m. on the fifteenth day preceding the date the petitions are due to be filed with the State Board of Elections, each petition shall be presented to the chairman of the board of elections of the county in which the signatures were obtained. Provided the petitions are timely submitted, the chairman shall examine the names on the petition and place a check mark on the petition by the name of each signer who is qualified and registered to vote in his county and shall attach to the petition his signed certificate. Said certificates shall state that the signatures on the petition have been checked against the registration records and shall indicate the number of signers to be qualified and registered to vote in his county. The chairman shall return each petition, together with the certificate required in this section, to the person who presented it to him for checking. Verification by the chairman of the county board of elections shall be completed within two weeks from the date such petitions are presented.

(2) If the office is a district office under the jurisdiction of the State Board of Elections under G.S. 163-182.4(b), file written petitions with the State Board of Elections supporting that voter's candidacy for a specified office. These petitions must be filed with the State Board of Elections on or before 12:00 noon on the last Friday in June preceding the general election and must be signed by qualified voters of the district equal in number to four percent (4%) of the total number of registered voters in the district as reflected by the voter registration records of the State Board of Elections as of January 1 of the year in which the general election is to be held. Each petition shall be presented to the chairman of the board of elections of the county in which the signatures were obtained. The chairman shall examine the names on the petition and the procedure for certification and deadline for submission to the county board shall be the same as specified in (1) above.

(3) If the office is a county office or a single county legislative district, file written petitions with the chairman or director of the county board of elections supporting his candidacy for a specified county office. These petitions must be filed with the county board of elections on or before 12:00 noon on the last Friday in June preceding the general election and must be signed by qualified voters of the county equal in number to four percent (4%) of the total number of registered voters in the county as reflected by the voter registration records of the State Board of Elections as of January 1 of the year in which the general election is to be held, except if the office is for a district consisting of less than the entire county and only the voters in that district vote for that office, the petitions must be signed by qualified voters of the district equal in number to four percent (4%) of the total number of voters in the district according to the voter registration records of the State Board of Elections as of January 1 of the year in which the general election is to be held. Each petition shall be presented to the chairman or director of the county board of elections. The chairman shall examine, or cause to be examined, the names on the petition and the procedure for certification shall be the same as specified in (1) above.

(4) If the office is a partisan municipal office, file written petitions with the chairman or director of the county board of elections in the county wherein the municipality is located supporting his candidacy for a specified municipal office. These petitions must be filed with the county board of elections on or before the time and date specified in G.S. 163-296 and must be signed by the number of qualified voters specified in G.S. 163-296. The procedure for certification shall be the same as specified in (1) above.

Upon compliance with the provisions of (1), (2), (3), or (4) of this subsection, the board of elections with which the petitions have been timely filed shall cause the unaffiliated candidate's name to be printed on the general election ballots in accordance with Article 14A of this Chapter.

An individual whose name appeared on the ballot in a primary election preliminary to the general election shall not be eligible to have his name placed on the general election ballot as an unaffiliated candidate for the same office in that year.

(b) Form of Petition. - Petitions requesting an unaffiliated candidate to be placed on the general election ballot shall contain on the heading of each page of the petition in bold print or in all capital letters the words: "THE UNDERSIGNED REGISTERED VOTERS IN _____ COUNTY HEREBY PETITION ON BEHALF OF _____ AS AN UNAFFILIATED CANDIDATE

FOR THE OFFICE OF _____ IN THE NEXT GENERAL ELECTION. THE UNDERSIGNED HEREBY PETITION THAT SUBJECT CANDIDATE BE PLACED ON THE APPROPRIATE BALLOT UPON COMPLIANCE WITH THE PROVISIONS CONTAINED IN G.S. 163-122."

(c) This section does not apply to elections under Article 25 of this Chapter.

(d) When any person files a petition with a board of elections under this section, the board of elections shall, immediately upon receipt of the petition, inspect the registration records of the county and cancel the petition of any person who does not meet the constitutional or statutory qualifications for the office, including residency.

The board shall give notice of cancellation to any person whose petition has been cancelled under this subsection by mail or by having the notice served on that person by the sheriff and to any other candidate filing for the same office. A person whose petition has been cancelled or another candidate for the same office affected by a substantiation under this subsection may request a hearing on the issue of constitutional or statutory qualifications for the office. If the person requests a hearing, the hearing shall be conducted in accordance with Article 11B of Chapter 163 of the General Statutes.

(e) Any candidate seeking to have that candidate's name printed on the general election ballot under this section shall pay a filing fee equal to that provided for candidates for the office in G.S. 163-107 or comply with the alternative available to candidates for the office in G.S. 163-107.1. (1929, c. 164, s. 6; 1931, c. 223; 1935, c. 236; 1967, c. 775, s. 1; 1973, c. 793, s. 50; 1977, c. 408, s. 3; 1979, c. 23, ss. 1, 3; c. 534, s. 2; 1981, c. 637; 1991, c. 297, s. 1; 1995, c. 243, s. 1; 1996, 2nd Ex. Sess., c. 9, s. 14; 1999-424, s. 5(b); 2002-159, s. 21(b); 2004-127, s. 8(a); 2006-155, s. 3; 2006-234, ss. 4, 5; 2007-391, s. 8(a); 2007-484, s. 21; 2008-187, s. 33(a).)

§ 163-123. Declaration of intent and petitions for write-in candidates in partisan elections.

(a) Procedure for Qualifying as a Write-In Candidate. - Any qualified voter who seeks to have write-in votes for him counted in a general election shall file a declaration of intent in accordance with subsection (b) of this section and petition(s) in accordance with subsection (c) of this section.

(b) Declaration of Intent. - The applicant for write-in candidacy shall file his declaration of intent at the same time and with the same board of elections as his petition, as set out in subsection (c) of this section. The declaration shall contain:

(1) Applicant's name,

(2) Applicant's residential address,

(3) Declaration of applicant's intent to be a write-in candidate,

(4) Title of the office sought,

(5) Date of the election,

(6) Date of the declaration,

(7) Applicant's signature.

(c) Petitions for Write-in Candidacy. - An applicant for write-in candidacy shall:

(1) If the office is a statewide office, file written petitions with the State Board of Elections supporting his candidacy for a specified office. These petitions shall be filed on or before noon on the 90th day before the general election. They shall be signed by 500 qualified voters of the State. No later than 5:00 p.m. on the fifteenth day preceding the date the petitions are due to be filed with the State Board of Elections, each petition shall be presented to the board of elections of the county in which the signatures were obtained. A petition presented to a county board of elections shall contain only names of voters registered in that county. Provided the petitions are timely submitted, the chairman of the county board of elections shall examine the names on the petition and place a check mark by the name of each signer who is qualified and registered to vote in his county. The chairman of the county board shall attach to the petition his signed certificate. On his certificate the chairman shall state that the signatures on the petition have been checked against the registration records and shall indicate the number of signers who are qualified and registered to vote in his county and eligible to vote for that office. The chairman shall return each petition, together with the certificate required in this section, to the person who presented it to him for checking. The chairman of the county

board shall complete the verification within two weeks from the date the petition is presented.

(2) If the office is a district office under the jurisdiction of the State Board of Elections under G.S. 163-182.4(b), file written petitions with the State Board of Elections supporting that applicant's candidacy for a specified office. These petitions must be filed with the State Board of Elections on or before noon on the 90th day before the general election and must be signed by 250 qualified voters. Before being filed with the State Board of Elections, each petition shall be presented to the board of elections of the county in which the signatures were obtained. A petition presented to a county board of elections shall contain only names of voters registered in that county who are eligible to vote for that office. The chairman of the county board shall examine the names on the petition and the procedure for certification shall be the same as specified in subdivision (1).

(3) If the office is a county office, or is a school administrative unit office elected on a partisan basis, or is a legislative district consisting of a single county or a portion of a county, file written petitions with the county board of elections supporting his candidacy for a specified office. A petition presented to a county board of elections shall contain only names of voters registered in that county. These petitions must be filed on or before noon on the 90th day before the general election and must be signed by 100 qualified voters who are eligible to vote for the office, unless fewer than 5,000 persons are eligible to vote for the office as shown by the most recent records of the appropriate board of elections. If fewer than 5,000 persons are eligible to vote for the office, an applicant's petition must be signed by not less than one percent (1%) of those registered voters. Before being filed with the county board of elections, each petition shall be presented to the county board of elections for examination. The chairman of the county board of elections shall examine the names on the petition and the procedure for certification shall be the same as specified in subdivision (1).

(d) Form of Petition. - Petitions requesting the qualification of a write-in candidate in a general election shall contain on the heading of each page of the petition in bold print or in capital letters the words: "THE UNDERSIGNED REGISTERED VOTERS IN _____ COUNTY HEREBY PETITION ON BEHALF OF _____ AS A WRITE-IN CANDIDATE IN THE NEXT GENERAL ELECTION. THE UNDERSIGNED HEREBY PETITION THAT SUBJECT CANDIDATE BE PLACED ON THE LIST OF QUALIFIED WRITE-IN

CANDIDATES WHOSE VOTES ARE TO BE COUNTED AND RECORDED IN ACCORDANCE WITH G.S. 163-123."

(e) Defeated Primary Candidate. - No person whose name appeared on the ballot in a primary election preliminary to the general election shall be eligible to have votes counted for him as a write-in candidate for the same office in that year.

(f) Counting and Recording of Votes. - If a qualified voter has complied with the provisions of subsections (a), (b), and (c) and is not excluded by subsection (e), the board of elections with which petition has been filed shall count votes for him according to the procedures set out in G.S. 163-182.1, and the appropriate board of elections shall record those votes on the official abstract. Write-in votes for names other than those of qualified write-in candidates shall not be counted for any purpose and shall not be recorded on the abstract.

(f1) When any person files a petition with a board of elections under this section, the board of elections shall, immediately upon receipt of the petition, inspect the registration records of the county and cancel the petition of any person who does not meet the constitutional or statutory qualifications for the office, including residency.

The board shall give notice of cancellation to any person whose petition has been cancelled under this subsection by mail or by having the notice served on that person by the sheriff. A person whose petition has been cancelled or another candidate for the same office affected by a substantiation under this subsection may request a hearing on the issue of constitutional or statutory qualifications for the office. If the person requests a hearing, the hearing shall be conducted in accordance with Article 11B of Chapter 163 of the General Statutes.

(g) Municipal and Nonpartisan Elections Excluded. - This section does not apply to municipal elections conducted under Subchapter IX of Chapter 163 of the General Statutes, and does not apply to nonpartisan elections except for elections under Article 25 of this Chapter. (1987, c. 393, ss. 1; 2; 1989, c. 92, s. 1; 1999-424, s. 5(c); 2001-319, s. 9(a); 2001-398, s. 7; 2001-403, s. 12; 2002-158, s. 13; 2004-127, s. 7; 2006-155, s. 4; 2007-391, s. 8(b); 2008-187, s. 33(a).)

§ 163-124. No run for two separate offices at the same time.

(a) No individual is eligible to have that individual's name on the general election ballot for two separate offices, unless one of the offices is for the remainder of the unexpired term for an office that requires an election to fill the unexpired portion of the term.

(b) This section shall apply to any individual nominated under Article 9 of this Chapter, filing under G.S. 163-106, or filing a petition under this Article. (2011-214, s. 1.)

Article 11A.

Resign-to-Run.

§ 163-125 through 163-127: Repealed by Session Laws 1995, c. 379, s. 18.

Article 11B.

Challenge to a Candidacy.

§ 163-127.1. Definitions.

As used in this Article, the following terms mean:

(1) Board. - State Board of Elections.

(2) Candidate. - A person having filed a notice of candidacy under the appropriate statute for any elective office in this State.

(3) Challenger. - Any qualified voter registered in the same district as the office for which the candidate has filed or petitioned.

(4) Office. - The elected office for which the candidate has filed or petitioned. (2006-155, s. 1; 2006-259, s. 48(a).)

§ 163-127.2. When and how a challenge to a candidate may be made.

(a) When. - A challenge to a candidate may be filed under this Article with the board of elections receiving the notice of the candidacy or petition no later than 10 business days after the close of the filing period for notice of candidacy or petition.

(b) How. - The challenge must be made in a verified affidavit by a challenger, based on reasonable suspicion or belief of the facts stated. Grounds for filing a challenge are that the candidate does not meet the constitutional or statutory qualifications for the office, including residency.

(c) If Defect Discovered After Deadline, Protest Available. - If a challenger discovers one or more grounds for challenging a candidate after the deadline in subsection (a) of this section, the grounds may be the basis for a protest under G.S. 163-182.9. (2006-155, s. 1.)

§ 163-127.3. Panel to conduct the hearing on a challenge.

Upon filing of a challenge, a panel shall hear the challenge, as follows:

(1) Single county. - If the district for the office subject to the challenge covers territory in all or part of only one county, the panel shall be the county board of elections of that county.

(2) Multicounty but less than entire State. - If the district for the office subject to the challenge contains territory in more than one county but is less than the entire State, the Board shall appoint a panel within two business days after the challenge is filed. The panel shall consist of at least one member of the county board of elections in each county in the district of the office. The panel shall have an odd number of members, no fewer than three and no more than five. In appointing members to the panel, the Board shall appoint members from each county in proportion to the relative total number of registered voters of the counties in the district for the office. If the district for the office subject to the challenge covers more than five counties, the panel shall consist of five members with at least one member from the county receiving the notice of candidacy or petition and at least one member from the county of residency of the challenger. The Board shall, to the extent possible, appoint members affiliated with different political parties in proportion to the representation of those parties on the county boards of elections in the district for the office. The Board shall designate a chair for the panel. A meeting of the Board to appoint a

panel under this subdivision shall be treated as an emergency meeting for purposes of G.S. 143-318.12.

(3) Entire State. - If the district for the office subject to the challenge consists of the entire State, the panel shall be the Board. (2006-155, s. 1.)

§ 163-127.4. Conduct of hearing by panel.

(a) The panel conducting a hearing under this Article shall do all of the following:

(1) Within five business days after the challenge is filed, designate and announce the time of the hearing and the facility where the hearing will be held. The hearing shall be held at a location in the district reasonably convenient to the public, and shall preferably be held in the county receiving the notice of the candidacy or petition. If the district for the office covers only part of a county, the hearing shall be at a location in the county convenient to residents of the district, but need not be in the district.

(2) Allow for depositions prior to the hearing, if requested by the challenger or candidate before the time of the hearing is designated and announced.

(3) Issue subpoenas for witnesses or documents, or both, upon request of the parties or upon its own motion.

(4) Render a written decision within 20 business days after the challenge is filed and serve that written decision on the parties.

(b) Notice of Hearing. - The panel shall give notice of the hearing to the challenger, to the candidate, other candidates filing or petitioning to be elected to the same office, to the county chair of each political party in every county in the district for the office, and to those persons who have requested to be notified. Each person given notice shall also be given a copy of the challenge or a summary of its allegations.

Failure to comply with the notice requirements in this subsection shall not delay the holding of a hearing nor invalidate the results if the individuals required by this section to be notified have been notified.

(c) Conduct of Hearing. - The hearing under this Article shall be conducted as follows:

(1) The panel may allow evidence to be presented at the hearing in the form of affidavits supporting documents, or it may examine witnesses. The chair or any two members of the panel may subpoena witnesses or documents. The parties shall be allowed to issue subpoenas for witnesses or documents, or both, including a subpoena of the candidate. Each witness must be placed under oath before testifying. The Board shall provide the wording of the oath to the panel.

(2) The panel may receive evidence at the hearing from any person with information concerning the subject of the challenge, and such presentation of evidence shall be subject to Chapter 8C of the General Statutes. The challenger shall be permitted to present evidence at the hearing, but the challenger shall not be required to testify unless subpoenaed by a party. The panel may allow evidence to be presented by a person who is present.

(3) The hearing shall be recorded by a reporter or by mechanical means, and the full record of the hearing shall be preserved by the panel until directed otherwise by the Board.

(d) Findings of Fact and Conclusions of Law by Panel. - The panel shall make a written decision on each challenge by separately stating findings of facts, conclusions of law, and an order.

(e) Rules by Board. - The Board shall adopt rules providing for adequate notice to parties, scheduling of hearings, and the timing of deliberations and issuance of decisions. (2006-155, s. 1.)

§ 163-127.5. Burden of proof.

(a) The burden of proof shall be upon the candidate, who must show by a preponderance of the evidence of the record as a whole that he or she is qualified to be a candidate for the office.

(b) If the challenge is based upon a question of residency, the candidate must show all of the following:

(1) An actual abandonment of the first domicile, coupled with an intent not to return to the first domicile.

(2) The acquisition of a new domicile by actual residence at another place.

(3) The intent of making the newer domicile a permanent domicile. (2006-155, s. 1.)

§ 163-127.6. Appeals.

(a) Appeals from Single or Multicounty Panel. - The decision of a panel created under G.S. 163-127.3(1) or G.S. 163-127.3(2) may be appealed as of right to the Board by any of the following:

(1) The challenger.

(2) A candidate adversely affected by the panel's decision.

Appeal must be taken within two business days after the panel serves the written decision on the parties. The written appeal must be delivered or deposited in the mail to the Board by the end of the second business day after the written decision was filed by the panel. The Board shall prescribe forms for filing appeals from a panel's decision in a challenge. The Board shall base its appellate decision on the whole record of the hearing conducted by the panel and render its opinion on an expedited basis. From the final order or decision by the Board under this subsection, appeal as of right lies directly to the Court of Appeals. Appeal shall be filed no later than two business days after the Board files its final order or decision in its office.

(b) Appeals from Statewide Panel. - The decision of a panel created under G.S. 163-127.3(3) may be appealed as of right to the Court of Appeals by any of the following:

(1) The challenger.

(2) A candidate adversely affected by the panel's decision.

Appeal must be taken within two business days after the panel files the written decision. The written appeal must be delivered or deposited in the mail to the

Court of Appeals by the end of the second business day after the written decision was filed by the panel. (2006-155, s. 1.)

SUBCHAPTER VI. CONDUCT OF PRIMARIES AND ELECTIONS.

Article 12.

Precincts and Voting Places.

§ 163-128. Election precincts and voting places established or altered.

(a)   Each county shall be divided into a convenient number of precincts for the purpose of voting. Upon a resolution adopted by the county board of elections and approved by the Executive Director of the State Board of Elections voters from a given precinct may be temporarily transferred, for the purpose of voting, to an adjacent precinct. Any such transfers shall be for the period of time equal only to the term of office of the county board of elections making such transfer. When such a resolution has been adopted by the county board of elections to assign voters from more than one precinct to the same precinct, then the county board of elections shall maintain separate registration and voting records, consistent with the procedure prescribed by the State Board of Elections, so as to properly identify the precinct in which such voters reside. The polling place for a precinct shall be located within the precinct or on a lot or tract adjoining the precinct.

Except as provided by Article 12A of this Chapter, the county board of elections shall have power from time to time, by resolution, to establish, alter, discontinue, or create such new election precincts or voting places as it may deem expedient. Upon adoption of a resolution establishing, altering, discontinuing, or creating a precinct or voting place, the board shall give 45 days' notice thereof prior to the next primary or election. Notice shall be given by advertisement in a newspaper having general circulation in the county, by posting a copy of the resolution at the courthouse door and at the office of the county board of elections, and by mailing a copy of the resolution to the chairman of every political party in the county. Notice may additionally be made on a radio or television station or both, but such notice shall be in addition to the newspaper and other required notice. No later than 30 days prior to the primary or election, the county board of elections shall mail a notice of precinct change to each registered voter who as a result of the change will be assigned to a different voting place.

(b) Each county board of elections shall prepare a map of the county on which the precinct boundaries are drawn or described, shall revise the map when boundaries are changed, and shall keep a copy of the current map on file and posted for public inspection at the office of the Board of Elections, and shall file a copy with the State Board of Elections. (Rev., s. 4313; 1913, c. 53; C.S., s. 5934; 1921, c. 180; 1933, c. 165, s. 3; 1967, c. 775, s. 1; 1969, c. 570; 1973, c. 793, ss. 51-53; 1975, c. 798, s. 2; 1979, c. 785; 1981, c. 515, s. 1; 1985, c. 757, s. 205(b); 1989, c. 93, s. 4; c. 440, s. 1; 1993 (Reg. Sess., 1994), c. 762, s. 33; 1995, c. 423, s. 1; 2001-353, s. 2; 2006-264, s. 20.)

§ 163-129. Structure at voting place; marking off limits of voting place.

At the voting place in each precinct established under the provisions of G.S. 163-128, the county board of elections shall provide or procure by lease or otherwise a suitable structure or part of a structure in which registration and voting may be conducted. To this end, the county board of elections shall be entitled to demand and use any school or other State, county, or municipal building, or a part thereof, or any other building, or a part thereof, which is supported or maintained, in whole or in part by or through tax revenues provided, however, that this section shall not be construed to permit any board of elections to demand and use any tax exempt church property for such purposes without the express consent of the individual church involved, for the purpose of conducting registration and voting for any primary or election, and it may require that the requisitioned premises, or a part thereof, be vacated for these purposes.

If a county board of elections requires that a tax-supported building be used as a voting place, that county board of elections may require that those in control of that building provide parking that is adequate for voters at the precinct, as determined by the county board of elections.

The county board of elections shall inspect each precinct voting place to ascertain how it should be arranged for voting purposes, and shall direct the chief judge and judges of any precinct to define the voting place by roping off the area or otherwise enclosing it or by marking its boundaries. The boundaries of the voting place shall at any point lie no more than 100 feet from each ballot box or voting machine. The space so roped off or enclosed or marked for the voting place may contain area both inside and outside the structure in which registration and voting are to take place. (1929, c. 164, s. 17; 1967, c. 775, s. 1;

1973, c. 793, s. 54; 1983, c. 411, s. 3; 1993 (Reg. Sess., 1994), c. 762, s. 34; 1999-426, s. 5(a).)

§ 163-130. Satellite voting places.

A county board of elections by unanimous vote may, upon approval of a request submitted in writing to the State Board of Elections, establish a plan whereby elderly or disabled voters in a precinct may vote at designated sites within the precinct other than the regular voting place for that precinct. Any approval under this section is only effective for one year and shall be annually reviewed for extension. The State Board of Elections shall approve a county board's proposed plan if:

(1)   All the satellite voting places to be used are listed in the county's written request;

(2)   The plan will in the State Board's judgment overcome a barrier to voting by the elderly or disabled;

(3)   Adequate security against fraud is provided for; and

(4)   The plan does not unfairly favor or disfavor voters with regard to race or party affiliation. (1991 (Reg. Sess., 1992), c. 1032, s. 10; 2013-381, s. 26.1(a).)

§ 163-130.1. Out-of-precinct voting places.

A county board of elections, by unanimous vote of all its members, may establish a voting place for a precinct that is located outside that precinct. The county board's proposal is subject to approval by the Executive Director of the State Board of Elections. The county board shall submit its proposal in writing to the Executive Director. Approval by the Executive Director of the county's proposed plan shall be conditioned upon the county board of elections' demonstrating that:

(1)   No facilities adequate to serve as a voting place are located in the precinct;

(2)   Adequate notification and publicity are provided to notify voters in the precinct of the new polling location;

(3) The plan does not unfairly favor or disfavor voters with regard to race or party affiliation;

(4) The new voting place meets all requirements for voting places including accessibility for elderly and disabled voters; and

(5) The proposal provides adequately for security against fraud.

Any approval granted by the Executive Director for a voting place outside the precinct is effective only for one primary and election and must be reevaluated by the county board of elections and the Executive Director annually to determine whether it is still the only available alternative for that precinct. (1999-426, s. 3(a); 2001-319, ss. 3(a), 11.)

§ 163-130.2. Temporary use of two voting places for certain precincts.

A county board of elections, by unanimous vote of all its members, may propose to designate two voting places to be used temporarily for the same precinct. The temporary designation of a voting place shall continue only for the term of office of the county board of elections making the designation. For any precinct that is temporarily given two voting places, the county board shall assign every voter to one or the other of those voting places.

The county board's proposal is subject to approval by the Executive Director of the State Board of Elections. The county board shall submit its proposal in writing to the Executive Director. The Executive Director shall approve that proposal only if it finds all of the following:

(1) That the precinct has more registered voters than can adequately be accommodated by any single potential voting place available for the precinct.

(2) That no boundary line that complies with Article 12A of this Chapter can be identified that adequately divides the precinct.

(3) That the county board can account for, by street address number, the location of every registered voter in the precinct and fix that voter's residence with certainty on a map.

(4) That no more than three other precincts in the same county will have two voting places.

(5)   That both voting places for the precinct would have adequate facilities for the elderly and disabled.

(6)   That the proposal provides adequately for security against fraud.

(7)   That the proposal does not unfairly favor or disfavor voters with regard to race or party affiliation.

The county board shall designate a full set of precinct officials, in the manner set forth in Article 5 of this Chapter, for each voting place designated for the precinct. (1999-426, s. 4(a); 2001-319, ss. 4(a), 4(b), 11.)

§ 163-131. Accessible polling places.

(a)   The State Board of Elections shall promulgate rules to assure that any disabled or elderly voter assigned to an inaccessible polling place, upon advance request of such voter, will be assigned to an accessible polling place. Such rules should allow the request to be made in advance of the day of the election.

(b)   Words in this section have the meanings prescribed by P.L. 98-435, except that the term "disabled" in this section has the same meaning as "handicapped" in P.L. 98-435. (1999-424, s. 3(b).)

§ 163-132. Reserved for future codification purposes.

Article 12A.

Precinct Boundaries.

§ 163-132.1: Repealed by Session Laws 2013-381, s. 27.1, effective January 1, 2014. (1985, c. 757, s. 205(a); 1987 (Reg. Sess., 1988), c. 1074, s. 2; 1993 (Reg. Sess., 1994), c. 762, s. 69; 1995, c. 423, s. 2; 1999-227, s. 1; 2000-140, s. 81; 2001-319, s. 11; 2005-428, s. 16; 2006-264, s. 75.5(a); repealed by 2013-381, s. 27.1, effective January 1, 2014.)

§ 163-132.1A: Repealed by Session Laws 1999-227, s. 1, effective June 25, 1999.

§ 163-132.1B. Participation in 2010 Census Redistricting Data Program of the United States Bureau of the Census.

(a) Purpose. - The State of North Carolina shall participate in the 2010 Census Redistricting Data Program, conducted pursuant to P.L. 94-171, of the United States Bureau of the Census, so that the State will receive 2010 Census data by voting precinct and be able to revise districts at all levels without splitting precincts and in compliance with the United States and North Carolina Constitutions and the Voting Rights Act of 1965, as amended.

(a1) Reporting of Voting Tabulation Districts. - The Executive Director of the State Board of Elections shall report to the Bureau of the Census as this State's voting tabulation districts the voting precincts as of January 1, 2008. In reporting the precincts, the Executive Director may make to the precincts the minimum of adjustments necessary to assure accurate election administration and the consistent reporting of election results from the precincts as they existed on January 1, 2008. Before making that report, the Executive Director shall consult with the Legislative Services Office concerning the accuracy of the voting precincts to be reported. The Legislative Services Office shall submit to the Executive Director its opinion as to whether the description of the precincts to be reported to the Bureau of the Census is accurate. The Executive Director shall submit the report to the Bureau of the Census in time to comply with the deadlines of that Bureau for the 2010 Census Redistricting Data Program. The Executive Director, with the assistance of the county boards of elections, shall participate in the Census Bureau's verification program and notify the Census Bureau of any errors in the entry of the voting tabulation districts in time for the Census Bureau to correct those errors.

(a2) Reporting From Unchanged Voting Tabulation Districts. - After January 1, 2008, every county board of elections shall report all election returns by voting tabulation districts as required by G.S. 163-132.5G. For purposes of this section and G.S. 163-132.5G, "voting tabulation districts" shall be the precincts as of January 1, 2008, as modified by the Executive Director of the State Board of Elections in reports to the Census Bureau in accordance with subsection (a1) of this section. No county board of elections may alter the voting tabulation districts. The county board of elections may change the boundaries of the county's precincts so that those precincts differ from the county's voting tabulation districts, but only to the extent permitted by G.S. 163-132.3.

(b)   Additional Rules. - In addition to directives promulgated by the Executive Director of the State Board of Elections under G.S. 163-132.4, the Legislative Services Commission may promulgate rules to implement this section. (2006-264, s. 75.5(b); 2007-391, s. 6(a); 2008-187, s. 33(b); 2009-541, s. 17.)

§ 163-132.2: Repealed by Session Laws 1999-227, s. 1, effective June 25, 1999.

§ 163-132.3. Alterations to approved precinct boundaries.

(a)   No county board of elections may change any precinct boundary unless the Executive Director of the State Board of Elections determines that the county board has a current capability of complying with G.S. 163-132.1B(a2) by reporting all election returns by voting tabulation district as required by G.S. 163-132.5G. If the Executive Director so determines, the county board may make any changes to precinct boundaries, provided that all proposed new precincts shall consist solely of contiguous territory. The State Board of Elections may set uniform standards for precinct boundaries, which the county boards of elections shall follow. The county board of elections shall report every change in precinct boundary to the Executive Director in a format required by the Executive Director.

The county boards of elections shall report precinct boundary changes to the Executive Director in the manner the Executive Director directs. No newly created or altered precinct boundary is effective until approved by the Executive Director of the State Board as being in compliance with this section.

(b)   The Executive Director of the State Board of Elections shall examine the maps of the proposed new or altered precincts and any required written descriptions. If the Executive Director of the State Board determines that all precinct boundaries are in compliance with this section, the Executive Director of the State Board shall approve the maps and written descriptions as filed and these precincts shall be the official precincts.

(c)   If the Executive Director of the State Board determines that the proposed precinct boundaries are not in compliance with subsection (a) of this section, the Executive Director shall not approve those precinct boundaries. The Executive Director shall notify the county board of elections of his disapproval specifying the reasons. The county board of elections may then resubmit new precinct maps and written descriptions to cure the reasons for their disapproval.

(d) Repealed by Session Laws 2004-127, s. 1(a), effective August 15, 2004, and applicable to precincts established or changed on or after that date.

(e) Repealed by Session Laws 2007-391, s. 6(b), effective January 1, 2008. (1985, c. 757, s. 205(a); 1987 (Reg. Sess., 1988), c. 1074, s. 2; 1991 (Reg. Sess., 1992), c. 927, s. 1; 1993, c. 352, s. 3; 1993 (Reg. Sess., 1994), c. 762, s. 71; 1995, c. 423, ss. 2, 3; 1999-227, ss. 1, 2; 2001-319, ss. 10.1, 11; 2001-487, s. 96; 2002-159, s. 56; 2003-434, 1st Ex. Sess., s. 13; 2004-127, s. 1(a); 2007-391, s. 6(b); 2008-187, s. 33(b).)

§ 163-132.3A. Alterations to precinct names.

No county board of elections shall assign to any precinct a name that has been used after January 1, 1999, for a precinct comprising different territory. That requirement does not apply to a precinct change made under G.S. 163-132.3(a)(3). The county board of elections shall submit to the Executive Director of the State Board of Elections for approval every proposed change to a precinct name, and the Executive Director shall approve a name change only if it complies with this section. (2004-127, s. 1(b).)

§ 163-132.4. Directives.

The Executive Director of the State Board of Elections may promulgate directives concerning its duties and those of the county boards of elections under this Article. (1985, c. 757, s. 205(a); 1987 (Reg. Sess., 1988), c. 1074, s. 2; 2001-319, s. 11.)

§ 163-132.5. Cooperation of State and local agencies.

The Office of State Budget and Management, the Department of Transportation and county and municipal planning departments shall cooperate and assist the Legislative Services Office, the Executive Director of the State Board of Elections and the county boards of elections in the implementation of this

Article. (1985, c. 757, s. 205(a); 1987, c. 715, s. 4; 1987 (Reg. Sess., 1988), c. 1074, s. 2; 1989, c. 440, s. 3, c. 770, s. 75.3; 2000-140, ss. 93.1(c); 2001-319, s. 11; 2001-424, s. 12.2(b).)

§ 163-132.5A: Repealed by Session Laws 1991 (Regular Session, 1992), c. 927, s. 1.

§ 163-132.5B. Exemption from Administrative Procedure Act.

The State Board of Elections is exempt from the provisions of Chapter 150B of the General Statutes while acting under the authority of this Article. Appeals from a final decision of the Executive Director of the State Board of Elections under this Article shall be taken to the State Board of Elections within 30 days of that decision. The State Board shall approve, disapprove or modify the Executive Director's decision within 30 days of receipt of notice of appeal. Failure of the State Board to act within 30 days of receipt of notice of appeal shall constitute a final decision approving that of the Executive Director. Appeals from a final decision of the State Board under this Article shall be taken to the Superior Court of Wake County. (1987, c. 715, s. 4; 1987 (Reg. Sess., 1988), c. 1074, s. 2; 2001-319, s. 11.)

§ 163-132.5C. Local acts and township lines.

(a) Notwithstanding the provisions of any local act, a county board of elections need not have the approval of any other county board or commission to make precinct boundary changes required by this Article.

(b) Precinct boundaries established, retained or changed under this Article, or changed to follow a district line where a precinct has been divided in a districting plan, may cross township lines. (1987, c. 715, s. 4; 1989, c. 440, s. 5; 1991 (Reg. Sess., 1992), c. 927, s. 1; 1995, c. 423, s. 2.)

§ 163-132.5D. Retention of precinct maps.

The Executive Director of the State Board of Elections shall retain the maps and written descriptions which he approves pursuant to G.S. 163-132.3. (1991 (Reg. Sess., 1992), c. 927, s. 1; 2001-319, s. 11.)

§ 163-132.5E. Repealed by Session Laws 1999-227, s. 1.

§ 163-132.5F. U.S. Census data by voting tabulation district.

The State shall request the U.S. Bureau of the Census for each decennial census to provide summaries of census data by voting tabulation district and shall participate in any U.S. Bureau of the Census' program to effectuate this provision. (1991 (Reg. Sess., 1992), c. 927, s. 1; 2007-391, s. 6(e); 2008-187, s. 33(b).)

§ 163-132.5G. Voting data maintained by voting tabulation district.

Each county board of elections shall maintain voting data by voting tabulation district as provided in G.S. 163-132.1B so that voting tabulation district returns for each item on the ballot shall include the votes cast by all residents of the voting tabulation district who voted, regardless of where they voted. The county board shall not be required to report returns by voting tabulation district for voters who voted other than at their precinct voting place on election day until 60 days after the election. In reporting returns, the county board shall not compromise the secrecy of an individual's ballot. The 60-day deadline for reporting returns by voting tabulation district does not relieve the county board of the duty to report all returns as soon as practicable after the election according to other categories specified by the State Board of Elections. The State Board of Elections shall adopt rules for the enforcement of this section. (2001-466, s. 2; 2003-183, s. 1; 2005-323, s. 1(e); 2007-391, s. 6(c); 2008-187, s. 33(b).)

§ 163-132.6: Repealed by Session Laws 1991 (Regular Session, 1992), c. 927, s. 1.

§ 116-133. Reserved for future codification purposes.

§ 116-134. Reserved for future codification purposes.

Article 13.

General Instructions.

§§ 163-135 through 163-159: Repealed by Session Laws 2001-460, s. 1, effective January 1, 2002.

Article 14.

Voting Systems.

§§ 163-160 through 163-164: Repealed by Session Laws 2001-460, s. 1, effective January 1, 2002.

Article 14A.

Voting.

Part 1. Definitions.

§ 163-165. Definitions.

In addition to the definitions stated below, the definitions set forth in Article 15A of Chapter 163 of the General Statutes also apply to this Article. As used in this Article:

(1) (Effective until January 1, 2018) "Ballot" means an instrument on which a voter indicates a choice so that it may be recorded as a vote for or against a certain candidate or referendum proposal. The term "ballot" may include a paper ballot to be counted by hand, a paper ballot to be counted on an electronic scanner, the face of a lever voting machine, the image on a direct record electronic unit, or a ballot used on any other voting system.

(1) (Effective January 1, 2018) "Ballot" means an instrument on which a voter indicates a choice so that it may be recorded as a vote for or against a certain candidate or referendum proposal. The term "ballot" may include a paper ballot to be counted by hand, a paper ballot to be counted on an electronic scanner, or a paper ballot used on any other voting system.

(2) "Ballot item" means a single item on a ballot in which the voters are to choose between or among the candidates or proposals listed.

(3) "Ballot style" means the version of a ballot within a jurisdiction that an individual voter is eligible to vote. For example, in a county that uses essentially the same official ballot, a group office such as county commissioner may be divided into districts so that different voters in the same county vote for commissioner in different districts. The different versions of the county's official ballot containing only those district ballot items one individual voter may vote are the county's different ballot styles.

(4) "Election" means the event in which voters cast votes in ballot items concerning proposals or candidates for office in this State or the United States. The term includes primaries, general elections, referenda, and special elections.

(5) "Official ballot" means a ballot that has been certified by the State Board of Elections and produced by or with the approval of the county board of elections. The term does not include a sample ballot or a specimen ballot.

(5a) (Effective January 1, 2018) "Paper ballot" means an individual paper document that bears marks made by the voter by hand or through electronic means.

(6) "Provisional official ballot" means an official ballot that is voted and then placed in an envelope that contains an affidavit signed by the voter certifying identity and eligibility to vote. Except for its envelope, a provisional official ballot shall not be marked to make it identifiable to the voter.

(7) "Referendum" means the event in which voters cast votes for or against ballot questions other than the election of candidates to office.

(8) "Voting booth" means the private space in which a voter is to mark an official ballot.

(9) "Voting enclosure" means the room within the voting place that is used for voting.

(10) "Voting place" means the building or area of the building that contains the voting enclosure.

(11) "Voting system" means a system of casting and tabulating ballots. The term includes systems of paper ballots counted by hand as well as systems utilizing mechanical and electronic voting equipment. (2001-460, s. 3; 2001-466, s. 3(a), (b); 2002-159, s. 21(h); 2006-262, s. 4; 2013-381, ss. 30.1, 30.2.)

Part 2. Ballots and Voting Systems.

§ 163-165.1. Scope and general rules.

(a)   Scope. - This Article shall apply to all elections in this State.

(b)   Requirements of Official Ballots in Voting. - In any election conducted under this Article:

(1)   All voting shall be by official ballot.

(2)   Only votes cast on an official ballot shall be counted.

(c)   Compliance With This Article. - All ballots shall comply with the provisions of this Article.

(d)   Other Uses Prohibited. - An official ballot shall not be used for any purpose not authorized by this Article.

(e)   Voted ballots and paper and electronic records of individual voted ballots shall be treated as confidential, and no person other than elections officials performing their duties may have access to voted ballots or paper or electronic records of individual voted ballots except by court order or order of the appropriate board of elections as part of the resolution of an election protest or investigation of an alleged election irregularity or violation. Voted ballots and paper and electronic records of individual voted ballots shall not be disclosed to members of the public in such a way as to disclose how a particular voter voted, unless a court orders otherwise. Any person who has access to an official voted ballot or record and knowingly discloses in violation of this section how an individual has voted that ballot is guilty of a Class 1 misdemeanor. (2001-460, s. 3; 2002-159, s. 55(o); 2005-323, s. 1(f); 2007-391, s. 9(a).)

§ 163-165.2. Sample ballots.

(a)   County Board to Produce and Distribute Sample Ballots. - The county board of elections shall produce sample ballots, in all the necessary ballot styles of the official ballot, for every election to be held in the county. The sample ballots shall be given an appearance that clearly distinguishes them from official ballots. The county board shall distribute sample ballots to the chief judge of every precinct in which the election is to be conducted. The chief judge shall post a sample ballot in the voting place and may use it for instructional purposes. The county board of elections may use the sample ballot for other informational purposes.

(b) Document Resembling an Official Ballot to Contain Disclaimer. - No person other than a board of elections shall produce or disseminate a document substantially resembling an official ballot unless the document contains on its face a prominent statement that the document was not produced by a board of elections and is not an official ballot. (2001-460, s. 3.)

§ 163-165.3. Responsibilities for preparing official ballots.

(a) State Board Responsibilities. - The State Board of Elections shall certify the official ballots and voter instructions to be used in every election that is subject to this Article. In conducting its certification, the State Board shall adhere to the following:

(1) No later than January 31 of every calendar year, the State Board shall establish a schedule for the certification of all official ballots and instructions during that year. The schedule shall include a time for county boards of elections to submit their official ballots and instructions to the State Board for certification and times for the State Board to complete the certification.

(2) The State Board of Elections shall compose model ballot instructions, which county boards of elections may amend subject to approval by the State Board as part of the certification process. The State Board of Elections may permit a county board of elections to place instructions elsewhere than on the official ballot itself, where placing them on the official ballot would be impractical.

(3) With regard only to multicounty ballot items on the official ballot, the State Board shall certify the accuracy of the content on the official ballot.

(4) With regard to the entire official ballot, the State Board shall certify that the content and arrangement of the official ballot are in substantial compliance with the provisions of this Article and standards adopted by the State Board.

(5) The State Board shall proofread the official ballot of every county, if practical, prior to final production.

(6) The State Board is not required to certify or review every official ballot style in the county but may require county boards to submit and may review a composite official ballot showing races that will appear in every district in the county.

The State Board shall be responsible for oversight of all ballot coding. In order to produce the data necessary for equipment programming, each county shall either contract with a qualified vendor certified by the State Board or be certified by the State Board to produce the data.

(b) County Board Responsibilities. - Each county board of elections shall prepare and produce official ballots for all elections in that county. The county board of elections shall submit the format of each official ballot and set of instructions to the State Board of Elections for review and certification in accordance with the schedule established by the State Board. The county board of elections shall follow the directions of the State Board in placing candidates, referenda, and other material on official ballots and in placing instructions.

(c) Late Changes in Ballots. - The State Board shall promulgate rules for late changes in ballots. The rules shall provide for the reprinting, where practical, of official ballots as a result of replacement candidates to fill vacancies in accordance with G.S. 163-114 or other late changes. If an official ballot is not reprinted, a vote for a candidate who has been replaced in accordance with G.S. 163-114 will count for the replacement candidate.

(d) Special Ballots. - The State Board of Elections, with the approval of a county board of elections, may produce special official ballots, such as those for disabled voters, where production by the State Board would be more practical than production by the county board. (2001-460, s. 3; 2007-391, s. 24(a); 2008-187, s. 33(a); 2009-541, s. 18(a).)

§ 163-165.4. Standards for official ballots.

The State Board of Elections shall ensure that official ballots throughout the State have all the following characteristics:

(1) Are readily understandable by voters.

(2) Present all candidates and questions in a fair and nondiscriminatory manner.

(3)   Allow every voter to cast a vote in every ballot item without difficulty.

(4)   Facilitate an accurate vote count.

(5)   Are uniform in content and format, subject to varied presentations required or made desirable by different voting systems. (2001-460, s. 3; 2013-381, s. 29.1.)

§ 163-165.4A. Punch-card ballots and lever machines.

(a)   No ballot may be used in any referendum, primary, or other election as an official ballot if it requires the voter to punch out a hole with a stylus or other tool.

(a1)   No lever machine voting system may be used in any referendum, primary, or other election as a means of voting the official ballot. A "lever machine voting system" is a voting system on which the voter casts a vote by pressing a lever and the vote is mechanically recorded by the machine.

(b)   In any counties that used punch-card ballots as official ballots or lever machines in the election of November 2000, and in any municipalities located in those counties, this section becomes effective January 1, 2006. It is the intent of the General Assembly that any county that uses county funds to replace voting equipment to satisfy this section shall be given priority in appropriations to counties for voting equipment. (2001-310, ss. 1, 3; 2003-226, s. 12.)

§ 163-165.4B. Butterfly ballots.

No butterfly ballot may be used as an official ballot in any referendum, primary, or other election. The term "butterfly ballot" means a ballot having more than one column listing ballot choices that share a common column for designating those choices. (2001-310, ss. 2, 3.)

§ 163-165.5. Contents of official ballots.

Each official ballot shall contain all the following elements:

(1) The heading prescribed by the State Board of Elections. The heading shall include the term "Official Ballot".

(2) The title of each office to be voted on and the number of seats to be filled in each ballot item.

(3) The names of the candidates as they appear on their notice of candidacy filed pursuant to G.S. 163-106 or G.S. 163-323, or on petition forms filed in accordance with G.S. 163-122. No title, appendage, or appellation indicating rank, status, or position shall be printed on the official ballot in connection with the candidate's name. Candidates, however, may use the title Mr., Mrs., Miss, or Ms. Nicknames shall be permitted on an official ballot if used in the notice of candidacy or qualifying petition, but the nickname shall appear according to standards adopted by the State Board of Elections. Those standards shall allow the presentation of legitimate nicknames in ways that do not mislead the voter or unduly advertise the candidacy. In the case of candidates for presidential elector, the official ballot shall not contain the names of the candidates for elector but instead shall contain the nominees for President and Vice President which the candidates for elector represent. The State Board of Elections shall establish a review procedure that local boards of elections shall follow to ensure that candidates' names appear on the official ballot in accordance with this subdivision.

(4) Party designations in partisan ballot items.

(5) A means by which the voter may cast write-in votes, as provided in G.S. 163-123. No space for write-ins is required unless a write-in candidate has qualified under G.S. 163-123 or unless the ballot item is exempt from G.S. 163-123.

(6) Instructions to voters, unless the State Board of Elections allows instructions to be placed elsewhere than on the official ballot.

(7) The printed title and facsimile signature of the chair of the county board of elections. (2001-460, s. 3; 2003-209, s. 1; 2007-391, s. 10; 2008-187, s. 33(a).)

§ 163-165.5A. Expired.

§ 163-165.5B. Ballots may be combined.

Notwithstanding any other statute or local act, a county board of elections, with the approval of the State Board of Elections, may combine ballot items on the same official ballot. (2007-391, s. 7; 2008-187, s. 33(a).)

§ 163-165.6. Arrangement of official ballots.

(a) Order of Precedence Generally. - Candidate ballot items shall be arranged on the official ballot before referenda.

(b) Order of Precedence for Candidate Ballot Items. - The State Board of Elections shall promulgate rules prescribing the order of offices to be voted on the official ballot. Those rules shall adhere to the following guidelines:

(1) Federal offices shall be listed before State and local offices. Member of the United States House of Representatives shall be listed immediately after United States Senator.

(2) State and local offices shall be listed according to the size of the electorate.

(3) Partisan offices, regardless of the size of the constituency, shall be listed before nonpartisan offices.

(4) When offices are in the same class, they shall be listed in alphabetical order by office name, or in numerical or alphabetical order by district name. Governor and Lieutenant Governor, in that order, shall be listed before other Council of State offices. Mayor shall be listed before other citywide offices. Chair of a board, where elected separately, shall be listed before other board seats having the same electorate. Chief Justice shall be listed before Associate Justices.

(5) Ballot items for full terms of an office shall be listed before ballot items for partial terms of the same office.

(c) Order of Candidates on Primary Official Ballots. - The order in which candidates shall appear on a county's official ballots in any primary ballot item shall be determined by the county board of elections using a process designed by the State Board of Elections for random selection.

(d) Order of Party Candidates on General Election Official Ballot. -

Candidates in any ballot item on a general election official ballot shall appear in the following order:

(1) Nominees of political parties that reflect at least five percent (5%) of statewide voter registration, according to the most recent statistical report published by the State Board of Elections, in alphabetical order by party beginning with the party whose nominee for Governor received the most votes in the most recent gubernatorial election, and in alphabetical order within the party.

(2) Nominees of other political parties, in alphabetical order by party and in alphabetical order within the party.

(3) Unaffiliated candidates, in alphabetical order.

(e) No Straight-Party Voting. - Each official ballot shall not contain any place that allows a voter with one mark to vote for the candidates of a party for more than one office.

(f) Write-In Voting. - Each official ballot shall be so arranged so that voters may cast write-in votes for candidates except where prohibited by G.S. 163-123 or other statutes governing write-in votes. Instructions for general election ballots shall clearly advise voters of the rules of this subsection and of the statutes governing write-in voting.

(g) Order of Precedence for Referenda. - The referendum questions to be voted on shall be arranged on the official ballot in the following order:

(1) Proposed amendments to the North Carolina Constitution, in the chronological order in which the proposals were approved by the General Assembly.

(2) Other referenda to be voted on by all voters in the State, in the chronological order in which the proposals were approved by the General Assembly.

(3) Referenda to be voted on by fewer than all the voters in the State, in the chronological order of the acts by which the referenda were properly authorized. (2001-460, s. 3; 2002-158, s. 14; 2013-381, ss. 31.1, 32.1.)

§ 163-165.7. Voting systems: powers and duties of State Board of Elections.

(a) (Effective until January 1, 2018) Only voting systems that have been certified by the State Board of Elections in accordance with the procedures and subject to the standards set forth in this section and that have not been subsequently decertified shall be permitted for use in elections in this State. Those certified voting systems shall be valid in any election held in the State or in any county, municipality, or other electoral district in the State. Subject to all other applicable rules adopted by the State Board of Elections and, with respect to federal elections, subject to all applicable federal regulations governing voting systems, paper ballots marked by the voter and counted by hand shall be deemed a certified voting system. The State Board of Elections shall certify optical scan voting systems, optical scan with ballot markers voting systems, and direct record electronic voting systems if any of those systems meet all applicable requirements of federal and State law. The State Board may certify additional voting systems only if they meet the requirements of the request for proposal process set forth in this section and only if they generate either a paper ballot or a paper record by which voters may verify their votes before casting them and which provides a backup means of counting the vote that the voter casts. Those voting systems may include optical scan and direct record electronic (DRE) voting systems. In consultation with the Office of Information Technology Services, the State Board shall develop the requests for proposal subject to the provisions of this Chapter and other applicable State laws. Among other requirements, the request for proposal shall require at least all of the following elements:

(1) That the vendor post a bond or letter of credit to cover damages resulting from defects in the voting system. Damages shall include, among other items, any costs of conducting a new election attributable to those defects.

(2) That the voting system comply with all federal requirements for voting systems.

(3) That the voting system must have the capacity to include in voting tabulation district returns the votes cast by voters outside of the voter's voting tabulation district as required by G.S. 163-132.5G.

(4) With respect to electronic voting systems, that the voting system generate a paper record of each individual vote cast, which paper record shall be maintained in a secure fashion and shall serve as a backup record for purposes of any hand-to-eye count, hand-to-eye recount, or other audit.

Electronic systems that employ optical scan technology to count paper ballots shall be deemed to satisfy this requirement.

(5) With respect to DRE voting systems, that the paper record generated by the system be viewable by the voter before the vote is cast electronically, and that the system permit the voter to correct any discrepancy between the electronic vote and the paper record before the vote is cast.

(6) With respect to all voting systems using electronic means, that the vendor provide access to all of any information required to be placed in escrow by a vendor pursuant to G.S. 163-165.9A for review and examination by the State Board of Elections; the Office of Information Technology Services; the State chairs of each political party recognized under G.S. 163-96; the purchasing county; and designees as provided in subdivision (9) of subsection (d) of this section.

(7) That the vendor must quote a statewide uniform price for each unit of the equipment.

(8) That the vendor must separately agree with the purchasing county that if it is granted a contract to provide software for an electronic voting system but fails to debug, modify, repair, or update the software as agreed or in the event of the vendor having bankruptcy filed for or against it, the source code described in G.S. 163-165.9A(a) shall be turned over to the purchasing county by the escrow agent chosen under G.S. 163-165.9A(a)(1) for the purposes of continuing use of the software for the period of the contract and for permitting access to the persons described in subdivision (6) of this subsection for the purpose of reviewing the source code.

In its request for proposal, the State Board of Elections shall address the mandatory terms of the contract for the purchase of the voting system and the maintenance and training related to that voting system.

If a voting system was acquired or upgraded by a county before August 1, 2005, the county shall not be required to go through the purchasing process described in this subsection if the county can demonstrate to the State Board of Elections compliance with the requirements in subdivisions (1) through (6) and subdivision (8) of this subsection, where those requirements are applicable to the type of voting system involved. If the county cannot demonstrate to the State Board of Elections that the voting system is in compliance with those subdivisions, the county board shall not use the system in an election during or after 2006, and the county shall be subject to the purchasing requirements of this subsection.

(a) (Effective January 1, 2018) Only voting systems that have been certified by the State Board of Elections in accordance with the procedures and subject to the standards set forth in this section and that have not been subsequently decertified shall be permitted for use in elections in this State. Those certified voting systems shall be valid in any election held in the State or in any county, municipality, or other electoral district in the State. Subject to all other applicable rules adopted by the State Board of Elections and, with respect to federal elections, subject to all applicable federal regulations governing voting systems, paper ballots marked by the voter and counted by hand shall be deemed a certified voting system. The State Board of Elections shall certify optical scan voting systems, optical scan with ballot markers voting systems, and direct record electronic voting systems if any of those systems meet all applicable requirements of federal and State law. The State Board may certify additional voting systems only if they meet the requirements of the request for proposal process set forth in this section and only if they generate a paper ballot which provides a backup means of counting the vote that the voter casts. Those voting systems may include optical scan and direct record electronic (DRE) voting systems that produce a paper ballot. In consultation with the Office of Information Technology Services, the State Board shall develop the requests for proposal subject to the provisions of this Chapter and other applicable State laws. Among other requirements, the request for proposal shall require at least all of the following elements:

(1) That the vendor post a bond or letter of credit to cover damages resulting from defects in the voting system. Damages shall include, among other items, any costs of conducting a new election attributable to those defects.

(2) That the voting system comply with all federal requirements for voting systems.

(3) That the voting system must have the capacity to include in voting tabulation district returns the votes cast by voters outside of the voter's voting tabulation district as required by G.S. 163-132.5G.

(4) With respect to electronic voting systems, that the voting system generate a paper ballot of each individual vote cast, which paper ballot shall be maintained in a secure fashion and shall serve as a backup record for purposes of any hand-to-eye count, hand-to-eye recount, or other audit. Electronic

systems that employ optical scan technology to count paper ballots shall be deemed to satisfy this requirement.

(5) With respect to DRE voting systems, that the paper ballot generated by the system be viewable by the voter before the vote is cast electronically, and that the system permit the voter to correct any discrepancy between the electronic vote and the paper ballot before the vote is cast.

(a1) Federal Assistance. - The State Board may use guidelines, information, testing reports, certification, decertification, recertification, and any relevant data produced by the Election Assistance Commission, its Standards Board, its Board of Advisors, or the Technical Guidelines Development Committee as established in Title II of the Help America Vote Act of 2002 with regard to any action or investigation the State Board may take concerning a voting system. The State Board may use, for the purposes of voting system certification, laboratories accredited by the Election Assistance Commission under the provisions of section 231(2) of the Help America Vote Act of 2002.

(b) The State Board may also, upon notice and hearing, decertify types, makes, and models of voting systems. Upon decertifying a type, make, or model of voting system, the State Board shall determine the process by which the decertified system is discontinued in any county. A county may appeal a decision by the State Board concerning the process by which the decertified system is discontinued in that county to the Superior Court of Wake County. The county has 30 days from the time it receives notice of the State Board's decision on the process by which the decertified system is discontinued in that county to make that appeal.

(c) Prior to certifying a voting system, the State Board of Elections shall review, or designate an independent expert to review, all source code made available by the vendor pursuant to this section and certify only those voting systems compliant with State and federal law. At a minimum, the State Board's review shall include a review of security, application vulnerability, application code, wireless security, security policy and processes, security/privacy program management, technology infrastructure and security controls, security organization and governance, and operational effectiveness, as applicable to that voting system. Any portion of the report containing specific information related to any trade secret as designated pursuant to G.S. 132-1.2 shall be confidential and shall be accessed only under the rules adopted pursuant to subdivision (9) of subsection (d) of this section. The State Board may hear and discuss the report of any such review under G.S. 143-318.11(a)(1).

(d) (Effective until January 1, 2018) Subject to the provisions of this Chapter, the State Board of Elections shall prescribe rules for the adoption, handling, operation, and honest use of certified voting systems, including all of the following:

(1) Procedures for county boards of elections to utilize when recommending the purchase of a certified voting system for use in that county.

(2) Form of official ballot labels to be used on voting systems.

(3) Operation and manner of voting on voting systems.

(4) Instruction of precinct officials in the use of voting systems.

(5) Instruction of voters in the use of voting systems.

(6) Assistance to voters using voting systems.

(7) Duties of custodians of voting systems.

(8) Examination and testing of voting systems in a public forum in the county before and after use in an election.

(9) Notwithstanding G.S. 132-1.2, procedures for the review and examination of any information placed in escrow by a vendor pursuant to G.S. 163-165.9A by only the following persons:

a. State Board of Elections.

b. Office of Information Technology Services.

c. The State chairs of each political party recognized under G.S. 163-96.

d. The purchasing county.

Each person listed in sub-subdivisions a. through d. of this subdivision may designate up to three persons as that person's agents to review and examine the information. No person shall designate under this subdivision a business competitor of the vendor whose proprietary information is being reviewed and examined. For purposes of this review and examination, any designees under this subdivision and the State party chairs shall be treated as public officials under G.S. 132-2.

(10) With respect to electronic voting systems, procedures to maintain the integrity of both the electronic vote count and the paper record. Those procedures shall at a minimum include procedures to protect against the alteration of the paper record after a machine vote has been recorded and procedures to prevent removal by the voter from the voting enclosure of any paper record or copy of an individually voted ballot or of any other device or item whose removal from the voting enclosure could permit compromise of the integrity of either the machine count or the paper record.

(11) Compliance with section 301 of the Help America Vote Act of 2002.

Any rules adopted under this subsection shall be in conjunction with procedures and standards adopted under G.S. 163-182.1, are exempt from Chapter 150B of the General Statutes, and are subject to the same procedures for notice and publication set forth in G.S. 163-182.1.

(d) (Effective January 1, 2018) Subject to the provisions of this Chapter, the State Board of Elections shall prescribe rules for the adoption, handling, operation, and honest use of certified voting systems, including all of the following:

(1) Procedures for county boards of elections to utilize when recommending the purchase of a certified voting system for use in that county.

(2) Form of official ballot labels to be used on voting systems.

(3) Operation and manner of voting on voting systems.

(4) Instruction of precinct officials in the use of voting systems.

(5) Instruction of voters in the use of voting systems.

(6) Assistance to voters using voting systems.

(7) Duties of custodians of voting systems.

(8) Examination and testing of voting systems in a public forum in the county before and after use in an election.

(9) Notwithstanding G.S. 132-1.2, procedures for the review and examination of any information placed in escrow by a vendor pursuant to G.S. 163-165.9A by only the following persons:

a. State Board of Elections.

b. Office of Information Technology Services.

c. The State chairs of each political party recognized under G.S. 163-96.

d. The purchasing county.

Each person listed in sub-subdivisions a. through d. of this subdivision may designate up to three persons as that person's agents to review and examine the information. No person shall designate under this subdivision a business competitor of the vendor whose proprietary information is being reviewed and examined. For purposes of this review and examination, any designees under this subdivision and the State party chairs shall be treated as public officials under G.S. 132-2.

(10) With respect to electronic voting systems, procedures to maintain the integrity of both the electronic vote count and the paper ballot. Those procedures shall at a minimum include procedures to protect against the alteration of the paper ballot after a machine vote has been recorded and procedures to prevent removal by the voter from the voting enclosure of any individually voted paper ballot or of any other device or item whose removal from the voting enclosure could permit compromise of the integrity of either the machine count or the paper ballot.

(e) The State Board of Elections shall facilitate training and support of the voting systems utilized by the counties. The training may be conducted through the use of videoconferencing or other technology. (2001-460, s. 3; 2003-226, s. 11; 2005-323, s. 1(a)-(d); 2006-264, s. 76(a); 2007-391, s. 6(d); 2008-187, s. 33(b); 2009-541, s. 19; 2013-381, s. 30.3.)

§ 163-165.8. Voting systems: powers and duties of board of county commissioners.

The board of county commissioners, with the approval of the county board of elections, may adopt and acquire only a voting system of a type, make, and model certified by the State Board of Elections for use in some or all voting places in the county at some or all elections.

The board of county commissioners may decline to adopt and acquire any voting system recommended by the county board of elections but may not adopt and acquire any voting system that has not been approved by the county board of elections. Article 8 of Chapter 143 of the General Statutes does not apply to the purchase of a voting system certified by the State Board of Elections. (2001-460, s. 3; 2005-323, s. 3.)

§ 163-165.9. Voting systems: powers and duties of county board of elections.

(a)   Before approving the adoption and acquisition of any voting system by the board of county commissioners, the county board of elections shall do all of the following:

(1)   Recommend to the board of county commissioners which type of voting system should be acquired by the county.

(2)   Witness a demonstration, in that county or at a site designated by the State Board of Elections, of the type of voting system to be recommended and also witness a demonstration of at least one other type of voting system certified by the State Board of Elections.

(3)   Test, during an election, the proposed voting system in at least one precinct in the county where the voting system would be used if adopted.

(b)   After the acquisition of any voting system, the county board of elections shall comply with any requirements of the State Board of Elections regarding training and support of the voting system by completing all of the following:

(1)   The county board of elections shall comply with all specifications of its voting system vendor for ballot printers. The county board of elections is authorized to contract with noncertified ballot printing vendors, so long as the noncertified ballot printing vendor meets all specifications and all quality assurance requirements as set by the State Board of Elections.

(2) The county board of elections shall annually maintain software license and maintenance agreements necessary to maintain the warranty of its voting system. A county board of elections may employ qualified personnel to maintain a voting system in lieu of entering into maintenance agreements necessary to maintain the warranty of its voting system. State Board of Elections is not required to provide routine maintenance to any county board of elections that does not maintain the warranty of its voting system. If the State Board of Elections provides any maintenance to a county that has not maintained the warranty of its voting system, the county shall reimburse the State for the cost. The State Board of Elections shall annually report to the House and Senate Committees on Appropriations, to the Fiscal Research Division, and to the Joint Legislative Commission on Governmental Operations on implementation of this subdivision. If requested by the county board of elections, the State Board of Elections may enter into contracts on behalf of that county under this subdivision, but such contracts must also be approved by the county board of elections. Any contract entered into under this subdivision shall be paid from non-State funds. Neither a county nor the State Board of Elections shall enter into any contract with any vendor for software license and maintenance agreements unless the vendor agrees to (i) operate a training program for qualification of county personnel under this subsection with training offered within the State of North Carolina and (ii) not dishonor warranties merely because the county is employing qualified personnel to maintain the voting system as long as the county:

a. Pays the costs of the annual software licensing agreement for that county.

b. Ensures that equipment (i) remains in full compliance with State certification requirements and (ii) remains in stock and supply available to the county for up to five years after the vendor discontinues distribution or sale of the equipment.

c. Maintains a tracking record to record and timely report all hardware issues and all repairs and provides those records for review by the vendor and by the State Board of Elections.

d. Provides that only parts provided by the vendor would be used to repair the vendor's equipment, contingent on (i) the county being able to purchase necessary parts in a timely manner from the vendor and (ii) the vendor providing the equipment at least at the lowest price at which it sells the equipment to any other customer in the United States.

e. Accepts financial responsibility for expenses related to voting equipment failure during an election if the failure is caused solely by work of the county technician.

(3) The county board of elections shall not replace any voting system, or any portion thereof, without approval of the State Board of Elections.

(4) The county board of elections may have its voting system repaired pursuant to its maintenance agreement but shall notify the State Board of Elections at the time of every repair, according to guidelines that shall be provided by the State Board of Elections. (2001-460, s. 3; 2005-323, s. 4; 2007-391, s. 25; 2008-187, s. 33(a); 2009-541, s. 20; 2011-145, s. 26.3(a); 2012-142, s. 23.3(a).)

§ 163-165.9A. Voting systems: requirements for voting systems vendors; penalties.

(a) Duties of Vendor. - Every vendor that has a contract to provide a voting system in North Carolina shall do all of the following:

(1) The vendor shall place in escrow with an independent escrow agent approved by the State Board of Elections all software that is relevant to functionality, setup, configuration, and operation of the voting system, including, but not limited to, a complete copy of the source and executable code, build scripts, object libraries, application program interfaces, and complete documentation of all aspects of the system including, but not limited to, compiling instructions, design documentation, technical documentation, user documentation, hardware and software specifications, drawings, records, and data. The State Board of Elections may require in its request for proposal that additional items be escrowed, and if any vendor that agrees in a contract to escrow additional items, those items shall be subject to the provisions of this section. The documentation shall include a list of programmers responsible for creating the software and a sworn affidavit that the source code includes all relevant program statements in low-level and high-level languages.

(2) The vendor shall notify the State Board of Elections of any change in any item required to be escrowed by subdivision (1) of this subsection.

(3) The chief executive officer of the vendor shall sign a sworn affidavit that the source code and other material in escrow is the same being used in its

voting systems in this State. The chief executive officer shall ensure that the statement is true on a continuing basis.

(4)   The vendor shall promptly notify the State Board of Elections and the county board of elections of any county using its voting system of any decertification of the same system in any state, of any defect in the same system known to have occurred anywhere, and of any relevant defect known to have occurred in similar systems.

(5)   The vendor shall maintain an office in North Carolina with staff to service the contract.

(b)   Penalties. - Willful violation of any of the duties in subsection (a) of this section is a Class G felony. Substitution of source code into an operating voting system without notification as provided by subdivision (a)(2) of this section is a Class I felony. In addition to any other applicable penalties, violations of this section are subject to a civil penalty to be assessed by the State Board of Elections in its discretion in an amount of up to one hundred thousand dollars ($100,000) per violation. A civil penalty assessed under this section shall be subject to the provisions of G.S. 163-278.34(e). (2005-323, s. 2(a).)

§ 163-165.10. Adequacy of voting system for each precinct.

The county board of elections shall make available for each precinct voting place an adequate quantity of official ballots or equipment. When the board of county commissioners has decided to adopt and purchase or lease a voting system for voting places under the provisions of G.S. 165-165.8, the board of county commissioners shall, as soon as practical, provide for each of those voting places sufficient equipment of the approved voting system in complete working order. If it is impractical to furnish each voting place with the equipment of the approved voting system, that which has been obtained may be placed in voting places chosen by the county board of elections. In that case, the county board of elections shall choose the voting places and allocate the equipment in a way that as nearly as practicable provides equal access to the voting system for each voter. The county board of elections shall appoint as many voting system custodians as may be necessary for the proper preparation of the system for each election and for its maintenance, storage, and care. The Executive Director of the State Board of Elections may permit a county board of elections to provide more than one type of voting system in a precinct, but only upon a finding that doing so is necessary to comply with federal or State law. (2001-460, s. 3; 2005-428, s. 2.)

Part 3. Procedures at the voting place.

§ 163-166: Repealed by Session Laws 1997-443, s. 31.

§ 163-166.01. Hours for voting.

In every election, the voting place shall be open at 6:30 A.M. and shall be closed at 7:30 P.M. If the polls are delayed in opening for more than 15 minutes, or are interrupted for more than 15 minutes after opening, the State Board of Elections may extend the closing time by an equal number of minutes. As authorized by law, the State Board of Elections shall be available either in person or by teleconference on the day of election to approve any such extension. If any voter is in line to vote at the time the polls are closed, that voter shall be permitted to vote. No voter shall be permitted to vote who arrives at the voting place after the closing of the polls.

Any voter who votes after the statutory poll closing time of 7:30 P.M. by virtue of a federal or State court order or any other lawful order, including an order of a county board of elections, shall be allowed to vote, under the provisions of that order, only by using a provisional official ballot. Any special provisional official ballots cast under this section shall be separated, counted, and held apart from other provisional ballots cast by other voters not under the effect of the order extending the closing time of the voting place. If the court order has not been reversed or stayed by the time of the county canvass, the total for that category of provisional ballots shall be added to the official canvass. (2001-460, s. 3; 2003-226, s. 14; 2013-381, s. 33.1.)

§ 163-166.1. Duties of county board of elections.

The county board of elections shall:

(1)   Provide for the timely delivery to each voting place of the supplies, records, and equipment necessary for the conduct of the election.

(2) Ensure that adequate procedures are in place at each voting place for a safe, secure, fair, and honest election.

(3) Respond to precinct officials' questions and problems where necessary.

(4) Provide adequate technical support for the voting system, which shall be done in conjunction with the State Board of Elections. (2001-460, s. 3; 2009-541, s. 21.)

§ 163-166.2. Arrangement of the voting enclosure.

Each voting enclosure shall contain at a minimum:

(1) A sufficient number of private spaces for all voters to mark their official ballots in secrecy.

(2) Adequate space and furniture for the separate functions of:

a. The checking of voter registration records.

b. The distribution of official ballots.

c. Private discussion with voters concerning irregular situations.

(3) A telephone or some facility for communication with the county board of elections.

The equipment and furniture in the voting enclosure shall be arranged so that it can be generally seen from the public space of the enclosure. (2001-460, s. 3.)

§ 163-166.3. Limited access to the voting enclosure.

(a) Persons Who May Enter Voting Enclosure. - During the time allowed for voting in the voting place, only the following persons may enter the voting enclosure:

(1) An election official.

(2) An observer appointed pursuant to G.S. 163-45.

(2a) A runner appointed pursuant to G.S. 163-45, but only to the extent necessary to announce that runner's presence and to receive the voter list as provided in G.S. 163-45.

(3) A person seeking to vote in that voting place on that day but only while in the process of voting or seeking to vote.

(4) A voter in that precinct while entering or explaining a challenge pursuant to G.S. 163-87 or G.S. 163-88.

(5) A person authorized under G.S. 163-166.8 to assist a voter but, except as provided in subdivision (6) of this section, only while assisting that voter.

(6) Minor children of the voter under the age of 18, or minor children under the age of 18 in the care of the voter, but only while accompanying the voter and while under the control of the voter.

(7) Persons conducting or participating in a simulated election within the voting place or voting enclosure, if that simulated election is approved by the county board of elections.

(8) Any other person determined by election officials to have an urgent need to enter the voting enclosure but only to the extent necessary to address that need.

(b) Photographing Voters Prohibited. - No person shall photograph, videotape, or otherwise record the image of any voter within the voting enclosure, except with the permission of both the voter and the chief judge of the precinct. If the voter is a candidate, only the permission of the voter is required. This subsection shall also apply to one-stop sites under G.S. 163-227.2. This subsection does not apply to cameras used as a regular part of the security of the facility that is a voting place or one-stop site.

(c) Photographing Voted Ballot Prohibited. - No person shall photograph, videotape, or otherwise record the image of a voted official ballot for any purpose not otherwise permitted under law. (2001-460, s. 3; 2005-428, s. 1(b); 2007-391, s. 23; 2008-187, s. 33(a).)

§ 163-166.4. Limitation on activity in the voting place and in a buffer zone around it.

(a) Buffer Zone. - No person or group of persons shall hinder access, harass others, distribute campaign literature, place political advertising, solicit votes, or otherwise engage in election-related activity in the voting place or in a buffer zone which shall be prescribed by the county board of elections around the voting place. In determining the dimensions of that buffer zone for each voting place, the county board of elections shall, where practical, set the limit at 50 feet from the door of entrance to the voting place, measured when that door is closed, but in no event shall it set the limit at more than 50 feet or at less than 25 feet.

(a1) Area for Election-Related Activity. - Except as provided in subsection (b) of this section, the county board of elections shall also provide an area adjacent to the buffer zone for each voting place in which persons or groups of persons may distribute campaign literature, place political advertising, solicit votes, or otherwise engage in election-related activity.

(b) Special Agreements About Election-Related Activity. - The Executive Director of the State Board of Elections may grant special permission for a county board of elections to enter into an agreement with the owners or managers of a nonpublic building to use the building as a voting place on the condition that election-related activity as described in subsection (a1) of this section not be permitted on their property adjacent to the buffer zone, if the Executive Director finds all of the following:

(1) That no other suitable voting place can be secured for the precinct.

(2) That the county board will require the chief judge of the precinct to monitor the grounds around the voting place to ensure that the restriction on election-related activity shall apply to all candidates and parties equally.

(3) That the pattern of voting places subject to agreements under this subsection does not disproportionately favor any party, racial or ethnic group, or candidate.

An agreement under this subsection shall be valid for as long as the nonpublic building is used as a voting place.

(c) Notice About Buffer Zone and Area for Election-Related Activity. - No later than 30 days before each election, the county board of elections shall make available to the public the following information concerning each voting place:

(1) The door from which the buffer zone is measured.

(2) The distance the buffer zone extends from that door.

(3) Any available information concerning where political activity, including sign placement, is permitted beyond the buffer zone.

(d) Buffer Zone and Area for Election-Related Activity at One-Stop Sites. - Except as modified in this subsection, the provisions of this section shall apply to one-stop voting sites in G.S. 163-227.2.

(1) Subsection (b) of this section shall not apply.

(2) The notice in subsection (c) of this section shall be provided no later than 10 days before the opening of one-stop voting at the site. (2001-460, s. 3; 2003-365, s. 1; 2007-391, s. 13; 2008-187, s. 33(a); 2009-541, s. 22(a).)

§ 163-166.5. Procedures at voting place before voting begins.

The State Board of Elections shall promulgate rules for precinct officials to set up the voting place before voting begins. Those rules shall emphasize:

(1) Continual participation or monitoring by officials of more than one party.

(2) Security of official ballots, records, and equipment.

(3) The appearance as well as the reality of care, efficiency, impartiality, and honest election administration.

The county boards of elections and precinct officials shall adhere to those procedures. (2001-460, s. 3.)

§ 163-166.6. Designation of tasks.

The State Board of Elections shall promulgate rules for the delegation of tasks among the election officials at each precinct. Those rules shall emphasize:

(1) The need to place primary managerial responsibility upon the chief judge.

(2) The need to have maximum multiparty participation in all duties where questions of partisan partiality might be raised.

(3) The need to provide flexibility of management to the county board of elections and to the chief judge, in consideration of different abilities of officials, the different availability of officials, and the different needs of voters precinct by precinct. (2001-460, s. 3.)

§ 163-166.7. Voting procedures.

(a) (Effective until January 1, 2016) Checking Registration. - A person seeking to vote shall enter the voting enclosure through the appropriate entrance. A precinct official assigned to check registration shall at once ask the voter to state current name and residence address. The voter shall answer by stating current name and residence address. In a primary election, that voter shall also be asked to state, and shall state, the political party with which the voter is affiliated or, if unaffiliated, the authorizing party in which the voter wishes to vote. After examination, that official shall state whether that voter is duly registered to vote in that precinct and shall direct that voter to the voting equipment or to the official assigned to distribute official ballots. If a precinct official states that the person is duly registered, the person shall sign the pollbook, other voting record, or voter authorization document in accordance with subsection (c) of this section before voting.

(a) (Effective January 1, 2016) Checking Registration. - A person seeking to vote shall enter the voting enclosure through the appropriate entrance. A precinct official assigned to check registration shall at once ask the voter to state current name and residence address. The voter shall answer by stating current name and residence address and presenting photo identification in accordance with G.S. 163-166.13. In a primary election, that voter shall also be asked to state, and shall state, the political party with which the voter is affiliated or, if unaffiliated, the authorizing party in which the voter wishes to vote. After examination, that official shall state whether that voter is duly registered to vote in that precinct and shall direct that voter to the voting equipment or to the official assigned to distribute official ballots. If a precinct official states that the person is duly registered, the person shall sign the pollbook, other voting record, or voter authorization document in accordance with subsection (c) of this section before voting.

(b) Distribution of Official Ballots. - If the voter is found to be duly registered and has not been successfully challenged, the official assigned to distribute the official ballots shall hand the voter the official ballot that voter is entitled to vote, or that voter shall be directed to the voting equipment that contains the official ballot. No voter in a primary shall be permitted to vote in more than one party's primary. The precinct officials shall provide the voter with any information the voter requests to enable that voter to vote as that voter desires.

(c) (Effective until January 1, 2018) The State Board of Elections shall promulgate rules for the process of voting. Those rules shall emphasize the appearance as well as the reality of dignity, good order, impartiality, and the convenience and privacy of the voter. Those rules, at a minimum, shall include procedures to ensure that all the following occur:

(1) The voting system remains secure throughout the period voting is being conducted.

(2) Only properly voted official ballots or paper records of individual voted ballots are introduced into the voting system.

(3) Except as provided by G.S. 163-166.9, no official ballots leave the voting enclosure during the time voting is being conducted there. The rules shall also provide that during that time no one shall remove from the voting enclosure any paper record or copy of an individually voted ballot or of any other device or item whose removal from the voting enclosure could permit compromise of the integrity of either the machine count or the paper record.

(4) All improperly voted official ballots or paper records of individual voted ballots are returned to the precinct officials and marked as spoiled.

(5) Voters leave the voting place promptly after voting.

(6) Voters not clearly eligible to vote in the precinct but who seek to vote there are given proper assistance in voting a provisional official ballot or guidance to another voting place where they are eligible to vote.

(7) Information gleaned through the voting process that would be helpful to the accurate maintenance of the voter registration records is recorded and delivered to the county board of elections.

(8) The registration records are kept secure. The State Board of Elections shall permit the use of electronic registration records in the voting place in lieu of or in addition to a paper pollbook or other registration record.

(9) Party observers are given access as provided by G.S. 163-45 to current information about which voters have voted.

(10) The voter, before voting, shall sign that voter's name on the pollbook, other voting record, or voter authorization document. If the voter is unable to sign, a precinct official shall enter the person's name on the same document before the voter votes.

(c) (Effective January 1, 2018) The State Board of Elections shall promulgate rules for the process of voting. Those rules shall emphasize the appearance as well as the reality of dignity, good order, impartiality, and the convenience and privacy of the voter. Those rules, at a minimum, shall include procedures to ensure that all the following occur:

(1) The voting system remains secure throughout the period voting is being conducted.

(2) Only properly voted official ballots are introduced into the voting system.

(3) Except as provided by G.S. 163-166.9, no official ballots leave the voting enclosure during the time voting is being conducted there. The rules shall also provide that during that time no one shall remove from the voting enclosure any paper record or copy of an individually voted ballot or of any other device or item whose removal from the voting enclosure could permit compromise of the integrity of either the machine count or the paper record.

(4) All improperly voted official ballots are returned to the precinct officials and marked as spoiled.

(5) Voters leave the voting place promptly after voting.

(6) Voters not clearly eligible to vote in the precinct but who seek to vote there are given proper assistance in voting a provisional official ballot or guidance to another voting place where they are eligible to vote.

(7) Information gleaned through the voting process that would be helpful to the accurate maintenance of the voter registration records is recorded and delivered to the county board of elections.

(8) The registration records are kept secure. The State Board of Elections shall permit the use of electronic registration records in the voting place in lieu of or in addition to a paper pollbook or other registration record.

(9) Party observers are given access as provided by G.S. 163-45 to current information about which voters have voted.

(10) The voter, before voting, shall sign that voter's name on the pollbook, other voting record, or voter authorization document. If the voter is unable to sign, a precinct official shall enter the person's name on the same document before the voter votes. (2001-460, s. 3; 2003-226, s. 14.1; 2005-323, s. 1(a1); 2005-428, s. 12; 2013-381, ss. 2.5, 30.4.)

§ 163-166.7A. Voter education and information.

(a) Posting the Information. - For each election that involves candidates for federal or State office, each county board of elections shall post at each active voting place the following information in a manner and format approved by the State Board of Elections:

(1) A sample ballot as required by G.S. 163-165.2.

(2) The date of the election and the hours the voting place will be open.

(3) Instructions on how to vote, including how to cast a vote or correct a vote on the voting systems available for use in that voting place.

(4) Instructions on how to cast a provisional ballot.

(5) Instructions to mail-in registrants and first-time voters on how to comply with the requirements in section 303(b) of the Help America Vote Act of 2002 concerning voter identifications.

(6) General information on voting rights under applicable federal and State law, including information on the right of an individual to cast a provisional ballot and instructions on how to contact the appropriate officials if the voter believes those rights have been violated.

(7) General information on federal and State laws that prohibit acts of fraud and misrepresentation as to voting and elections.

(b) Intent. - The posting required by subsection (a) of this section is intended to meet the mandate of the voting information requirements in section 302(b) of the Help America Vote Act of 2002. (2003-226, s. 8.)

§ 163-166.8. Assistance to voters.

(a) Any registered voter qualified to vote in the election shall be entitled to assistance with entering and exiting the voting booth and in preparing ballots in accordance with the following rules:

(1) Any voter is entitled to assistance from the voter's spouse, brother, sister, parent, grandparent, child, grandchild, mother-in-law, father-in-law, daughter-in-law, son-in-law, stepparent, or stepchild, as chosen by the voter.

(2) A voter in any of the following four categories is entitled to assistance from a person of the voter's choice, other than the voter's employer or agent of that employer or an officer or agent of the voter's union:

a. A voter who, on account of physical disability, is unable to enter the voting booth without assistance.

b. A voter who, on account of physical disability, is unable to mark a ballot without assistance.

c. A voter who, on account of illiteracy, is unable to mark a ballot without assistance.

d. A voter who, on account of blindness, is unable to enter the voting booth or mark a ballot without assistance.

(b) A qualified voter seeking assistance in an election shall, upon arriving at the voting place, request permission from the chief judge to have assistance, stating the reasons. If the chief judge determines that such assistance is appropriate, the chief judge shall ask the voter to point out and identify the person the voter desires to provide such assistance. If the identified person meets the criteria in subsection (a) of this section, the chief judge shall request the person indicated to render the assistance. The chief judge, one of the judges, or one of the assistants may provide aid to the voter if so requested, if the election official is not prohibited by subdivision (a) (2) of this section. Under no circumstances shall any precinct official be assigned to assist a voter qualified for assistance, who was not specified by the voter.

(c) A person rendering assistance to a voter in an election shall be admitted to the voting booth with the voter being assisted. The State Board of Elections shall promulgate rules governing voter assistance, and those rules shall adhere to the following guidelines:

(1) The person rendering assistance shall not in any manner seek to persuade or induce any voter to cast any vote in any particular way.

(2) The person rendering assistance shall not make or keep any memorandum of anything which occurs within the voting booth.

(3) The person rendering assistance shall not, directly or indirectly, reveal to any person how the assisted voter marked ballots, unless the person rendering assistance is called upon to testify in a judicial proceeding for a violation of the election laws. (2001-460, s. 3.)

§ 163-166.9. (Effective until January 1, 2016) Curbside voting.

In any election or referendum, if any qualified voter is able to travel to the voting place, but because of age or physical disability and physical barriers encountered at the voting place is unable to enter the voting enclosure to vote in person without physical assistance, that voter shall be allowed to vote either in the vehicle conveying that voter or in the immediate proximity of the voting place. The State Board of Elections shall promulgate rules for the administration of this section. (2001-460, s. 3.)

§ 163-166.9. (Effective January 1, 2016) Curbside voting.

(a)   In any election or referendum, if any qualified voter is able to travel to the voting place, but because of age or physical disability and physical barriers encountered at the voting place is unable to enter the voting enclosure to vote in person without physical assistance, that voter shall be allowed to vote either in the vehicle conveying that voter or in the immediate proximity of the voting place.

(b)   Any qualified voter voting under this section shall comply with G.S. 163-166.13(a) by one of the following means:

(1)   Presenting photo identification in accordance with G.S. 163-166.13.

(2)   Presenting a copy of a document listed in G.S. 163-166.12(a)(2).

(c)   The State Board of Elections shall adopt rules for the administration of this section. (2001-460, s. 3; 2013-381, s. 2.6.)

§ 163-166.10. Procedures after the close of voting.

The State Board of Elections shall promulgate rules for closing the voting place and delivering voting information to the county board of elections for counting, canvassing, and record maintenance. Those rules shall emphasize the need for the appearance as well as the reality of security, accuracy, participation by representatives of more than one political party, openness of the process to public inspection, and honesty. The rules, at a minimum, shall include procedures to ensure all of the following:

(1)   The return and accurate accounting of all official ballots, regular, provisional, voted, unvoted, and spoiled, according to the provisions of Article 15A of this Chapter.

(2)   The certification of ballots and voter-authorization documents by precinct officials of more than one political party.

(3)   The delivery to the county board of elections of registration documents and information gleaned through the voting process that would be helpful in the accurate maintenance of the voter registration records.

(4)   The return to the county board of all issued equipment.

(5) The restoration of the voting place to the condition in which it was found. (2001-460, ss. 3, 3.1.)

§ 163-166.11. Provisional voting requirements.

If an individual seeking to vote claims to be a registered voter in a jurisdiction as provided in G.S. 163-82.1 and though eligible to vote in the election does not appear on the official list of eligible registered voters in the voting place, that individual may cast a provisional official ballot as follows:

(1) An election official at the voting place shall notify the individual that the individual may cast a provisional official ballot in that election.

(2) The individual may cast a provisional official ballot at that voting place upon executing a written affirmation before an election official at the voting place, stating that the individual is a registered voter in the jurisdiction as provided in G.S. 163-82.1 in which the individual seeks to vote and is eligible to vote in that election.

(2a) A voter who has moved within the county more than 30 days before election day but has not reported the move to the board of elections shall not be required on that account to vote a provisional ballot at the one-stop site, as long as the one-stop site has available all the information necessary to determine whether a voter is registered to vote in the county and which ballot the voter is eligible to vote based on the voter's proper residence address. The voter with that kind of unreported move shall be allowed to vote the same kind of absentee ballot as other one-stop voters as provided in G.S. 163-227.2(e2).

(3) At the time the individual casts the provisional official ballot, the election officials shall provide the individual written information stating that anyone casting a provisional official ballot can ascertain whether and to what extent the ballot was counted and, if the ballot was not counted in whole or in part, the reason it was not counted. The State Board of Elections or the county board of elections shall establish a system for so informing a provisional voter. It shall make the system available to every provisional voter without charge, and it shall build into it reasonable procedures to protect the security, confidentiality, and integrity of the voter's personal information and vote.

(4) The cast provisional official ballot and the written affirmation shall be secured by election officials at the voting place according to guidelines and

procedures adopted by the State Board of Elections. At the close of the polls, election officials shall transmit the provisional official ballots cast at that voting place to the county board of elections for prompt verification according to guidelines and procedures adopted by the State Board of Elections.

(5) The county board of elections shall count the individual's provisional official ballot for all ballot items on which it determines that the individual was eligible under State or federal law to vote, except that the ballot shall not be counted if the voter did not vote in the proper precinct under G.S. 163-55, including a central location as provided by that section. (2003-226, s. 15; 2005-2, s. 4; 2005-428, s. 6(b); 2013-381, s. 49.3.)

§ 163-166.11A. Notation on provisional ballot.

Whenever a voter is permitted to vote a provisional ballot, the election official issuing the ballot shall annotate in writing or other means on the ballot that it is a provisional ballot. (2013-381, s. 52.1.)

§ 163-166.12. Requirements for certain voters who register by mail.

(a) Voting in Person. - An individual who has registered to vote by mail on or after January 1, 2003, and has not previously voted in an election that includes a ballot item for federal office in North Carolina, shall present to a local election official at a voting place before voting there one of the following:

(1) A current and valid photo identification.

(2) A copy of one of the following documents that shows the name and address of the voter: a current utility bill, bank statement, government check, paycheck, or other government document.

(b) Voting Mail-In Absentee. - An individual who has registered to vote by mail on or after January 1, 2003, and has not previously voted in an election that includes a ballot item for federal office in North Carolina, in order to cast a mail-in absentee vote, shall submit with the mailed-in absentee ballot one of the following:

(1) A copy of a current and valid photo identification.

(2) A copy of one of the following documents that shows the name and address of the voter: a current utility bill, bank statement, government check, paycheck, or other government document.

(b1) Notation of Identification Proof. - The county board of elections shall note the type of identification proof submitted by the voter under the provisions of subsection (a) or (b) of this section and may dispose of the tendered copy of identification proof as soon as the type of proof is noted in the voter registration records.

(b2) Voting When Identification Numbers Do Not Match. - Regardless of whether an individual has registered by mail or by another method, if the individual has provided with the registration form a drivers license number or last four digits of a Social Security number but the computer validation of the number as required by G.S. 163-82.12 did not result in a match, and the number has not been otherwise validated by the board of elections, in the first election in which the individual votes that individual shall submit with the ballot the form of identification described in subsection (a) or subsection (b) of this section, depending upon whether the ballot is voted in person or absentee. If that identification is provided and the board of elections does not determine that the individual is otherwise ineligible to vote a ballot, the failure of identification numbers to match shall not prevent that individual from registering to vote and having that individual's vote counted.

(c) The Right to Vote Provisionally. - If an individual is required under subsection (a), (b), or (b2) of this section to present identification in order to vote, but that individual does not present the required identification, that individual may vote a provisional official ballot. If the voter is at the voting place, the voter may vote provisionally there without unnecessary delay. If the voter is voting by mail-in absentee ballot, the mailed ballot without the required identification shall be treated as a provisional official ballot.

(d) Exemptions. - This section does not apply to any of the following:

(1) An individual who registers by mail and submits as part of the registration application either of the following:

a. A copy of a current and valid photo identification.

b. A copy of one of the following documents that shows the name and address of the voter: a current utility bill, bank statement, government check, paycheck, or other government document.

(2) An individual who registers by mail and submits as part of the registration application the individual's drivers license number or at least the last four digits of the individual's social security number where an election official matches either or both of the numbers submitted with an existing State identification record bearing the same number, name, and date of birth contained in the submitted registration. If any individual's number does not match, the individual shall provide identification as required in subsection (b2) of this section in the first election in which the individual votes.

(3) An individual who is entitled to vote by absentee ballot under the Uniformed and Overseas Citizens Absentee Voting Act.

(4) An individual who is entitled to vote otherwise than in person under section 3(b)(2)(B)(ii) of the Voting Accessibility for the Elderly and Handicapped Act.

(5) An individual who is entitled to vote otherwise than in person under any other federal law. (2003-226, s. 16; 2004-127, s. 3; 2007-391, s. 21(a); 2008-187, s. 33(a); 2013-381, s. 16.4; 2013-410, s. 14(b).)

§ 163-166.13. (Effective January 1, 2016 - see note) Photo identification requirement for voting in person.

(a) Every qualified voter voting in person in accordance with this Article, G.S. 163-227.2, or G.S. 163-182.1A shall present photo identification bearing any reasonable resemblance to that voter to a local election official at the voting place before voting, except as follows:

(1) For a registered voter voting curbside, that voter shall present identification under G.S. 163-166.9.

(2) For a registered voter who has a sincerely held religious objection to being photographed and has filed a declaration in accordance with G.S. 163-82.7A at least 25 days before the election in which that voter is voting in person, that voter shall not be required to provide photo identification.

(3) For a registered voter who is a victim of a natural disaster occurring within 60 days before election day that resulted in a disaster declaration by the President of the United States or the Governor of this State who declares the lack of photo identification due to the natural disaster on a form provided by the State Board, that voter shall not be required to provide photo identification in any county subject to such declaration. The form shall be available from the State Board of Elections, from each county board of elections in a county subject to the disaster declaration, and at each polling place and one-stop early voting site in that county. The voter shall submit the completed form at the time of voting.

(b) Any voter who complies with subsection (a) of this section shall be permitted to vote.

(c) Any voter who does not comply with subsection (a) of this section shall be permitted to vote a provisional official ballot which shall be counted in accordance with G.S. 163-182.1A.

(d) The local election official to whom the photo identification is presented shall determine if the photo identification bears any reasonable resemblance to the voter presenting the photo identification. If it is determined that the photo identification does not bear any reasonable resemblance to the voter, the local election official shall comply with G.S. 163-166.14.

(e) As used in this section, "photo identification" means any one of the following that contains a photograph of the registered voter. In addition, the photo identification shall have a printed expiration date and shall be unexpired, provided that any voter having attained the age of 70 years at the time of presentation at the voting place shall be permitted to present an expired form of any of the following that was unexpired on the voter's 70th birthday. Notwithstanding the previous sentence, in the case of identification under subdivisions (4) through (6) of this subsection, if it does not contain a printed expiration date, it shall be acceptable if it has a printed issuance date that is not more than eight years before it is presented for voting:

(1) A North Carolina drivers license issued under Article 2 of Chapter 20 of the General Statutes, including a learner's permit or a provisional license.

(2) A special identification card for nonoperators issued under G.S. 20-37.7.

(3) A United States passport.

(4) A United States military identification card, except there is no requirement that it have a printed expiration or issuance date.

(5) A Veterans Identification Card issued by the United States Department of Veterans Affairs for use at Veterans Administration medical facilities facilities, except there is no requirement that it have a printed expiration or issuance date.

(6) A tribal enrollment card issued by a federally recognized tribe.

(7) A tribal enrollment card issued by a tribe recognized by this State under Chapter 71A of the General Statutes, provided that card meets all of the following criteria:

a. Is issued in accordance with a process approved by the State Board of Elections that requires an application and proof of identity equivalent to the requirements for issuance of a special identification card by the Division of Motor Vehicles under G.S. 20-7 and G.S. 20-37.7.

b. Is signed by an elected official of the tribe.

(8) A drivers license or nonoperators identification card issued by another state, the District of Columbia, or a territory or commonwealth of the United States, but only if the voter's voter registration was within 90 days of the election. (2013-381, s. 2.1.)

§ 163-166.14. (Effective January 1, 2016 - see note) Evaluation of determination of nonreasonable resemblance of photo identification.

(a) Any local election official that determines the photo identification presented by a voter in accordance with G.S. 163-166.13 does not bear any reasonable resemblance to that voter shall notify the judges of election of the determination.

(b) When notified under subsection (a) of this section, the judges of election present shall review the photo identification presented and the voter to determine if the photo identification bears any reasonable resemblance to that voter. The judges of election present may consider information presented by the voter in addition to the photo identification and shall construe all evidence presented in a light most favorable to the voter.

(c) A voter subject to subsections (a) and (b) of this section shall be permitted to vote unless the judges of election present unanimously agree that the photo identification presented does not bear any reasonable resemblance to that voter. The failure of the judges of election present to unanimously agree that photo identification presented by a voter does not bear any reasonable resemblance to that voter shall be dispositive of any challenges that may otherwise be made under G.S. 163-85(c)(10).

(d) A voter subject to subsections (a) and (b) of this section shall be permitted to vote a provisional ballot in accordance with G.S. 163-88.1 if the judges of election present unanimously agree that the photo identification presented does not bear any reasonable resemblance to that voter.

(e) At any time a voter presents photo identification to a local election official other than on election day, the county board of elections shall have available to the local election official judges of election for the review required under subsection (b) of this section, appointed with the same qualifications as is in Article 5 of this Chapter, except that the individuals (i) may reside anywhere in the county or (ii) be an employee of the county or the State. Neither the local election official nor the judges of election may be a county board member. The county board is not required to have the same judges of election available throughout the time period a voter may present photo identification other than on election day but shall have at least two judges, who are not of the same political party affiliation, available at all times during that period.

(f) Any local or State employee appointed to serve as a judge of election may hold that office in addition to the number permitted by G.S. 128-1.1.

(g) The county board of elections shall cause to be made a record of all voters subject to subsection (c) of this section. The record shall include all of the following:

(1) The name and address of the voter.

(2) The name of the local election official under subsection (a) of this section.

(3)   The names and a record of how each judge of election voted under subsection (b) of this section.

(4)   The date of the determinations under subsections (a) and (b) of this section.

(5)   A brief description of the photo identification presented by the voter.

(h)   For purposes of this section, the term "judges of election" shall have the following meanings:

(1)   On election day, the chief judge and judges of election as appointed under Article 5 of this Chapter.

(2)   Any time other than on election day, the individuals appointed under subsection (e) of this section.

(i)   The State Board shall adopt rules for the administration of this section. (2013-381, s. 2.2.)

§ 163-167: Reserved for future codification purposes.

Article 15.

Counting Ballots, Canvassing Votes, and Certifying Results in Precinct and County.

§§ 163-168 through 163-181: Repealed by Session Laws 2001-398, s. 1, effective January 1, 2002.

Article 15A.

Counting Official Ballots, Canvassing Votes, Hearing Protests, and Certifying Results.

§ 163-182. Definitions.

In addition to the definitions stated below, the definitions set forth in Article 14A of Chapter 163 of the General Statutes also apply to this Article. As used in this Article, the following definitions apply:

(1) "Abstract" means a document signed by the members of the board of elections showing the votes for each candidate and ballot proposal on the official ballot in the election. The abstract shall show a total number of votes for each candidate in each precinct and a total for each candidate in the county. It shall also show the number of votes for each candidate among the absentee official ballots, among the provisional official ballots, and in any other category of official ballots that is not otherwise reported.

(2) "Certificate of election" means a document prepared by the official or body with the legal authority to do so, conferring upon a candidate the right to assume an elective office as a result of being elected to it.

(3) "Composite abstract" means a document signed by the members of the State Board of Elections showing the total number of votes for each candidate and ballot proposal and the number of votes in each county. A composite abstract does not include precinct returns.

(4) "Protest" means a complaint concerning the conduct of an election which, if supported by sufficient evidence, may require remedy by one or more of the following:

a. A correction in the returns.

b. A discretionary recount as provided in G.S. 163-182.7.

c. A new election as provided in G.S. 163-182.13. (2001-398, s. 3; 2010-96, ss. 19, 35.)

§ 163-182.1. (Effective until January 1, 2018) Principles and rules for counting official ballots.

(a) General Principles That Shall Apply. - The following general principles shall apply in the counting of official ballots, whether the initial count or any recount:

(1) Only official ballots shall be counted.

(2) No official ballot shall be rejected because of technical errors in marking it, unless it is impossible to clearly determine the voter's choice.

(3) If it is impossible to clearly determine a voter's choice in a ballot item, the official ballot shall not be counted for that ballot item, but shall be counted in all other ballot items in which the voter's choice can be clearly determined.

(4) If an official ballot is marked in a ballot item with more choices than there are offices to be filled or propositions that may prevail, the official ballot shall not be counted for that ballot item, but shall be counted in all other ballot items in which there is no overvote and the voter's choice can be clearly determined.

(5) If an official ballot is rejected by a scanner or other counting machine, but human counters can clearly determine the voter's choice, the official ballot shall be counted by hand and eye.

(6) Write-in votes shall not be counted in party primaries or in referenda, but shall be counted in general elections if all of the following are true:

a. The write-in vote is written by the voter or by a person authorized to assist the voter pursuant to G.S. 163-166.8.

b. The write-in vote is not cast for a candidate who has failed to qualify under G.S. 163-123 as a write-in candidate.

c. The voter's choice can be clearly determined.

(7) Repealed by Session Laws 2013-381, s. 32.2, effective January 1, 2014.

(b) Procedures and Standards. - The State Board of Elections shall adopt uniform and nondiscriminatory procedures and standards for voting systems. The standards shall define what constitutes a vote and what will be counted as a vote for each category of voting system used in the State. The State Board shall adopt those procedures and standards at a meeting occurring not earlier than 15 days after the State Board gives notice of the meeting. The procedures and standards adopted shall apply to all elections occurring in the State and shall be subject to amendment or repeal by the State Board acting at any meeting where notice that the action has been proposed has been given at least 15 days before the meeting. These procedures and standards shall not be considered to be rules subject to Article 2A of Chapter 150B of the General Statutes. However, the State Board shall publish in the North Carolina Register the procedures and standards and any changes to them after adoption, with that publication noted as information helpful to the public under G.S. 150B-21.17(a)(6). Copies of those procedures and standards shall be made available to the public upon request or otherwise by the State Board. For optical scan and direct record electronic voting systems, and for any other voting systems in which ballots are counted other than on paper by hand and eye, those procedures and standards shall do both of the following:

(1) Provide for a sample hand-to-eye count of the paper ballots or paper records of a statewide ballot item in every county. The presidential ballot item shall be the subject of the sampling in a presidential election. If there is no statewide ballot item, the State Board shall provide a process for selecting district or local ballot items to adequately sample the electorate. The State Board shall approve in an open meeting the procedure for randomly selecting the sample precincts for each election. The random selection of precincts for any county shall be done publicly after the initial count of election returns for that county is publicly released or 24 hours after the polls close on election day, whichever is earlier. The sample chosen by the State Board shall be of one or more full precincts, full counts of mailed absentee ballots, full counts of one or more one-stop early voting sites, or a combination. The size of the sample of each category shall be chosen to produce a statistically significant result and shall be chosen after consultation with a statistician. The actual units shall be chosen at random. In the event of a material discrepancy between the electronic or mechanical count and a hand-to-eye count, the hand-to-eye count shall control, except where paper ballots or records have been lost or destroyed or where there is another reasonable basis to conclude that the hand-to-eye count is not the true count. If the discrepancy between the hand-to-eye count and the mechanical or electronic count is significant, a complete hand-to-eye count shall be conducted.

(2) Provide that if the voter selects votes for more than the number of candidates to be elected or proposals to be approved in a ballot item, the voting system shall do all the following:

a. Notify the voter that the voter has selected more than the correct number of candidates or proposals in the ballot item.

b. Notify the voter before the vote is accepted and counted of the effect of casting overvotes in the ballot item.

c.   Provide the voter with the opportunity to correct the official ballot before it is accepted and counted. (2001-398, s. 3; 2003-226, s. 13; 2005-323, s. 5(a); 2006-192, s. 7(a); 2006-264, s. 76(b); 2013-381, s. 32.2.)

§ 163-182.1. (Effective January 1, 2018) Principles and rules for counting official ballots.

(a)   General Principles That Shall Apply. - The following general principles shall apply in the counting of official ballots, whether the initial count or any recount:

(1)   Only official ballots shall be counted.

(2)   No official ballot shall be rejected because of technical errors in marking it, unless it is impossible to clearly determine the voter's choice.

(3)   If it is impossible to clearly determine a voter's choice in a ballot item, the official ballot shall not be counted for that ballot item, but shall be counted in all other ballot items in which the voter's choice can be clearly determined.

(4)   If an official ballot is marked in a ballot item with more choices than there are offices to be filled or propositions that may prevail, the official ballot shall not be counted for that ballot item, but shall be counted in all other ballot items in which there is no overvote and the voter's choice can be clearly determined.

(5)   If an official ballot is rejected by a scanner or other counting machine, but human counters can clearly determine the voter's choice, the official ballot shall be counted by hand and eye.

(6)   Write-in votes shall not be counted in party primaries or in referenda, but shall be counted in general elections if all of the following are true:

a.   The write-in vote is written by the voter or by a person authorized to assist the voter pursuant to G.S. 163-166.8.

b.   The write-in vote is not cast for a candidate who has failed to qualify under G.S. 163-123 as a write-in candidate.

c.   The voter's choice can be clearly determined.

(7) Repealed by Session Laws 2013-381, s. 32.2, effective January 1, 2014.

(b) Procedures and Standards. - The State Board of Elections shall adopt uniform and nondiscriminatory procedures and standards for voting systems. The standards shall define what constitutes a vote and what will be counted as a vote for each category of voting system used in the State. The State Board shall adopt those procedures and standards at a meeting occurring not earlier than 15 days after the State Board gives notice of the meeting. The procedures and standards adopted shall apply to all elections occurring in the State and shall be subject to amendment or repeal by the State Board acting at any meeting where notice that the action has been proposed has been given at least 15 days before the meeting. These procedures and standards shall not be considered to be rules subject to Article 2A of Chapter 150B of the General Statutes. However, the State Board shall publish in the North Carolina Register the procedures and standards and any changes to them after adoption, with that publication noted as information helpful to the public under G.S. 150B-21.17(a)(6). Copies of those procedures and standards shall be made available to the public upon request or otherwise by the State Board. For optical scan and direct record electronic voting systems, and for any other voting systems in which ballots are counted other than on paper by hand and eye, those procedures and standards shall do both of the following:

(1) Provide for a sample hand-to-eye count of the paper ballots of a statewide ballot item in every county. The presidential ballot item shall be the subject of the sampling in a presidential election. If there is no statewide ballot item, the State Board shall provide a process for selecting district or local ballot items to adequately sample the electorate. The State Board shall approve in an open meeting the procedure for randomly selecting the sample precincts for each election. The random selection of precincts for any county shall be done publicly after the initial count of election returns for that county is publicly released or 24 hours after the polls close on election day, whichever is earlier. The sample chosen by the State Board shall be of one or more full precincts, full counts of mailed absentee ballots, full counts of one or more one-stop early voting sites, or a combination. The size of the sample of each category shall be chosen to produce a statistically significant result and shall be chosen after consultation with a statistician. The actual units shall be chosen at random. In the event of a material discrepancy between the electronic or mechanical count and a hand-to-eye count, the hand-to-eye count shall control, except where paper ballots have been lost or destroyed or where there is another reasonable basis to conclude that the hand-to-eye count is not the true count. If the

discrepancy between the hand-to-eye count and the mechanical or electronic count is significant, a complete hand-to-eye count shall be conducted.

(2) Provide that if the voter selects votes for more than the number of candidates to be elected or proposals to be approved in a ballot item, the voting system shall do all the following:

a. Notify the voter that the voter has selected more than the correct number of candidates or proposals in the ballot item.

b. Notify the voter before the vote is accepted and counted of the effect of casting overvotes in the ballot item.

c. Provide the voter with the opportunity to correct the official ballot before it is accepted and counted. (2001-398, s. 3; 2003-226, s. 13; 2005-323, s. 5(a); 2006-192, s. 7(a); 2006-264, s. 76(b); 2013-381, ss. 30.5, 32.2.)

§ 163-182.1A. (Effective January 1, 2016 - see note) Counting of provisional official ballots cast due to failure to provide photo identification when voting in person.

(a) Unless disqualified for some other reason provided by law, the county board of elections shall find that a voter's provisional official ballot cast as a result of failing to present photo identification when voting in person in accordance with G.S. 163-166.13 is valid and direct that the provisional ballot be opened and counted in accordance with this Chapter if the voter complies with this section.

(b) A voter who casts a provisional official ballot wholly or partly as a result of failing to present photo identification when voting in person in accordance with G.S. 163-166.13 may comply with this section by appearing in person at the county board of elections and doing one of the following:

(1) Presenting photo identification as defined in G.S. 163-166.13(e) that bears any reasonable resemblance to the voter. The local election official to whom the photo identification is presented shall determine if the photo identification bears any reasonable resemblance to that voter. If not, that local election official shall comply with G.S. 163-166.14.

(2) Presenting any of the documents listed in G.S. 163-166.12(a)(2) and declaring that the voter has a sincerely held religious objection to being photographed. That voter shall also be offered an opportunity to execute a declaration under G.S. 163-82.7A for future elections.

(c) All identification under subsection (b) of this section shall be presented to the county board of elections not later than 12:00 noon the day prior to the time set for the convening of the election canvass pursuant to G.S. 163-182.5.

(d) If the county board of elections determines that a voter has also cast a provisional official ballot for a cause other than the voter's failure to provide photo identification in accordance with G.S. 163-166.13, the county board shall do all of the following:

(1) Note on the envelope containing the provisional official ballot that the voter has complied with the proof of identification requirement.

(2) Proceed to determine any other reasons for which the provisional official ballot was cast provisionally before ruling on the validity of the voter's provisional official ballot. (2013-381, s. 2.8.)

§ 163-182.2. Initial counting of official ballots.

(a) The initial counting of official ballots shall be conducted according to the following principles:

(1) Vote counting at the precinct shall occur immediately after the polls close and shall be continuous until completed.

(2) Vote counting at the precinct shall be conducted with the participation of precinct officials of all political parties then present. Vote counting at the county board of elections shall be conducted in the presence or under the supervision of board members of all political parties then present.

(3) Any member of the public wishing to witness the vote count at any level shall be allowed to do so. No witness shall interfere with the orderly counting of the official ballots. Witnesses shall not participate in the official counting of official ballots.

(4) Provisional official ballots shall be counted by the county board of elections before the canvass. If the county board finds that an individual voting a provisional official ballot is not eligible to vote in one or more ballot items on the official ballot, the board shall not count the official ballot in those ballot items, but shall count the official ballot in any ballot items for which the individual is eligible to vote. Eligibility shall be determined by whether the voter is registered in the county as provided in G.S. 163-82.1 and whether the voter is qualified by residency to vote in the precinct as provided in G.S. 163-55 and G.S. 163-57. If a voter was properly registered to vote in the election by the county board, no mistake of an election official in giving the voter a ballot or in failing to comply with G.S. 163-82.15 or G.S. 163-166.11 shall serve to prevent the counting of the vote on any ballot item the voter was eligible by registration and qualified by residency to vote.

(5) Precinct officials shall provide a preliminary report of the vote counting to the county board of elections as quickly as possible. The preliminary report shall be unofficial and has no binding effect upon the official county canvass to follow.

(6) In counties that use any certified mechanical or electronic voting system, subject to the sample counts under G.S. 163-182.1 and subdivision (1a) of subsection (b) of this section, and of a hand-to-eye recount under G.S. 163-182.7 and G.S. 163-182.7A, a board of elections shall rely in its canvass on the mechanical or electronic count of the vote rather than the full hand-to-eye count of the paper ballots or records. In the event of a material discrepancy between the electronic or mechanical count and a hand-to-eye count or recount, the hand-to-eye count or recount shall control, except where paper ballots or records have been lost or destroyed or where there is another reasonable basis to conclude that the hand-to-eye count is not the true count.

(b) The State Board of Elections shall promulgate rules for the initial counting of official ballots. All election officials shall be governed by those rules. In promulgating those rules, the State Board shall adhere to the following guidelines:

(1) For each voting system used, the rules shall specify the role of precinct officials and of the county board of elections in the initial counting of official ballots.

(1a) (Effective until January 1, 2018) For optical scan and direct record electronic voting systems, and for any other voting systems in which ballots are counted other than on paper by hand and eye, those rules shall provide for a sample hand-to-eye count of the paper ballots or paper records of a sampling of a statewide ballot item in every county. The presidential ballot item shall be the subject of the sampling in a presidential election. If there is no statewide ballot item, the State Board shall provide a process for selecting district or local ballot items to adequately sample the electorate. The State Board shall approve in an open meeting the procedure for randomly selecting the sample precincts for each election. The random selection of precincts for any county shall be done publicly after the initial count of election returns for that county is publicly released or 24 hours after the polls close on election day, whichever is earlier. The sample chosen by the State Board shall be of one or more full precincts, full counts of mailed absentee ballots, and full counts of one or more one-stop early voting sites. The size of the sample of each category shall be chosen to produce a statistically significant result and shall be chosen after consultation with a statistician. The actual units shall be chosen at random. In the event of a material discrepancy between the electronic or mechanical count and a hand-to-eye count, the hand-to-eye count shall control, except where paper ballots or records have been lost or destroyed or where there is another reasonable basis to conclude that the hand-to-eye count is not the true count. If the discrepancy between the hand-to-eye count and the mechanical or electronic count is significant, a complete hand-to-eye count shall be conducted. The sample count need not be done on election night.

(1a)   (Effective January 1, 2018) For optical scan and direct record electronic voting systems, and for any other voting systems in which ballots are counted other than on paper by hand and eye, those rules shall provide for a sample hand-to-eye count of the paper ballots of a sampling of a statewide ballot item in every county. The presidential ballot item shall be the subject of the sampling in a presidential election. If there is no statewide ballot item, the State Board shall provide a process for selecting district or local ballot items to adequately sample the electorate. The State Board shall approve in an open meeting the procedure for randomly selecting the sample precincts for each election. The random selection of precincts for any county shall be done publicly after the initial count of election returns for that county is publicly released or 24 hours after the polls close on election day, whichever is earlier. The sample chosen by the State Board shall be of one or more full precincts, full counts of mailed absentee ballots, and full counts of one or more one-stop early voting sites. The size of the sample of each category shall be chosen to produce a statistically significant result and shall be chosen after consultation with a statistician. The actual units shall be chosen at random. In the event of a material discrepancy between the electronic or mechanical count and a hand-to-eye count, the hand-to-eye count shall control, except where paper ballots have been lost or destroyed or where there is another reasonable basis to conclude that the hand-to-eye count is not the true count. If the discrepancy between the hand-to-eye count and the mechanical or electronic count is significant, a complete hand-to-eye count shall be conducted. The sample count need not be done on election night.

(2) The rules shall provide for accurate unofficial reporting of the results from the precinct to the county board of elections with reasonable speed on the night of the election.

(3) The rules shall provide for the prompt and secure transmission of official ballots from the voting place to the county board of elections.

The State Board shall direct the county boards of elections in the application of the principles and rules in individual circumstances. (2001-398, s. 3; 2005-2, s. 5; 2005-323, s. 5(b); 2006-192, s. 7(b); 2006-264, s. 76(c); 2013-381, ss. 30.6, 49.4.)

§ 163-182.3. Responsibility of chief judge.

The chief judge of each precinct shall be responsible for the adherence of the precinct officials to the State Board rules for counting, reporting, and transmitting official ballots. (2001-398, s. 3.)

§ 163-182.4. Jurisdiction for certain ballot items.

(a) Jurisdiction of County Board of Elections. - As used in this Article, the county board of elections shall have jurisdiction over the following:

(1) Offices of that county, including clerk of superior court and register of deeds.

(2) Membership in either house of the General Assembly from a district lying entirely within that county.

(3) Offices of municipalities, unless the municipality has a valid board of election.

(4) Referenda in which only residents of that county are eligible to vote.

(b)   Jurisdiction of State Board of Elections. - As used in this Article, the State Board of Elections shall have jurisdiction over the following:

(1)   National offices.

(2)   State offices.

(3)   District offices (including General Assembly seats) in which the district lies in more than one county.

(4)   Superior court judge, district court judge, and district attorney, regardless of whether the district lies entirely in one county or in more than one county.

(5)   Referenda in which residents of more than one county are eligible to vote.

(c)   For the purposes of this Article, having jurisdiction shall mean that the appropriate board shall do all of the following with regard to the ballot item:

(1)   Canvass for the entire electorate for the ballot item.

(2)   Prepare abstracts or composite abstracts for the entire electorate for the ballot item.

(3)   Issue certificates of nomination and election. (2001-398, s. 3.)

§ 163-182.5. Canvassing votes.

(a)   The Canvass. - As used in this Article, the term "canvass" means the entire process of determining that the votes have been counted and tabulated correctly, culminating in the authentication of the official election results. The board of elections conducting a canvass has authority to send for papers and persons and to examine them and pass upon the legality of disputed ballots.

(b)   Canvassing by County Board of Elections. - The county board of elections shall meet at 11:00 A.M. on the tenth day after every election held on the same day as a general election in November of the even-numbered year, and at 11:00 A.M. on the seventh day after every other election, to complete the canvass of votes cast and to authenticate the count in every ballot item in the county by determining that the votes have been counted and tabulated correctly. If, despite due diligence by election officials, the initial counting of all the votes has not been completed by that time, the county board may hold the canvass meeting a reasonable time thereafter. The canvass meeting shall be at the county board of elections office, unless the county board, by unanimous vote of all its members, designates another site within the county. The county board shall examine the returns from precincts, from absentee official ballots, from the sample hand-to-eye paper ballot counts, and from provisional official ballots and shall conduct the canvass.

(c) Canvassing by State Board of Elections. - After each general election, the State Board of Elections shall meet at 11:00 A.M. on the Tuesday three weeks after election day to complete the canvass of votes cast in all ballot items within the jurisdiction of the State Board of Elections and to authenticate the count in every ballot item in the county by determining that the votes have been counted and tabulated correctly. After each primary, the State Board shall fix the date of its canvass meeting. If, by the time of its scheduled canvass meeting, the State Board has not received the county canvasses, the State Board may adjourn for not more than 10 days to secure the missing abstracts. In obtaining them, the State Board is authorized to secure the originals or copies from the appropriate clerks of superior court or county boards of elections, at the expense of the counties. (2001-398, s. 3; 2003-278, s. 10(a); 2005-323, s. 5(c); 2005-428, s. 11(a).)

§ 163-182.6. Abstracts.

(a) Abstracts to Be Prepared by County Board of Elections. - As soon as the county canvass has been completed, the county board of elections shall prepare abstracts of all the ballot items in a form prescribed by the State Board of Elections. The county board shall prepare those abstracts in triplicate originals. The county board shall retain one of the triplicate originals, and shall distribute one each to the clerk of superior court for the county and the State Board of Elections. The State Highway Patrol may, upon request of the State Board of Elections, be responsible for the delivery of the abstracts from each county to the State Board of Elections. The State Board of Elections shall forward the original abstract it receives to the Secretary of State.

(b) Composite Abstracts to Be Prepared by the State Board of Elections. - As soon as the State canvass has been completed, the State Board shall prepare composite abstracts of all those ballot items. It shall prepare those composite abstracts in duplicate originals. It shall retain one of the originals and shall send the other original to the Secretary of State.

(c) Duty of the Secretary of State. - The Secretary of State shall maintain the certified copies of abstracts received from the county and State boards of elections. The Secretary shall keep the abstracts in a form readily accessible and useful to the public.

(d) Forms by State Board of Elections. - The State Board of Elections shall prescribe forms for all abstracts. Those forms shall be uniform and shall, at a minimum, state the name of each candidate and the office sought and each referendum proposal, the number of votes cast for each candidate and proposal, the candidate or proposal determined to have prevailed, and a statement authenticating the count. (2001-398, s. 3.)

§ 163-182.7. Ordering recounts.

(a) Discretionary Recounts. - The county board of elections or the State Board of Elections may order a recount when necessary to complete the canvass in an election. The county board may not order a recount where the State Board of Elections has already denied a recount to the petitioner.

(b) Mandatory Recounts for Ballot Items Within the Jurisdiction of the County Board of Elections. - In a ballot item within the jurisdiction of the county board of elections, a candidate shall have the right to demand a recount of the votes if the difference between the votes for that candidate and the votes for a prevailing candidate is not more than one percent (1%) of the total votes cast in the ballot item, or in the case of a multiseat ballot item not more than one percent (1%) of the votes cast for those two candidates. The demand for a recount must be made in writing and must be received by the county board of elections by 5:00 P.M. on the first business day after the canvass. The recount shall be conducted under the supervision of the county board of elections.

(c) Mandatory Recounts for Ballot Items Within the Jurisdiction of the State Board of Elections. - In a ballot item within the jurisdiction of the State Board of Elections, a candidate shall have the right to demand a recount of the votes if the difference between the votes for that candidate and the votes for a prevailing candidate are not more than the following:

(1) For a nonstatewide ballot item, one percent (1%) of the total votes cast in the ballot item, or in the case of a multiseat ballot item, one percent (1%) of the votes cast for those two candidates.

(2) For a statewide ballot item, one-half of one percent (0.5%) of the votes cast in the ballot item, or 10,000 votes, whichever is less.

The demand for a recount must be in writing and must be received by the State Board of Elections by noon on the second business day after the county canvass. If at that time the available returns show a candidate not entitled to a mandatory recount, but the Executive Director determines subsequently that the margin is within the threshold set out in this subsection, the Executive Director shall notify the eligible candidate immediately and that candidate shall be entitled to a recount if that candidate so demands within 48 hours of notice. The recount shall be conducted under the supervision of the State Board of Elections.

(d) Rules for Conducting Recounts. - The State Board of Elections shall promulgate rules for conducting recounts. Those rules shall be subject to the following guidelines:

(1) The rules shall specify, with respect to each type of voting system, when and to what extent the recount shall consist of machine recounts and hand-to-eye recounts. Hand-to-eye recounts shall also be ordered as provided by G.S. 163-182.7A.

(2) The rules shall provide guidance in interpretation of the voter's choice.

(3) The rules shall specify how the goals of multipartisan participation, opportunity for public observation, and good order shall be balanced. (2001-398, s. 3; 2003-278, ss. 10(b), 10(c); 2005-323, s. 6(a); 2005-428, s. 11(b).)

§ 163-182.7A. Additional provisions for hand-to-eye recounts.

(a) The rules promulgated by the State Board of Elections for recounts shall provide that if the initial recount is not hand-to-eye, and if the recount does not reverse the results, the candidate who had originally been entitled to a recount may, within 24 hours of the completion of the first recount, demand a second recount on a hand-to-eye basis in a sample of precincts. If the initial recount was not hand-to-eye and it reversed the results, the candidate who had initially been the winner shall have the same right to ask for a hand-to-eye recount in a sample of precincts.

That sample shall be all the ballots in three percent (3%) of the precincts casting ballots in each county in the jurisdiction of the office, rounded up to the next whole number of precincts. For the purpose of that calculation, each one-stop (early) voting site shall be considered to be a precinct. The precincts to be recounted by a hand-to-eye count shall be chosen at random within each county. If the results of the hand-to-eye recount differ from the previous results within those precincts to the extent that extrapolating the amount of the change to the entire jurisdiction (based on the proportion of ballots recounted to the total votes cast for that office) would result in the reversing of the results, then the State Board of Elections shall order a hand-to-eye recount of the entire jurisdiction in which the election is held. There shall be no cost to the candidate for that recount in the entire jurisdiction.

(b)   Recounts under this section shall be governed by rules adopted under G.S. 163-182.7(d).

(c)   No complete hand-to-eye recount shall be conducted under this section if one has already been done under another provision of law. (2005-323, s. 6(b).)

§ 163-182.8. Determining result in case of a tie.

If the count, upon completion of canvass by the proper board of elections, shows a tie vote other than in a primary, the tie shall be resolved as follows:

(1)   If more than 5,000 voters cast official ballots in the ballot item, the State Board of Elections shall order a new election in which only the candidates or positions tied will be on the official ballot. The State Board of Elections shall set the schedule for publication of the notice, preparation of absentee official ballots, and the other actions necessary to conduct the election. Eligibility to vote in the new election shall be determined by the voter's eligibility at the time of the new election.

(2)   If 5,000 or fewer voters cast official ballots in the ballot item, the board of elections with jurisdiction to certify the election shall break the tie by a method of random selection to be determined by the State Board of Elections. (2001-398, s. 3.)

§ 163-182.9. Filing an election protest.

(a) Who May File a Protest With County Board. - A protest concerning the conduct of an election may be filed with the county board of elections by any registered voter who was eligible to vote in the election or by any person who was a candidate for nomination or election in the election.

(b) How Protest May Be Filed. - The following principles shall apply to the filing of election protests with the county board of elections:

(1) The protest shall be in writing and shall be signed by the protester. It shall include the protester's name, address, and telephone number and a statement that the person is a registered voter in the jurisdiction or a candidate.

(2) The protest shall state whether the protest concerns the manner in which votes were counted and results tabulated or concerns some other irregularity.

(3) The protest shall state what remedy the protester is seeking.

(4) The timing for filing a protest shall be as follows:

a. If the protest concerns the manner in which votes were counted or results tabulated, the protest shall be filed before the beginning of the county board of election's canvass meeting.

b. If the protest concerns the manner in which votes were counted or results tabulated and the protest states good cause for delay in filing, the protest may be filed until 5:00 P.M. on the second business day after the county board of elections has completed its canvass and declared the results.

c. If the protest concerns an irregularity other than vote counting or result tabulation, the protest shall be filed no later than 5:00 P.M. on the second business day after the county board has completed its canvass and declared the results.

d. If the protest concerns an irregularity on a matter other than vote counting or result tabulation and the protest is filed before election day, the protest proceedings shall be stayed, unless a party defending against the protest moves otherwise, until after election day if any one of the following conditions exists:

1. The ballot has been printed.

2. The voter registration deadline for that election has passed.

3. Any of the proceedings will occur within 30 days before election day.

(c) State Board to Prescribe Forms. - The State Board of Elections shall prescribe forms for filing protests. (2001-398, s. 3; 2005-428, s. 4.)

§ 163-182.10. Consideration of protest by county board of elections.

(a) Preliminary Consideration. - The following principles shall apply to the initial consideration of election protests by the county board of elections:

(1) The county board shall, as soon as possible after the protest is filed, meet to determine whether the protest substantially complies with G.S. 163-182.9 and whether it establishes probable cause to believe that a violation of election law or irregularity or misconduct has occurred. If the board determines that one or both requirements are not met, the board shall dismiss the protest. The board shall notify both the protester and the State Board of Elections. The protester may file an amended protest or may appeal to the State Board. If the board determines that both requirements are met, it shall schedule a hearing.

(2) If a protest was filed before the canvass and concerns the counting and tabulating of votes, the county board shall resolve the protest before the canvass is completed. If necessary to provide time to resolve the protest, the county board may recess the canvass meeting, but shall not delay the completion of the canvass for more than three days unless approved by the State Board of Elections. Resolution of the protest shall not delay the canvass of ballot items unaffected by the protest. The appeal of a dismissal shall not delay the canvass.

(3) If a protest concerns an irregularity other than the counting or tabulating of votes, that protest shall not delay the canvass.

(b) Notice of Hearing. - The county board shall give notice of the protest hearing to the protester, any candidate likely to be affected, any election official alleged to have acted improperly, and those persons likely to have a significant interest in the resolution of the protest. Each person given notice shall also be given a copy of the protest or a summary of its allegations. The manner of notice shall be as follows:

(1)   If the protest concerns the manner in which the votes were counted or the results tabulated, the protester shall be told at the time of filing that the protest will be heard at the time of the canvass. Others shall be notified as far in advance of the canvass as time permits.

(2)   If the protest concerns a matter other than the manner in which votes were counted or results tabulated, the county board shall comply with rules to be promulgated by the State Board of Elections concerning reasonable notice of the hearing.

Failure to comply with the notice requirements in this subsection shall not delay the holding of a hearing nor invalidate the results if it appears reasonably likely that all interested persons were aware of the hearing and had an opportunity to be heard.

(c)   Conduct of Hearing. - The following principles shall apply to the conduct of a protest hearing before the county board of elections:

(1)   The county board may allow evidence to be presented at the hearing in the form of affidavits or it may examine witnesses. The chair or any two members of the board may subpoena witnesses or documents. Each witness must be placed under oath before testifying.

(2)   The county board may receive evidence at the hearing from any person with information concerning the subject of the protest. The person who made the protest shall be permitted to present allegations and introduce evidence at the hearing. Any other person to whom notice of hearing was given, if present, shall be permitted to present evidence. The board may allow evidence by affidavit. The board may permit evidence to be presented by a person to whom notice was not given, if the person apparently has a significant interest in the resolution of the protest that is not adequately represented by other participants.

(3)   The hearing shall be recorded by a reporter or by mechanical means, and the full record of the hearing shall be preserved by the county board until directed otherwise by the State Board.

(d) Findings of Fact and Conclusions of Law by County Board. - The county board shall make a written decision on each protest which shall state separately each of the following:

(1) Findings of fact. - The findings of fact shall be based exclusively on the evidence and on matters officially noticed. Findings of fact, if set forth in statutory language, shall be accompanied by a concise and explicit statement of the underlying facts supporting them.

(2) Conclusions of law. - The conclusions the county board may state, and their consequences for the board's order, are as follows:

a. "The protest should be dismissed because it does not substantially comply with G.S. 163-182.9." If the board makes this conclusion, it shall order the protest dismissed.

b. "The protest should be dismissed because there is not substantial evidence of a violation of the election law or other irregularity or misconduct." If the county board makes this conclusion, it shall order the protest dismissed.

c. "The protest should be dismissed because there is not substantial evidence of any violation, irregularity, or misconduct sufficient to cast doubt on the results of the election." If the county board makes this conclusion, it shall order the protest dismissed.

d. "There is substantial evidence to believe that a violation of the election law or other irregularity or misconduct did occur, and might have affected the outcome of the election, but the board is unable to finally determine the effect because the election was a multicounty election." If the county board makes this conclusion, it shall order that the protest and the county board's decision be sent to the State Board for action by it.

e. "There is substantial evidence to believe that a violation of the election law or other irregularity or misconduct did occur and that it was sufficiently serious to cast doubt on the apparent results of the election." If the county board makes this conclusion, it may order any of the following as appropriate:

1. That the vote total as stated in the precinct return or result of the canvass be corrected and new results declared.

2. That votes be recounted.

3. That the protest and the county board's decision be sent to the State Board for action by it.

4. Any other action within the authority of the county board.

(3) An order. - Depending on the conclusion reached by the county board, its order shall be as directed in subdivision (c)(2). If the county board is not able to determine what law is applicable to the Findings of Fact, it may send its findings of fact to the State Board for it to determine the applicable law.

(e) Rules by State Board of Elections. - The State Board of Elections shall promulgate rules providing for adequate notice to parties, scheduling of hearings, and the timing of deliberations and issuance of decision. (2001-398, s. 3.)

§ 163-182.11. Appeal of a protest decision by the county board to the State Board of Elections.

(a) Notice and Perfection of Appeal. - The decision by the county board of elections on an election protest may be appealed to the State Board of Elections by any of the following:

(1) The person who filed the protest.

(2) A candidate or elected official adversely affected by the county board's decision.

(3) Any other person who participated in the hearing and has a significant interest adversely affected by the county board's decision.

Written notice of the appeal must be given to the county board within 24 hours after the county board files the written decision at its office. The appeal to the State Board must be in writing. The appeal must be delivered or deposited in the mail, addressed to the State Board, by the appropriate one of the following: (i) the end of the second day after the day the decision was filed by the county board in its office, if the decision concerns a first primary; or (ii) the end of the fifth day after the day the decision was filed in the county board office, if the decision concerns an election other than a first primary.

The State Board shall prescribe forms for filing appeals from the county board.

(b) Consideration of Appeal by State Board. - In its consideration of an appeal from a decision of a county board of elections on a protest, the State Board of Elections may do any of the following:

(1) Decide the appeal on the basis of the record from the county board, as long as the county board has made part of the record a transcript of the evidentiary hearing.

(2) Request the county board or any interested person to supplement the record from the county board, and then decide the appeal on the basis of that supplemented record.

(3) Receive additional evidence and then decide the appeal on the basis of the record and that additional evidence.

(4) Hold its own hearing on the protest and resolve the protest on the basis of that hearing.

(5) Remand the matter to the county board for further proceedings in compliance with an order of the State Board.

The State Board shall follow the procedures set forth in subsections (c) and (d) of G.S. 163-182.10 except where they are clearly inapplicable.

The State Board shall give notice of its decision as required by G.S. 163-182.14, and may notify the county board and other interested persons in its discretion. (2001-398, s. 3.)

§ 163-182.12. Authority of State Board of Elections over protests.

The State Board of Elections may consider protests that were not filed in compliance with G.S. 163-182.9, may initiate and consider complaints on its own motion, may intervene and take jurisdiction over protests pending before a county board, and may take any other action necessary to assure that an election is determined without taint of fraud or corruption and without irregularities that may have changed the result of an election. Where a known group of voters cast votes that were lost beyond retrieval or where a known group of voters was given an incorrect ballot style, the State Board of Elections may authorize a county board of elections to allow those voters to recast their votes during a period of two weeks after the canvass by the State Board of

Elections required in G.S. 163-182.5(c). If there is no State Board canvass after the election, the State Board may authorize the county board to allow the recasting of votes during the two weeks after the county canvass set in G.S. 163-182.5(a). If the State Board approves a recasting of votes under this section, any procedures the county board uses to contact those voters and allow them to recast their votes shall be subject to approval by the State Board. Those recast votes shall be added to the returns and included in the canvass. The recasting of those votes shall not be deemed a new election for purposes of G.S. 163-182.13. (2001-398, s. 3; 2005-428, s. 17; 2007-391, s. 12; 2008-187, s. 33(a).)

§ 163-182.13. New elections.

(a) When State Board May Order New Election. - The State Board of Elections may order a new election, upon agreement of at least four of its members, in the case of any one or more of the following:

(1) Ineligible voters sufficient in number to change the outcome of the election were allowed to vote in the election, and it is not possible from examination of the official ballots to determine how those ineligible voters voted and to correct the totals.

(2) Eligible voters sufficient in number to change the outcome of the election were improperly prevented from voting.

(3) Other irregularities affected a sufficient number of votes to change the outcome of the election.

(4) Irregularities or improprieties occurred to such an extent that they taint the results of the entire election and cast doubt on its fairness.

(b) State Board to Set Procedures. - The State Board of Elections shall determine when a new election shall be held and shall set the schedule for publication of the notice, preparation of absentee official ballots, and the other actions necessary to conduct the election.

(c) Eligibility to Vote in New Election. - Eligibility to vote in the new election shall be determined by the voter's eligibility at the time of the new election, except that in a primary, no person who voted in the initial primary of one party shall vote in the new election in the primary of another party. The State Board of Elections shall promulgate rules to effect the provisions of this subsection.

(d)   Jurisdiction in Which New Election Held. - The new election shall be held in the entire jurisdiction in which the original election was held.

(e)   Which Candidates to Be on Official Ballot. - All the candidates who were listed on the official ballot in the original election shall be listed in the same order on the official ballot for the new election, except in either of the following:

(1)   If a candidate dies or otherwise becomes ineligible between the time of the original election and the new election, that candidate may be replaced in the same manner as if the vacancy occurred before the original election.

(2)   If the election is for a multiseat office, and the irregularities could not have affected the election of one or more of the candidates, the new election, upon agreement of at least four members of the State Board, may be held among only those candidates whose election could have been affected by the irregularities.

(f)   Tie Votes. - If ineligible voters voted in an election and it is possible to determine from the official ballots the way in which those votes were cast and to correct the results, and consequently the election ends in a tie, the provisions of G.S. 163-182.8 concerning tie votes shall apply. (2001-398, s. 3; 2003-278, s. 8(a); 2008-150, s. 2(a).)

§ 163-182.13A. Contested elections for Council of State offices.

(a)   Application of Procedures. - A contested election for any elective office established by Article III of the Constitution shall be determined by joint ballot of both houses of the General Assembly under Article VI, Section 5 of the Constitution in accordance with the provisions of this section. Except as provided by this section, the provisions of Article 3 of Chapter 120 shall apply to contested elections under this section and shall govern standing, notice of intent to contest, answers, service of process, evidence, the petition, procedures, grounds, and relief except as provided in this section. All filings shall be with the Principal Clerk of the House of Representatives.

(b)   Notice of Intent. - Notice of the intent to contest the election under this section shall be filed with the Principal Clerk of the House of Representatives as if it were a contested election for the House of Representatives as prescribed in Article 3 of Chapter 120.

(c) Jurisdiction. - When a contest arises out of the general election, the General Assembly elected at the same time shall hear and decide it. Any other contest shall be heard by the General Assembly sitting at the time of the election.

(d) Committee. - A contest filed under this section shall initially be heard before a select committee consisting of five Senators appointed by the President Pro Tempore and five Representatives appointed by the Speaker of the House of Representatives. Not more than three members of the Senate appointed by the President Pro Tempore shall be members of the same political party. Not more than three members of the House of Representatives appointed by the Speaker shall be members of the same political party. That committee shall have the same power as a committee under Article 3 of Chapter 120 and may adopt supplemental rules as necessary to govern its proceedings. The committee shall report its findings as to the law and the facts and make recommendations to the General Assembly for its action.

(e) Final Determination. - The final determination on the recommendations of the committee shall be made by the General Assembly, both houses sitting in joint session in the Hall of the House of Representatives, with the Speaker of the House of Representatives presiding. The vote shall be taken as provided by Article VI, Section 5 of the Constitution. In order to find for the contestant or contestee and order the contestant or contestee elected, the vote on the joint ballot must include the affirmative vote of a majority of the members of the General Assembly voting on the issue. The ballots shall be in writing and are subject to the provisions of G.S. 143-318.13(b).

(f) Basis for Decision. -

(1) If the contest is as to the eligibility or qualifications of the contestee, the General Assembly shall determine if the contestee is eligible and qualified. If it determines that the contestee is not eligible or not qualified, it shall order a new election.

(2) If the contest is as to the conduct or results of the election, the General Assembly shall determine which candidate received the highest number of votes. If it can determine which candidate received the highest number of votes, it shall declare that candidate to be elected. If it cannot determine which

candidate received the highest number of votes, it may order a new election, or may order such other relief as may be necessary and proper. If it determines that two or more candidates shall be equal and highest in votes, the provisions of G.S. 147-4 shall apply.

(g) Final Determination. - A copy of the final determination of the General Assembly under this section shall be filed with the Secretary of State and with the State Board of Elections.

(h) Copies. - The Principal Clerk of the House of Representatives shall make copies of any filings and transmit them to the Principal Clerk for the Senate.

(i) Applicability. - This section applies only to a general or special election and does not apply to the primary or any other part of the nominating process.

(j) Judicial Proceedings Abated. - Notwithstanding any other provision of law, upon the initiation of a contest under this Article, any judicial proceedings involving either the contestant or the contestee encompassing the issues set forth in the notice of intent or an answer thereto concerning the election that is the subject of the contest shall abate. The clerk shall file a copy of the notice of intent and final determination with the court in any judicial proceeding pending prior to the filing of the notice of intent.

(k) General Assembly Determination Not Reviewable. - The decision of the General Assembly in determining the contest of the election pursuant to this section may not be reviewed by the General Court of Justice.

(l) Definition. - As used in this section, "contest" means a challenge to the apparent election for any elective office established by Article III of the Constitution or to request the decision of an undecided election to any elective office established by Article III of the Constitution, where the challenge or the request is filed in accordance with the timing and procedures of this section. (2005-3, s. 3(a).)

§ 163-182.14. Appeal of a final decision to superior court; appeal to the General Assembly or a house thereof.

(a) Final Decision. - A copy of the final decision of the State Board of Elections on an election protest shall be served on the parties personally or through delivery by U.S. mail or a designated delivery service authorized under 26 U.S.C. § 7502(f)(2) if that delivery provides a record of the date and time of delivery to the address provided by the party. A decision to order a new election is considered a final decision for purposes of seeking review of the decision.

(b) Timing of Right of Appeal. - Except in the case of a general or special election to either house of the General Assembly or to an office established by Article III of the Constitution, an aggrieved party has the right to appeal the final decision to the Superior Court of Wake County within 10 days of the date of service.

After the decision by the State Board of Elections has been served on the parties, the certification of nomination or election or the results of the referendum shall issue pursuant to G.S. 163-182.15 unless an appealing party obtains a stay of the certification from the Superior Court of Wake County within 10 days after the date of service. The court shall not issue a stay of certification unless the petitioner shows the court that the petitioner has appealed the decision of the State Board of Elections, that the petitioner is an aggrieved party, and that the petitioner is likely to prevail in the appeal.

If service is by mail or a designated delivery service, the additional time after service provided in Rule 6(e) of the North Carolina Rules of Civil Procedure shall apply to both the time for appeal and the time to obtain a stay under this subsection.

(c) Contests for General Assembly and Executive Branch Offices. - In the case of a general or special election to either house of the General Assembly or to an office established by Article III of the Constitution, an unsuccessful candidate has the right to appeal the final decision to the General Assembly in accordance with Article 3 of Chapter 120 and G.S. 163-182.13A, as appropriate.

After the decision by the State Board of Elections has been served on the parties, the certification of nomination or election shall issue pursuant to G.S. 163-182.15 unless a contest of the election is initiated pursuant to Article 3 of Chapter 120 or G.S. 163-182.13A, as appropriate.

(d) Attorney's fees shall not be awarded against the State Board of Elections in any election protest brought under this Article. (2001-398, s. 3; 2003-278, s. 8(b); 2005-3, s. 4; 2008-150, s. 4(a); 2009-541, s. 27.)

§ 163-182.15. Certificate of nomination or election, or certificate of the results of a referendum.

(a) Issued by County Board of Elections. - In ballot items within the jurisdiction of the county board of elections, the county board shall issue a certificate of nomination or election, or a certificate of the results of the referendum, as appropriate. The certificate shall be issued by the county board six days after the completion of the canvass pursuant to G.S. 163-182.5, unless there is an election protest pending. If there is an election protest, the certificate of nomination or election or the certificate of the result of the referendum shall be issued in one of the following ways, as appropriate:

(1) The certificate shall be issued five days after the protest is dismissed or denied by the county board of elections, unless that decision has been appealed to the State Board of Elections.

(2) The certificate shall be issued on the tenth day after the final decision of the State Board, unless the State Board has ordered a new election or the issuance of the certificate is stayed by the Superior Court of Wake County pursuant to G.S. 163-182.14.

(3) If the decision of the State Board has been appealed to the Superior Court of Wake County and the court has stayed the certification, the certificate shall be issued five days after the entry of a final order in the case in the Superior Court of Wake County, unless that court or an appellate court orders otherwise.

(4) No certificate of election need be issued for any member of the General Assembly following a contest of the election pursuant to Article 3 of Chapter 120.

(b) Issued by State Board of Elections. - In ballot items within the jurisdiction of the State Board of Elections, the State Board of Elections shall issue a certificate of nomination or election, or a certificate of the results of the referendum, as appropriate. The certificate shall be issued by the State Board six days after the completion of the canvass pursuant to G.S. 163-182.5, unless there is an election protest pending. If there is an election protest, the certificate of nomination or election or the certificate of the result of the referendum shall be issued in one of the following ways, as appropriate:

(1) The certificate shall be issued 10 days after the final decision of the State Board on the election protest, unless the State Board has ordered a new election or the issuance of the certificate is stayed by the Superior Court of Wake County pursuant to G.S. 163-182.14.

(2) If the decision of the State Board has been appealed to the Superior Court of Wake County and the court has stayed the certification, the certificate shall be issued five days after the entry of a final order in the case in the Superior Court of Wake County, unless that court or an appellate court orders otherwise.

(3) The certificate shall be issued immediately upon the filing of a copy of the determination of the General Assembly with the State Board of Elections in contested elections involving any elective office established by Article III of the Constitution.

(4) No certificate of election need be issued for any member of the General Assembly following a contest of the election pursuant to Article 3 of Chapter 120.

(c) Copy to Secretary of State. - The State Board of Elections shall provide to the Secretary of State a copy of each certificate of nomination or election, or certificate of the results of a referendum, issued by it. The Secretary shall keep the certificates in a form readily accessible and useful to the public.

(d) Determining Results. - In a primary for party nomination, the results shall be determined in accordance with G.S. 163-111. In a general election, the individuals having the highest number of votes for each office shall be declared elected to the office, and the certificate shall be issued accordingly. In a referendum, the ballot proposal receiving the highest number of votes shall be declared to have prevailed, and the certificate shall be issued accordingly. (2001-398, s. 3; 2003-278, s. 10(k); 2005-3, s. 5; 2005-428, s. 13; 2007-391, s. 11; 2007-484, s. 22; 2008-187, s. 33(a).)

§ 163-182.16. Governor to issue commissions for certain offices.

The Secretary of State shall send a notice to the Governor that a certificate of election has been issued for any of the following offices, and upon receiving the notice, the Governor shall provide to each such elected official a commission attesting to that person's election:

(1)   Members of the United States House of Representatives.

(2)   Justices, judges, and district attorneys of the General Court of Justice. (2001-398, s. 3.)

§ 163-182.17. Summary of officials' duties under this Article.

(a)   This Section a Summary. - The provisions of this section provide a nonexclusive summary of the duties given to officials under this Article. The legal duty is contained, not in this section, but in the other sections of this Article.

(b)   Duties of the Precinct Officials. - Precinct officials, in accordance with rules of the State Board of Elections and under the supervision of the county board of elections, shall perform all of the following:

(1)   Count votes when votes are required to be counted at the voting place. G.S. 163-182.2.

(2)   Make an unofficial report of returns to the county board of elections. G.S. 163-182.2.

(3)   Certify the integrity of the vote and the security of the official ballots at the voting place. G.S. 163-182.2.

(4)   Return official ballots and equipment to the county board of elections. G.S. 163-182.2.

(c)   Duties of the County Board of Elections. - The county board of elections, in accordance with rules of the State Board of Elections, shall perform all of the following:

(1)   Count absentee and provisional official ballots and other official ballots required to be initially counted by the county board of elections. G.S. 163-182.2.

(2)   Canvass results in all ballot items on the official ballot in the county. G.S. 163-182.5.

(3) Order a recount in any ballot item on the official ballot in the county, where necessary to complete the canvass, and where not prohibited from doing so. G.S. 163-182.7.

(4) Conduct any recount that has been ordered by the county board of elections or the State Board of Elections or that has been properly demanded in accordance with G.S. 163-182.7(b).

(5) Conduct hearings in election protests as provided in G.S. 163-182.10.

(6) Prepare abstracts of returns in all the ballot items in the county. G.S. 163-182.6.

(7) Retain one original abstract and distribute the other two originals as follows:

a. One to the clerk of superior court in the county.

b. One to the State Board of Elections. G.S. 163-182.6.

(8) Issue a certificate of nomination or election or a certificate of the results of a referendum in each ballot item within the jurisdiction of the county board of elections. Provide a copy of the certificate to the clerk of court. G.S. 163-182.15.

(d) Duties of the State Board of Elections. - The State Board of Elections shall perform all the following:

(1) Promulgate rules as directed in this Article. G.S. 163-182.1, 163-182.2, 163-182.7, 163-182.10, and 163-182.13.

(2) Provide supervisory direction to the county boards of elections as provided in this Article. G.S. 163-182.1 and G.S. 163-182.2.

(3) Canvass the results in ballot items within the jurisdiction of the State Board of Elections. G.S. 163-182.5.

(4) Order and supervise a recount in any ballot item within the jurisdiction of the State Board of Elections, where necessary to complete the canvass. G.S. 163-182.7.

(5) Hear and decide appeals from decisions of county boards of elections in election protests. G.S. 163-182.11.

(6) Order new elections in accordance with G.S. 163-182.15.

(7) Prepare, in duplicate originals, composite abstracts of ballot items within the jurisdiction of the State Board of Elections. G.S. 163-182.6.

(8) Retain one original of the composite abstract and deliver to the Secretary of State the other original composite abstract of the results of ballot items within the jurisdiction of the State Board of Elections. G.S. 163-182.6.

(9) Certify the results of any election within the jurisdiction of the State Board of Elections and provide a copy to the Secretary of State. G.S. 163-182.15.

(e) Duties of the Secretary of State. - The Secretary of State shall retain and compile in a useful form all the abstracts and returns provided by the county boards of elections and the State Board of Elections. G.S. 163-182.6.

(f) Duty of the Governor. - The Governor shall issue a commission to any person elected to an office listed in G.S. 163-182.16 upon notification from the Secretary of State that a certificate of election has been issued to the person. G.S. 163-182.16. (2001-398, s. 3.)

§§ 116-183 through 116-186. Reserved for future codification purposes.

Article 16.

Canvass of Returns for Higher Offices and Preparation of State Abstracts.

§§ 163-187 through 163-200: Repealed by Session Laws 2001-398, s. 1.

Article 17.

Members of United States House of Representatives.

§ 163-201. Congressional districts specified.

(a) For purposes of nominating and electing members of the House of Representatives of the Congress of the United States in 2012 and every two years thereafter; the State of North Carolina shall be divided into 13 districts as follows:

District 1: Beaufort County: VTD: PSJW3, VTD: WASH1, VTD: WASH2; Bertie County, Chowan County: VTD: 1, VTD: 2, VTD: 4; Craven County: VTD: 06, VTD: 07, VTD: 08, VTD: 09, VTD: N1, VTD: N2, VTD: N4, VTD: N5; Durham County: VTD: 01, VTD: 02, VTD: 03, VTD: 05, VTD: 06, VTD: 07, VTD: 08, VTD: 09, VTD: 10, VTD: 12, VTD: 13, VTD: 14, VTD: 15, VTD: 17, VTD: 18, VTD: 19, VTD: 20, VTD: 21, VTD: 22, VTD: 23, VTD: 24, VTD: 29, VTD: 30-1, VTD: 30-2, VTD: 31, VTD: 34, VTD: 40, VTD: 41, VTD: 42, VTD: 46, VTD: 47, VTD: 52, VTD: 54, VTD: 55; Edgecombe County: VTD: 0101, VTD: 0102, VTD: 0104, VTD: 0201, VTD: 0301, VTD: 0401, VTD: 0501, VTD: 0601, VTD: 0701, VTD: 0901: Block(s) 0650216003018; VTD: 1101: 0650213001009, 0650213002000, 0650213002001, 0650213002002, 0650213002003, 0650213002004, 0650213002005, 0650213002006, 0650213002007, 0650213002008, 0650213002009, 0650213002010, 0650213002011, 0650213002012, 0650213002013, 0650213002014, 0650213002015, 0650213002016, 0650213002017, 0650213002018, 0650213002019, 0650213002022, 0650213002025, 0650213002026, 0650213002027, 0650213002028, 0650213002029, 0650213002036, 0650213002037; VTD: 1201, VTD: 1202, VTD: 1203: Block(s) 0650202001034, 0650202001035, 0650202001037, 0650202004015, 0650202004027, 0650202004028, 0650202004029, 0650202004031, 0650202004032, 0650202005021, 0650202005022, 0650202005023, 0650202005028, 0650202006000, 0650202006001, 0650202006002, 0650202006003, 0650202006005, 0650202006006, 0650202006007, 0650202006008, 0650202006009, 0650202006010, 0650202006011, 0650202006013, 0650202006017, 0650202006018, 0650202006023, 0650202006024, 0650202006025, 0650202006026, 0650202006027, 0650202006028, 0650202006029, 0650202006030, 0650202006031, 0650202006032, 0650202006035, 0650202006036, 0650202006038, 0650202006039, 0650202006040, 0650202006041, 0650202006043, 0650202006052, 0650203004000, 0650203004001, 0650203004002, 0650203004003, 0650203004010, 0650203004011, 0650203004012, 0650203004013, 0650203004014, 0650203004015, 0650203004016, 0650203004017, 0650203004018, 0650203004019, 0650203004020, 0650203004021, 0650203004022, 0650203004023, 0650203004024, 0650203004025, 0650203004026, 0650203004033, 0650203004034, 0650203004050, 0650203004051, 0650203004052, 0650204005000, 0650204005001, 0650204005008,

0650204005009, 0650204005010, 0650204005011, 0650204005012, 0650204005013, 0650204005014, 0650204005015, 0650204005016, 0650204005017, 0650204005019, 0650204005020, 0650204005021, 0650204005022, 0650204005050, 0650204005051, 0650204005052, 0650204005053, 0650204005054, 0650204005055, 0650204005056, 0650204005063, 0650204005064, 0650213001000, 0650213001001, 0650213001002, 0650213001003, 0650213001004, 0650213001005, 0650213001006, 0650213001007, 0650213001008, 0650213001010, 0650213001011, 0650213001012, 0650213001013, 0650213001014, 0650213001015, 0650213001016, 0650213001017, 0650213001018, 0650213001019, 0650213001022, 0650213001023, 0650213001024, 0650213001026, 0650213001027, 0650213001028, 0650213001029, 0650213001041, 0650213001042, 0650213002020, 0650213002021, 0650213002023, 0650213002024, 0650213002030, 0650213002031, 0650213002032, 0650213002033, 0650213002034; VTD: 1204, VTD: 1205; Franklin County: VTD: 01, VTD: 02, VTD: 03: Block(s) 0690604011000, 0690604011001, 0690604011002, 0690604011003, 0690604011004, 0690604011026, 0690604011027, 0690604011028, 0690604011029, 0690604011035, 0690604011036, 0690604021016, 0690604021022, 0690604021037, 0690604021038, 0690604021039, 0690604021040, 0690604021041, 0690604021042, 0690604021043, 0690604021044, 0690604021050, 0690604021051, 0690604021052, 0690604021053, 0690604021054, 0690604021055, 0690604021057, 0690604021058, 0690604021059, 0690604021060, 0690604021061, 0690604021063, 0690604021064, 0690604021065, 0690604021066, 0690604021067, 0690604021068, 0690604021069, 0690604021070, 0690604021071, 0690604021072, 0690604021073, 0690604021074, 0690604021075, 0690604021076, 0690604021077, 0690604021078, 0690604021079, 0690604021080, 0690604021081, 0690604021082, 0690604021083, 0690604021084, 0690604021085, 0690604021086, 0690604021087, 0690604021088, 0690604021089, 0690604021090, 0690604021091, 0690604021092, 0690604021093, 0690604021094, 0690604021095, 0690604021096, 0690604021097, 0690604021098, 0690604021099, 0690604021101, 0690604021102, 0690604021104, 0690604023007, 0690604023008, 0690604023009, 0690604023010, 0690604023011, 0690604023012, 0690604023013, 0690604023014, 0690604023016, 0690604023017, 0690604023019, 0690604023022, 0690604023029, 0690604023037, 0690604023038, 0690604023039, 0690604023040, 0690604023041, 0690604023042, 0690604023043, 0690604023044, 0690604023045, 0690604023046, 0690604023047, 0690604023048, 0690604023051, 0690604023052, 0690604023053, 0690604023054,

0690604023055, 0690604023056, 0690604023058, 0690604023059, 0690604023074, 0690604023078, 0690604023079, 0690604023082, 0690604023083, 0690604023084, 0690604023085, 0690604023087, 0690604023088, 0690604023089, 0690604023091, 0690604023096, 0690605011018, 0690605011019; VTD: 10, VTD: 11, VTD: 15, VTD: 16; Gates County: VTD: 1, VTD: 4S; Granville County: VTD: ANTI, VTD: BTNR, VTD: CORI, VTD: CRDL, VTD: EAOX, VTD: SALM, VTD: SOOX, VTD: TYHO, VTD: WOEL; Greene County: VTD: ARBA, VTD: BULL, VTD: SH1, VTD: SHIN, VTD: SUGG, VTD: WALS: Block(s) 0799501011000, 0799501011001, 0799501011002, 0799501011003, 0799501011004, 0799501011005, 0799501011006, 0799501011007, 0799501011008, 0799501011009, 0799501011010, 0799501011011, 0799501011012, 0799501011013, 0799501011014, 0799501011015, 0799501011027, 0799501011028, 0799501011029, 0799501011031, 0799501011032, 0799501011033, 0799501011034, 0799501011035, 0799501011036, 0799501011037, 0799501011038, 0799501011040, 0799501011041, 0799501011042, 0799501011043, 0799501011057, 0799501011068, 0799501011081, 0799501011082, 0799501011084, 0799501011090, 0799501011091, 0799501011093, 0799501011094, 0799501012000, 0799501012001, 0799501012002, 0799501012003, 0799501012004, 0799501012005, 0799501012006, 0799501012007, 0799501012008, 0799501012009, 0799501012010, 0799501012011, 0799501012012, 0799501012013, 0799501012014, 0799501012015, 0799501012016, 0799501012020, 0799501012021, 0799501012022, 0799501012023, 0799501012040, 0799501012041; Halifax County, Hertford County, Lenoir County: VTD: K1, VTD: K2, VTD: K3, VTD: K5, VTD: K6, VTD: K7, VTD: K8, VTD: K9, VTD: MH, VTD: SH, VTD: V: Block(s) 1070108001002, 1070108001006, 1070108001007, 1070108001034, 1070109001000, 1070109001001, 1070109001002, 1070109001003, 1070109001004, 1070109001005, 1070109001006, 1070109001007, 1070109001008, 1070109001009, 1070109001010, 1070109001011, 1070109001012, 1070109001013, 1070109001014, 1070109001015, 1070109001016, 1070109001017, 1070109001018, 1070109001019, 1070109001020, 1070109002000, 1070109002001, 1070109002002, 1070109002003, 1070109002004, 1070109002005, 1070109002006, 1070109002007, 1070109002008, 1070109002009, 1070109002010, 1070109002011, 1070109002012, 1070109002013, 1070109002014, 1070109002015, 1070109002016, 1070109002017, 1070109002018, 1070109002019, 1070109002020, 1070109002021, 1070109002022, 1070109002023, 1070109002024, 1070109002025, 1070109002026, 1070109002027, 1070109002028, 1070109002029, 1070109002030, 1070109002031, 1070109002032, 1070109002033,

1070109002034; Martin County: VTD: GN, VTD: HM, VTD: HS, VTD: J: Block(s) 1179701001000, 1179701001001, 1179701001002, 1179701001003, 1179701001004, 1179701001005, 1179701001006, 1179701001007, 1179701001008, 1179701001009, 1179701001010, 1179701001012, 1179701001013, 1179701001014, 1179701001015, 1179701001016, 1179701001017, 1179701001018, 1179701001019, 1179701001021, 1179701001022, 1179701001023, 1179701001024, 1179701001025, 1179701001026, 1179701001027, 1179701001028, 1179701001029, 1179701001030, 1179701001031, 1179701001064, 1179701001065, 1179701001066, 1179701001067, 1179701001068, 1179701001071, 1179701001072, 1179701001081, 1179701001082; VTD: R1, VTD: R2, VTD: W1, VTD: W2; Nash County: VTD: 0002, VTD: 0003, VTD: 0007, VTD: 0011, VTD: 0021, VTD: 0022, VTD: 0025: Block(s) 1270105043015, 1270105043016, 1270105043017, 1270105043037; VTD: 0031, VTD: 0032, VTD: 0033, VTD: 0034, VTD: 0037: Block(s) 1270105032002, 1270105032005, 1270105032006, 1270105032007, 1270105032008, 1270105032009, 1270105032010, 1270105032011, 1270105032032, 1270105042008, 1270105042009, 1270105043000, 1270105043001, 1270105043002, 1270105043003, 1270105043005, 1270105043006, 1270105043007, 1270105043008, 1270105043009, 1270105043010, 1270105043012, 1270105043013, 1270105043014, 1270105043018, 1270105043019, 1270105043033; VTD: 0038, VTD: 0040; Northampton County, Pasquotank County: VTD: 1-A, VTD: 1-B: Block(s) 1399602001000, 1399602001001, 1399602001002, 1399602001003, 1399602001004, 1399602001005, 1399602001006, 1399602001007, 1399602001008, 1399602001009, 1399602001010, 1399602001011, 1399602001012, 1399602001013, 1399602001014, 1399602001015, 1399602001016, 1399602001017, 1399602001018, 1399602001019, 1399602001020, 1399602001021, 1399602001022, 1399602001023, 1399602001024, 1399602001025, 1399602001026, 1399602001027, 1399602001028, 1399602001029, 1399602001030, 1399602001031, 1399602001032, 1399602001033, 1399602001034, 1399602001035, 1399602001036, 1399602001037, 1399602001038, 1399602001039, 1399602001040, 1399602001041, 1399602003000, 1399602003001, 1399602003002, 1399602003003, 1399602003004, 1399602003005, 1399602003006, 1399602003008, 1399602003013, 1399607012002, 1399607012004, 1399607012005, 1399607012006, 1399607012007, 1399607012008, 1399607012009, 1399607012010, 1399607012011, 1399607012012, 1399607012013, 1399607012014, 1399607012015; VTD: 2-A: 1399601001001, 1399601001003, 1399601001004, 1399601001005, 1399601001006, 1399601001007, 1399601001008, 1399601001009, 1399601001010, 1399601001011, 1399601001012,

1399601001013, 1399601001014, 1399601001015, 1399601001016, 1399601001017, 1399601001019, 1399601001020, 1399601001021, 1399601001022, 1399601001023, 1399601001024, 1399601001025, 1399601001026, 1399601001027, 1399601001028, 1399601001029, 1399601001030, 1399601001031, 1399601001032, 1399601001033, 1399601001034, 1399601001035, 1399601001036, 1399601001037, 1399601001038, 1399601001039, 1399601001040; VTD: 2-B, VTD: 3-A, VTD: 3-B, VTD: 4-A: Block(s) 1399602002000, 1399602002001, 1399602002002, 1399602002003, 1399602002004, 1399602002005, 1399602002006, 1399602002007, 1399602002008, 1399602002009, 1399602002010, 1399602002011, 1399602002012, 1399602002013, 1399602002014, 1399602002015, 1399602002016, 1399602002017, 1399602002018, 1399602002019, 1399602002020, 1399602002021, 1399602002022, 1399602002023, 1399602002024, 1399602002025, 1399602002026, 1399602002027, 1399602002028, 1399602002029, 1399602002030, 1399602002031, 1399602002032, 1399602002033, 1399602002034, 1399602002035, 1399602002036, 1399602002037, 1399602002038, 1399602002039, 1399602002040, 1399602002041, 1399602002042, 1399603002035, 1399607011000, 1399607011001, 1399607011002, 1399607011003, 1399607011004, 1399607011005, 1399607011006, 1399607011008, 1399607011009, 1399607011010, 1399607011011, 1399607011012, 1399607011013, 1399607011014, 1399607011015, 1399607011016, 1399607011030, 1399607011031, 1399607011032, 1399607011050; VTD: 4-B: 1399602003007, 1399602003009, 1399602003010, 1399602003011, 1399602003012, 1399602003014, 1399602003015, 1399602003016, 1399602003017, 1399602003018, 1399602003019, 1399602003020, 1399602004000, 1399602004003, 1399602004004, 1399602004005, 1399602004006, 1399602004007, 1399602004008, 1399602004009, 1399602004010, 1399602004011, 1399602004012, 1399602004017, 1399602004018, 1399602004019, 1399602004020, 1399602004021, 1399602004022, 1399602004023, 1399602004024, 1399602004025, 1399602004026, 1399602004027, 1399602004028, 1399602004029, 1399602004030; VTD: MH, VTD: NEW: Block(s) 1399605031022, 1399605031028, 1399605031030, 1399605031031, 1399605031034, 1399605031035, 1399605031036, 1399605031037, 1399605031038, 1399605031039, 1399605031040, 1399605031045, 1399605031046, 1399605031050, 1399605031051, 1399605031052, 1399605031057, 1399605031074, 1399605031075, 1399605031076, 1399605031080, 1399605031084, 1399605031085, 1399605031086, 1399605031087, 1399605031088, 1399605031090, 1399605031091; VTD: PRO: 1399605022000, 1399605022001, 1399605022002, 1399605022003,

1399605022004, 1399605022005, 1399605022006, 1399605022008, 1399605022009, 1399605022011, 1399605022012, 1399605022013, 1399605022018, 1399605022032, 1399605022033, 1399605022036, 1399605022037, 1399605022038, 1399605031053, 1399605031054, 1399605031055, 1399605031056, 1399605031058, 1399605031059, 1399605031060, 1399605031061, 1399605031062, 1399605031063, 1399605031064, 1399605031065, 1399605031066, 1399605031067, 1399605031068, 1399605031069, 1399605031070, 1399605031071, 1399605031072, 1399605031073, 1399605031077, 1399605031078, 1399605031079, 1399605031081, 1399605031082, 1399605031083; Perquimans County: VTD: EAST H, VTD: PARKVI, VTD: WEST H; Pitt County: VTD: 0301, VTD: 0501: Block(s) 1470020021045, 1470020021065, 1470020021066, 1470020021067, 1470020025056, 1470020025057, 1470020025058, 1470020025062, 1470020025070, 1470020025072, 1470020025073, 1470020025081, 1470020025082, 1470020025083, 1470020025084, 1470020025085, 1470020025086, 1470020025096; VTD: 0701: 1470006011005, 1470006011006, 1470006011007, 1470017001000, 1470017001001, 1470017001002, 1470017001007, 1470017001015, 1470017001028, 1470017001029, 1470017001047, 1470017001048, 1470017001049, 1470017001050, 1470017001076, 1470019002006, 1470019003000, 1470019003001, 1470019003002, 1470019003003, 1470019003004, 1470019003005, 1470019003006, 1470019003009, 1470019003010, 1470019003011, 1470019003012, 1470019003013, 1470019003015, 1470019003016, 1470019003017, 1470019003018, 1470019003022, 1470019003023, 1470019003024, 1470019003025, 1470019003026, 1470019003027, 1470019003028, 1470019003029, 1470019003030, 1470019003031, 1470019003032, 1470019003033, 1470019003034, 1470019003035, 1470019003036, 1470019003037, 1470019003038, 1470019003039, 1470019003040, 1470019003041, 1470019003042, 1470019003043, 1470019003044, 1470019003045, 1470019003046; VTD: 0800A: 1470019001043, 1470019001044; VTD: 0901, VTD: 1101, VTD: 1201: Block(s) 1470008002000, 1470008002001, 1470008002011, 1470008002018, 1470008002019, 1470008002020, 1470008002021, 1470008002022, 1470008002023, 1470008002024, 1470008002025, 1470008002026, 1470008002027, 1470008002028, 1470008002029, 1470008002030, 1470008002031, 1470008002032, 1470008002033, 1470008002034, 1470008002035, 1470008002036, 1470008002037, 1470008002038, 1470008002039, 1470008002040, 1470008002041, 1470008002042, 1470008002050, 1470008002051, 1470008002052, 1470008002053, 1470008002054, 1470008002055, 1470008002056, 1470008002057, 1470008002060, 1470008002061,

1470008002062, 1470008002063, 1470008002065, 1470008002066, 1470008002067, 1470008002068, 1470008002134, 1470008002135, 1470008002136, 1470008002137, 1470008002138, 1470008002139, 1470008002140, 1470008002141, 1470008002142, 1470008002143, 1470008002144, 1470008002145, 1470008002146, 1470008002147, 1470008002148, 1470009001048, 1470009001051, 1470009002000, 1470009002001, 1470009002002, 1470009002003, 1470009002004, 1470009002005, 1470009002006, 1470009002007, 1470009002008, 1470009002009, 1470009002010, 1470009002011, 1470009002012, 1470009002013, 1470009002014, 1470009002015, 1470009002016, 1470009002017, 1470009002018, 1470009002019, 1470009002020, 1470009002021, 1470009002022, 1470009002023, 1470009002024, 1470009002025, 1470009002026, 1470009002027, 1470009002031, 1470009002032, 1470009002033, 1470009002034, 1470009002035, 1470009002036, 1470009002037, 1470009002038, 1470009002039, 1470009002040, 1470009002041, 1470009002042, 1470009002044, 1470009002045, 1470009002046, 1470009002047, 1470009002048, 1470009002049, 1470009002050, 1470009002051, 1470009002052, 1470009002053, 1470009002054, 1470009002055, 1470009002056, 1470009002057, 1470009002058, 1470009002073, 1470009002076, 1470009002077, 1470009002078, 1470009002079, 1470009002080, 1470009002081, 1470009002082, 1470009002083, 1470009002084, 1470009002093, 1470009002094, 1470009002095, 1470009002096, 1470009002097, 1470009002098, 1470009002099, 1470009002100, 1470009002101, 1470009002107, 1470009002108, 1470009003041, 1470009003042, 1470009003043, 1470009003044, 1470009003045, 1470009003046, 1470009003047, 1470009003050, 1470009003051, 1470009003052, 1470009003053, 1470009003054, 1470009003055, 1470009003056, 1470009003057, 1470009003058, 1470009003060, 1470009003065, 1470009003068; VTD: 1403A: 1470006032029, 1470006032037, 1470013011000, 1470013011001, 1470013011002, 1470013011003, 1470013011004, 1470013011005, 1470013011006, 1470013011030, 1470013011031, 1470013011032, 1470013011036, 1470013011037, 1470013011038, 1470013011081, 1470013012000, 1470013012001, 1470013012002, 1470013012003, 1470013012004, 1470013012005, 1470013012006, 1470013012007, 1470013012008, 1470013012012, 1470013012013, 1470013012014, 1470013012015, 1470013012019, 1470013012020, 1470013012021, 1470013012022, 1470013012023, 1470013012024, 1470013012025, 1470013012028, 1470013012029, 1470013012030, 1470013012031, 1470013012032, 1470013012033, 1470013012034, 1470013012035, 1470013012036,

1470013012037; VTD: 1403B: 1470013022035, 1470013022040, 1470013022041, 1470013022042, 1470013022043, 1470013022055, 1470013022056, 1470013022058, 1470013022059, 1470013022060, 1470013022061, 1470013022065; VTD: 1501, VTD: 1503, VTD: 1504, VTD: 1505A, VTD: 1505B, VTD: 1506: Block(s) 1470001003029, 1470001003030, 1470001003031, 1470001003032, 1470001003039, 1470001003040, 1470001003041, 1470001003042, 1470001003043, 1470001003044, 1470001003045, 1470001003046, 1470001003047, 1470001003048, 1470001003049, 1470001003050, 1470001003051, 1470001003055, 1470001003056, 1470001003057, 1470001003058, 1470001003059, 1470001003060, 1470001003061, 1470001003062, 1470001003063, 1470001003064, 1470001003065, 1470001004000, 1470001004001, 1470001004002, 1470001004003, 1470001004004, 1470001004005, 1470001004006, 1470001004007, 1470001004008, 1470001004009, 1470001004010, 1470001004011, 1470001004012, 1470001004013, 1470001004014, 1470001004015, 1470001004016, 1470001004017, 1470001004018, 1470001004019, 1470001004020, 1470001004021, 1470001004022, 1470001004023, 1470001004024, 1470001004025, 1470001004026, 1470001004027, 1470001004028, 1470001005005, 1470001005006, 1470001005007, 1470001005008, 1470001005012, 1470001005013, 1470001005014, 1470001005015, 1470001005019, 1470001005020, 1470001005021, 1470001005022, 1470001005023, 1470004004013; VTD: 1508A: 1470001003009, 1470001003010, 1470001003011, 1470001003017, 1470001003018, 1470001003019, 1470001003020, 1470001003023, 1470001003024, 1470001003025, 1470001003026; VTD: 1509: 1470009002028, 1470009002029, 1470009002030, 1470009002043, 1470009002059, 1470009002060, 1470009002061, 1470009002062, 1470009002063, 1470009002064, 1470009002065, 1470009002066, 1470009002067, 1470009002068, 1470009002069, 1470009002070, 1470009002071, 1470009002072, 1470009002074, 1470009002075, 1470009002102, 1470009002103, 1470009002104, 1470009002105, 1470009002106; VTD: 1512A: 1470006031000, 1470006031001, 1470006031002, 1470006031004, 1470006031005, 1470006031006, 1470006031008, 1470006031009, 1470006031010, 1470006031011, 1470006031012, 1470006032000, 1470006032001, 1470006032002, 1470006032003, 1470006032004, 1470006032005, 1470006032006, 1470006032007, 1470006032008, 1470006032030, 1470006032031, 1470006032032, 1470006032033; VTD: 1512B: 1470006033031, 1470006033032, 1470006033033, 1470006034000, 1470006034002; Vance County: VTD: DABN, VTD: EH1, VTD: EH2, VTD: HTOP, VTD: MIDD, VTD: NH1, VTD: NH2, VTD: SH1, VTD: SH2, VTD: TWNS,

VTD: WH1, VTD: WH2, VTD: WMSB; Warren County, Washington County: VTD: LM, VTD: P1, VTD: P2, VTD: P3: Block(s) 1879502002017, 1879502002018, 1879502002021, 1879502002022, 1879502002023, 1879502005000, 1879502005001, 1879502005002, 1879502005003, 1879502005004, 1879502005005, 1879502005006, 1879502005007, 1879502005008, 1879502005009, 1879502005010, 1879502005011, 1879502005012, 1879502005013, 1879502005014, 1879502005015, 1879502005016, 1879502005017, 1879502005018, 1879502005019, 1879502005020, 1879502005021, 1879502005022, 1879502005023, 1879502005024, 1879502005025, 1879502005026, 1879502006003, 1879502006009, 1879502006010, 1879502006011, 1879502006012, 1879502006013, 1879502006014, 1879502006015, 1879502006016, 1879502006017, 1879502006018, 1879502006019, 1879503002025, 1879503002026; Wayne County: VTD: 07, VTD: 10, VTD: 11, VTD: 12, VTD: 13, VTD: 17, VTD: 18, VTD: 19, VTD: 20, VTD: 21, VTD: 22, VTD: 25: Block(s) 1910008001016, 1910008001017, 1910008001018, 1910008001019, 1910008001020, 1910008001021, 1910008001026, 1910008001027, 1910008001028, 1910008001029, 1910008001030, 1910008001031, 1910008001035, 1910008001036, 1910008001037, 1910008001038, 1910008001039, 1910008001040, 1910008001041, 1910008001042, 1910008001071; VTD: 26, VTD: 27, VTD: 29, VTD: 30: Block(s) 1910007001000, 1910007001001, 1910007001002, 1910007001003, 1910007001004, 1910007001005, 1910007001006, 1910007001007, 1910007001008, 1910007001009, 1910007001010, 1910007001011, 1910007001012, 1910007001013, 1910007001014, 1910007001015, 1910007001016, 1910007001017, 1910007001018, 1910007001019, 1910007001020, 1910007001021, 1910007001024, 1910007001025, 1910007001026, 1910007001027, 1910007001028, 1910007001029, 1910007001030, 1910007001031, 1910007001032, 1910007001033, 1910007001034, 1910007001035, 1910007001036, 1910007002000, 1910007002001, 1910007002002, 1910007002003, 1910007002004, 1910007002005, 1910007002006, 1910007002007, 1910007002008, 1910007002009, 1910007002010, 1910007002011, 1910007002012, 1910007002013, 1910007002014, 1910007002015, 1910007002016, 1910007002017, 1910007002018, 1910007002019, 1910007002020, 1910007002021, 1910007002022, 1910007002023, 1910007002024, 1910007002025, 1910007002026, 1910007002027, 1910007002028, 1910007002029, 1910007002030, 1910007002031, 1910007002032, 1910007002033, 1910007002034, 1910007002035, 1910007002036, 1910007002037, 1910007002038, 1910007002039, 1910007002040, 1910007002041, 1910007002042, 1910007002043, 1910007002044,

1910007002045, 1910007002046, 1910007003013, 1910007003017, 1910007003018, 1910007003019, 1910007003026, 1910007003027, 1910007003030, 1910007003031, 1910007003032, 1910007003033, 1910007003034, 1910007003035, 1910007003039, 1910007003042, 1910007003043, 1910007003044, 1910007003045, 1910007003046, 1910007003047, 1910007003048, 1910007003049, 1910007003050, 1910007003051, 1910007003052, 1910008001025, 1910008001043, 1910008001044, 1910008001045, 1910008001046, 1910008001049, 1910008001050, 1910008001051, 1910008001052, 1910008001053, 1910008001054, 1910008001056, 1910008001057, 1910008001059, 1910008001060, 1910008001062, 1910008001063, 1910008001064, 1910008001065, 1910008001066, 1910008001067, 1910008001070, 1910008002009, 1910008002010; Wilson County: VTD: PRGA: Block(s) 1950007001065, 1950007001066, 1950007001067, 1950012001031, 1950012001032, 1950012002000, 1950012002001, 1950012002002, 1950012002003, 1950012002004, 1950012002005, 1950012002006, 1950012002007, 1950012002008, 1950012002009, 1950012002010, 1950012002011, 1950012002012, 1950012002013, 1950012002014, 1950012002015, 1950012002016, 1950012003003, 1950012003004, 1950012003005, 1950012003006, 1950012003007, 1950012003008, 1950012003009, 1950012003010, 1950012003011, 1950012003012, 1950012003013, 1950012003014, 1950012003015, 1950012003016, 1950012003017, 1950012003018, 1950012003019, 1950012003021; VTD: PRSA: 1950011001002, 1950011001003, 1950011001004, 1950011001005, 1950011001006, 1950011001007, 1950011001008, 1950011001009, 1950011001010, 1950011001011, 1950011001012, 1950011001013, 1950011001014, 1950011001015, 1950011001016, 1950011001017, 1950011001018, 1950011001019, 1950011001020, 1950011001021, 1950011001022, 1950011001023, 1950011001024, 1950011001025, 1950011001026, 1950011001027, 1950011001028, 1950011001029, 1950011001030, 1950011001031, 1950011001032, 1950011001033, 1950011001034, 1950011001035, 1950011001036, 1950011001037, 1950011001038, 1950011001039, 1950011001040, 1950011001041, 1950011001042, 1950011001043, 1950011001044, 1950011001045, 1950011001046, 1950011001047, 1950011001048, 1950011001049, 1950011001050, 1950011002000, 1950011002001, 1950011002002, 1950011002003, 1950011002004, 1950011002005, 1950011002006, 1950011002007, 1950011002008, 1950011002009, 1950011002010, 1950011002011, 1950011002012, 1950011002013, 1950011002014, 1950011002015, 1950011002016, 1950011002017, 1950011002018, 1950011002019, 1950011002020, 1950011002021, 1950011002022,

1950011002023, 1950011002024, 1950011002025, 1950011002026,
1950011002027, 1950011002028, 1950011002029, 1950011002030,
1950011002031, 1950011002032, 1950011002033, 1950011002034,
1950011002035; VTD: PRWA: 1950001001004, 1950001001005,
1950001001007, 1950001001008, 1950001001009, 1950001001012,
1950001001016, 1950001001017, 1950001001018, 1950001001019,
1950001001020, 1950001002006, 1950001002007, 1950001002008,
1950001002009, 1950001002010, 1950001002014, 1950001002015,
1950001002016, 1950001002017, 1950001002018, 1950001002019,
1950001002020, 1950001002021, 1950001002022, 1950001002023,
1950001003000, 1950001003001, 1950001003002, 1950001003003,
1950001003009, 1950001003010, 1950001003011, 1950001003012,
1950001003013, 1950001003014, 1950001003016, 1950001003017,
1950001003018, 1950001003019, 1950001004000, 1950001004001,
1950001004002, 1950001004003, 1950001004004, 1950001004010,
1950001004011, 1950001004012, 1950001004013, 1950001004014,
1950001004015, 1950001004016, 1950001004018, 1950001004020; VTD:
PRWB, VTD: PRWC, VTD: PRWD: Block(s) 1950005011061; VTD: PRWE,
VTD: PRWH, VTD: PRWI, VTD: PRWJ: Block(s) 1950004001001,
1950004001002, 1950004001004, 1950004001005, 1950004001006,
1950004001007, 1950004001008; VTD: PRWM: 1950006001000,
1950006001002, 1950006001005, 1950006001006, 1950006001007,
1950006001014, 1950006002002, 1950006004000, 1950006004001,
1950006004002, 1950006004003, 1950006005026; VTD: PRWN, VTD: PRWQ,
VTD: PRWR.

District 2: Alamance County: VTD: 01; Chatham County: VTD: 18, VTD: 21,
VTD: 24, VTD: 3, VTD: 30, VTD: 42, VTD: 45, VTD: 6, VTD: 75, VTD: 85, VTD:
9, VTD: ESC114; Cumberland County: VTD: CC01: Block(s) 0510008003013;
VTD: CC04: 0510008001001, 0510008001008, 0510008001009,
0510008001010, 0510008001011, 0510008001013, 0510008001014,
0510008001015, 0510008001016, 0510008001017, 0510008001021,
0510008001022, 0510008001023, 0510008001024, 0510008001025,
0510008001026, 0510008001029, 0510008001030, 0510008002001,
0510008002002, 0510008002003, 0510008002004, 0510008002005,
0510008002006, 0510008002007, 0510008002008, 0510008002009,
0510008002010, 0510008002011, 0510008002012, 0510008002013,
0510008003000, 0510008003001, 0510008003006, 0510008003007,
0510008003008, 0510008003009, 0510008003010, 0510008003011,
0510008003012, 0510038002008, 0510038002009, 0510038002010,
0510038002011, 0510038002012, 0510038002013, 0510038002014,

0510038002015, 0510038002016, 0510038002017, 0510038002018, 0510038002019; VTD: CC06, VTD: CC07, VTD: CC08: Block(s) 0510007021000, 0510007021001, 0510007021002, 0510007021003, 0510007021004, 0510007021007, 0510007021008, 0510007021009, 0510007021010, 0510007021011, 0510007021012, 0510007021013, 0510007021014, 0510007021015, 0510007021016, 0510007021017, 0510007021018, 0510007021019, 0510007021020, 0510007021021, 0510007021022, 0510007021023, 0510007021024, 0510007021025, 0510007022000, 0510007022001, 0510007022002, 0510007022003, 0510007022004, 0510007022005, 0510007022009, 0510007022012, 0510008003003, 0510008003014, 0510008003015, 0510008003020, 0510008003029, 0510008003030, 0510008003031, 0510008003036, 0510008003037; VTD: CC10, VTD: CC12, VTD: CC13: Block(s) 0510010002033; VTD: CC14, VTD: CC15, VTD: CC18, VTD: CC24, VTD: CC31, VTD: CC34, VTD: CU02, VTD: EO61-1, VTD: EO61-2, VTD: G1, VTD: G10, VTD: G11, VTD: G3, VTD: G4, VTD: G7, VTD: G8, VTD: G9, VTD: SH77; Harnett County: VTD: PR01, VTD: PR07, VTD: PR08, VTD: PR16, VTD: PR24, VTD: PR25, VTD: PR26, VTD: PR27, VTD: PR28: Block(s) 0850708011023, 0850710011000, 0850710011001, 0850710011002, 0850710011003, 0850710011004, 0850710011005, 0850710011006, 0850710011007, 0850710011008, 0850710011009, 0850710011010, 0850710011011, 0850710011012, 0850710011013, 0850710011014, 0850710011015, 0850710011016, 0850710011017, 0850710011019, 0850710011020, 0850710011021, 0850710011022, 0850710011023, 0850710011024, 0850710011025, 0850710011026, 0850710011027, 0850710011028, 0850710012000, 0850710012001, 0850710012002, 0850710012003, 0850710012004, 0850710012005, 0850710012006, 0850710012007, 0850710012008, 0850710012009, 0850710012010, 0850710012011, 0850710012012, 0850710012013, 0850710012014, 0850710012015, 0850710012016, 0850710012017, 0850710012018, 0850710012019, 0850710012020, 0850710012022, 0850710021000, 0850710021001, 0850710021002, 0850710021003, 0850710021004, 0850710021005, 0850710021006, 0850710021007, 0850710021008, 0850710021009, 0850710021010, 0850710021011, 0850710021012, 0850710021013, 0850710021014, 0850710021015, 0850710021016, 0850710021017, 0850710021018, 0850710021019, 0850710021020, 0850710021021, 0850710021022, 0850710021023, 0850710021024, 0850710021025, 0850710021026, 0850710021027, 0850710021028, 0850710021029, 0850710021030, 0850710021031, 0850710021032, 0850710021033, 0850710021034, 0850710021035, 0850710021036, 0850710021037, 0850710021038, 0850710021039, 0850710021040, 0850710021041,

0850710021042, 0850710021043, 0850710021044, 0850710021045, 0850710021046, 0850710021047, 0850710021048, 0850710021049, 0850710021050, 0850710021051, 0850710021052, 0850710021053, 0850710021054, 0850710021055, 0850710021058, 0850710021059, 0850710021060, 0850710022000, 0850710022001, 0850710022002, 0850710022003, 0850710022004, 0850710022005, 0850710022006, 0850710022007, 0850710022008, 0850710022009, 0850710022010, 0850710022011, 0850710022012, 0850710022013, 0850710022014, 0850710022015, 0850710022016, 0850710022017, 0850710022018, 0850710022019, 0850710022020; VTD: PR29; Hoke County: VTD: 04, VTD: 05, VTD: 06, VTD: 12, VTD: 13, VTD: 63; Lee County, Moore County, Randolph County: VTD: 01, VTD: 02, VTD: 03, VTD: 04, VTD: 05, VTD: 06, VTD: 07, VTD: 08, VTD: 09, VTD: 10, VTD: 11, VTD: 12, VTD: 13, VTD: 14, VTD: 15, VTD: 16: Block(s) 1510306001009, 1510306001011, 1510306001013; VTD: 17, VTD: 19, VTD: 20, VTD: 21, VTD: 22, VTD: 23, VTD: 25, VTD: 26, VTD: 27, VTD: 28, VTD: 29, VTD: 30, VTD: 31, VTD: 32, VTD: 33, VTD: 34, VTD: 35, VTD: 37, VTD: 38, VTD: 39, VTD: 40; Wake County: VTD: 03-00, VTD: 04-01, VTD: 04-02, VTD: 04-04, VTD: 04-08, VTD: 04-09, VTD: 04-13, VTD: 04-14, VTD: 04-15, VTD: 04-16, VTD: 04-17, VTD: 04-18, VTD: 04-19, VTD: 04-20, VTD: 05-01, VTD: 05-03, VTD: 05-06, VTD: 06-01, VTD: 20-01, VTD: 20-02, VTD: 20-06, VTD: 20-10, VTD: 20-11, VTD: 20-12.

District 3: Beaufort County: VTD: AUROR, VTD: BEADM, VTD: BELHV, VTD: BLCK, VTD: CHOCO, VTD: EDWAR, VTD: GILEA, VTD: HB, VTD: NCRK, VTD: OLDF, VTD: PANTE, VTD: PINET, VTD: RVRD, VTD: SURBA, VTD: TCRK, VTD: WASH4, VTD: WASHP, VTD: WDPD; Camden County, Carteret County, Chowan County: VTD: 3, VTD: 5, VTD: 6; Craven County: VTD: 03, VTD: 04, VTD: 05, VTD: 10, VTD: 11, VTD: 12, VTD: 13, VTD: 14, VTD: 15, VTD: 16, VTD: 17, VTD: 18, VTD: 19, VTD: 20, VTD: 21, VTD: 22, VTD: 23, VTD: N3, VTD: N6; Currituck County, Dare County, Gates County: VTD: 2, VTD: 3, VTD: 4N, VTD: 5; Greene County: VTD: BEAR, VTD: CAST, VTD: HOOK, VTD: MAUR, VTD: WALS: Block(s) 0799501011039, 0799501011044, 0799501011045, 0799501011046, 0799501011047, 0799501011055, 0799501011056, 0799501011058, 0799501011059, 0799501011060, 0799501011063, 0799501011064, 0799501011065, 0799501011066, 0799501011067, 0799501011069, 0799501011070, 0799501011071, 0799501011072, 0799501011073, 0799501011074, 0799501011075, 0799501011076, 0799501011077, 0799501011078, 0799501011079, 0799501011080, 0799501011083, 0799501011089, 0799501012017, 0799501012019, 0799501012024, 0799501012025, 0799501012028, 0799501012029, 0799501012030, 0799501013005, 0799501013006; Hyde

County, Jones County, Lenoir County: VTD: C, VTD: V: Block(s)
1070109003000, 1070109003001, 1070109003002, 1070109003003,
1070109003004, 1070109003005, 1070109003006, 1070109003007,
1070109003008, 1070109003009, 1070109003010, 1070109003011,
1070109003012, 1070109003013, 1070109003014, 1070109003015,
1070109003016, 1070109003017, 1070109003018, 1070109003019,
1070109003020, 1070109003021, 1070109003022, 1070109003023,
1070109003024, 1070109003025, 1070109003026, 1070109003027; Martin
County: VTD: BG, VTD: CR, VTD: GR, VTD: J: Block(s) 1179701001011,
1179701001020, 1179701001032, 1179701001033, 1179701001034,
1179701001035, 1179701001036, 1179701001037, 1179701001038,
1179701001039, 1179701001040, 1179701001041, 1179701001042,
1179701001043, 1179701001044, 1179701001045, 1179701001046,
1179701001047, 1179701001048, 1179701001049, 1179701001050,
1179701001051, 1179701001052, 1179701001053, 1179701001054,
1179701001055, 1179701001056, 1179701001057, 1179701001058,
1179701001059, 1179701001060, 1179701001061, 1179701001062,
1179701001063, 1179701001069, 1179701001070, 1179701001073,
1179701001074, 1179701001075, 1179701001076, 1179701001077,
1179701001078, 1179701001079, 1179701001080, 1179701003000,
1179701003001, 1179701003002, 1179701003003, 1179701003004,
1179701003005, 1179701003006, 1179701003007, 1179701003008,
1179701003009, 1179701003010, 1179701003011, 1179701003012,
1179701003013, 1179701003014, 1179701003015, 1179701003016,
1179701003017, 1179701003018, 1179701003019, 1179701003020,
1179701003021, 1179701003022, 1179701003023, 1179701003024,
1179701003025, 1179701003026, 1179701003027, 1179701003028,
1179701003029, 1179701003030, 1179701003035, 1179701003036,
1179701003064, 1179701003065, 1179701003070, 1179701003071,
1179701003072, 1179701003073, 1179701003077, 1179701003078,
1179701003080, 1179701003081, 1179701003102; VTD: PP, VTD: W; New
Hanover County: VTD: CF01, VTD: W03, VTD: W08, VTD: W13, VTD: W15,
VTD: W24, VTD: W25, VTD: W26, VTD: W27, VTD: W28: Block(s)
1290105021023, 1290105021024, 1290105021025, 1290105021026,
1290105021027, 1290105021028, 1290105021029, 1290105021030,
1290105021031, 1290105021032, 1290105021033, 1290105021034,
1290105021035, 1290105021036, 1290105021037, 1290105021038,
1290105021039, 1290105021040, 1290105021041, 1290105021047,
1290105021049, 1290105021050, 1290105021051, 1290105022000,
1290105022001, 1290105022002, 1290105022003, 1290105022004,
1290105022005, 1290105022006, 1290105022007, 1290105022008,

1290105022009, 1290105022010, 1290105022011, 1290105022012, 1290105022013, 1290105023000, 1290105023001, 1290105023002, 1290105023003, 1290105023004, 1290105023005, 1290105023006, 1290105023007, 1290105023008, 1290105023009, 1290105023011, 1290105023014, 1290105023015, 1290105023016, 1290105023017, 1290105023018, 1290105023019, 1290105024000, 1290105024001, 1290105024002, 1290105024003, 1290105024006, 1290105024007, 1290105024008, 1290105024009, 1290105024010, 1290105024011, 1290105024012, 1290105024013, 1290105024014, 1290105024015, 1290105024016, 1290105024018, 1290105024019, 1290105024020, 1290105024021, 1290105024022, 1290105024023, 1290105024027, 1290105024028, 1290105024029, 1290105024030, 1290105024031, 1290119021024, 1290119021033, 1290119021034; VTD: W29; Onslow County, Pamlico County, Pasquotank County: VTD: 1-B: Block(s) 1399607012042, 1399607012043, 1399607012044, 1399607012045, 1399607012046, 1399607012047, 1399607012048, 1399607012049, 1399607012050, 1399607012052, 1399607012053, 1399607012054, 1399607012058, 1399607012060, 1399607012088, 1399607012089; VTD: 2-A: 1399601001000, 1399601001002, 1399601001018, 1399604005002, 1399604005016, 1399604005017, 1399604005018, 1399604005038, 1399604005039, 1399604005040, 1399604005058, 1399604005059, 1399605012023, 1399605012024, 1399605012025, 1399605012026, 1399605012027, 1399605012028, 1399605012029, 1399605012030, 1399605012035, 1399605012036, 1399605012038, 1399605012039, 1399605012040, 1399605012041, 1399605021023, 1399605021024, 1399605021025, 1399605021026, 1399605021027, 1399605021028, 1399605021029, 1399605021030, 1399605021031, 1399605021032, 1399605021033, 1399605021034, 1399605021035, 1399605021036; VTD: 4-A: 1399607011017, 1399607011018, 1399607011019, 1399607011025, 1399607011026, 1399607011027, 1399607011045, 1399607011048; VTD: 4-B: 1399602004001, 1399602004002, 1399602004013, 1399602004014; VTD: NEW: 1399605011000, 1399605011001, 1399605011002, 1399605011014, 1399605031000, 1399605031001, 1399605031002, 1399605031003, 1399605031004, 1399605031005, 1399605031006, 1399605031007, 1399605031008, 1399605031009, 1399605031010, 1399605031011, 1399605031012, 1399605031013, 1399605031014, 1399605031015, 1399605031016, 1399605031017, 1399605031018, 1399605031019, 1399605031020, 1399605031021, 1399605031023, 1399605031024, 1399605031025, 1399605031026, 1399605031027, 1399605031029, 1399605031032, 1399605031033, 1399605031041, 1399605031042, 1399605031043, 1399605031044, 1399605031047, 1399605031048,

1399605031049, 1399605031092; VTD: NIX, VTD: PRO: Block(s) 1399604005000, 1399604005001, 1399604005003, 1399604005004, 1399604005005, 1399604005006, 1399604005007, 1399604005008, 1399604005009, 1399604005010, 1399604005011, 1399604005012, 1399604005013, 1399604005014, 1399604005015, 1399604005019, 1399604005020, 1399604005021, 1399604005022, 1399604005026, 1399604005027, 1399604005028, 1399604005029, 1399604005030, 1399604005031, 1399604005066, 1399605011003, 1399605011004, 1399605011005, 1399605011006, 1399605011007, 1399605011008, 1399605011009, 1399605011010, 1399605011011, 1399605011012, 1399605011013, 1399605011015, 1399605011016, 1399605011017, 1399605011018, 1399605011019, 1399605011020, 1399605012000, 1399605012001, 1399605012002, 1399605012003, 1399605012004, 1399605012005, 1399605012006, 1399605012007, 1399605012008, 1399605012009, 1399605012010, 1399605012011, 1399605012012, 1399605012013, 1399605012014, 1399605012015, 1399605012016, 1399605012017, 1399605012018, 1399605012019, 1399605012020, 1399605012021, 1399605012022, 1399605012031, 1399605012032, 1399605012033, 1399605012034, 1399605012037, 1399605012042, 1399605021000, 1399605021001, 1399605021002, 1399605021003, 1399605021004, 1399605021005, 1399605021006, 1399605021007, 1399605021008, 1399605021009, 1399605021010, 1399605021011, 1399605021012, 1399605021013, 1399605021014, 1399605021015, 1399605021016, 1399605021017, 1399605021018, 1399605021019, 1399605021020, 1399605021021, 1399605021022, 1399605022007, 1399605022010, 1399605022014, 1399605022015, 1399605022016, 1399605022017, 1399605022019, 1399605022020, 1399605022021, 1399605022022, 1399605022023, 1399605022024, 1399605022025, 1399605022026, 1399605022027, 1399605022028, 1399605022029, 1399605022030, 1399605022031, 1399605022034, 1399605022035, 1399605022039, 1399606001000, 1399606001001, 1399606001002, 1399606001003, 1399606001004, 1399606001005, 1399606001006, 1399606001007, 1399606001008, 1399606001009, 1399606001010, 1399606001011, 1399606001026; VTD: SAL; Pender County: VTD: CF11, VTD: CL05, VTD: CS04, VTD: CT03, VTD: GR06, VTD: LC09, VTD: LU16, VTD: MH07, VTD: NB01, VTD: PL10, VTD: RP20, VTD: SB02, VTD: UH08, VTD: UU17; Perquimans County: VTD: BELVID, VTD: BETHEL, VTD: NEW HO, VTD: NICANO; Pitt County: VTD: 0101, VTD: 0200A, VTD: 0200B, VTD: 0401, VTD: 0501: Block(s) 1470009001000, 1470009001001, 1470009001002, 1470009001003, 1470009001004, 1470009001005, 1470009001006, 1470009001007, 1470009001008, 1470009001009, 1470009001010,

1470009001011, 1470009001012, 1470009001013, 1470009001014, 1470009001015, 1470009001016, 1470009001017, 1470009001058, 1470009003000, 1470009003001, 1470009003002, 1470009003003, 1470009003004, 1470009003006, 1470009003009, 1470009003010, 1470009003011, 1470009003012, 1470009003017, 1470009003018, 1470009003019, 1470009003066, 1470009003067, 1470020021000, 1470020021001, 1470020021002, 1470020021003, 1470020021004, 1470020021005, 1470020021006, 1470020021007, 1470020021008, 1470020021009, 1470020021010, 1470020021016, 1470020021017, 1470020021018, 1470020021019, 1470020021023, 1470020021024, 1470020021025, 1470020021026, 1470020021027, 1470020021028, 1470020021029, 1470020021030, 1470020021031, 1470020021035, 1470020021036, 1470020021037, 1470020021041, 1470020021042, 1470020021043, 1470020021044, 1470020021046, 1470020021047, 1470020021048, 1470020021049, 1470020021050, 1470020021051, 1470020021052, 1470020021053, 1470020021054, 1470020021055, 1470020021056, 1470020021057, 1470020021058, 1470020021059, 1470020021060, 1470020021061, 1470020021062, 1470020021063, 1470020021064, 1470020022000, 1470020022001, 1470020022050, 1470020022057, 1470020022058, 1470020022059; VTD: 0601, VTD: 0701: Block(s) 1470017001003, 1470017001004, 1470017001005, 1470017001006, 1470017001011, 1470017001017, 1470017001019, 1470017001021, 1470017001025, 1470017001026, 1470017001027, 1470017001030, 1470017001031, 1470017001032, 1470017001033, 1470017001034, 1470017001035, 1470017001036, 1470017001037, 1470017001038, 1470017001039, 1470017001040, 1470017001041, 1470017001042, 1470017001043, 1470017001044, 1470017001045, 1470017001046, 1470017001056, 1470017001061, 1470017001065, 1470017001074, 1470017001075; VTD: 0800A: 1470018001000, 1470018001001, 1470018001002, 1470018001003, 1470018001004, 1470018001005, 1470018001006, 1470018001007, 1470018001008, 1470018001009, 1470018001010, 1470018001011, 1470018001012, 1470018001013, 1470018001014, 1470018001015, 1470018001016, 1470018001017, 1470018001018, 1470018001019, 1470018001020, 1470018001021, 1470018001022, 1470018001023, 1470018001024, 1470018001025, 1470018001026, 1470018001027, 1470018001028, 1470018001029, 1470018001030, 1470018001031, 1470018001032, 1470018001033, 1470018001034, 1470018001035, 1470018001036, 1470018001037, 1470018001038, 1470018001039, 1470018001040, 1470018001041, 1470018001042, 1470018001043, 1470018001044, 1470018001045, 1470018001046, 1470018001047, 1470018001048, 1470018001049,

1470018001050, 1470018001051, 1470018001052, 1470018001053, 1470018001054, 1470018001055, 1470018001056, 1470018001057, 1470018001058, 1470018001059, 1470018001060, 1470018001061, 1470018001062, 1470018001063, 1470018001064, 1470018001065, 1470018001066, 1470018001067, 1470018001068, 1470018001069, 1470018001070, 1470018001071, 1470018001080, 1470018001081, 1470018001082, 1470018001083, 1470018001084, 1470018001085, 1470018001086, 1470018001087, 1470018001088, 1470018002000, 1470018002001, 1470018002002, 1470018002003, 1470018002004, 1470018002005, 1470018002006, 1470018002007, 1470018002008, 1470018002009, 1470018002010, 1470018002011, 1470018002012, 1470018002016, 1470018002018, 1470018002019, 1470018002020, 1470018002021, 1470018002022, 1470018002023, 1470018002024, 1470018002025, 1470018002026, 1470018002027, 1470018002028, 1470018002029, 1470018002032, 1470018002033, 1470018002034, 1470018002035, 1470018002036, 1470018002037, 1470018002038, 1470018002039, 1470018002040, 1470018002041, 1470018002042, 1470018002043, 1470018002044, 1470018002047, 1470018003001, 1470018003002, 1470018003003, 1470018003004, 1470018003005, 1470018003007, 1470018003008, 1470018003009, 1470018003010, 1470018003011, 1470018003012, 1470018003013, 1470018003014, 1470018003015, 1470018003016, 1470018003017, 1470018003019, 1470018003020, 1470018003021, 1470018003022, 1470018003023, 1470018003024, 1470018003025, 1470018003026, 1470018003028, 1470018003029, 1470018003030, 1470018003031, 1470018003033, 1470018003034, 1470018003035, 1470019001038, 1470019001041, 1470019001045, 1470019001046, 1470019001047, 1470019001048, 1470019001049, 1470019001050, 1470019001051, 1470019001052, 1470019001053, 1470019001054, 1470019001056, 1470019002040, 1470019002041, 1470019002042, 1470019002043, 1470019002044, 1470019002048, 1470019002050, 1470019002051; VTD: 0800B, VTD: 1001, VTD: 1102A, VTD: 1102B, VTD: 1201: Block(s) 1470009001018, 1470009001019, 1470009001020, 1470009001021, 1470009001022, 1470009001023, 1470009001024, 1470009001025, 1470009001026, 1470009001027, 1470009001028, 1470009001029, 1470009001030, 1470009001031, 1470009001032, 1470009001033, 1470009001034, 1470009001035, 1470009001036, 1470009001037, 1470009001038, 1470009001039, 1470009001040, 1470009001041, 1470009001042, 1470009001043, 1470009001044, 1470009001045, 1470009001046, 1470009001047, 1470009001049, 1470009001050, 1470009001052, 1470009001053, 1470009001054, 1470009001055, 1470009001056,

1470009001057, 1470009002085, 1470009002086, 1470009002087, 1470009002088, 1470009002089, 1470009002090, 1470009002091, 1470009002092, 1470009003005, 1470009003007, 1470009003008, 1470009003013, 1470009003014, 1470009003015, 1470009003016, 1470009003020, 1470009003021, 1470009003022, 1470009003023, 1470009003024, 1470009003025, 1470009003026, 1470009003027, 1470009003028, 1470009003029, 1470009003030, 1470009003031, 1470009003032, 1470009003033, 1470009003034, 1470009003035, 1470009003036, 1470009003037, 1470009003038, 1470009003039, 1470009003040, 1470009003048, 1470009003049, 1470009003059, 1470009003061, 1470009003062, 1470009003063, 1470009003064, 1470009003069, 1470009003070, 1470009003071, 1470009003072; VTD: 1301, VTD: 1402A, VTD: 1402B, VTD: 1403A: Block(s) 1470012001047, 1470013011007, 1470013011008, 1470013011009, 1470013011010, 1470013011011, 1470013011012, 1470013011013, 1470013011014, 1470013011015, 1470013011016, 1470013011017, 1470013011018, 1470013011019, 1470013011020, 1470013011021, 1470013011022, 1470013011023, 1470013011024, 1470013011025, 1470013011026, 1470013011027, 1470013011028, 1470013011029, 1470013011033, 1470013011034, 1470013011035, 1470013011039, 1470013011040, 1470013011041, 1470013011042, 1470013011043, 1470013011044, 1470013011045, 1470013011046, 1470013011047, 1470013011048, 1470013011049, 1470013011050, 1470013011051, 1470013011052, 1470013011053, 1470013011054, 1470013011055, 1470013011056, 1470013011057, 1470013011058, 1470013011059, 1470013011060, 1470013011061, 1470013011062, 1470013011063, 1470013011064, 1470013011065, 1470013011066, 1470013011069, 1470013011070, 1470013011071, 1470013011072, 1470013011073, 1470013011074, 1470013011075, 1470013011076, 1470013011077, 1470013011078, 1470013011079, 1470013011080, 1470013011082, 1470013012009, 1470013012010, 1470013012011, 1470013012016, 1470013012017, 1470013012018, 1470013012026, 1470013012027, 1470013021000, 1470013021001, 1470013021002, 1470013021003, 1470013021004, 1470013021005, 1470013021006, 1470013021007, 1470013021008, 1470013021009, 1470013021010, 1470013021011, 1470013021012, 1470013021013, 1470013021014, 1470013021015, 1470013021016, 1470013021017, 1470013021018, 1470013021019, 1470013021020, 1470013021021, 1470013021022, 1470013021023, 1470013021024, 1470013021025, 1470013021026, 1470013021027, 1470013021028, 1470013021029, 1470013021030, 1470013021031, 1470013021032, 1470013021033, 1470013021034, 1470013021035, 1470013021036,

1470013021037, 1470013021038, 1470013021039, 1470013021040, 1470013021041, 1470013021042, 1470013021043, 1470013021044, 1470013021045, 1470013021046, 1470013021047, 1470013021048, 1470013021049, 1470013021050, 1470013021051, 1470013021052, 1470013021053, 1470013021054, 1470013031044, 1470013031048, 1470013031049, 1470013031050, 1470013031051, 1470013031052, 1470013031055, 1470014011000, 1470014011001, 1470014011002, 1470014011003, 1470014011067, 1470014011068, 1470014022000, 1470014022001, 1470014022002, 1470014022003, 1470014022004, 1470014022005, 1470014022006, 1470014022007, 1470014022024, 1470014022026, 1470016003019, 1470016003020, 1470016003021, 1470016003027, 1470016003028, 1470016003029, 1470016003030, 1470016003031, 1470016003032, 1470016003033, 1470016003034, 1470016003035, 1470016003036, 1470016003037, 1470016003042, 1470016003047, 1470016003048, 1470016003049, 1470016003050, 1470016003051, 1470016003052, 1470016003053, 1470016003054, 1470016004000, 1470016004001, 1470016004002, 1470016004003, 1470016004004, 1470016004006, 1470016004007, 1470016004008; VTD: 1403B: 1470013022000, 1470013022001, 1470013022002, 1470013022003, 1470013022004, 1470013022005, 1470013022006, 1470013022007, 1470013022008, 1470013022009, 1470013022010, 1470013022011, 1470013022012, 1470013022013, 1470013022014, 1470013022015, 1470013022016, 1470013022017, 1470013022018, 1470013022019, 1470013022020, 1470013022021, 1470013022022, 1470013022023, 1470013022024, 1470013022025, 1470013022026, 1470013022027, 1470013022028, 1470013022029, 1470013022030, 1470013022031, 1470013022032, 1470013022033, 1470013022034, 1470013022036, 1470013022037, 1470013022038, 1470013022039, 1470013022044, 1470013022045, 1470013022046, 1470013022047, 1470013022048, 1470013022049, 1470013022050, 1470013022051, 1470013022052, 1470013022053, 1470013022054, 1470013022057, 1470013022062, 1470013022063, 1470013022064, 1470013022066, 1470013022067, 1470013022068, 1470013022069, 1470013031000, 1470013031001, 1470013031002, 1470013031003, 1470013031004, 1470013031005, 1470013031006, 1470013031007, 1470013031008, 1470013031009, 1470013031010, 1470013031011, 1470013031012, 1470013031013, 1470013031014, 1470013031015, 1470013031016, 1470013031017, 1470013031019, 1470013031020, 1470013031021, 1470013031022, 1470013031023, 1470013031024, 1470013031025, 1470013031026, 1470013031027, 1470013031028, 1470013031029, 1470013031030, 1470013031031, 1470013031032, 1470013031040, 1470013031041,

1470013031042, 1470013031045, 1470013031053, 1470013031054, 1470013031056, 1470013031057; VTD: 1506: 1470001003033, 1470001003053, 1470001003054, 1470001003066, 1470001004029, 1470001005009, 1470001005011, 1470001005016, 1470001005017, 1470001005018, 1470004004006, 1470004004007, 1470004004008, 1470004004009, 1470004004010, 1470004004011, 1470004004012, 1470004004014, 1470004004015, 1470005011000, 1470005011001, 1470005011002, 1470005011003, 1470005011004, 1470005011005, 1470005011006, 1470005011007, 1470005011008, 1470005011009, 1470005011010, 1470005011026, 1470005011027, 1470005011028, 1470005011029, 1470005011030; VTD: 1507, VTD: 1507B, VTD: 1508A: Block(s) 1470001001003, 1470001001004, 1470001001005, 1470001001006, 1470001001007, 1470001001008, 1470001001009, 1470001001010, 1470001001011, 1470001001012, 1470001001013, 1470001001014, 1470001001015, 1470001001016, 1470001001017, 1470001001018, 1470001001019, 1470001001020, 1470001001021, 1470001001022, 1470001001023, 1470001001024, 1470001001025, 1470001002000, 1470001002001, 1470001002002, 1470001002003, 1470001002004, 1470001002005, 1470001002006, 1470001002007, 1470001002008, 1470001002009, 1470001002010, 1470001002011, 1470001002012, 1470001002013, 1470001002014, 1470001002015, 1470001002016, 1470001002017, 1470001002018, 1470001002019, 1470001002020, 1470001002021, 1470001002022, 1470001002023, 1470001002024, 1470001002025, 1470001002026, 1470001002027, 1470001003000, 1470001003003, 1470001003004, 1470001003005, 1470001003006, 1470001003007, 1470001003008, 1470001003021, 1470001003022, 1470001003034, 1470001003035, 1470001003036, 1470001003037, 1470001003038, 1470002012002, 1470002012015, 1470002012016, 1470002012017, 1470002014006, 1470002014007, 1470002014008; VTD: 1508B, VTD: 1509: Block(s) 1470001005024, 1470002021024, 1470002021025, 1470002021026, 1470003021000, 1470003021001, 1470003021002, 1470003021003, 1470003021004, 1470003021005, 1470003021006, 1470003021007, 1470003021008, 1470003021009, 1470003021010, 1470003021011, 1470003021012, 1470003021013, 1470003021014, 1470003021015, 1470003021016, 1470003022000, 1470003022001, 1470003022002, 1470003022003, 1470003022004, 1470003022005, 1470003022006, 1470003022007, 1470003022008, 1470003022009, 1470003022010, 1470003022011, 1470003022012, 1470003022013, 1470003022014, 1470003022015, 1470003022016, 1470003022017, 1470003022018, 1470003022019, 1470003022020, 1470003022021, 1470003023000, 1470003023001, 1470003023002,

1470003023003, 1470003023004, 1470003023005, 1470003023006, 1470003023007, 1470003023008, 1470003023009, 1470003023010, 1470003023013, 1470003023014, 1470003023025, 1470003023026, 1470004003005, 1470004003010, 1470004003011, 1470004003012, 1470004003013, 1470004003014, 1470004003015, 1470004003016, 1470004003017, 1470004003018, 1470004003019, 1470004003020, 1470004003021, 1470004003022, 1470004003023, 1470004003024, 1470004003025, 1470004003026, 1470004003027, 1470004003028, 1470004003029, 1470004003030, 1470004003031, 1470004004003, 1470004004004, 1470004004005, 1470010011033, 1470010011034, 1470010011035, 1470010011036, 1470010011037, 1470010011038, 1470010011039, 1470010011040, 1470010011041, 1470010011042, 1470010011043, 1470010011044, 1470010011045, 1470010011046, 1470010011047, 1470010011048, 1470010011049, 1470010011050; VTD: 1510A, VTD: 1510B, VTD: 1511A, VTD: 1511B, VTD: 1512A: Block(s) 1470006031003, 1470006031007, 1470006031013, 1470006031014, 1470006031015, 1470006031016, 1470006031017, 1470006031018, 1470006031019, 1470006031020, 1470006031021, 1470006031022, 1470006031023, 1470006031024, 1470006031025, 1470006031026, 1470006031027, 1470006031028, 1470006031029, 1470006031030, 1470006031031, 1470006031032, 1470006031033, 1470006031034, 1470006031035, 1470006031036, 1470006031037, 1470006031038, 1470006031039, 1470006031040, 1470006031041, 1470006031042, 1470006031043, 1470006031044, 1470006031045, 1470006031046, 1470006031047, 1470006031048, 1470006031049, 1470006031050, 1470006031051, 1470006031052, 1470006032009, 1470006032010, 1470006032011, 1470006032012, 1470006032013, 1470006032014, 1470006032015, 1470006032016, 1470006032017, 1470006032018, 1470006032019, 1470006032020, 1470006032021, 1470006032022, 1470006032023, 1470006032024, 1470006032025, 1470006032026, 1470006032027, 1470006032028, 1470006032034, 1470006032035, 1470006032036, 1470016003008, 1470016003009, 1470016003010, 1470016003011, 1470016003012, 1470016003023, 1470016003024, 1470016003043, 1470016003044, 1470016003045, 1470016003046; VTD: 1512B: 1470006033000, 1470006033001, 1470006033002, 1470006033003, 1470006033004, 1470006033005, 1470006033006, 1470006033007, 1470006033008, 1470006033009, 1470006033010, 1470006033011, 1470006033012, 1470006033013, 1470006033014, 1470006033015, 1470006033016, 1470006033017, 1470006033018, 1470006033019, 1470006033020, 1470006033021, 1470006033022, 1470006033023, 1470006033024, 1470006033025, 1470006033026, 1470006033027,

1470006033028, 1470006033029, 1470006033030, 1470006033034, 1470006033035, 1470006033036, 1470006033037, 1470006033038, 1470006033039, 1470006034001, 1470006034003, 1470006034004, 1470006034005, 1470006034006, 1470006034007, 1470006034008; Tyrrell County, Washington County: VTD: P3: Block(s) 1879502002000, 1879502002001, 1879502002002, 1879502002004, 1879502002006, 1879502002008, 1879502002009, 1879502002013, 1879502002014, 1879502002015, 1879502002016, 1879502006000, 1879502006001, 1879502006002, 1879502006004, 1879502006005, 1879502006006, 1879502006007, 1879502006008, 1879502006020, 1879502006021, 1879502006022, 1879502006023, 1879503002016, 1879503002017, 1879503002018, 1879503002019, 1879503002020, 1879503002021, 1879503002022, 1879503002023, 1879503002027, 1879503002028, 1879503002029, 1879503002031, 1879503002032, 1879503002033, 1879503002034, 1879503002035; VTD: SC, VTD: SK.

District 4: Alamance County: VTD: 063, VTD: 06N, VTD: 11, VTD: 127, VTD: 128, VTD: 12E, VTD: 12N, VTD: 12S, VTD: 13: Block(s) 0010203005000, 0010203005002, 0010203005003, 0010203005004, 0010203005006, 0010203005009, 0010203005010, 0010203005011, 0010203005016, 0010203005017, 0010203005018, 0010203005051, 0010203005052, 0010203005053, 0010203005054, 0010203005055, 0010203005056, 0010203005057, 0010203005058, 0010203005059, 0010203005060, 0010203005061, 0010203005062, 0010203005063, 0010203005064, 0010203005065, 0010210002000, 0010210002001, 0010211011000, 0010211011001, 0010211011002, 0010211011003, 0010211011004, 0010211011010, 0010211012000, 0010211012001, 0010211012002, 0010211012003, 0010211012004, 0010211012062, 0010212011001, 0010212011002, 0010212011003, 0010212011004, 0010212011005, 0010212011006, 0010212011007, 0010212011010, 0010212011011, 0010212011012, 0010212011013, 0010212011014, 0010212011015, 0010212011016, 0010212011017, 0010212011018, 0010212011019, 0010212011020, 0010212011021, 0010212011022, 0010212011023, 0010212011024, 0010212011025, 0010212011026, 0010212011027, 0010212011028, 0010212011029, 0010212011030, 0010212011031, 0010212011032, 0010212011033, 0010212011034, 0010212011035, 0010212011036, 0010212011037, 0010212011038, 0010212011039, 0010212011040, 0010212011041, 0010212011042, 0010212011043, 0010212011044, 0010212011045, 0010212011046, 0010212011047, 0010212011048, 0010212011049, 0010212011050, 0010212011051, 0010212011052, 0010212011053, 0010212011054, 0010212011055,

0010212011056, 0010212011057, 0010212011058, 0010212011059,
0010212011060, 0010212011061, 0010212011062, 0010212011063,
0010212011064, 0010212011065, 0010212011066, 0010212011067,
0010212011068, 0010212011069, 0010212011070, 0010212011071,
0010212011072, 0010212011073, 0010212011074, 0010212011075,
0010212011076, 0010212011078, 0010212012004, 0010212012005,
0010212012006, 0010212012007, 0010212012008, 0010212012009,
0010212012010, 0010212012011, 0010212012012, 0010212012013,
0010212012016, 0010212012017, 0010212012018, 0010212012019,
0010212012020, 0010212012021, 0010212012022, 0010212012023,
0010212012041, 0010212012043, 0010212012044, 0010212012045,
0010212012046, 0010212012047, 0010212012048, 0010212012049,
0010212012050, 0010212012051, 0010212012052, 0010212012053,
0010212012054, 0010212012055, 0010212012056, 0010212012057,
0010212012058, 0010212012059, 0010212012060, 0010212012061,
0010212012062, 0010212012063, 0010212012064, 0010212012065,
0010212012066, 0010212012067, 0010212012068, 0010212012069,
0010212012070, 0010212012071, 0010212012072, 0010212012075,
0010212012076, 0010212012077, 0010212012078, 0010212012079,
0010212012080, 0010212012081, 0010212012082, 0010212012083,
0010212012084, 0010212012085, 0010212012086, 0010212012087,
0010212012088, 0010212012089, 0010212012090, 0010212012091,
0010212012092, 0010212012093, 0010212012094, 0010212012095,
0010212012096, 0010212012097, 0010212012098, 0010212012099,
0010212012100, 0010212012101, 0010212013000, 0010212013001,
0010212013002, 0010212013003, 0010212013004, 0010212013005,
0010212013006, 0010212013007, 0010212013008, 0010212013009,
0010212013010, 0010212013011, 0010212013012, 0010212013013,
0010212013014, 0010212013015, 0010212013016, 0010212013017,
0010212013018, 0010212013019, 0010212013020, 0010212013021,
0010212013022, 0010212013023, 0010212013024, 0010212013025,
0010212013027, 0010212013039, 0010212013040, 0010212013041,
0010212013042, 0010212013052, 0010212013053, 0010212013054,
0010212013055, 0010212013056, 0010212013057, 0010212013058,
0010213005012, 0010213005013, 0010213005014, 0010213005015,
0010213005016, 0010213005017, 0010213005023, 0010213005024,
0010213005025, 0010213005026, 0010213005027, 0010213005028,
0010213005029, 0010213005030, 0010213005031, 0010213005032,
0010213005033; Chatham County: VTD: 15, VTD: 20, VTD: 78, VTD: MCH110,
VTD: NWM117, VTD: PIT113; Cumberland County: VTD: AH49, VTD: CC01:
Block(s) 0510002001009, 0510002001010, 0510002001011, 0510002001012,

0510002001013, 0510002001017, 0510002001018, 0510002001019,
0510002001021, 0510002001022, 0510002001023, 0510002001024,
0510002001025, 0510002001026, 0510002001027, 0510002001028,
0510002001029, 0510002001030, 0510002001031, 0510002001032,
0510002001033, 0510002001034, 0510002001035, 0510002001036,
0510002002000, 0510002002001, 0510002002002, 0510002002003,
0510002002004, 0510002002005, 0510002002006, 0510002002007,
0510002002008, 0510002002009, 0510002002010, 0510002002011,
0510002002012, 0510002002013, 0510002002014, 0510002002015,
0510002002016, 0510002002017, 0510002002018, 0510002002019,
0510002002020, 0510002002021, 0510002002022, 0510002002023,
0510002002024, 0510002002025, 0510002002026, 0510002002027,
0510002003000, 0510002003001, 0510002003002, 0510002003003,
0510002003004, 0510002003005, 0510002003006, 0510002003007,
0510002003008, 0510002003009, 0510002003010, 0510002003011,
0510002003012, 0510002003013, 0510002003014, 0510002003015,
0510002003016, 0510002003017, 0510002003018, 0510002003019,
0510002003020, 0510002003021, 0510002003022, 0510002003023,
0510002003024, 0510002003025, 0510002003026, 0510002003027,
0510002003028, 0510002003029, 0510002003030, 0510002003031,
0510002003032, 0510002003033, 0510002003034, 0510002003035,
0510002003036, 0510002003037, 0510002003038, 0510002003039,
0510002003040, 0510002003041, 0510002003042, 0510002003043,
0510002003044, 0510002003047, 0510002003048, 0510002003049,
0510002003050, 0510002003051, 0510002003052, 0510005003000,
0510007022027, 0510007022028, 0510008001027, 0510008001028,
0510008001031, 0510008003022, 0510008003023, 0510008003024,
0510008003025, 0510008003026, 0510008003027, 0510008003028,
0510008003032, 0510008003033, 0510015001006, 0510038002020,
0510038002021, 0510038002022, 0510038002023, 0510038002024,
0510038002025, 0510038002026, 0510038002027, 0510038002028,
0510038002029, 0510038002030, 0510038002031, 0510038002032,
0510038002033, 0510038002034, 0510038002035, 0510038002036,
0510038002037, 0510038002038, 0510038002039, 0510038002040,
0510038002041, 0510038002042, 0510038002043, 0510038002044,
0510038002045, 0510038002046, 0510038002047, 0510038002048,
0510038002049, 0510038002050, 0510038002051, 0510038002052,
0510038002053, 0510038002054, 0510038002055, 0510038002056,
0510038002057, 0510038002058, 0510038002059, 0510038002060,
0510038002061, 0510038002062, 0510038002063, 0510038002064,
0510038002065, 0510038002066, 0510038002067, 0510038002068,

0510038002069, 0510038002070, 0510038002071, 0510038002072, 0510038002073, 0510038002074, 0510038002075, 0510038002076, 0510038002077, 0510038002078, 0510038002079, 0510038002080, 0510038002081, 0510038002082, 0510038002083, 0510038002084, 0510038002085, 0510038003000, 0510038003001, 0510038003002, 0510038003003, 0510038003004, 0510038003005, 0510038003006, 0510038003007, 0510038003008, 0510038003009, 0510038003010, 0510038003011, 0510038003012, 0510038003013, 0510038003014, 0510038003015, 0510038003016, 0510038003017, 0510038003018, 0510038003019, 0510038003020, 0510038003021, 0510038003022, 0510038003023, 0510038003024, 0510038003025, 0510038003026, 0510038003027, 0510038003028, 0510038003029, 0510038003039, 0510038003040, 0510038003041, 0510038003042, 0510038003043, 0510038003044, 0510038003045, 0510038003046, 0510038003047, 0510038003048, 0510038003049, 0510038003050, 0510038003062, 0510038003063; VTD: CC03, VTD: CC04: Block(s) 0510008001012; VTD: CC05, VTD: CC08: Block(s) 0510008003021; VTD: CC13: 0510008001000, 0510008001002, 0510008001003, 0510008001004, 0510008001018, 0510008001019, 0510009004000, 0510009004020, 0510010001001, 0510010001002, 0510010001003, 0510010001004, 0510010001005, 0510010001006, 0510010001007, 0510010002000, 0510010002001, 0510010002002, 0510010002003, 0510010002010, 0510010002014, 0510010002015, 0510010002016, 0510010002017, 0510010002018, 0510010002019, 0510010002020, 0510010002021, 0510010002022, 0510010002023, 0510010002024, 0510010002025, 0510010002026, 0510010002027, 0510010002028, 0510010002029, 0510010002030, 0510010002031, 0510010002032, 0510010002034, 0510011003017, 0510011003018, 0510011003019, 0510011003020, 0510011003021, 0510011003022, 0510011003023, 0510011003024, 0510011003025, 0510011003026; VTD: CC16, VTD: CC17, VTD: CC19, VTD: CC21, VTD: CC25, VTD: CC26, VTD: CC27, VTD: CC29, VTD: CC32, VTD: CC33, VTD: CL57, VTD: G2, VTD: G5, VTD: LI65, VTD: LR63, VTD: MB62, VTD: MR02; Durham County: VTD: 04, VTD: 16, VTD: 27, VTD: 33, VTD: 35, VTD: 36, VTD: 38, VTD: 39, VTD: 43, VTD: 48, VTD: 50, VTD: 51, VTD: 53-1, VTD: 53-2; Harnett County: VTD: PR17, VTD: PR20, VTD: PR23, VTD: PR28: Block(s) 0850710021056, 0850710021057; Orange County: VTD: BC, VTD: BP, VTD: CA, VTD: CB, VTD: CC, VTD: CF, VTD: CH, VTD: CO, VTD: CS1, VTD: CX, VTD: DA, VTD: DM, VTD: EA, VTD: EH, VTD: ES, VTD: GB, VTD: GL, VTD: GR, VTD: H, VTD: HF, VTD: KM, VTD: LC, VTD: LI, VTD: MF, VTD: NC, VTD: NS, VTD: OG, VTD: OW, VTD: PA, VTD: RF, VTD: SJ, VTD: TH, VTD: WC, VTD: WD, VTD: WH, VTD: WW; Wake County: VTD: 01-01, VTD: 01-02:

Block(s) 1830514001006, 1830514001007, 1830514001012, 1830514001013, 1830514001014, 1830514002001, 1830514002002, 1830514002003, 1830514002006, 1830514002007, 1830514002010, 1830514002011, 1830514003000, 1830514003001, 1830514003002, 1830514003003, 1830514003004, 1830514003005, 1830514003006, 1830514003007, 1830514003008, 1830514003009, 1830514003010, 1830514003011, 1830514003012, 1830514003013, 1830514003014, 1830514003015, 1830514004000, 1830514004001, 1830514004002, 1830514004003, 1830514004004, 1830514004005, 1830514004006, 1830514004016, 1830515022025, 1830515022026, 1830524012000, 1830524012001, 1830524012002, 1830524012010, 1830524012013, 1830524012014; VTD: 01-06, VTD: 01-07, VTD: 01-09, VTD: 01-10, VTD: 01-12, VTD: 01-13, VTD: 01-14, VTD: 01-16: Block(s) 1830524012003, 1830524012004, 1830524012005, 1830524012006, 1830524012008, 1830524012009, 1830524012015, 1830525041000, 1830525041001, 1830525041002, 1830525041003, 1830525041004, 1830525041005, 1830525041006, 1830525041007, 1830525041008, 1830525041009, 1830525041010, 1830525041011, 1830525041012, 1830525041013, 1830525041014, 1830525041015, 1830525041016, 1830525041017, 1830525041018, 1830525041019, 1830525042000, 1830525042001, 1830525042002, 1830525042003, 1830525042004, 1830525042005, 1830525042006, 1830525042007, 1830525042008, 1830525042009, 1830525042010, 1830525042011, 1830525042012, 1830525042013; VTD: 01-18: 1830527012002; VTD: 01-19, VTD: 01-20, VTD: 01-21: Block(s) 1830521011007, 1830521011008, 1830521011009, 1830521011010, 1830528031020, 1830545002001, 1830545002002, 1830545002003, 1830545002004, 1830545002005, 1830545002006, 1830545002007, 1830545002008, 1830545002009, 1830545002010, 1830545002011, 1830545002012, 1830545002013, 1830545002014, 1830545002015, 1830545002016, 1830545002017, 1830545002018, 1830545002019, 1830545002020, 1830545002021, 1830545002022, 1830545002023, 1830545002024, 1830545002025, 1830545002026, 1830545002027, 1830545002028, 1830545002029, 1830545002030, 1830545002031, 1830545002032, 1830545002033, 1830545002034, 1830545002035, 1830545002036, 1830545002037, 1830545002038, 1830545002039, 1830545002040, 1830545002041, 1830545002042, 1830545002043, 1830545002044, 1830545002045, 1830545002046, 1830545002047, 1830545002048, 1830545002049, 1830545002050, 1830545002051, 1830545002053, 1830545002054, 1830545002057, 1830545002061, 1830545002062, 1830545002063, 1830545002064, 1830545002080, 1830545002081, 1830545002082, 1830545002083, 1830545002084, 1830545002085, 1830545002086,

1830545002087, 1830545002088, 1830545002089, 1830545002093, 1830545003000, 1830545003001, 1830545003002, 1830545003003, 1830545003004, 1830545003005, 1830545003006, 1830545003007, 1830545003008, 1830545003009, 1830545003010, 1830545003011, 1830545003012, 1830545003013, 1830545003014, 1830545003015, 1830545003016, 1830545003017, 1830545003018, 1830545003019, 1830545003020, 1830545003021, 1830545003022, 1830545003023, 1830545003024, 1830545003025, 1830545003026, 1830545003027, 1830545003028, 1830545003029, 1830545003030, 1830545003031, 1830545003032, 1830545003033, 1830545004000, 1830545004001, 1830545004002, 1830545004003, 1830545004004, 1830545004005, 1830545004006, 1830545004007, 1830545004008, 1830545004009, 1830545004010, 1830545004011, 1830545004012, 1830545004013, 1830545004014, 1830545004015, 1830545004016, 1830545004017, 1830545004018, 1830545004019; VTD: 01-22, VTD: 01-23, VTD: 01-25, VTD: 01-26, VTD: 01-27, VTD: 01-28, VTD: 01-31, VTD: 01-32, VTD: 01-33: Block(s) 1830515012008, 1830515012009, 1830515012010, 1830515012011, 1830515012012, 1830515012013, 1830515012014, 1830515012015, 1830515012025, 1830515012026, 1830515012027, 1830515021000, 1830515021001, 1830515021002, 1830515021003, 1830515021004, 1830515021005, 1830515021006, 1830515021007, 1830515022010, 1830515022011, 1830515022012, 1830515022013, 1830515022014, 1830515022027; VTD: 01-34, VTD: 01-35, VTD: 01-36: Block(s) 1830526032014, 1830526032015, 1830527013010, 1830527013011, 1830527013013, 1830527013014, 1830527013019, 1830527013020, 1830527013021, 1830527013025; VTD: 01-38, VTD: 01-39: Block(s) 1830537151011, 1830537161000, 1830537161001, 1830537161002, 1830537161003, 1830537161004, 1830537161005, 1830537161006, 1830537161007, 1830537162000, 1830537162001, 1830537162002, 1830537162003, 1830537162007, 1830537162008, 1830537162011, 1830537162012, 1830537162013, 1830537163000, 1830537163001, 1830537163002, 1830537163003, 1830537163004, 1830537163005, 1830537163006, 1830537163007, 1830537163008; VTD: 01-40, VTD: 01-41, VTD: 01-43, VTD: 01-44, VTD: 01-46, VTD: 01-48, VTD: 01-49, VTD: 01-50, VTD: 01-51, VTD: 04-03, VTD: 04-05, VTD: 04-11, VTD: 04-21, VTD: 05-04, VTD: 05-05, VTD: 07-04, VTD: 07-10, VTD: 08-06, VTD: 08-09, VTD: 11-01, VTD: 13-01, VTD: 13-05, VTD: 13-07, VTD: 13-08, VTD: 13-09, VTD: 16-02: Block(s) 1830521011023, 1830521011024, 1830521011025, 1830521011026, 1830521011027, 1830521011028, 1830521011031, 1830521011034, 1830528031000, 1830528031001, 1830528031002, 1830528031003, 1830528031004, 1830528031005, 1830528031006, 1830528031007,

1830528031008, 1830528031009, 1830528031010, 1830528031011, 1830528031012, 1830528031013, 1830528031014, 1830528031015, 1830528031016, 1830528031017, 1830528031018, 1830528031019, 1830528031021, 1830528031022, 1830528031023, 1830528031024, 1830528031025, 1830528031026, 1830528031027, 1830528031028, 1830528031029, 1830528031030, 1830528031031, 1830528031032, 1830528031033, 1830528031034, 1830528031035, 1830528031036, 1830528032000, 1830528032001, 1830528032002, 1830528032003, 1830528032004, 1830528032005, 1830528032006, 1830528032007, 1830528032012, 1830528032013, 1830528032017, 1830528032018, 1830528032019, 1830528032022, 1830528032023, 1830528032024, 1830528032025, 1830528032026, 1830528032027, 1830528032028, 1830528032030, 1830528032031, 1830528032032, 1830528032033, 1830528032034, 1830528032035, 1830528032036, 1830528032037, 1830528032038, 1830528032039, 1830528032040, 1830528032041, 1830528032042, 1830528032043, 1830528032044, 1830528032045, 1830528032046, 1830528032047, 1830528032048, 1830528032049, 1830528032050, 1830528032055, 1830528032056, 1830528033000, 1830528033001, 1830528033002, 1830528033003, 1830528033004, 1830528033005, 1830528033006, 1830528033007, 1830528033008, 1830528033009, 1830528033010, 1830528033011, 1830528033012, 1830528033013, 1830528033014, 1830528033015, 1830528033016, 1830528033017, 1830528033018, 1830528033019, 1830528033020, 1830528033044, 1830528033045, 1830528033046, 1830528033047, 1830528033048, 1830528033049, 1830528033050, 1830528033051, 1830528033052, 1830528033053, 1830528033054, 1830528033055, 1830528033056, 1830528033057, 1830528033058, 1830528033059, 1830528033060, 1830528033061, 1830528033062, 1830528033063, 1830528033064, 1830528033065, 1830528033066, 1830528033067, 1830528033068, 1830528033069, 1830528033070, 1830528033071, 1830528033072, 1830528061019, 1830528061020, 1830528061021, 1830528061022, 1830528061026, 1830528061027, 1830528061028, 1830528061029, 1830545002055, 1830545002056, 1830545002065, 1830545002066, 1830545002072, 1830545002073, 1830545002090; VTD: 16-03, VTD: 16-06, VTD: 16-08, VTD: 17-01, VTD: 17-03, VTD: 17-05, VTD: 17-07, VTD: 17-09, VTD: 17-10, VTD: 17-11, VTD: 18-01, VTD: 18-06.

District 5: Alexander County, Alleghany County, Ashe County, Catawba County: VTD: 04, VTD: 11, VTD: 12, VTD: 13: Block(s) 0350105011054, 0350105011055, 0350105011057, 0350105011061, 0350105011064, 0350105011065, 0350105011066, 0350105011067, 0350105011068,

0350106003019, 0350106003023, 0350106003050, 0350106003052, 0350106003054, 0350106003055, 0350106003059, 0350106003060, 0350106003061, 0350106003062, 0350106003063, 0350106003064, 0350106003065, 0350106003066, 0350106003067, 0350106003068, 0350106003069, 0350106003070, 0350106003071, 0350106003072, 0350106004004, 0350106004005, 0350106004006, 0350106004007, 0350106004008, 0350106004009, 0350106004010, 0350106004048, 0350106004049, 0350106004050, 0350106004051, 0350106004052, 0350106004053, 0350106004059, 0350106004060, 0350106004065, 0350106004066, 0350107001004, 0350107001005, 0350107001006, 0350107001007, 0350107001008, 0350107001009, 0350107001010, 0350107001030, 0350107001031, 0350107001032, 0350107001033, 0350107001034, 0350107001035, 0350107001036, 0350107001037, 0350107001038, 0350107001039, 0350107001043, 0350107001044, 0350107002000, 0350107002001, 0350107002002, 0350107002003, 0350107002004, 0350107002005, 0350107002006, 0350107002007, 0350107002008, 0350107002009, 0350107002010, 0350107002011, 0350107002012, 0350107002013, 0350107002014, 0350107002015, 0350107002016, 0350107002017, 0350107002018, 0350107002019, 0350107002020, 0350107002021, 0350107002022, 0350107002023, 0350107002024, 0350107002025, 0350107002026, 0350107002027, 0350107002028, 0350107002029, 0350107002031, 0350107002038, 0350107002039, 0350107002040, 0350107002041, 0350107002042, 0350107002043, 0350107002044, 0350107002045, 0350107002046, 0350107002047, 0350107002048, 0350107002049, 0350107002050, 0350107002051, 0350109001005, 0350109001006, 0350109001007, 0350109001008, 0350109001009, 0350109001010, 0350109001011, 0350109001016, 0350109001017, 0350109001018, 0350109001019, 0350109001020, 0350109001021, 0350109001022, 0350109001023, 0350109001024, 0350109001025, 0350109001026, 0350109001027, 0350109001028, 0350109001029, 0350109001030, 0350109001031, 0350109001038; VTD: 15, VTD: 16, VTD: 37, VTD: 38; Davidson County: VTD: 02, VTD: 04, VTD: 16, VTD: 24, VTD: 26, VTD: 34, VTD: 44, VTD: 46, VTD: 48, VTD: 50, VTD: 78, VTD: 82, VTD: 84; Davie County, Forsyth County: VTD: 011, VTD: 012, VTD: 013, VTD: 014, VTD: 015, VTD: 021, VTD: 031, VTD: 032, VTD: 033, VTD: 034, VTD: 043, VTD: 051, VTD: 052, VTD: 053, VTD: 054, VTD: 055, VTD: 061, VTD: 062, VTD: 063, VTD: 064, VTD: 065, VTD: 066, VTD: 067, VTD: 068, VTD: 071, VTD: 072, VTD: 073, VTD: 074, VTD: 075, VTD: 081, VTD: 082, VTD: 083, VTD: 091, VTD: 092, VTD: 101, VTD: 111, VTD: 112, VTD: 122, VTD: 123, VTD: 131, VTD: 132, VTD: 133, VTD: 201, VTD: 207, VTD: 306, VTD: 503, VTD: 506, VTD: 507, VTD: 601, VTD: 602,

VTD: 603, VTD: 604, VTD: 605, VTD: 606, VTD: 607, VTD: 701, VTD: 702, VTD: 703, VTD: 704, VTD: 705, VTD: 706, VTD: 707, VTD: 708, VTD: 709, VTD: 801, VTD: 802, VTD: 803, VTD: 804, VTD: 805, VTD: 806, VTD: 807, VTD: 808, VTD: 809, VTD: 901, VTD: 902, VTD: 903, VTD: 904, VTD: 905, VTD: 906, VTD: 907, VTD: 908, VTD: 909; Iredell County: VTD: CH-A, VTD: CH-B: Block(s) 0970606031000, 0970606031001, 0970606031002, 0970606031003, 0970606031004, 0970606031005, 0970606031006, 0970606031007, 0970606031023, 0970606031024, 0970606031030, 0970606031031, 0970606031032, 0970606031033, 0970606031034, 0970606031035, 0970606031038, 0970607012019, 0970607012021, 0970607012023, 0970607012025, 0970607012026, 0970607012027, 0970607012028, 0970607012036, 0970607012037, 0970607012062, 0970607012063, 0970607012064, 0970607012065, 0970612013025, 0970612013027, 0970613011002, 0970613011003, 0970613011005, 0970613011006, 0970613011007, 0970613011008, 0970613011010, 0970613011011, 0970613011012, 0970613011018, 0970613011019, 0970613011020, 0970613011021, 0970613011035; VTD: CS, VTD: EM, VTD: NH, VTD: ST1, VTD: ST2, VTD: ST3, VTD: ST4, VTD: ST5, VTD: ST6, VTD: TB, VTD: UG; Rowan County: VTD: 07, VTD: 11, VTD: 12, VTD: 21, VTD: 24, VTD: 27, VTD: 29, VTD: 32, VTD: 39, VTD: 40, VTD: 41, VTD: 45; Watauga County, Wilkes County, Yadkin County.

District 6: Alamance County: VTD: 02, VTD: 035, VTD: 03C, VTD: 03N, VTD: 03S, VTD: 03W, VTD: 04, VTD: 05, VTD: 064, VTD: 06E, VTD: 06S, VTD: 06W, VTD: 07, VTD: 08N, VTD: 08S, VTD: 09N, VTD: 09S, VTD: 103, VTD: 10N, VTD: 10S, VTD: 1210, VTD: 124, VTD: 125, VTD: 126, VTD: 129, VTD: 12W, VTD: 13: Block(s) 0010212011077, 0010212013026, 0010212013028, 0010212013029, 0010212013030, 0010212013031, 0010212013032, 0010212013033, 0010212013034, 0010212013035, 0010212013036, 0010212013037, 0010212013038, 0010212013043, 0010212013044, 0010212013045, 0010212013046, 0010212013047, 0010212013048, 0010212013049, 0010212013050, 0010212013051, 0010212013059, 0010212013060, 0010212013061, 0010212013062, 0010212013063, 0010212013064, 0010212013065, 0010212013066, 0010212013067, 0010212013068, 0010212013069, 0010212013070, 0010212013071, 0010212013072, 0010212013073, 0010212013074, 0010220011000, 0010220011001, 0010220011002; Caswell County, Durham County: VTD: 25, VTD: 26, VTD: 28, VTD: 37, VTD: 44, VTD: 45; Granville County: VTD: BERE, VTD: OKHL, VTD: SASS; Guilford County: VTD: CG1, VTD: CG2, VTD: CG3A, VTD: CG3B, VTD: FEN2, VTD: FR1, VTD: FR2, VTD: FR3, VTD: FR4, VTD: FR5, VTD: G11, VTD: G12, VTD: G13, VTD: G14, VTD: G15, VTD: G16, VTD:

G17, VTD: G18, VTD: G19, VTD: G20, VTD: G21, VTD: G22, VTD: G23, VTD: G24, VTD: G25, VTD: G27, VTD: G28, VTD: G29, VTD: G30, VTD: G31, VTD: G32, VTD: G33, VTD: G34, VTD: G35, VTD: G36, VTD: G38, VTD: G39, VTD: G40A1, VTD: G40A2, VTD: G40B, VTD: G41, VTD: G42, VTD: G44, VTD: G45, VTD: G46: Block(s) 0810108002075, 0810108002078, 0810114003000; VTD: G48, VTD: G60: Block(s) 0810126094014; VTD: G62, VTD: G63, VTD: G64: Block(s) 0810160111024, 0810160111025, 0810160111026, 0810160111027, 0810160111028, 0810160111029, 0810160111030, 0810160111031, 0810160111032, 0810160111033, 0810160111034, 0810160111035, 0810160111038, 0810160111039, 0810160111040, 0810160111044, 0810160111045, 0810160111046, 0810160111047, 0810160111048, 0810160111049, 0810160111050, 0810160111056, 0810160111057, 0810160111058, 0810160111059, 0810160111060, 0810160111061, 0810160114001, 0810160114002, 0810160114003, 0810160114004, 0810160114005, 0810164051000, 0810164051009, 0810164051010, 0810164051044, 0810164051045, 0810164051046, 0810164051047, 0810164051048, 0810164051051, 0810165031000, 0810165031001, 0810165031002, 0810165031003, 0810165031004, 0810165031006, 0810165031008, 0810165031009, 0819801001037, 0819801001038, 0819801001039; VTD: G65, VTD: G66, VTD: GIB, VTD: GR, VTD: H02, VTD: H04, VTD: H06, VTD: H13, VTD: H14, VTD: H15, VTD: H16, VTD: H20A, VTD: H20B, VTD: H21, VTD: H22, VTD: H23, VTD: H24, VTD: H25, VTD: H26, VTD: H27, VTD: JAM1, VTD: JAM2, VTD: JAM3: Block(s) 0810126094004, 0810126094005, 0810126094006, 0810126094007, 0810126094008, 0810126094009, 0810126094010, 0810126094017, 0810126094018, 0810126094019, 0810126094020, 0810126094021, 0810126094022, 0810126094023, 0810126094024, 0810126094025, 0810126094026, 0810126094027, 0810126094028, 0810126094029, 0810126094032, 0810126094033, 0810165021002, 0810165021004, 0810165021005, 0810165021006, 0810165021007, 0810165021008, 0810165021009, 0810165021010, 0810165021012, 0810165021013, 0810165021014, 0810165021015, 0810165021016, 0810165021017, 0810165021018, 0810165021019, 0810165021020, 0810165021021, 0810165021022, 0810165021023, 0810165021024, 0810165021025, 0810165021026, 0810165021027, 0810165021028, 0810165021029, 0810165021030, 0810165021031, 0810165021032, 0810165021033, 0810165021034, 0810165021035, 0810165021036, 0810165021037, 0810165021038, 0810165021039, 0810165021040, 0810165021041, 0810165021042, 0810165021043, 0810165021044, 0810165021045, 0810165021046, 0810165021047, 0810165021048, 0810165021049, 0810165021050, 0810165021051, 0810165021052, 0810165021053, 0810165021054,

0810165021055, 0810165021056, 0810165021057, 0810165021058, 0810165021059, 0810165021060, 0810165021061, 0810165021062, 0810165021063, 0810165023000, 0810165023002, 0810165023003, 0810165023010, 0810165023011, 0810165023028, 0810165023044, 0810165023045, 0810165024001, 0810165024002, 0810165024003, 0810165024004, 0810165024005, 0810165024006, 0810165024007, 0810165024008, 0810165024009, 0810165024010, 0810165024012, 0810165024013, 0810165024014, 0810165024015, 0810165024016, 0810165024017, 0810165024018, 0810165024019, 0810165024020; VTD: JAM4, VTD: JAM5, VTD: JEF1, VTD: JEF2, VTD: JEF4, VTD: MON1, VTD: MON3, VTD: NCGR1, VTD: NCGR2, VTD: NCLAY1, VTD: NCLAY2, VTD: NDRI, VTD: NMAD, VTD: NWASH, VTD: OR1, VTD: OR2, VTD: PG1, VTD: PG2, VTD: RC1, VTD: RC2, VTD: SCLAY, VTD: SDRI, VTD: SF1, VTD: SF2, VTD: SF3, VTD: SF4, VTD: SMAD, VTD: STOK, VTD: SUM2, VTD: SUM3, VTD: SUM4, VTD: SWASH; Orange County: VTD: CG, VTD: CP, VTD: CW, VTD: EF, VTD: ENO, VTD: SM, VTD: TO; Person County, Rockingham County, Stokes County, Surry County.

District 7: Bladen County, Brunswick County, Columbus County, Cumberland County: VTD: AL51, VTD: G6; Duplin County, Hoke County: VTD: 01, VTD: 02, VTD: 03, VTD: 61, VTD: 62, VTD: 64, VTD: 65; Johnston County, Lenoir County: VTD: FC, VTD: I, VTD: K4, VTD: N, VTD: PH1, VTD: PH2, VTD: SW, VTD: T1, VTD: T2, VTD: W; New Hanover County: VTD: CF02, VTD: CF03, VTD: FP01, VTD: FP02, VTD: FP03, VTD: FP04, VTD: FP05, VTD: H01, VTD: H02, VTD: H03, VTD: H04, VTD: H05, VTD: H06, VTD: H07, VTD: H08, VTD: H09, VTD: M02, VTD: M03, VTD: M04, VTD: M05, VTD: W12, VTD: W16, VTD: W17, VTD: W18, VTD: W21, VTD: W28: Block(s) 1290105021042, 1290105021043, 1290105021044, 1290105021048, 1290105023012, 1290105023013, 1290119021038, 1290119021039, 1290119021040, 1290119021041; VTD: W30, VTD: W31, VTD: WB; Pender County: VTD: LT18, VTD: MT19, VTD: SC13, VTD: SH12, VTD: SP15, VTD: UT14; Robeson County: VTD: 10, VTD: 21, VTD: 27, VTD: 33, VTD: 34; Sampson County.

District 8: Anson County, Cabarrus County: VTD: 01-02, VTD: 01-04, VTD: 01-06, VTD: 01-07, VTD: 01-08, VTD: 01-09, VTD: 01-10, VTD: 02-01, VTD: 02-02, VTD: 02-03, VTD: 02-05, VTD: 02-06, VTD: 02-07, VTD: 04-01, VTD: 04-02, VTD: 04-03, VTD: 04-04, VTD: 04-05, VTD: 04-06, VTD: 04-07, VTD: 04-08, VTD: 04-09, VTD: 04-10, VTD: 05-00, VTD: 06-00, VTD: 07-00, VTD: 08-00, VTD: 09-00, VTD: 10-00, VTD: 11-01, VTD: 11-02, VTD: 12-01, VTD: 12-02, VTD: 12-03, VTD: 12-04, VTD: 12-05, VTD: 12-06, VTD: 12-07, VTD: 12-08, VTD: 12-09, VTD: 12-10, VTD: 12-11, VTD: 12-12; Davidson County: VTD: 08,

VTD: 10: Block(s) 0570618032000, 0570618032001, 0570618032002, 0570618032009, 0570618032010, 0570618032011, 0570618032012, 0570618032013, 0570618032014, 0570618032026, 0570618032027, 0570618032028, 0570618032029, 0570618032030, 0570618032031, 0570618032032, 0570618032033, 0570618032034, 0570618032035, 0570618032036, 0570618032037, 0570618032043, 0570618032044, 0570618033000, 0570618033001, 0570618033002, 0570618033003, 0570618033004, 0570618033005, 0570618033006, 0570618033007, 0570618033008, 0570618033009, 0570618033010, 0570618033011, 0570618033012, 0570618033013, 0570618033014, 0570618033015, 0570618033016, 0570618033017, 0570618033018, 0570618033019, 0570618033020, 0570618034007, 0570618034009, 0570618034018, 0570618034020, 0570618034027, 0570618034028, 0570618034035, 0570618034036, 0570618034037, 0570618034038, 0570618034039, 0570618034040, 0570618034041, 0570618034042, 0570618034046, 0570618034047, 0570618034050, 0570618034051, 0570618034052, 0570618034053, 0570618034054, 0570618034055, 0570618034056, 0570618034057, 0570618041012, 0570618041013, 0570618041014, 0570618041034, 0570618041035, 0570618041036, 0570618041037, 0570618041038, 0570618041039, 0570618041067, 0570618041068, 0570618041069, 0570618044000, 0570618044001, 0570618044002, 0570618044003, 0570618044004, 0570618044005, 0570618044006, 0570618044007, 0570618044008, 0570618044009, 0570618044010, 0570618044011, 0570618044012, 0570618044013, 0570618044014, 0570618044015, 0570618044016, 0570618044017, 0570618044018, 0570618044029, 0570618044030, 0570618044031, 0570618044032, 0570618045000, 0570618045001, 0570618045002, 0570618045003, 0570618045004, 0570618045005, 0570618045006, 0570618045007, 0570618045008, 0570618045009, 0570618045010, 0570618045017, 0570618045018; VTD: 12, VTD: 14, VTD: 18, VTD: 20, VTD: 40, VTD: 42, VTD: 52, VTD: 54, VTD: 56, VTD: 58, VTD: 60, VTD: 66, VTD: 68, VTD: 74, VTD: 76; Mecklenburg County: VTD: 083, VTD: 095, VTD: 201; Montgomery County, Randolph County: VTD: 16: Block(s) 1510305041041, 1510305041042, 1510305041062, 1510305041063, 1510306001000, 1510306001001, 1510306001002, 1510306001003, 1510306001004, 1510306001005, 1510306001006, 1510306001007, 1510306001008, 1510306001010, 1510306001012, 1510306001014, 1510306001015, 1510306001016, 1510306001017, 1510306001018, 1510306001021, 1510306001022, 1510306001023, 1510306001024, 1510306001025, 1510306001026, 1510306001027, 1510306001028, 1510306001029, 1510306001030, 1510306001032, 1510306001033, 1510306001034, 1510306001035,

1510306001036, 1510306001037, 1510306001038, 1510306001039, 1510306001044, 1510306001045, 1510306001046, 1510306001048, 1510306001049, 1510306001050, 1510306001051, 1510306001052, 1510306001053, 1510306001054, 1510306001055, 1510306001056, 1510306001057, 1510306001058, 1510306001059, 1510306001060, 1510306001061, 1510306001062, 1510306001063, 1510306001064, 1510306001065, 1510306001069, 1510306002025, 1510306002026, 1510306002027, 1510306002028, 1510306002029, 1510306002030, 1510306002038, 1510306002039, 1510306002040, 1510306002041, 1510306002042, 1510306002043, 1510306002044, 1510306002045, 1510306002046, 1510306002047, 1510306002048, 1510306002049, 1510306002050, 1510306002051, 1510306003010, 1510306003011, 1510306003012, 1510306003013, 1510307003008, 1510307003009, 1510307003010, 1510307003011, 1510307003012, 1510307003014, 1510307003015, 1510307003019, 1510307003020; VTD: 18, VTD: 24, VTD: 36; Richmond County, Robeson County: VTD: 01, VTD: 02, VTD: 03, VTD: 04, VTD: 05, VTD: 06, VTD: 07, VTD: 08, VTD: 09, VTD: 11, VTD: 12, VTD: 13, VTD: 14, VTD: 15, VTD: 16, VTD: 17, VTD: 18A, VTD: 19, VTD: 20, VTD: 22, VTD: 23, VTD: 24, VTD: 25, VTD: 26, VTD: 28, VTD: 29, VTD: 30, VTD: 31, VTD: 32, VTD: 35, VTD: 36, VTD: 37, VTD: 38, VTD: 39, VTD: 40, VTD: 41; Rowan County: VTD: 01, VTD: 02, VTD: 03, VTD: 05, VTD: 06, VTD: 09, VTD: 10, VTD: 13, VTD: 14, VTD: 15, VTD: 16, VTD: 17, VTD: 19, VTD: 20, VTD: 22, VTD: 23, VTD: 25, VTD: 26, VTD: 31, VTD: 33, VTD: 46; Scotland County, Stanly County, Union County: VTD: 001, VTD: 002, VTD: 003, VTD: 004, VTD: 005: Block(s) 1790204031000, 1790204031001, 1790204031002, 1790204031003, 1790204031004, 1790204031005, 1790204031006, 1790204031007, 1790204031008, 1790204031009, 1790204031010, 1790204031011, 1790204031012, 1790204031013, 1790204031014, 1790204031015, 1790204031016, 1790204031017, 1790204041000, 1790204041001, 1790204041002, 1790204041003, 1790204041004, 1790204041005, 1790204041006, 1790204041007, 1790204041008, 1790204041009, 1790204041010, 1790204041011, 1790204041012, 1790204041013, 1790204041014, 1790204041015, 1790204041016, 1790204042028, 1790204042029, 1790204042030, 1790204042031, 1790204042032, 1790204042034, 1790204042035; VTD: 006, VTD: 007: Block(s) 1790205011003, 1790205011004, 1790205011005, 1790205011006, 1790205011007, 1790205011008, 1790205011009, 1790205011010, 1790205011017, 1790205011018, 1790205011019, 1790205011020, 1790205011021, 1790205011022, 1790205011023, 1790205011024, 1790205011025, 1790205011026, 1790205011027, 1790205011028, 1790205011029, 1790205011030, 1790205011031, 1790205011032,

1790205011033, 1790205011034, 1790205011035, 1790205011036, 1790205011037, 1790205011038, 1790205011039, 1790205011040, 1790205011041, 1790205011042, 1790205011043, 1790205011044, 1790205011045, 1790205011046, 1790205011047, 1790205011048, 1790205011067, 1790205011068, 1790209022000, 1790209022001, 1790209022002, 1790209022007, 1790209022008, 1790209022009, 1790210051002, 1790210051003, 1790210051039, 1790210052000, 1790210052001, 1790210052002, 1790210052003, 1790210052004, 1790210052005, 1790210052006, 1790210052007, 1790210052008, 1790210052009, 1790210052010, 1790210052011, 1790210052012, 1790210052013, 1790210052014, 1790210052015, 1790210052016, 1790210052017, 1790210052027, 1790210052031, 1790210052032, 1790210052033, 1790210052034, 1790210052035, 1790210052036, 1790210052037, 1790210052038, 1790210052039, 1790210052040, 1790210052041, 1790210052049; VTD: 008, VTD: 009, VTD: 010, VTD: 011, VTD: 012, VTD: 013, VTD: 016, VTD: 021: Block(s) 1790209022003, 1790209022004, 1790209022005, 1790209022006, 1790209022015; VTD: 023, VTD: 024, VTD: 025, VTD: 026, VTD: 027, VTD: 030, VTD: 031: Block(s) 1790204033000, 1790204033001, 1790204033002, 1790204033003, 1790204033004, 1790204033005, 1790204033006, 1790204033007, 1790204033008, 1790204033009, 1790210051000, 1790210051001; VTD: 032, VTD: 034, VTD: 035: Block(s) 1790203051000, 1790203051018, 1790203051025, 1790203051057, 1790203051058, 1790203051061, 1790203091018, 1790203091019, 1790203091020, 1790203091021, 1790203091022, 1790203091023, 1790203091024, 1790203091025; VTD: 036, VTD: 037A: Block(s) 1790203102025, 1790203102026, 1790203102027, 1790203102028, 1790203103000, 1790203103001, 1790203103002, 1790203103004, 1790203103005, 1790203103028, 1790203103029; VTD: 038A, VTD: 038B, VTD: 039, VTD: 042: Block(s) 1790204032000, 1790204032001, 1790204032002, 1790204032003, 1790204032004, 1790204032005, 1790204032006, 1790204032007, 1790204032008, 1790204032009, 1790204032010, 1790204032011, 1790204032012, 1790204032013, 1790204032014, 1790204032015, 1790204032016, 1790204032018, 1790204032019, 1790204032020, 1790204032021, 1790204032022, 1790204032023, 1790204032026, 1790204032027, 1790204032028, 1790204032029, 1790204032030, 1790204032031, 1790204032032, 1790204032033, 1790204032034, 1790204032035, 1790204042036, 1790205012009; VTD: 043.

District 9: Iredell County: VTD: BA, VTD: BE, VTD: CC1, VTD: CC2, VTD: CC3, VTD: CC4, VTD: CD, VTD: CH-B: Block(s) 0970606032053, 0970606032054,

0970607012020, 0970607012022, 0970607012029, 0970607012030,
0970607012031, 0970607012032, 0970607012033, 0970607012034,
0970607012035, 0970607012038, 0970607012039, 0970607012040,
0970607012041, 0970607012042, 0970607012043, 0970607012044,
0970607012045, 0970607012048, 0970607012049, 0970607012050,
0970607012051, 0970607012052, 0970607012053, 0970607012055,
0970607012057, 0970607012058, 0970607012059, 0970607012060,
0970607012061, 0970607012066, 0970607012067, 0970607012069,
0970613011000, 0970613011004, 0970613011024, 0970613011028,
0970613011040, 0970613012000, 0970613012001, 0970613012002,
0970613012003, 0970613012004, 0970613012005, 0970613012006,
0970613012007, 0970613012008, 0970613012009, 0970613012010,
0970613012014, 0970613012015, 0970613013000, 0970613013001,
0970613013002, 0970613013003, 0970613013004, 0970613013005,
0970613013006, 0970613013007, 0970613013008, 0970613013009,
0970613013010, 0970613013011, 0970613022000, 0970613022002,
0970613023000, 0970613023001, 0970613023002, 0970613023003,
0970613023004, 0970613023005, 0970613023006, 0970613023007,
0970613023008, 0970613023009; VTD: DV1-A, VTD: DV1-B, VTD: DV2-A,
VTD: DV2-B, VTD: FT, VTD: OL, VTD: SB, VTD: SH-A, VTD: SH-B;
Mecklenburg County: VTD: 001, VTD: 002: Block(s) 1190024001000,
1190024001001, 1190024001002, 1190024001003, 1190024001004,
1190024001005, 1190024001006, 1190024001007, 1190024001009,
1190024001010, 1190024001011, 1190024001012, 1190024001013,
1190024001014, 1190024001015, 1190024001017, 1190024001018,
1190024001019, 1190024002000, 1190024002001, 1190024002002,
1190024002003, 1190024002004, 1190024002005, 1190024002006,
1190024002007, 1190024002008, 1190024002009, 1190024002010,
1190024002011, 1190024002012, 1190024003000, 1190024003001,
1190024003002, 1190024003003, 1190024003004, 1190024003007,
1190024003008, 1190024003018, 1190025001013, 1190025001014,
1190025001015, 1190025001016, 1190025001017, 1190025001018,
1190025001019, 1190025001020, 1190025002027, 1190025002029,
1190025002030, 1190025002031, 1190025002032, 1190025002041,
1190025002042, 1190025002043, 1190026001000, 1190026001001,
1190026001002, 1190026001003, 1190026001004, 1190026001005,
1190026001006, 1190026001007, 1190026001008, 1190026001009,
1190026001010, 1190026001011, 1190026001012, 1190026001013,
1190026001014, 1190026001015, 1190026001016, 1190026001017,
1190026001018, 1190026001019, 1190026001020, 1190026001021,
1190026001022, 1190026001023, 1190026001024, 1190026001025,

1190026001026, 1190026001027, 1190026001028, 1190026001029, 1190026001030, 1190026001032; VTD: 007, VTD: 008, VTD: 009, VTD: 010, VTD: 015, VTD: 018, VTD: 019, VTD: 020, VTD: 021, VTD: 032, VTD: 034, VTD: 035, VTD: 036, VTD: 037, VTD: 038, VTD: 044, VTD: 047, VTD: 048, VTD: 049, VTD: 050, VTD: 051, VTD: 057, VTD: 058, VTD: 059, VTD: 064, VTD: 065, VTD: 066, VTD: 067, VTD: 068, VTD: 069, VTD: 070, VTD: 071, VTD: 072, VTD: 073, VTD: 074, VTD: 075, VTD: 076, VTD: 080, VTD: 085, VTD: 086, VTD: 087, VTD: 088, VTD: 089, VTD: 090, VTD: 091, VTD: 092, VTD: 093, VTD: 094, VTD: 096, VTD: 100, VTD: 101, VTD: 102, VTD: 103, VTD: 106, VTD: 109, VTD: 110, VTD: 111, VTD: 112, VTD: 113, VTD: 114, VTD: 115, VTD: 118, VTD: 119, VTD: 121, VTD: 122, VTD: 127, VTD: 128, VTD: 129, VTD: 131, VTD: 133, VTD: 134, VTD: 136, VTD: 137, VTD: 139.1, VTD: 140, VTD: 142, VTD: 143, VTD: 144, VTD: 145, VTD: 148, VTD: 150, VTD: 200, VTD: 202, VTD: 206, VTD: 207, VTD: 208, VTD: 209, VTD: 214, VTD: 215, VTD: 216, VTD: 217, VTD: 218, VTD: 219, VTD: 220, VTD: 221, VTD: 223.1, VTD: 224, VTD: 225, VTD: 226, VTD: 227, VTD: 228, VTD: 229, VTD: 230, VTD: 231, VTD: 232, VTD: 233, VTD: 234, VTD: 235, VTD: 236, VTD: 238.1, VTD: 239, VTD: 240, VTD: 241, VTD: 242, VTD: 243; Union County: VTD: 005: Block(s) 1790203071025, 1790203071029, 1790203071030, 1790203071031, 1790203071032, 1790203071033, 1790203071034, 1790203071035, 1790203071038, 1790203071039, 1790203071040, 1790203071041, 1790203071043, 1790203071046, 1790203071047, 1790203071048, 1790203071050, 1790203071051, 1790203071052, 1790203071053, 1790203071054, 1790203071055, 1790203071056, 1790203071057, 1790203071058, 1790203071059, 1790203071060, 1790203071061, 1790203071062, 1790203071063, 1790203071064, 1790203071065, 1790203071066, 1790203071067, 1790203071068, 1790203071069, 1790203071070, 1790203071072, 1790203071073, 1790203071074, 1790203071075, 1790203071076, 1790203071077, 1790203071078, 1790203071079, 1790203072008, 1790203072011, 1790203072012, 1790203072013, 1790203072014, 1790203072015, 1790203072016, 1790203072027, 1790203072029, 1790203073000, 1790203073001, 1790203073002, 1790203073003, 1790203073004, 1790203073005, 1790203073006, 1790203073007, 1790203073008, 1790203073009, 1790203073012, 1790203073013, 1790203073014, 1790203073015, 1790203073016, 1790203073020, 1790203073021, 1790203073022, 1790203073026, 1790203073027, 1790203073028, 1790203073029, 1790203073030, 1790203073031; VTD: 007: 1790210051027, 1790210051028, 1790210052018, 1790210052019, 1790210052020, 1790210052025, 1790210052026, 1790210052042, 1790210052043, 1790210052044, 1790210052046, 1790210053010,

1790210053011, 1790210053012, 1790210053013, 1790210053015, 1790210053022, 1790210053023; VTD: 014, VTD: 015, VTD: 017A, VTD: 017B, VTD: 018, VTD: 019, VTD: 020A, VTD: 020B, VTD: 021: Block(s) 1790209022011, 1790209022012, 1790209022013, 1790209022014, 1790209022016, 1790209022017, 1790209022018, 1790209022019, 1790209022020, 1790209022021, 1790209022022, 1790209022023, 1790209022024, 1790209022025, 1790209022026, 1790209022027, 1790209022028, 1790209022029, 1790209022036, 1790209022037, 1790209023000, 1790209023001, 1790209023002, 1790209023003, 1790209023004, 1790209023010, 1790209023011, 1790209023012, 1790209023013, 1790209023014, 1790209023015, 1790209023016, 1790209023017, 1790209023018, 1790209023019, 1790209023020, 1790209023021, 1790209023022, 1790209023023, 1790209023024, 1790209023025, 1790209023026, 1790209023027, 1790209023029, 1790209023030, 1790209023031, 1790209023032, 1790209023033, 1790209023034, 1790209023035, 1790209023036, 1790209023037, 1790209023038, 1790209023039, 1790209023040, 1790209023041, 1790209023042, 1790209023045, 1790209023046, 1790209023047, 1790209023048, 1790209023049, 1790209023050, 1790209023051, 1790209023052, 1790209023053, 1790209023054, 1790209023055, 1790209023056, 1790210053014, 1790210053024, 1790210053025, 1790210053026, 1790210053027, 1790210053028, 1790210053029, 1790210053030, 1790210053031, 1790210053032, 1790210053033, 1790210053034, 1790210053035, 1790210053036, 1790210053037, 1790210053038, 1790210053039, 1790210053042, 1790210053043, 1790210053044, 1790210053045, 1790210152000, 1790210152001, 1790210152002, 1790210152003, 1790210152008, 1790210152009, 1790210152010, 1790210152011, 1790210152012, 1790210152013, 1790210152014, 1790210152015, 1790210152019, 1790210152020, 1790210152021, 1790210152022; VTD: 022, VTD: 028, VTD: 029A, VTD: 029B, VTD: 029C, VTD: 031: Block(s) 1790203082004, 1790203082005, 1790203082006, 1790203082007, 1790203082009, 1790203082010, 1790203082011, 1790203082012, 1790203082013, 1790203082014, 1790203082016, 1790203082017, 1790203082018, 1790203082019, 1790203083000, 1790203083001, 1790203083002, 1790203083003, 1790203083004, 1790203083005, 1790203083006, 1790203083007, 1790203083008, 1790203083009, 1790203083010, 1790203083011, 1790203083012, 1790203083013, 1790203083014, 1790203083015, 1790203083016, 1790203083017, 1790203083018, 1790203083019, 1790203083020, 1790203083021, 1790203083022, 1790203083023, 1790203083024; VTD: 033, VTD: 035: Block(s) 1790203091000,

1790203091001, 1790203091002, 1790203091003, 1790203091004, 1790203091005, 1790203091006, 1790203091007, 1790203091008, 1790203091009, 1790203091010, 1790203091011, 1790203091012, 1790203091013, 1790203091014, 1790203091015, 1790203091016, 1790203091017, 1790203091026, 1790203091027, 1790203091028, 1790203091029, 1790203091030, 1790203091031, 1790203091032, 1790203091033, 1790203091034, 1790203091035, 1790203091036, 1790203091037, 1790203091038, 1790203091039, 1790203091040, 1790203091041; VTD: 037A: 1790203102000, 1790203102001, 1790203102002, 1790203102003, 1790203102004, 1790203102005, 1790203102006, 1790203102007, 1790203102008, 1790203102009, 1790203102010, 1790203102011, 1790203102012, 1790203102013, 1790203102014, 1790203102015, 1790203102016, 1790203102017, 1790203102018, 1790203102019, 1790203102020, 1790203102021, 1790203102022, 1790203102023, 1790203102024, 1790203103003, 1790203103006, 1790203103007, 1790203103008, 1790203103009, 1790203103010, 1790203103011, 1790203103012, 1790203103013, 1790203103014, 1790203103015, 1790203103016, 1790203103017, 1790203103018, 1790203103019, 1790203103020, 1790203103021, 1790203103022, 1790203103023, 1790203103024, 1790203103025, 1790203103026, 1790203103027, 1790203111000, 1790203111001, 1790203111002, 1790203111003, 1790203111004, 1790203111005, 1790203111006, 1790203111007, 1790203111008, 1790203111009, 1790203111010, 1790203111011, 1790203111012, 1790203111013, 1790203111014, 1790203111015, 1790203111016, 1790203111017, 1790203111018, 1790203111019, 1790203111020, 1790203111021, 1790203111022, 1790203111023, 1790203111024, 1790203111025, 1790203111026, 1790203112000, 1790203112003, 1790203112004, 1790203112005, 1790203112006, 1790203112009, 1790203112010, 1790203112011, 1790203112012, 1790203112013, 1790203112014, 1790203112016, 1790203112017, 1790203112018, 1790203112019, 1790203112020, 1790203112021, 1790203121000, 1790203121001, 1790203121002, 1790203121003, 1790203121004, 1790203121005, 1790203121012, 1790203121013, 1790203121014, 1790203121015, 1790203121016, 1790203121017, 1790203121018, 1790203121019, 1790203121020, 1790203121021, 1790203121022, 1790203121023, 1790203121036, 1790203121037, 1790203121038, 1790203121039, 1790203121040, 1790203121041, 1790203121042, 1790203121043, 1790203121063, 1790203121064; VTD: 037B, VTD: 040, VTD: 041, VTD: 042: Block(s) 1790203081000, 1790203081001, 1790203081002, 1790203081003, 1790203081004, 1790203081005, 1790203081020, 1790203081021,

1790203081022, 1790203081023, 1790203081024, 1790203081025,
1790203081026, 1790203081027, 1790203081028, 1790203081029,
1790203081030, 1790203081031, 1790203081033, 1790203081034,
1790203081036, 1790203081037, 1790203081038, 1790203081039,
1790203081040, 1790203081041, 1790203082000, 1790203082001,
1790203082002, 1790203082003, 1790203082008, 1790203082015,
1790203082020, 1790203082021, 1790203082022, 1790203082023,
1790203082024, 1790203082025, 1790203082026, 1790203082027,
1790203082028.

District 10: Buncombe County: VTD: 01.1, VTD: 02.1, VTD: 03.1, VTD: 04.1, VTD: 05.1, VTD: 06.1, VTD: 07.1, VTD: 09.1, VTD: 10.1, VTD: 100.1, VTD: 103.1, VTD: 104.1, VTD: 105.1, VTD: 106.1: Block(s) 0210011001021,
0210011001022, 0210011001024, 0210011001025, 0210011001026,
0210011001032, 0210011001033, 0210011001034, 0210012001001,
0210012001003, 0210012001004, 0210012001005, 0210012001006,
0210012001007, 0210012001008, 0210012001009, 0210012001010,
0210012001011, 0210012001012, 0210012001013, 0210012001014,
0210012001015, 0210012001016, 0210012001017, 0210012001018,
0210012001019, 0210012001020, 0210012001021, 0210012001022,
0210012002000, 0210012002001, 0210012002002, 0210012002003,
0210012002004, 0210012002005, 0210012002006, 0210012002007,
0210012002009, 0210012002010, 0210012002015, 0210012002016,
0210012003000, 0210012003001, 0210012003002, 0210012003003,
0210012003008, 0210012003009, 0210013001000, 0210013001007,
0210013001008, 0210013001009, 0210013001012, 0210013002002,
0210013002003, 0210013002004, 0210013002005, 0210013002006,
0210013002007, 0210013002008, 0210013002009, 0210013002010,
0210013002011, 0210013002012, 0210013002013, 0210013002014,
0210013002015, 0210013002016, 0210013002017, 0210013002018,
0210013002019, 0210013002020, 0210013002021, 0210013002022,
0210013002023, 0210013002024, 0210013002026, 0210013002027,
0210013002028, 0210013002029, 0210013002030, 0210013002031,
0210013002032, 0210013002033, 0210013002034, 0210013002037,
0210013002038, 0210013002039, 0210013002040, 0210013002041,
0210014005002, 0210014005003, 0210014005023, 0210014005024,
0210014005025, 0210025062000, 0210025062001, 0210025062002,
0210025062003, 0210025062004, 0210025062005, 0210025062006,
0210025062007, 0210025062008, 0210025062009, 0210025062010,
0210025062011, 0210025062012, 0210025062013, 0210025062027,
0210025062029, 0210025062030, 0210025062031, 0210025063000,

0210025063001, 0210025063002, 0210025063003, 0210025063004, 0210025063006, 0210026052050, 0210026052052, 0210026052053, 0210026052054, 0210026052055, 0210026052057; VTD: 11.1, VTD: 12.1, VTD: 13.1, VTD: 14.2, VTD: 15.1: Block(s) 0210011002001, 0210011002002, 0210011002004, 0210011002005, 0210011002006, 0210011002007, 0210011002008, 0210011002009, 0210011002010, 0210011002011, 0210011002012, 0210011002013, 0210011002014, 0210011002015, 0210011002016, 0210011002017, 0210011002018, 0210011002021, 0210011002022, 0210011002023, 0210011002028, 0210011002029, 0210011002030, 0210012003004, 0210012003010, 0210012003011, 0210012003012, 0210012003013, 0210012003014; VTD: 17.1, VTD: 20.1, VTD: 25.1, VTD: 28.1, VTD: 31.1, VTD: 32.1, VTD: 33.2, VTD: 33.3, VTD: 34.1, VTD: 35.1, VTD: 36.1, VTD: 37.1, VTD: 38.2, VTD: 38.3, VTD: 39.1, VTD: 55.1, VTD: 57.1, VTD: 60.2, VTD: 61.1, VTD: 62.1, VTD: 64.1, VTD: 65.1, VTD: 66.1, VTD: 70.1; Catawba County: VTD: 01, VTD: 02, VTD: 03, VTD: 05, VTD: 06, VTD: 07, VTD: 08, VTD: 09, VTD: 10, VTD: 13: Block(s) 0350106002013, 0350106002015, 0350106002017, 0350106002018, 0350106002019, 0350106002022, 0350106002023, 0350106002027, 0350106002028, 0350106003024, 0350106003025, 0350106003026, 0350106003027, 0350106004011, 0350106004046, 0350106004047, 0350107001029, 0350107001042; VTD: 14, VTD: 17, VTD: 19, VTD: 20, VTD: 21, VTD: 22, VTD: 23, VTD: 24, VTD: 25, VTD: 26, VTD: 27, VTD: 28, VTD: 29, VTD: 30, VTD: 31, VTD: 32, VTD: 33, VTD: 34, VTD: 35, VTD: 36, VTD: 39, VTD: 40, VTD: 41; Cleveland County, Gaston County, Lincoln County, Polk County, Rutherford County.

District 11: Avery County, Buncombe County: VTD: 101.1, VTD: 102.1, VTD: 106.1: Block(s) 0210012002008; VTD: 107.1, VTD: 15.1: Block(s) 0210012002017, 0210012002018, 0210012003005, 0210012003006, 0210012003007, 0210012003015, 0210012003016, 0210012003017, 0210012003018, 0210012003019, 0210012003020, 0210012003021, 0210012004000, 0210012004017, 0210012004018, 0210012004019; VTD: 19.1, VTD: 24.1, VTD: 26.1, VTD: 30.1, VTD: 41.1, VTD: 44.1, VTD: 45.1, VTD: 46.1, VTD: 47.1, VTD: 48.1, VTD: 49.1, VTD: 50.1, VTD: 52.1, VTD: 53.1, VTD: 58.1, VTD: 59.1, VTD: 63.1, VTD: 67.1, VTD: 68.1, VTD: 69.1, VTD: 71.1; Burke County, Caldwell County, Cherokee County, Clay County, Graham County, Haywood County, Henderson County, Jackson County, Macon County, Madison County, McDowell County, Mitchell County, Swain County, Transylvania County, Yancey County.

District 12: Cabarrus County: VTD: 02-08, VTD: 02-09, VTD: 03-00; Davidson County: VTD: 06, VTD: 10: Block(s) 0570618032024, 0570618032025, 0570618032038, 0570618032039, 0570618032040, 0570618032041, 0570618032042, 0570618032045, 0570618032046, 0570618041011; VTD: 22, VTD: 28, VTD: 30, VTD: 32, VTD: 36, VTD: 38, VTD: 62, VTD: 64, VTD: 70, VTD: 72, VTD: 80; Forsyth County: VTD: 042, VTD: 203, VTD: 204, VTD: 205, VTD: 206, VTD: 301, VTD: 302, VTD: 303, VTD: 304, VTD: 305, VTD: 401, VTD: 402, VTD: 403, VTD: 404, VTD: 405, VTD: 501, VTD: 502, VTD: 504, VTD: 505; Guilford County: VTD: FEN1, VTD: G01, VTD: G02, VTD: G03, VTD: G04, VTD: G05, VTD: G06, VTD: G07, VTD: G08, VTD: G09, VTD: G10, VTD: G26, VTD: G37, VTD: G43, VTD: G46: Block(s) 0810108002079, 0810113002011, 0810113002012, 0810114001001, 0810114001002, 0810114001004, 0810114001006, 0810114001007, 0810114001008, 0810114001009, 0810114001010, 0810114001011, 0810114001012, 0810114001013, 0810114001014, 0810114001016, 0810114001017, 0810114001018, 0810114001019, 0810114001020, 0810114001021, 0810114001022, 0810114002000, 0810114002001, 0810114002002, 0810114002003, 0810114002004, 0810114002005, 0810114002006, 0810114002007, 0810114002008, 0810114002009, 0810114002010, 0810114003001, 0810114003002, 0810114003003, 0810114003004, 0810114003005, 0810114003006, 0810114003007, 0810114003008, 0810114003009, 0810114003010, 0810114003011, 0810114003012, 0810114003013, 0810114003014, 0810114003015, 0810114004000, 0810114004001, 0810114004002, 0810114004003, 0810114004004, 0810114004005, 0810114004006, 0810114004007, 0810114005000, 0810114005001, 0810114005002, 0810114005003, 0810114005004, 0810114005005, 0810114005006, 0810114005007, 0810114005008, 0810114005009, 0810114006000, 0810114006001, 0810114006002, 0810114006003, 0810114006004, 0810114006005, 0810114006006, 0810114006007, 0810115001000, 0810115001001, 0810115001006, 0810115001007, 0810115001008, 0810115002000, 0810115002004; VTD: G47, VTD: G49, VTD: G50, VTD: G51, VTD: G52, VTD: G53, VTD: G54, VTD: G55, VTD: G56, VTD: G57, VTD: G58, VTD: G59, VTD: G60: Block(s) 0810126081002, 0810126081003, 0810126081004, 0810126081005, 0810126081006, 0810126081014, 0810126081016, 0810126081017, 0810126081018, 0810126081019, 0810126081020, 0810126092001, 0810126092002, 0810126092003, 0810126092004, 0810126093001, 0810126093002, 0810126093004, 0810126093005, 0810126093006, 0810126093007, 0810126093008, 0810126093009, 0810126093010, 0810126093011, 0810126093012, 0810126093024, 0810126093025, 0810126093026, 0810126094000, 0810126094012, 0810126094013,

0810126094015, 0810126094030, 0810126094031, 0810165022009,
0810165022010, 0810165024000, 0810165024011; VTD: G61, VTD: G64:
Block(s) 0810160111014, 0810160111019, 0810160111020, 0810160111021,
0810160111022, 0810160111023, 0810160111036, 0810160111037,
0810160111055, 0810160111062, 0810160111064, 0810160111065,
0810160111066, 0810160111067, 0810160111068, 0810160111069,
0810160111070, 0810160111071, 0810160111072, 0810160111073,
0810160111074, 0810160111075, 0810160111076, 0810160111077,
0810160111078, 0810160111079, 0810160112000, 0810160112001,
0810160112002, 0810160112003, 0810160112004, 0810160112005,
0810160112006, 0810160112007, 0810160112008, 0810160112009,
0810160112010, 0810160112011, 0810160112012, 0810160112013,
0810160112014, 0810160112015, 0810160112016, 0810160112017,
0810160112018, 0810160113000, 0810160113001, 0810160113002,
0810160113003, 0810160113004, 0810160113006, 0810160113007,
0810160113008, 0810160114000, 0810162041000, 0810162041001,
0810162041005, 0810162041017, 0810162041018, 0810162041019,
0810162041020, 0810162041021, 0810162041022, 0810162041024,
0810162041039, 0810164051001, 0810164051002, 0810164051003,
0810164051004, 0810164051005, 0810164051006, 0810164051007,
0810164051008, 0810164051011, 0810164051012, 0810164051013,
0810164051014, 0810164051015, 0810164051016, 0810164051017,
0810164051018, 0810164051019, 0810164051020, 0810164051021,
0810164051022, 0810164051023, 0810164051024, 0810164051026,
0810164051030, 0810164051031, 0810164051032, 0810164051038,
0810164051049, 0810164051050, 0810164051052, 0810164051053,
0810164051059, 0810164051060, 0810164051063, 0810164061000,
0810164061001; VTD: G67, VTD: G68, VTD: G69, VTD: G70, VTD: G71, VTD:
G72, VTD: G73, VTD: G74, VTD: G75, VTD: H01, VTD: H03, VTD: H05, VTD:
H07, VTD: H08, VTD: H09, VTD: H10, VTD: H11, VTD: H12, VTD: H17, VTD:
H18, VTD: H19A, VTD: H19B, VTD: HP, VTD: JAM3: Block(s) 0810126094001,
0810126094011, 0810126094016; VTD: JEF3, VTD: MON2, VTD: SUM1;
Mecklenburg County: VTD: 002: Block(s) 1190024001016; VTD: 003, VTD: 004,
VTD: 005, VTD: 006, VTD: 011, VTD: 012, VTD: 013, VTD: 014, VTD: 016,
VTD: 017, VTD: 022, VTD: 023, VTD: 024, VTD: 025, VTD: 026, VTD: 027,
VTD: 028, VTD: 029, VTD: 030, VTD: 031, VTD: 033, VTD: 039, VTD: 040,
VTD: 041, VTD: 042, VTD: 043, VTD: 045, VTD: 046, VTD: 052, VTD: 053,
VTD: 054, VTD: 055, VTD: 056, VTD: 060, VTD: 061, VTD: 062, VTD: 063,
VTD: 077, VTD: 078.1, VTD: 079, VTD: 081, VTD: 082, VTD: 084, VTD: 097,
VTD: 098, VTD: 099, VTD: 104, VTD: 105, VTD: 107.1, VTD: 108, VTD: 116,
VTD: 117, VTD: 120, VTD: 123, VTD: 124, VTD: 125, VTD: 126, VTD: 130,

VTD: 132, VTD: 135, VTD: 138, VTD: 141, VTD: 146, VTD: 147, VTD: 149, VTD: 151, VTD: 203, VTD: 204.1, VTD: 205, VTD: 210, VTD: 211, VTD: 212, VTD: 213, VTD: 222, VTD: 237; Rowan County: VTD: 04, VTD: 08, VTD: 18, VTD: 28, VTD: 30, VTD: 34, VTD: 35, VTD: 36, VTD: 38, VTD: 42, VTD: 44.

District 13: Durham County: VTD: 32; Edgecombe County: VTD: 0103, VTD: 0801, VTD: 0901: Block(s) 0650215003023, 0650216002000, 0650216002001, 0650216002002, 0650216002003, 0650216002004, 0650216002005, 0650216002006, 0650216002007, 0650216002008, 0650216002010, 0650216002011, 0650216002012, 0650216002013, 0650216002014, 0650216002015, 0650216002016, 0650216002017, 0650216002018, 0650216002019, 0650216002020, 0650216002021, 0650216002022, 0650216002023, 0650216002024, 0650216002025, 0650216002026, 0650216002027, 0650216002028, 0650216002029, 0650216002030, 0650216002031, 0650216002032, 0650216002033, 0650216002034, 0650216002035, 0650216002036, 0650216002037, 0650216002038, 0650216002039, 0650216003000, 0650216003001, 0650216003002, 0650216003003, 0650216003004, 0650216003005, 0650216003006, 0650216003007, 0650216003008, 0650216003009, 0650216003010, 0650216003011, 0650216003012, 0650216003013, 0650216003014, 0650216003015, 0650216003016, 0650216003017, 0650216003019, 0650216003020, 0650216003021, 0650216003022, 0650216003023, 0650216003024, 0650216003025, 0650216003026, 0650216003027; VTD: 1001, VTD: 1101: Block(s) 0650213001034, 0650213001035, 0650213002035, 0650213002038, 0650213002039, 0650213002040, 0650213002041, 0650213002042, 0650213002043, 0650213002044, 0650213002045, 0650213002046, 0650213002048, 0650213002049, 0650213002050, 0650213002051, 0650213002052, 0650213002053, 0650213002054, 0650213002055, 0650213002056, 0650213002057, 0650213002058, 0650213002059, 0650213002060, 0650213002061, 0650213002062, 0650213002063, 0650213002064, 0650213002065, 0650213002066, 0650213002067, 0650213002068, 0650213002069, 0650213002070, 0650213002071, 0650213002072, 0650213002073, 0650213002074, 0650213002075, 0650213002076, 0650213002077, 0650213002078, 0650213002079, 0650213002080, 0650213002081, 0650213002082, 0650213002087, 0650213002088; VTD: 1203: 0650202004030, 0650202005026, 0650202006004, 0650202006014, 0650202006015, 0650202006016, 0650202006019, 0650202006020, 0650202006021, 0650202006022, 0650202006033, 0650202006034, 0650202006037, 0650202006042, 0650202006050, 0650202006051, 0650213001020, 0650213001021, 0650213001025, 0650213001030, 0650213001031,

0650213001032, 0650213001033, 0650213001036, 0650213001037, 0650213001038, 0650213001039, 0650213001040, 0650213002047, 0650214001000, 0650214001001, 0650214001012; VTD: 1301, VTD: 1401; Franklin County: VTD: 03: Block(s) 0690604011005, 0690604011006, 0690604011007, 0690604011008, 0690604011009, 0690604011010, 0690604011011, 0690604011012, 0690604011013, 0690604011014, 0690604011015, 0690604011016, 0690604011017, 0690604011018, 0690604011019, 0690604011020, 0690604011021, 0690604011022, 0690604011023, 0690604011024, 0690604011025, 0690604011030, 0690604011031, 0690604011032, 0690604011033, 0690604011034, 0690605011000, 0690605011001, 0690605011002, 0690605011003, 0690605011004, 0690605011005, 0690605011006, 0690605011014, 0690605011015, 0690605011017; VTD: 05, VTD: 06, VTD: 07, VTD: 08, VTD: 09, VTD: 12, VTD: 13, VTD: 14, VTD: 17, VTD: 18, VTD: 19; Granville County: VTD: CRDM, VTD: MTEN, VTD: WILT; Nash County: VTD: 0001, VTD: 0004, VTD: 0005, VTD: 0006, VTD: 0008, VTD: 0012, VTD: 0015, VTD: 0025: Block(s) 1270103005004, 1270103005005, 1270103005006, 1270103005007, 1270103005008, 1270103005009, 1270103005017, 1270103005018, 1270103005019, 1270103006032, 1270103006033, 1270103006034, 1270103006035, 1270103006037, 1270103006038, 1270103006039, 1270103006040, 1270103006041, 1270103006042, 1270103006045, 1270105043020, 1270105043021, 1270105043022, 1270105043023, 1270105043024, 1270105043025, 1270105043026, 1270105043027, 1270105043028, 1270105043029, 1270105043030, 1270105043031, 1270105043032, 1270105043034, 1270105043035, 1270105043036, 1270105043038, 1270105043039, 1270105043040, 1270105043041, 1270105043042, 1270105043043, 1270105043044, 1270108002146, 1270111011000, 1270111011001, 1270111011002, 1270111011003, 1270111011004, 1270111011005, 1270111011006, 1270111011007, 1270111011008, 1270111011009, 1270111011010, 1270111011011, 1270111011012, 1270111011013, 1270111011014, 1270111011015, 1270111011016, 1270111011017, 1270111011018, 1270111011019, 1270111011020, 1270111011021, 1270111011022, 1270111011023, 1270111011024, 1270111011025, 1270111011026, 1270111011027, 1270111011028, 1270111011029, 1270111011030, 1270111011031, 1270111011032, 1270111011033, 1270111011034, 1270111011035, 1270111011036, 1270111011037, 1270111011038, 1270111011039, 1270111011040, 1270111011041, 1270111011042, 1270111011043, 1270111011044, 1270111011045, 1270111011046, 1270111011047, 1270111011048, 1270111011049, 1270111011050, 1270111011051, 1270111011052, 1270111011053, 1270111011054, 1270111011055,

1270111011056, 1270111011057, 1270111012000, 1270111012001, 1270111012002, 1270111012003, 1270111012004, 1270111012005, 1270111012011, 1270111012051, 1270111012052, 1270111012053, 1270111012054, 1270111012055, 1270111012056, 1270111012057, 1270111012058, 1270111012059, 1270111012060, 1270111012061, 1270111012062, 1270111012063, 1270111012064, 1270111012065, 1270111012066, 1270111012067, 1270111012068, 1270111012069, 1270111012070, 1270111012071, 1270111012072, 1270111012073, 1270111012074, 1270111012075, 1270111012076, 1270111012077, 1270111012081, 1270111024000, 1270111025000, 1270111025001, 1270112001000, 1270112001001, 1270112001002, 1270112001003, 1270112001004, 1270112001005, 1270112001006, 1270112001013, 1270112001014, 1270112001015, 1270112001016, 1270112001017, 1270112001018, 1270112001019, 1270112001020, 1270112001021, 1270112001026, 1270112001027, 1270112001028; VTD: 0026, VTD: 0035, VTD: 0036, VTD: 0037: Block(s) 1270105023004, 1270105023005, 1270105023008, 1270105023009, 1270105023010, 1270105023011, 1270105023012, 1270105023017, 1270105024009, 1270105024010, 1270105024011, 1270105024012, 1270105024013, 1270105024014, 1270105024024, 1270105024025, 1270105024026, 1270105024027, 1270105024028, 1270105024029, 1270105024043, 1270105024044, 1270105024045, 1270105024046, 1270105024047, 1270105025006, 1270105025007, 1270105025008, 1270105032000, 1270105032001, 1270105032003, 1270105032004, 1270105032012, 1270105032013, 1270105032014, 1270105032015, 1270105032016, 1270105032017, 1270105032019, 1270105032020, 1270105032021, 1270105032022, 1270105032023, 1270105032024, 1270105032025, 1270105032026, 1270105032027, 1270105032028, 1270105032029, 1270105032030, 1270105032031, 1270105032033, 1270105032034, 1270105032035, 1270105032036, 1270105032037, 1270105032038, 1270105032039, 1270105042000, 1270105042001, 1270105042002, 1270105042003, 1270105042004, 1270105042005, 1270105042006, 1270105042007, 1270105042010, 1270105042011, 1270105042012, 1270105042013, 1270105042014, 1270105042015, 1270105042016, 1270105042017, 1270105042018, 1270105042019, 1270105042020, 1270105042021, 1270105042022, 1270105042023, 1270105043004, 1270105043011; VTD: 0039, VTD: 0041; Vance County: VTD: KITT, VTD: SCRK, VTD: WATK; Wake County: VTD: 01-02: Block(s) 1830515022022, 1830515022023, 1830515022024; VTD: 01-03, VTD: 01-04, VTD: 01-05, VTD: 01-11, VTD: 01-15, VTD: 01-16: Block(s) 1830515011000, 1830515011001, 1830515011004, 1830515011005, 1830515011006, 1830515011007, 1830515011008,

1830515011011, 1830515011012, 1830515011013, 1830515011031, 1830515011032, 1830515011033, 1830515011034, 1830515011035, 1830525043012, 1830525043035, 1830525043036, 1830525052021; VTD: 01-17, VTD: 01-18: Block(s) 1830527011000, 1830527011001, 1830527011002, 1830527011003, 1830527011004, 1830527011005, 1830527011006, 1830527011007, 1830527011008, 1830527011009, 1830527011010, 1830527011011, 1830527011012, 1830527011013, 1830527011014, 1830527011015, 1830527011016, 1830527011017, 1830527011018, 1830527011019, 1830527011020, 1830527011021, 1830527012003, 1830527012004, 1830527012005, 1830527012006, 1830527012007, 1830527012008, 1830527012009, 1830527012010, 1830527012012, 1830527012013, 1830527012014, 1830527012016, 1830527012017, 1830527012020, 1830527012021, 1830527012025, 1830527012026, 1830527012027, 1830527012028, 1830527012029, 1830527012030, 1830527012031, 1830527012032, 1830527012033, 1830527012034, 1830527012035, 1830527012036, 1830527012037, 1830527012038, 1830527012039, 1830527013000, 1830527013001, 1830527013002, 1830527013003, 1830527013004, 1830527013005, 1830527013006, 1830527013007, 1830527013008, 1830527013009; VTD: 01-21: 1830545002058, 1830545002059, 1830545002060; VTD: 01-29, VTD: 01-30, VTD: 01-33: Block(s) 1830515022008, 1830515022009, 1830515022015, 1830515022016, 1830515022017, 1830515022018, 1830515022019, 1830515022020, 1830515022021; VTD: 01-36: 1830526012016, 1830526031000, 1830526031001, 1830526031009, 1830526031010, 1830526031011, 1830526031012, 1830526031013, 1830526031014, 1830526031015, 1830526032000, 1830526032001, 1830526032002, 1830526032003, 1830526032004, 1830526032005, 1830526032006, 1830526032007, 1830526032008, 1830526032009, 1830526032010, 1830526032011, 1830526032012, 1830526032013, 1830526032016, 1830526032017, 1830526032018, 1830527013012; VTD: 01-37, VTD: 01-39: Block(s) 1830537162009; VTD: 01-42, VTD: 01-45, VTD: 01-47, VTD: 02-01, VTD: 02-02, VTD: 02-03, VTD: 02-04, VTD: 02-05, VTD: 02-06, VTD: 04-06, VTD: 04-07, VTD: 04-10, VTD: 04-12, VTD: 06-04, VTD: 06-05, VTD: 06-06, VTD: 06-07, VTD: 07-01, VTD: 07-02, VTD: 07-03, VTD: 07-05, VTD: 07-06, VTD: 07-07, VTD: 07-09, VTD: 07-11, VTD: 07-12, VTD: 07-13, VTD: 08-02, VTD: 08-03, VTD: 08-04, VTD: 08-05, VTD: 08-07, VTD: 08-08, VTD: 08-10, VTD: 08-11, VTD: 09-01, VTD: 09-02, VTD: 09-03, VTD: 10-01, VTD: 10-02, VTD: 10-03, VTD: 10-04, VTD: 11-02, VTD: 12-01, VTD: 12-02, VTD: 12-04, VTD: 12-05, VTD: 12-06, VTD: 12-07, VTD: 12-08, VTD: 12-09, VTD: 13-02, VTD: 13-06, VTD: 13-10, VTD: 13-11, VTD: 14-01, VTD: 14-02, VTD: 15-01, VTD: 15-02, VTD: 15-03, VTD: 15-04, VTD: 16-01, VTD: 16-02: Block(s)

1830545002067, 1830545002068, 1830545002070, 1830545002075, 1830545002076, 1830545002077; VTD: 16-04, VTD: 16-05, VTD: 16-07, VTD: 16-09, VTD: 17-02, VTD: 17-04, VTD: 17-06, VTD: 17-08, VTD: 18-02, VTD: 18-03, VTD: 18-04, VTD: 18-05, VTD: 18-07, VTD: 18-08, VTD: 19-03, VTD: 19-04, VTD: 19-05, VTD: 19-06, VTD: 19-07, VTD: 19-09, VTD: 19-10, VTD: 19-11, VTD: 19-12, VTD: 19-16, VTD: 19-17, VTD: 20-03, VTD: 20-04, VTD: 20-05, VTD: 20-08, VTD: 20-09; Wayne County: VTD: 01, VTD: 02, VTD: 03, VTD: 04, VTD: 05, VTD: 06, VTD: 08, VTD: 09, VTD: 14, VTD: 15, VTD: 16, VTD: 23, VTD: 24, VTD: 25: Block(s) 1910008001000, 1910008001001, 1910008001002, 1910008001003, 1910008001004, 1910008001005, 1910008001006, 1910008001007, 1910008001008, 1910008001009, 1910008001010, 1910008001011, 1910008001012, 1910008001013, 1910008001014, 1910008001015, 1910008001022, 1910008001023, 1910008001024, 1910008001032, 1910008001033, 1910008001034, 1910008001047, 1910008001048, 1910008001055, 1910008001072, 1910008001073, 1910008002000, 1910008002001, 1910008002002, 1910008002003, 1910008002004, 1910008002005, 1910008002006, 1910008002007, 1910008002008, 1910008002011, 1910008002012, 1910008002013, 1910008002014, 1910008002015, 1910008002016, 1910008002017, 1910008002018, 1910008002019, 1910008002020, 1910008002021, 1910008002022, 1910008002023, 1910008002024, 1910008002025, 1910008002026, 1910008002027, 1910008002028, 1910008002029, 1910008002030, 1910008002031, 1910008002032, 1910008002033, 1910008002034, 1910008002035, 1910008002036, 1910008002037, 1910008002038, 1910008002039, 1910008002040, 1910008002041, 1910008002042, 1910008002043, 1910008002044, 1910008002045, 1910008002046, 1910008002047, 1910008002048, 1910008002049, 1910008002050, 1910008002051, 1910008002052, 1910008002053, 1910008002054, 1910008002055, 1910008002056, 1910008002057, 1910008002058, 1910008002059, 1910008002060, 1910008002061, 1910008002062, 1910008002063, 1910008002064, 1910008002065, 1910008002066, 1910008002067, 1910008002068, 1910008002069, 1910008002070, 1910008002071, 1910008002072, 1910008002073, 1910008002074, 1910008002075, 1910008002076, 1910008002077, 1910008002078, 1910008002079, 1910008002080, 1910008002081, 1910009021010, 1910009021011, 1910009021012, 1910009021013, 1910009021015, 1910009021016, 1910009021017, 1910009021018, 1910009021019, 1910009021020, 1910009021021, 1910009021022, 1910009021023, 1910009021024, 1910009021025, 1910009021026, 1910009021036, 1910009021037, 1910009021038, 1910009021039, 1910009021040, 1910009021041, 1910009021044, 1910009021051,

1910009021052, 1910009021053, 1910009021054, 1910009021055, 1910009021066, 1910009021067, 1910009021068, 1910009021069, 1910009021070, 1910009021071, 1910009021072, 1910009021073, 1910009021074, 1910009021075, 1910009021076, 1910009021077, 1910009021078, 1910009021079, 1910009021080, 1910009021081, 1910009021082, 1910009021085, 1910009021086, 1910009021087, 1910009021088, 1910009021089, 1910009021090, 1910009021091, 1910009023048; VTD: 28, VTD: 30: Block(s) 1910007001022, 1910007001023, 1910007001037, 1910007001038, 1910007001039, 1910007001040, 1910007001041, 1910007002047, 1910007003016, 1910007003036, 1910007003037, 1910007003038, 1910007003053, 1910008001058, 1910008001061, 1910008001068, 1910008001069; Wilson County: VTD: PRBL, VTD: PRCR, VTD: PRGA: Block(s) 1950012001000, 1950012001001, 1950012001002, 1950012001003, 1950012001012, 1950012001013, 1950012001014, 1950012001015, 1950012001016, 1950012001017, 1950012001018, 1950012001019, 1950012001020, 1950012001021, 1950012001022, 1950012001023, 1950012001025, 1950012001026, 1950012001033, 1950012001034, 1950012001035, 1950012001036, 1950012001038, 1950012003000, 1950012003001, 1950012003002, 1950012003020; VTD: PROL, VTD: PRSA: Block(s) 1950011001000, 1950011001001; VTD: PRSP, VTD: PRST, VTD: PRTA, VTD: PRTO, VTD: PRWA: Block(s) 1950001001006; VTD: PRWD: 1950005011002, 1950005011003, 1950005011004, 1950005011005, 1950005011006, 1950005011007, 1950005011008, 1950005011009, 1950005011010, 1950005011011, 1950005011012, 1950005011013, 1950005011014, 1950005011015, 1950005011016, 1950005011017, 1950005011018, 1950005011019, 1950005011020, 1950005011021, 1950005011022, 1950005011023, 1950005011024, 1950005011025, 1950005011026, 1950005011027, 1950005011028, 1950005011029, 1950005011030, 1950005011031, 1950005011032, 1950005011033, 1950005011034, 1950005011035, 1950005011036, 1950005011037, 1950005011038, 1950005011039, 1950005011040, 1950005011041, 1950005011042, 1950005011043, 1950005011044, 1950005011045, 1950005011046, 1950005011047, 1950005011048, 1950005011049, 1950005011050, 1950005011051, 1950005011052, 1950005011053, 1950005011054, 1950005011055, 1950005011056, 1950005011057, 1950005011058, 1950005011059, 1950005011060, 1950005011062, 1950006001019, 1950006001020, 1950006001021, 1950006001022, 1950006001023, 1950006001024, 1950006001025, 1950006001026; VTD: PRWJ: 1950004001000, 1950004001003, 1950004001009, 1950004001010, 1950004001011, 1950004002014, 1950004002015, 1950004002016,

1950004002017, 1950004002018, 1950004002019, 1950004002020, 1950004002021, 1950004002022, 1950004002023, 1950004002024, 1950004002025, 1950004002026, 1950004002027, 1950004002028, 1950004002029, 1950004002030, 1950004002031, 1950004002032, 1950004002033, 1950004002034, 1950004004000, 1950004004001, 1950004004002, 1950004004003, 1950004004004, 1950004004005, 1950004004006, 1950004004007, 1950004004008, 1950004004009, 1950004004010, 1950004004011, 1950004004012, 1950004004013, 1950004004014, 1950004004015, 1950004004016, 1950004004017, 1950004004018, 1950004004019, 1950004004020, 1950004004021, 1950004004022, 1950004004023, 1950004004024, 1950004004025, 1950004004026, 1950004004027, 1950004004028, 1950004004029, 1950004004030, 1950004004031, 1950004004032, 1950004004033, 1950004004034, 1950004004035, 1950004004036, 1950004004037, 1950004004038, 1950004004039, 1950004004040, 1950004004041, 1950004004042, 1950004004043, 1950004004044, 1950004004045, 1950004004046, 1950004004047, 1950004004048, 1950004004049, 1950004004050, 1950004004051, 1950004004052, 1950004004054, 1950004004055, 1950004004056, 1950004004057, 1950004004058, 1950004004059, 1950004004074, 1950004004076, 1950004004093, 1950004004099, 1950004004100, 1950004004102, 1950004004103; VTD: PRWK, VTD: PRWL, VTD: PRWM: Block(s) 1950006001001, 1950006001003, 1950006001004, 1950006001008, 1950006001009, 1950006001010, 1950006001011, 1950006001012, 1950006001013, 1950006001015, 1950006001016, 1950006001017, 1950006001018, 1950006002003, 1950006005000, 1950006005001, 1950006005002, 1950006005003, 1950006005004, 1950006005005, 1950006005006, 1950006005007, 1950006005008, 1950006005009, 1950006005010, 1950006005011, 1950006005012, 1950006005013, 1950006005014, 1950006005015, 1950006005016, 1950006005017, 1950006005018, 1950006005024, 1950006005025, 1950006005027, 1950006005028, 1950006005029, 1950006005030, 1950006005031, 1950006005032, 1950006005033, 1950006005034, 1950006005035, 1950006005036, 1950006005037, 1950006005038, 1950006005039, 1950006005040, 1950006005041, 1950006005042, 1950006005043, 1950006005044, 1950006005045, 1950006005046, 1950006005047, 1950006005048, 1950006005049, 1950006005050, 1950006005051, 1950006005052, 1950006005053, 1950006005054, 1950006005055, 1950006005056, 1950006005057, 1950006005058, 1950006005059, 1950006005060, 1950006005061, 1950006005062, 1950006005063, 1950006005064, 1950006005065, 1950006005066, 1950006005067, 1950006005068, 1950006005069,

1950006005070, 1950006005071, 1950006005072, 1950006005073, 1950006005074, 1950006005076; VTD: PRWP.

(b) The names and boundaries of voting tabulation districts, tracts, block groups, and blocks specified in this section are as shown on the 2010 Census Redistricting TIGER/Line Shapefiles.

(c) If any voting tabulation district boundary is changed, that change shall not change the boundary of a congressional district, which shall remain the same as it is depicted by the 2010 Census Redistricting TIGER/Line Shapefiles.

(d) Repealed by Session Laws 2011-414, s. 2, effective November 7, 2011.

(e) The Legislative Services Officer shall certify a true copy of the block assignment file associated with any mapping software used to generate the language in subsection (a) of this section. The certified true copy of the block assignment file shall be delivered by the Legislative Services Officer to the Principal Clerk of the Senate and the Principal Clerk of the House of Representatives. If any area within North Carolina is not assigned to a specific district by subsection (a) of this section, the certified true copy of the block assignment file delivered to the Principal Clerk of the Senate and the Principal Clerk of the House of Representatives shall control. (Rev., s. 4366; 1911, c. 97; C.S., s. 6004; 1931, c. 216; 1941, c. 3; 1961, c. 864; 1966, Ex. Sess., c. 7, s. 1; 1967, c. 775, s. 1; c. 1109; 1971, c. 257; 1981, c. 894; 1982, Ex. Sess., c. 7; 1991, c. 601, s. 1; c. 761, s. 33(a), (b); 1991, Ex. Sess., c. 7, s. 1; 1993, c. 553, s. 66; 1997-11, ss. 1, 2; 1997-456, ss. 27, 52; 1998-2, ss. 1, 1.1; 2001-471, s. 1; 2001-479, ss. 1, 2; 2011-403, s. 1; 2011-414, s. 2.)

§ 163-201.1. Severability of congressional apportionment acts.

If any provision of any act of the General Assembly that apportions congressional districts is held invalid by any court of competent jurisdiction, the invalidity shall not affect other provisions that can be given effect without the invalid provision; and to this end the provisions of any said act are severable. (1981, c. 771, s. 2.)

§ 163-201.2: Repealed by G.S. 120-30.9J, as enacted by Session Laws 2013-343, s. 1, effective July 23, 2013.

§ 163-202. Election after reapportionment of members of House of Representatives.

Whenever, by a new apportionment of members of the United States House of Representatives, the number of Representatives from North Carolina shall be changed, and neither the Congress nor the General Assembly shall provide for electing them, the following procedures shall apply:

(1) If the number of Representatives is increased, the Representative from each of the existing congressional districts shall be elected by the qualified voters of his district, and the additional Representatives apportioned to North Carolina shall be elected on a single ballot by the qualified voters of the whole State.

(2) If the number of Representatives is decreased, existing congressional district lines shall be ignored, and all Representatives apportioned to North Carolina shall be elected on a single ballot by the qualified voters of the whole State. (1901, c. 89, s. 58; Rev., s. 4368; C.S., s. 6006; 1967, c. 775, s. 1.)

§§ 163-203 through 163-207. Reserved for future codification purposes.

Article 18.

Presidential Electors.

§ 163-208. Conduct of presidential election.

Unless otherwise provided, the election of presidential electors shall be conducted and the returns made in the manner prescribed by this Chapter for the election of State officers. (1901, c. 89, s. 79; Rev., s. 4371; C.S., s. 6009; 1933, c. 165, s. 11; 1967, c. 775, s. 1.)

§ 163-209. Names of presidential electors not printed on ballots; notification.

(a) The names of candidates for electors of President and Vice-President nominated by any political party recognized in this State under G.S. 163-96, or nominated under G.S. 163-1(c) by a candidate for President of the United States who has qualified to have his or her name printed on the general election ballot as an unaffiliated candidate under G.S. 163-122, shall be filed with the Secretary of State but shall not be printed on the ballot. In the case of the unaffiliated candidate, the names of candidates for electors must be filed with the Secretary of State no later than 12:00 noon on the first Friday in August. In place of their names, there shall be printed on the ballot the names of the candidates for President and Vice-President of each political party recognized in this State, and the name of any candidate for President who has qualified to have his or her name printed on the general election ballot under G.S. 163-122. A candidate for President who has qualified for the general election ballot as an unaffiliated candidate under G.S. 163-122 shall, no later than 12:00 noon on the first Friday in August, file with the State Board of Elections the name of a candidate for Vice-President, whose name shall also be printed on the ballot. A vote for the candidates named on the ballot shall be a vote for the electors of the party or unaffiliated candidate by which those candidates were nominated and whose names have been filed with the Secretary of State.

(b) Upon receiving the filing of a name as a candidate for elector under this section, the Secretary of State shall notify that candidate of the dual-office holding requirements of the North Carolina Constitution and the General Statutes, including specifically that if a person elected as elector holds another elective office at the time of taking the oath of office as elector, that other office is vacated upon taking the oath of office. (1901, c. 89, s. 78; Rev., s. 4372; C.S., s. 6010; 1933, c. 165, s. 11; 1949, c. 672, s. 2; 1967, c. 775, s. 1; 1991 (Reg. Sess., 1992), c. 782, s. 2; 2001-460, s. 5; 2009-96, s. 2.)

§ 163-209.1. Notification of political parties of dual-office holding rules.

During January of each year in which electors are elected, the Secretary of State shall notify each political party authorized to nominate electors of (i) the requirement under G.S. 163-1(c) to nominate first and second alternate electors, and (ii) the dual-office holding requirements of the North Carolina Constitution and the General Statutes, including specifically that if a person elected as elector holds another elective office at the time of taking the oath of office as elector, that other office is vacated upon taking the oath of office. (2009-96, s. 3.)

§ 163-209.2. Elector may be held in addition to other appointive offices.

The office of elector may be held in addition to the maximum number of appointive offices allowed by G.S. 128-1.1. (2009-96, s. 1.)

§ 163-210. Governor to proclaim results; casting State's vote for President and Vice-President.

Upon receipt of the certifications prepared by the State Board of Elections and delivered in accordance with G.S. 163-182.15, the Secretary of State, under seal of the office, shall notify the Governor of the names of the persons elected to the office of elector for President and Vice-President of the United States as stated in the abstracts of the State Board of Elections. Thereupon, the Governor shall immediately issue a proclamation setting forth the names of the electors and instructing them to be present in the old Hall of the House of Representatives in the State Capitol in the City of Raleigh at noon on the first Monday after the second Wednesday in December next after their election, at which time the electors shall meet and vote on behalf of the State for President and Vice-President of the United States. The Governor shall cause this proclamation to be published in the daily newspapers published in the City of Raleigh. Notice may additionally be made on a radio or television station or both, but such notice shall be in addition to the newspaper and other required notice. The Secretary of State is responsible for making the actual arrangements for the meeting, preparing the agenda, and inviting guests.

Before the date fixed for the meeting of the electors, the Governor shall send by registered mail to the Archivist of the United States, either three duplicate original certificates, or one original certificate and two authenticated copies of the Certificates of Ascertainment, under the great seal of the State setting forth the names of the persons chosen as presidential electors for this State and the number of votes cast for each. These Certificates of Ascertainment should be sent as soon as possible after the election, but must be received before the Electoral College meeting. At the same time the Governor shall deliver to the electors six duplicate originals of the same certificate, each bearing the great seal of the State. At any time prior to receipt of the certificate of the Governor or within 48 hours thereafter, any person elected to the office of elector may resign by submitting his resignation, written and duly verified, to the Governor. Failure to so resign shall signify consent to serve and to cast his vote for the candidate of the political party which nominated such elector.

In case of the absence, ineligibility or resignation of any elector chosen, or if the proper number of electors shall for any cause be deficient, the first and second alternates, respectively, who were nominated under G.S. 163-1(c), shall fill the first two vacancies. If the alternates are absent, ineligible, resign, or were not chosen, or if there are more than two vacancies, then the electors present at the required meeting shall forthwith elect from the citizens of the State a sufficient number of persons to fill the deficiency, and the persons chosen shall be deemed qualified electors to vote for President and Vice-President of the United States. (1901, c. 89, s. 81; Rev., s. 4374; 1917, c. 176, s. 2; C.S., ss. 5916, 6012; 1923, c. 111, s. 12; 1927, c. 260, s. 17; 1933, c. 165, s. 11; 1935, c. 143, s. 2; 1967, c. 775, s. 1; 1969, c. 949, ss. 1, 2; 1981, c. 35, s. 1; 1989, c. 93, s. 5; 1993 (Reg. Sess., 1994), c. 738, s. 1; 2001-398, s. 8.)

§ 163-211. Compensation of presidential electors.

Presidential electors shall be paid, for attending the meeting held in the City of Raleigh on the first Monday after the second Wednesday in December next after their election, the sum of forty-four dollars ($44.00) per day and traveling expenses at the rate of seventeen cents (17¢) per mile in going to and returning home from the required meeting. (1901, c. 89, s. 84; Rev., s. 2761; C.S., s. 3878; 1933, c. 5; 1967, c. 775, s. 1; 1979, c. 1008.)

§ 163-212. Penalty for failure of presidential elector to attend and vote.

Any presidential elector having previously signified his consent to serve as such, who fails to attend and vote for the candidate of the political party which nominated such elector, for President and Vice-President of the United States at the time and place directed in G.S. 163-210 (except in case of sickness or other unavoidable accident) shall forfeit and pay to the State five hundred dollars ($500.00), to be recovered by the Attorney General in the Superior Court of Wake County. In addition to such forfeiture, refusal or failure to vote for the candidates of the political party which nominated such elector shall constitute a resignation from the office of elector, his vote shall not be recorded, and the remaining electors shall forthwith fill such vacancy as hereinbefore provided.

The clear proceeds of forfeitures provided for in this section shall be remitted to the Civil Penalty and Forfeiture Fund in accordance with G.S. 115C-457.2. (1901, c. 89, s. 83; Rev., s. 4375; C.S., s. 6013; 1933, c. 165, s. 11; 1967, c. 775, s. 1; 1969, c. 949, s. 3; 1998-215, s. 131.)

§ 163-213. Appointment of Presidential Electors by General Assembly in certain circumstances, by the Governor in certain other circumstances.

(a) Appointment by General Assembly if No Proclamation by Six Days Before Electors' Meeting Day. - As permitted by 3 U.S.C. § 2, whenever the appointment of any Presidential Elector has not been proclaimed under G.S. 163-210 before noon on the date for settling controversies specified by 3 U.S.C. § 5, and upon the call of an extra session pursuant to the North Carolina Constitution for the purposes of this section, the General Assembly may fill the position of any Presidential Electors whose election is not yet proclaimed.

(b) Appointment by Governor if No Appointment by the Day Before Electors' Meeting Day. - If the appointment of any Presidential Elector has not been proclaimed under G.S. 163-210 before noon on the date for settling controversies specified by 3 U.S.C. § 5, nor appointed by the General Assembly by noon on the day before the day set for the meeting of Presidential Electors by 3 U.S.C. § 7, then the Governor shall appoint that Elector.

(c) Standard for Decision by General Assembly and Governor. - In exercising their authority under subsections (a) and (b) of this section, the General Assembly and the Governor shall designate Electors in accord with their best judgment of the will of the electorate. The decisions of the General Assembly or Governor under subsections (a) and (b) of this section are not subject to judicial review, except to ensure that applicable statutory and constitutional procedures were followed. The judgment itself of what was the will of the electorate is not subject to judicial review.

(d) Proclamation Before Electors' Meeting Day Controls. - If the proclamation of any Presidential Elector under G.S. 163-210 is made any time before noon on the day set for the meeting of Presidential Electors by 3 U.S.C. § 7, then that proclamation shall control over an appointment made by the General Assembly or the Governor. This section does not preclude litigation otherwise provided by law to challenge the validity of the proclamation or the procedures that resulted in that proclamation. (2001-289, s. 2.)

Article 18A.

Presidential Preference Primary Act.

§ 163-213.1. Short title.

This Article may be cited as the "Presidential Preference Primary Act." (1971, c. 225; 1975, c. 744.)

§ 163-213.2. Primary to be held; date; qualifications and registration of voters.

On the Tuesday after the first Monday in May, 1992, and every four years thereafter, the voters of this State shall be given an opportunity to express their preference for the person to be the presidential candidate of their political party, except that if South Carolina holds its presidential primary before the 15th day of March, the North Carolina presidential preference primary shall be held on the Tuesday after the first South Carolina presidential preference primary of that year.

Any person otherwise qualified who will become qualified by age to vote in the general election held in the same year of the presidential preference primary shall be entitled to register and vote in the presidential preference primary. Such persons may register not earlier than 60 days nor later than the last day for making application to register under G.S. 163-82.6 prior to the said primary. In addition, persons who will become qualified by age to register and vote in the general election for which the primary is held, who do not register during the special period may register to vote after such period as if they were qualified on the basis of age, but until they are qualified by age to vote, they may vote only in primary elections. (1971, c. 225; 1975, c. 744; c. 844, s. 18; 1977, c. 19; c. 661, s. 7; 1983, c. 331, s. 5; 1985 (Reg. Sess., 1986), c. 927, s. 1; 1987, c. 457, s. 3; 1991, c. 689, s. 15(a); 1991 (Reg. Sess., 1992), c. 1032, s. 6; 1999-424, s. 7(j); 2013-381, s. 35.1.)

§ 163-213.3. Conduct of election.

The presidential preference primary election shall be conducted and canvassed by the same authority and in the manner provided by law for the conduct and canvassing of the primary election for the office of Governor and all other offices enumerated in G.S. 163-182.4(b) and under the same provisions stipulated in G.S. 163-182.5(c). The State Board of Elections shall have authority to promulgate reasonable rules and regulations, not inconsistent with provisions contained herein, pursuant to the administration of this Article. (1971, c. 225; 1975, c. 744; 1987, c. 81, s. 2; 1991, c. 689, s. 15(b); 2001-398, s. 9.)

§ 163-213.4. Nomination by State Board of Elections.

No later than 90 days preceding the North Carolina presidential preference primary, the chair of each political party shall submit to the State Board of Elections a list of its presidential candidates to be placed on the presidential preference primary ballot. The list must be comprised of candidates whose candidacy is generally advocated and recognized in the news media throughout the United States or in North Carolina, unless any such candidate executes and files with the chair of the political party an affidavit stating without qualification that the candidate is not and does not intend to become a candidate for nomination in the North Carolina Presidential Preference Primary Election. The State Board of Elections shall prepare and publish a list of the names of the presidential candidates submitted. The State Board of Elections shall convene in Raleigh on the first Tuesday in March preceding the presidential preference primary election. At the meeting required by this section, the State Board of Elections shall nominate as presidential primary candidates all candidates affiliated with a political party, recognized pursuant to the provisions of Article 9 of Chapter 163 of the General Statutes, who have been submitted to the State Board of Elections. Additionally, the State Board of Elections, by vote of at least three of its members in the affirmative, may nominate as a presidential primary candidate any other person affiliated with a political party that it finds is generally advocated and recognized in the news media throughout the United States or in North Carolina as candidates for the nomination by that party. Immediately upon completion of these requirements, the Board shall release to the news media all such nominees selected. Provided, however, nothing shall prohibit the partial selection of nominees prior to the meeting required by this section, if all provisions herein have been complied with. (1971, c. 225; 1975, c. 744; 1983, c. 729; 1987, c. 81, s. 1; c. 549, s. 6.1; 1991, c. 689, s. 15(c); 2003-278, s. 9(a); 2007-391, s. 33; 2008-187, s. 33(a); 2013-381, ss. 35.2, 36.1.)

§ 163-213.5. Nomination by petition.

Any person seeking the endorsement by the national political party for the office of President of the United States, or any group organized in this State on behalf of, and with the consent of, such person, may file with the State Board of Elections petitions signed by 10,000 persons who, at the time they signed are registered and qualified voters in this State and are affiliated, by such registration, with the same political party as the candidate for whom the petitions are filed. Such petitions shall be presented to the county board of elections 10 days before the filing deadline and shall be certified promptly by the chairman of the board of elections of the county in which the signatures were obtained and shall be filed by the petitioners with the State Board of Elections no later than 5:00 P.M. on the Monday prior to the date the State Board of Elections is required to meet as directed by G.S. 163-213.4.

The petitions must state the name of the candidate for nomination, along with a letter of approval signed by such candidate. Said petitions must also state the name and address of the chairman of any such group organized to circulate petitions authorized under this section. The requirement for signers of such petitions shall be the same as now required under provisions of G.S. 163-96(b)(1) and (2). The requirement of the respective chairmen of county boards of elections shall be the same as now required under the provisions of G.S. 163-96 as they relate to the chairman of the county board of elections.

The State Board of Elections shall forthwith determine the sufficiency of petitions filed with it and shall immediately communicate its determination to the chairman of such group organized to circulate petitions. The form and style of petition shall be as prescribed by the State Board of Elections. (1971, c. 225; 1975, c. 744; 2002-159, s. 55(e); 2003-278, s. 9(b); 2004-127, s. 6.)

§ 163-213.6. Notification to candidates.

The State Board of Elections shall forthwith contact each person who has been nominated by the Board or by petition and notify him in writing that his name will be printed as a candidate of a specified political party on the North Carolina presidential preference primary ballot. A candidate who participates in the North Carolina presidential preference primary of a particular party shall have his name placed on the general election ballot only as a nominee of that political party. The board shall send a copy of the "Presidential Preference Primary Act" to each candidate with the notice specified above. (1971, c. 225; 1975, c. 744; 1987, c. 549, s. 6.2.)

§ 163-213.7. Voting in presidential preference primary; ballots.

The names of all candidates in the presidential preference primary shall appear at an appropriate place on the ballot or voting machine. In addition the State Board of Elections shall provide a category on the ballot or voting machine allowing voters in each political party to vote an "uncommitted" or "no preference" status. The voter shall be able to cast his ballot for one of the presidential candidates of a political party or for an "uncommitted" or "no preference" status, but shall not be permitted to vote for candidates or "uncommitted" status of a political party different from his registration. Persons registered as "Unaffiliated" shall not participate in the presidential primary except as provided in G.S. 163-119. (1971, c. 225; 1975, c. 744; 1993 (Reg. Sess., 1994), c. 762, s. 52; 2004-127, s. 11.)

§ 163-213.8. Allocation of delegate positions to reflect division of votes in the primary.

(a) Upon completion and certification of the primary results by the State Board of Elections, the Secretary of State shall certify the results to the State chairman of each political party.

Each political party shall allocate delegate positions in a manner which reflects the division of votes of the party primary consistent with the national party rules of that political party.

(b) In case of conflict between subsection (a) of this section and the national rules of a political party, the State executive committee of that party has the authority to resolve the conflict by adopting for that party the national rules, which shall then supercede any provision in subsection (a) of this section with which it conflicts, provided that the executive committee shall take only such action under this subsection necessary to resolve the conflict. (1971, c. 225; 1975, c. 744; 1979, c. 800; 1983, c. 216, ss. 1, 2.)

§ 163-213.9. National committee to be notified of provisions under this Article.

It shall be the responsibility of the State chairman of each political party, qualified under the laws of this State, to notify his party's national committee no later than January 30 of each year in which such presidential preference primary shall be conducted of the provisions contained under this Article. (1971, c. 225; 1975, c. 744.)

§ 163-213.10. Transferred to § 163-213.9 by Session Laws 1975, c. 744.

§ 163-213.11: Repealed by Session Laws 1991, c. 689, s. 15.

§§ 163-214 through 163-217. Reserved for future codification purposes.

Article 19.

Petitions for Elections and Referenda.

§ 163-218. Registration of notice of circulation of petition.

From and after July 1, 1957, notice of circulation of a petition calling for any election or referendum shall be registered with the county board of elections with which the petition is to be filed, and the date of registration of the notice shall be the date of issuance and commencement of circulation of the petition. (1957, c. 1239, s. 1; 1967, c. 775, s. 1.)

§ 163-219. Petition void after one year from registration.

Petitions calling for elections and referenda shall be and become void and of no further effect one year after the date the notice of circulation is registered with the county board of elections with which it is required to be filed; and notwithstanding any public, special, local, or private act to the contrary, no election or referendum shall thereafter be called or held pursuant to or based upon any such void petition. (1957, c. 1239, s. 2; 1967, c. 775, s. 1.)

§ 163-220. Limitation on petitions circulated prior to July 1, 1957.

Petitions calling for elections or referenda which were circulated prior to July 1, 1957, shall be and become void and of no further force and effect one year after the date of issuance of such petitions for circulation; and notwithstanding any public, special, local, or private act to the contrary, no election or referendum shall be called or held pursuant to or based upon any such void petition from and after July 1, 1957. (1957, c. 1239, s. 3; 1967, c. 775, s. 1.)

§ 163-221. Persons may not sign name of another to petition.

(a) No person may sign the name of another person to any of the following:

(1) Any petition calling for an election or referendum.

(2) Any petition under G.S. 163-96 for the formulation of a new political party.

(3) Any petition under G.S. 163-107.1 requesting a person to be a candidate.

(4) Any petition under G.S. 163-122 to have the name of an unaffiliated candidate placed on the general election ballot, or under G.S. 163-296 to have the name of an unaffiliated or nonpartisan candidate placed on the regular municipal election ballot.

(5) Any petition under G.S. 163-213.5 to place a name on the ballot under the Presidential Preference Primary Act.

(6) Any petition under G.S. 163-123 to qualify as a write-in candidate.

(b) Any name signed on a petition, in violation of this section, shall be void.

(c) Any person who willfully violates this section is guilty of a Class 2 misdemeanor. (1977, c. 218, s. 1; 1979, c. 534, s. 1; 1987, c. 565, s. 6; 1993, c. 539, s. 1104; 1994, Ex. Sess., c. 24, s. 14(c); 2003-278, s. 7.)

§ 163-222. Reserved for future codification purposes.

§ 163-223. Reserved for future codification purposes.

§ 163-224. Reserved for future codification purposes.

§ 163-225. Reserved for future codification purposes.

SUBCHAPTER VII. ABSENTEE VOTING.

Article 20.

Absentee Ballot.

§ 163-226. Who may vote an absentee ballot.

(a)	Who May Vote Absentee Ballot; Generally. - Any qualified voter of the State may vote by absentee ballot in a statewide primary, general, or special election on constitutional amendments, referenda or bond proposals, and any qualified voter of a county is authorized to vote by absentee ballot in any primary or election conducted by the county board of elections, in the manner provided in this Article.

(a1)	Repealed by Session Laws 2001-337, s. 1, effective January 1, 2002.

(a2)	Annual Request by Person With Sickness or Physical Disability. - If the applicant so requests and reports in the application that the voter has a sickness or physical disability that is expected to last the remainder of the calendar year, the application shall constitute a request for an absentee ballot for all of the primaries and elections held during the calendar year when the application is received.

(b)	Absentee Ballots; Exceptions. - Notwithstanding the authority contained in G.S. 163-226(a), absentee ballots shall not be permitted in fire district elections.

(c)	The Term "Election". - As used in this Subchapter, unless the context clearly requires otherwise, the term "election" includes a general, primary, second primary, runoff election, bond election, referendum, or special election.

(d)	The Term "Verifiable Legal Guardian." - An individual appointed guardian under Chapter 35A of the General Statutes. For a corporation appointed as a guardian under that Chapter, the corporation may submit a list of 10 named individuals to the State Board of Elections who may act for that corporation under this Article. (1939, c. 159, s. 1; 1963, c. 457, s. 1; 1967, c. 775, s. 1; c. 952, s. 1; 1973, c. 536, s. 1; c. 1018; 1977, c. 469, s. 1; 1979, c. 140, s. 1; 1995 (Reg. Sess., 1996), c. 561, s. 1; c. 734, s. 5; 1999-455, s. 1; 2001-337, s. 1; 2001-507, s. 1; 2013-381, s. 4.5.)

§ 163-226.1. Absentee voting in primary.

A qualified voter may vote by absentee ballot in a partisan primary provided the qualified voter is affiliated, at the time the qualified voter makes application for absentee ballots, with the political party in whose primary the qualified voter wishes to vote, except that an unaffiliated voter may vote in a party primary if permitted under G.S. 163-119. The official registration records of the county in which the voter is registered shall be proof of whether the qualified voter is affiliated with a political party and of the party, if any, with which the qualified voter is affiliated. (1977, c. 469, s. 1; 1999-455, s. 2.)

§ 163-226.2. Absentee voting in municipal elections.

Absentee voting by qualified voters residing in a municipality shall be in accordance with the authorization specified in G.S. 163-302. (1977, c. 469, s. 1.)

§ 163-226.3. Certain acts declared felonies.

(a)   Any person who shall, in connection with absentee voting in any election held in this State, do any of the acts or things declared in this section to be unlawful, shall be guilty of a Class I felony. It shall be unlawful:

(1)   For any person except the voter's near relative or the voter's verifiable legal guardian to assist the voter to vote an absentee ballot when the voter is voting an absentee ballot other than under the procedure described in G.S. 163-227.2; provided that if there is not a near relative or legal guardian available to assist the voter, the voter may request some other person to give assistance;

(2)   For any person to assist a voter to vote an absentee ballot under the absentee voting procedure authorized by G.S. 163-227.2 except as provided in that section;

(3)   For a voter who votes an absentee ballot under the procedures authorized by G.S. 163-227.2 to vote that voter's absentee ballot outside of the voting booth or private room provided to the voter for that purpose in or adjacent to the office of the county board of elections or at the additional site provided by G.S. 163-227.2(f1), or to receive assistance except as provided in G.S. 163-227.2;

(4)   For any owner, manager, director, employee, or other person, other than the voter's near relative or verifiable legal guardian, to (i) make a written request pursuant to G.S. 163-230.1 or (ii) sign an application or certificate as a witness, on behalf of a registered voter, who is a patient in any hospital, clinic, nursing home or rest home in this State or for any owner, manager, director, employee,

or other person other than the voter's near relative or verifiable legal guardian, to mark the voter's absentee ballot or assist such a voter in marking an absentee ballot. This subdivision does not apply to members, employees, or volunteers of the county board of elections, if those members, employees, or volunteers are working as part of a multipartisan team trained and authorized by the county board of elections to assist voters with absentee ballots. Each county board of elections shall train and authorize such teams, pursuant to procedures which shall be adopted by the State Board of Elections. If neither the voter's near relative nor a verifiable legal guardian is available to assist the voter, and a multipartisan team is not available to assist the voter within seven calendar days of a telephonic request to the county board of elections, the voter may obtain such assistance from any person other than (i) an owner, manager, director, employee of the hospital, clinic, nursing home, or rest home in which the voter is a patient or resident; (ii) an individual who holds any elective office under the United States, this State, or any political subdivision of this State; (iii) an individual who is a candidate for nomination or election to such office; or (iv) an individual who holds any office in a State, congressional district, county, or precinct political party or organization, or who is a campaign manager or treasurer for any candidate or political party; provided that a delegate to a convention shall not be considered a party office. None of the persons listed in (i) through (iv) of this subdivision may sign the application or certificate as a witness for the patient.

(5) Repealed by Session Laws 1987, c. 583, s. 8.

(6) For any person to take into that person's possession for delivery to a voter or for return to a county board of elections the absentee ballot of any voter, provided, however, that this prohibition shall not apply to a voter's near relative or the voter's verifiable legal guardian;

(7) Except as provided in subsections (1), (2), (3) and (4) of this section, G.S. 163-231(a), G.S. 163-250(a), and G.S. 163-227.2(e), for any voter to permit another person to assist the voter in marking that voter's absentee ballot, to be in the voter's presence when a voter votes an absentee ballot, or to observe the voter mark that voter's absentee ballot.

(b) The State Board of Elections or a county board of elections, upon receipt of a sworn affidavit from any qualified voter of the State or the county, as the case may be, attesting to first-person knowledge of any violation of subsection (a) of this section, shall transmit that affidavit to the appropriate district attorney, who shall investigate and prosecute any person violating subsection (a). (1979, c. 799, s. 4; 1983, c. 331, s. 2; 1985, c. 563, s. 4; 1987, c. 565, s. 7; c. 583, ss. 8, 10; 1995, c. 243, s. 1; 1999-455, s. 3; 2005-428, s. 5(b); 2007-391, s. 29(a); 2013-381, s. 4.6(a).)

§ 163-227. Repealed by Session Laws 1999-455, s. 4.

§ 163-227.1. Second primary; applications for absentee ballots for voting in second primary.

A voter applying for an absentee ballot for a primary election who will be eligible to vote under this Article on the day of the primary and second primary shall be permitted by the county board of elections to indicate that fact on that voter's application and that voter shall automatically be issued an application and absentee ballot for the second primary if one is called. The county board of elections shall consider that indication a separate request for application for the second primary and, at the proper time, shall enter that voter's name in the absentee register along with the listing of other applicants for absentee ballots for the second primary.

In addition, a voter entitled to absentee ballots under the provisions of this Article who did not make application for the primary or who failed to apply for a second primary ballot at the time of application for a first primary ballot may make a written request for absentee ballots for a second primary not earlier than the day a second primary is called and not later than the date and time provided by G.S. 163-230.1.

All procedures with respect to absentee ballots in a second primary shall be the same as with respect to absentee ballots in a first primary except as otherwise provided by this section. (1973, c. 536, s. 1; 1977, c. 469, s. 1; 1981, c. 560, s. 1; 1985, c. 600, s. 3; 1999-455, s. 5.)

§ 163-227.2. Alternate procedures for requesting application for absentee ballot; "one-stop" voting procedure in board office.

(a)   Any voter eligible to vote by absentee ballot under G.S. 163-226 may request an application for absentee ballots, complete the application, and vote under the provisions of this section.

(a1) Repealed by Session Laws 2001-337, s. 2, effective January 1, 2002.

(b) (Effective until January 1, 2016) Not earlier than the second Thursday before an election, in which absentee ballots are authorized, in which a voter seeks to vote and not later than 1:00 P.M. on the last Saturday before that election, the voter shall appear in person only at the office of the county board of elections, provided in subsection (g) of this section. A county board of elections shall conduct one-stop voting on the last Saturday before the election until 1:00 P.M. That voter shall enter the voting enclosure at the board office through the appropriate entrance and shall at once state his or her name and place of residence to an authorized member or employee of the board. In a primary election, the voter shall also state the political party with which the voter affiliates and in whose primary the voter desires to vote, or if the voter is an unaffiliated voter permitted to vote in the primary of a particular party under G.S. 163-119, the voter shall state the name of the authorizing political party in whose primary he wishes to vote. The board member or employee to whom the voter gives this information shall announce the name and residence of the voter in a distinct tone of voice. After examining the registration records, an employee of the board shall state whether the person seeking to vote is duly registered. If the voter is found to be registered that voter may request that the authorized member or employee of the board furnish the voter with an application form as specified in G.S. 163-227. The voter shall complete the application in the presence of the authorized member or employee of the board, and shall deliver the application to that person.

(b) (Effective January 1, 2016) Not earlier than the second Thursday before an election, in which absentee ballots are authorized, in which a voter seeks to vote and not later than 1:00 P.M. on the last Saturday before that election, the voter shall appear in person only at the office of the county board of elections, except as provided in subsection (g) of this section. A county board of elections shall conduct one-stop voting on the last Saturday before the election until 1:00 P.M. That voter shall enter the voting enclosure at the board office through the appropriate entrance and shall at once state his or her name and place of residence to an authorized member or employee of the board and present photo identification in accordance with G.S. 163-166.13. In a primary election, the voter shall also state the political party with which the voter affiliates and in whose primary the voter desires to vote, or if the voter is an unaffiliated voter permitted to vote in the primary of a particular party under G.S. 163-119, the voter shall state the name of the authorizing political party in whose primary he wishes to vote. The board member or employee to whom the voter gives this information shall announce the name and residence of the voter in a distinct tone of voice. After examining the registration records, an employee of the board shall state whether the person seeking to vote is duly registered. If the voter is found to be registered that voter may request that the authorized member or employee of the board furnish the voter with an application form as specified in G.S. 163-227. The voter shall complete the application in the presence of the authorized member or employee of the board, and shall deliver the application to that person.

(c) If the application is properly filled out, the authorized member or employee shall enter the voter's name in the register of absentee requests, applications, and ballots issued and shall furnish the voter with the ballots to which the application for absentee ballots applies. The voter thereupon shall vote in accordance with subsection (e) of this section.

All actions required by this subsection shall be performed in the office of the board of elections, except that the voting may take place in an adjacent room as provided by subsection (e) of this section. The application under this subsection shall be signed in the presence of the chair, member, director of elections of the board, or full-time employee, authorized by the board who shall sign the application and certificate as the witness and indicate the official title held by him or her. Notwithstanding G.S. 163-231(a), in the case of this subsection, only one witness shall be required on the certificate.

(d) Only the chairman, member, employee, or director of elections of the board shall keep the voter's application for absentee ballots in a safe place, separate and apart from other applications and container-return envelopes. If the voter's application for absentee ballots is disapproved by the board, the board shall so notify the voter stating the reason for disapproval by first-class mail addressed to the voter at that voter's residence address and at the address shown in the application for absentee ballots; and the board shall enter a challenge under G.S. 163-89.

(e) The voter shall vote that voter's absentee ballot in a voting booth in the office of the county board of elections, and the county board of elections shall provide a voting booth for that purpose, provided however, that the county board of elections may in the alternative provide a private room for the voter adjacent to the office of the board, in which case the voter shall vote that voter's absentee ballot in that room. A voter at a one-stop site shall be entitled to the same assistance as a voter at a voting place on election day under G.S. 163-166.8. The State Board of Elections shall, where appropriate, adapt the rules it adopts under G.S. 163-166.8 to one-stop voting.

(e1) (Effective until January 1, 2018) If a county uses a voting system with retrievable ballots, that county's board of elections may by resolution elect to conduct one-stop absentee voting according to the provisions of this subsection. In a county in which the board has opted to do so, a one-stop voter shall cast the ballot and then shall deposit the ballot in the ballot box or voting system in the same manner as if such box or system was in use in a precinct on election day. At the end of each business day, or at any time when there will be no employee or officer of the board of elections on the premises, the ballot box or system shall be secured in accordance with a plan approved by the State Board of Elections, which shall include that no additional ballots have been placed in the box or system. Any county board desiring to conduct one-stop voting according to this subsection shall submit a plan for doing so to the State Board of Elections. The State Board shall adopt standards for conducting one-stop voting under this subsection and shall approve any county plan that adheres to its standards. The county board shall adhere to its State Board-approved plan. The plan shall provide that each one-stop ballot shall have a ballot number on it in accordance with G.S. 163-230.1(a2), or shall have an equivalent identifier to allow for retrievability. The standards shall address retrievability in one-stop voting on direct record electronic equipment where no paper ballot is used.

(e1) (Effective January 1, 2018) If a county uses a voting system with retrievable ballots, that county's board of elections may by resolution elect to conduct one-stop absentee voting according to the provisions of this subsection. In a county in which the board has opted to do so, a one-stop voter shall cast the ballot and then shall deposit the ballot in the ballot box or voting system in the same manner as if such box or system was in use in a precinct on election day. At the end of each business day, or at any time when there will be no employee or officer of the board of elections on the premises, the ballot box or system shall be secured in accordance with a plan approved by the State Board of Elections, which shall include that no additional ballots have been placed in the box or system. Any county board desiring to conduct one-stop voting according to this subsection shall submit a plan for doing so to the State Board of Elections. The State Board shall adopt standards for conducting one-stop voting under this subsection and shall approve any county plan that adheres to its standards. The county board shall adhere to its State Board-approved plan. The plan shall provide that each one-stop ballot shall have a ballot number on it in accordance with G.S. 163-230.1(a2), or shall have an equivalent identifier to allow for retrievability.

(e2) A voter who has moved within the county more than 30 days before election day but has not reported the move to the board of elections shall not be required on that account to vote a provisional ballot at the one-stop site, as long as the one-stop site has available all the information necessary to determine whether a voter is registered to vote in the county and which ballot the voter is eligible to vote based on the voter's proper residence address. The voter with that kind of unreported move shall be allowed to vote the same kind of absentee ballot as other one-stop voters.

(f) Notwithstanding the exception specified in G.S. 163-36, counties which operate a modified full-time office shall remain open five days each week during regular business hours consistent with daily hours presently observed by the county board of elections, commencing with the date prescribed in G.S. 163-227.2(b) and continuing until 5:00 P.M. on the Friday prior to that election and shall also be open on the last Saturday before the election. A county board may conduct one-stop absentee voting during evenings or on weekends, as long as the hours are part of a plan submitted and approved according to subsection (g) of this section. The boards of county commissioners shall provide necessary funds for the additional operation of the office during that time.

(g) Notwithstanding any other provision of this section, a county board of elections by unanimous vote of all its members may provide for one or more sites in that county for absentee ballots to be applied for and cast under this section. Every individual staffing any of those sites shall be a member or full-time employee of the county board of elections or an employee of the county board of elections whom the board has given training equivalent to that given a full-time employee. Those sites must be approved by the State Board of Elections as part of a Plan for Implementation approved by both the county board of elections and by the State Board of Elections which shall also provide adequate security of the ballots and provisions to avoid allowing persons to vote who have already voted. The Plan for Implementation shall include a provision for the presence of political party observers at each one-stop site equivalent to the provisions in G.S. 163-45 for party observers at voting places on election day. A county board of elections may propose in its Plan not to offer one-stop voting at the county board of elections office; the State Board may approve that proposal in a Plan only if the Plan includes at least one site reasonably proximate to the county board of elections office and the State Board finds that the sites in the Plan as a whole provide adequate coverage of the county's electorate. If a county board of elections has considered a proposed Plan or Plans for Implementation and has been unable to reach unanimity in favor of a Plan, a member or members of that county board of elections may petition the State Board of Elections to adopt a plan for it. If petitioned, the State Board may also receive and consider alternative petitions from another member or members of that county board. The State Board of Elections may adopt a Plan for that county. The State Board, in that plan, shall take into consideration factors including geographic, demographic, and partisan interests of that county. Any plan adopted by either the county board of elections or the State Board of Elections under this subsection shall provide for the same days of operation and same number of hours of operation on each day for all sites in that county for that election. The requirement of the previous sentence does not apply to the county board of elections office itself nor, if one-stop voting is not conducted at the county board of elections office, to the reasonably proximate alternate site approved under this subsection.

(g1)   The State Board of Elections shall not approve, either in a Plan approved unanimously by a county board of elections or in an alternative Plan proposed by a member or members of that board, a one-stop site in a building that the county board of elections is not entitled under G.S. 163-129 to demand and use as an election-day voting place, unless the State Board of Elections finds that other equally suitable sites were not available and that the use of the sites chosen will not unfairly advantage or disadvantage geographic, demographic, or partisan interests of that county. In providing the site or sites for one-stop absentee voting under this section, the county board of elections shall make a request to the State, county, city, local school board, or other entity in control of the building that is supported or maintained, in whole or in part, by or through tax revenues at least 90 days prior to the start of one-stop absentee voting under this section. The request shall clearly identify the building, or any specific portion thereof, requested the dates and times for which that building or specific portion thereof is requested and the requirement of an area for election related activity. If the State, local governing board, or other entity in control of the building does not respond to the request within 20 days, the building or specific portion thereof may be used for one-stop absentee voting as stated in the request. If the State, local governing board, or other entity in control of the building or specific portion thereof responds negatively to the request within 20 days, that entity and the county board of elections shall, in good faith, work to identify a building or specific portion thereof in which to conduct one-stop absentee voting under this section. If no building or specific portion thereof has been agreed upon within 45 days from the date the county board of elections received a response to the request, the matter shall be resolved by the State Board of Elections.

(g2)   Notwithstanding the requirements of subsection (g) and (g1) of this section, for any county board of elections that provided for one or more sites as provided in subsection (g) of this section during the 2010 or 2012 general election, that county shall provide, at a minimum, the following:

(1)   The county board of elections shall calculate the cumulative total number of scheduled voting hours at all sites during the 2012 primary and general elections, respectively, that the county provided for absentee ballots to be applied for and voted under this section. For elections which include a presidential candidate on the ballot, the county shall ensure that at least the same number of hours offered in 2012 is offered for absentee ballots to be applied for and voted under this section through a combination of hours and numbers of one-stop sites during the primary or general election, correspondingly.

(2)   The county board of elections shall calculate the cumulative total number of scheduled voting hours at all sites during the 2010 primary and general elections, respectively, that the county provided for absentee ballots to be applied for and voted under this section. For elections which do not include a presidential candidate on the ballot, the county shall ensure that at least the same number of hours offered in 2010 is offered for absentee ballots to be applied for and voted under this section through a combination of hours and numbers of one-stop sites during the primary or general election, correspondingly.

The State Board of Elections, to ensure compliance with this subsection, may approve a one-stop site in a building that the county board of elections is not entitled under G.S. 163-129 to demand and use as an election-day voting place, but may deny approval if a member of that board presents evidence that other equally suitable sites were available and the use of the sites chosen would unfairly advantage or disadvantage geographic, demographic, or partisan interests of that county.

(g3)   A county board of elections by unanimous vote of the board, with all members present and voting, may submit a request to the State Board to reduce the number of hours established in subsection (g2) of this section for a primary or a general election. The reduction shall take effect for that primary or general election only if approved by unanimous vote of the State Board with all members present and voting.

(h)   Notwithstanding the provisions of G.S. 163-89(a) and (b), a challenge may be entered against a voter at a one-stop site under subsection (g) of this section or during one-stop voting at the county board office. The challenge may be entered by a person conducting one-stop voting under this section or by another registered voter who resides in the same precinct as the voter being challenged. If challenged at the place where one-stop voting occurs, the voter shall be allowed to cast a ballot in the same way as other voters. The challenge shall be made on forms prescribed by the State Board of Elections. The challenge shall be heard by the county board of elections in accordance with the procedures set forth in G.S. 163-89(e).

(i) At any site where one-stop absentee voting is conducted, there shall be a curtained or otherwise private area where the voter may mark the ballot unobserved. (1973, c. 536, s. 1; 1975, c. 844, s. 12; 1977, c. 469, s. 1; c. 626, s. 1; 1979, c. 107, s. 14; c. 799, ss. 1-3; 1981, c. 305, s. 2; 1985, c. 600, s. 4; 1987, c. 583, s. 4; 1989, c. 520; 1989 (Reg. Sess., 1990), c. 991, s. 2; 1993 (Reg. Sess., 1994), c. 762, s. 53; 1995, c. 243, s. 1; c. 509, ss. 117, 118; 1995 (Reg. Sess., 1996), c. 561, s. 4; 1997-510, s. 2; 1999-455, s. 6; 2000-136, s. 2; 2001-319, s. 5(a)-(c); 2001-337, s. 2; 2001-353, s. 9; 2003-278, s. 11; 2005-428, ss. 5(a), 6(a), 7; 2007-253, s. 3; 2007-391, s. 34(a); 2009-541, s. 23; 2013-381, ss. 2.7, 16.5, 25.1, 25.2, 25.3, 30.7.)

§ 163-227.3. Date by which absentee ballots must be available for voting.

(a) A board of elections shall provide absentee ballots of the kinds needed 60 days prior to the statewide general election in even-numbered years and 50 days prior to the date on which any other election shall be conducted, unless 45 days is authorized by the State Board of Elections under G.S. 163-22(k) or there shall exist an appeal before the State Board or the courts not concluded, in which case the board shall provide the ballots as quickly as possible upon the conclusion of such an appeal. Provided, in a presidential election year, the board of elections shall provide general election ballots no later than three days after nomination of the presidential and vice presidential candidates if that nomination occurs later than 63 days prior to the statewide general election and makes compliance with the 60-day deadline impossible. However, in the case of municipal elections, absentee ballots shall be made available no later than 30 days before an election. In every instance the board of elections shall exert every effort to provide absentee ballots, of the kinds needed by the date on which absentee voting is authorized to commence.

(b) Second Primary. - The board of elections shall provide absentee ballots, of the kinds needed, as quickly as possible after the ballot information for a second primary has been determined. (1973, c. 1275; 1977, c. 469, s. 1; 1985

(Reg. Sess., 1986), c. 986, s. 2; 1987, c. 485, ss. 2, 5; c. 509, s. 9; 1989, c. 635, s. 5; 2001-353, s. 4; 2002-159, s. 55(i); 2009-537, s. 2; 2013-381, s. 17(a).)

§ 163-228. Register of absentee requests, applications, and ballots issued; a public record.

The State Board of Elections shall approve an official register in which the county board of elections in each county of the State shall record the following information:

(1) Name of voter for whom application and ballots are being requested, and, if applicable, the name and address of the voter's near relative or verifiable legal guardian who requested the application and ballots for the voter.

(2) Number of assigned voter's application when issued.

(3) Precinct in which applicant is registered.

(4) Address to which ballots are to be mailed, or, if the voter voted pursuant to G.S. 163-227.2, a notation of that fact.

(5) Repealed by Session Laws 2009-537, s. 3, effective January 1, 2010, and applicable with respect to elections held on or after that date.

(6) Date request for application for ballots is received by the county board of elections.

(7) The voter's party affiliation.

(8) The date the ballots were mailed or delivered to the voter.

(9) Whatever additional information and official action may be required by this Article.

The State Board of Elections may provide for the register to be kept by electronic data processing equipment, and a copy shall be printed out each business day or a supplement printed out each business day of new information.

The register of absentee requests, applications and ballots issued shall constitute a public record and shall be opened to the inspection of any registered voter of the county within 60 days before and 30 days after an election in which absentee ballots were authorized, or at any other time when good and sufficient reason may be assigned for its inspection. (1939, c. 159, ss. 3, 9; 1945, c. 758, s. 8; 1953, c. 1114; 1963, c. 457, s. 3; 1965, c. 1208; 1967, c. 775, s. 1; c. 952, s. 4; 1973, c. 536, s. 1; 1977, c. 469, s. 1; 1991, c. 636, s. 21; 1999-455, s. 7; 2009-537, s. 3.)

§ 163-229. Absentee ballots, applications on container-return envelopes, and instruction sheets.

(a) Absentee Ballot Form. - In accordance with the provisions of G.S. 163-230.1, persons entitled to vote by absentee ballot shall be furnished with official ballots.

(b) Application on Container-Return Envelope. - In time for use not later than 60 days before a statewide general election in an even-numbered year, and not later than 50 days before a statewide primary, other general election or county bond election, the county board of elections shall print a sufficient number of envelopes in which persons casting absentee ballots may transmit their marked ballots to the county board of elections. However, in the case of municipal elections, sufficient container-return envelopes shall be made available no later than 30 days before an election. Each container-return envelope shall have printed on it an application which shall be designed and prescribed by the State Board of Elections, providing for all of the following:

(1) The voter's certification of eligibility to vote the enclosed ballot and of having voted the enclosed ballot in accordance with this Article.

(2) A space for identification of the envelope with the voter and the voter's signature.

(3) A space for the identification of the two persons witnessing the casting of the absentee ballot in accordance with G.S. 163-231, those persons' signatures, and those persons' addresses.

(4) A space for the name and address of any person who, as permitted under G.S. 163-226.3(a), assisted the voter if the voter is unable to complete and sign the certification and that individual's signature.

(5) A space for approval by the county board of elections.

(6) A space to allow reporting of a change of name as provided by G.S. 163-82.16.

(7) A prominent display of the unlawful acts under G.S. 163-226.3 and G.S. 163-275, except if there is not room on the envelope, the State Board of Elections may provide for that disclosure to be made on a separate piece of paper to be included along with the container-return envelope.

The container-return envelope shall be printed in accordance with the instructions of the State Board of Elections.

(c) Instruction Sheets. - In time for use not later than 60 days before a statewide general election in an even-numbered year, and not later than 50 days before a statewide primary, other general or county bond election, the county board of elections shall prepare and print a sufficient number of sheets of instructions on how voters are to prepare absentee ballots and return them to the county board of elections. However, in the case of municipal elections, instruction sheets shall be made available no later than 30 days before an election. (1929, c. 164, s. 39; 1939, c. 159, ss. 3, 4; 1943, c. 751, s. 2; 1963, c. 457, ss. 3, 4; 1965, c. 1208; 1967, c. 775, s. 1; c. 851, s. 1; c. 952, s. 5; 1973, c. 536, s. 1; 1975, c. 844, s. 13; 1977, c. 469, s. 1; 1985, c. 562, ss. 3, 4; 1985 (Reg. Sess., 1986), c. 986, s. 2; 1987, c. 485, ss. 2, 5; c. 509, s. 9; c. 583, s. 3; 1989, c. 635, s. 5; 1995 (Reg. Sess., 1996), c. 561, s. 5; 1999-455, s. 8; 2009-537, s. 4; 2013-381, s. 4.1.)

§ 163-230. Repealed by Session Laws 1999-455, s. 9.

§ 163-230.1. Simultaneous issuance of absentee ballots with application.

(a) A qualified voter who desires to vote by absentee ballot, or that voter's near relative or verifiable legal guardian, shall complete a request form for an absentee application and absentee ballots so that the county board of elections receives that completed request form not later than 5:00 P.M. on the Tuesday before the election. That completed written request form shall be in compliance with G.S. 163-230.2. The county board of elections shall enter in the register of absentee requests, applications, and ballots issued the information required in G.S. 163-228 as soon as each item of that information becomes available. Upon receiving the completed request form, the county board of elections shall cause to be mailed to that voter a single package that includes all of the following:

(1)   The official ballots that voter is entitled to vote.

(2)   A container-return envelope for the ballots, printed in accordance with G.S. 163-229.

(3)   Repealed by Session Laws 1999-455, s. 10.

(4)   An instruction sheet.

The ballots, envelope, and instructions shall be mailed to the voter by the county board's chairman, member, officer, or employee as determined by the board and entered in the register as provided by this Article.

(a1)   Absence for Sickness or Physical Disability. - Notwithstanding the provisions of subsection (a) of this section, if a voter expects to be unable to go to the voting place to vote in person on election day because of that voter's sickness or other physical disability, that voter or that voter's near relative or verifiable legal guardian may make the request under subsection (a) of this section in person to the board of elections of the county in which the voter is registered after 5:00 p.m. on the Tuesday before the election but not later than 5:00 p.m. on the day before the election. The county board of elections shall treat that completed request form in the same manner as a request under subsection (a) of this section but may personally deliver the application and ballots to the voter or that voter's near relative or verifiable legal guardian.

(a2)   Delivery of Absentee Ballots and Container-Return Envelope to Applicant. - When the county board of elections receives a completed request form for applications and absentee ballots, the board shall promptly issue and transmit them to the voter in accordance with the following instructions:

(1)   On the top margin of each ballot the applicant is entitled to vote, the chair, a member, officer, or employee of the board of elections shall write or type the words "Absentee Ballot No. ____ " or an abbreviation approved by the State Board of Elections and insert in the blank space the number assigned the applicant's application in the register of absentee requests, applications, and ballots issued. That person shall not write, type, or print any other matter upon the ballots transmitted to the absentee voter. Alternatively, the board of

elections may cause to be barcoded on the ballot the voter's application number, if that barcoding system is approved by the State Board of Elections.

(2) The chair, member, officer, or employee of the board of elections shall fold and place the ballots (identified in accordance with the preceding instruction) in a container-return envelope and write or type in the appropriate blanks thereon, in accordance with the terms of G.S. 163-229(b), the absentee voter's name, the absentee voter's application number, and the designation of the precinct in which the voter is registered. If the ballot is barcoded under this section, the envelope may be barcoded rather than having the actual number appear. The person placing the ballots in the envelopes shall leave the container-return envelope holding the ballots unsealed.

(3) The chair, member, officer, or employee of the board of elections shall then place the unsealed container-return envelope holding the ballots together with printed instructions for voting and returning the ballots, in an envelope addressed to the voter at the post office address stated in the request, seal the envelope, and mail it at the expense of the county board of elections: Provided, that in case of a request received after 5:00 p.m. on the Tuesday before the election under the provisions of subsection (a1) of this section, in lieu of transmitting the ballots to the voter in person or by mail, the chair, member, officer, or employee of the board of elections may deliver the sealed envelope containing the instruction sheet and the container-return envelope holding the ballots to a near relative or verifiable legal guardian of the voter.

The county board of elections may receive completed written request forms for applications at any time prior to the election but shall not mail applications and ballots to the voter or issue applications and ballots in person earlier than 60 days prior to the statewide general election in an even-numbered year, or earlier than 50 days prior to any other election, except as provided in G.S. 163-227.2. No election official shall issue applications for absentee ballots except in compliance with this Article.

(b) The application shall be completed and signed by the voter personally, the ballots marked, the ballots sealed in the container-return envelope, and the certificate completed as provided in G.S. 163-231.

(c) At its next official meeting after return of the completed container-return envelope with the voter's ballots, the county board of elections shall determine whether the container-return envelope has been properly executed. If the board determines that the container-return envelope has been properly executed, it shall approve the application and deposit the container-return envelope with other container-return envelopes for the envelope to be opened and the ballots counted at the same time as all other container-return envelopes and absentee ballots.

(c1)   Required Meeting of County Board of Elections. - During the period commencing on the third Tuesday before an election, in which absentee ballots are authorized, the county board of elections shall hold one or more public meetings each Tuesday at 5:00 p.m. for the purpose of action on applications for absentee ballots. At these meetings, the county board of elections shall pass upon applications for absentee ballots.

If the county board of elections changes the time of holding its meetings or provides for additional meetings in accordance with the terms of this subsection, notice of the change in hour and notice of the schedule of additional meetings, if any, shall be published in a newspaper circulated in the county at least 30 days prior to the election.

At the time the county board of elections makes its decision on an application for absentee ballots, the board shall enter in the appropriate column in the register of absentee requests, applications, and ballots issued opposite the name of the applicant a notation of whether the applicant's application was "Approved" or "Disapproved".

The decision of the board on the validity of an application for absentee ballots shall be final subject only to such review as may be necessary in the event of an election contest. The county board of elections shall constitute the proper official body to pass upon the validity of all applications for absentee ballots received in the county; this function shall not be performed by the chairman or any other member of the board individually.

(d)   Repealed by Session Laws 1999-455, s. 10.

(e)   The State Board of Elections, by rule or by instruction to the county board of elections, shall establish procedures to provide appropriate safeguards in the implementation of this section.

(f)   For the purpose of this Article, "near relative" means spouse, brother, sister, parent, grandparent, child, grandchild, mother-in-law, father-in-law, daughter-in-law, son-in-law, stepparent, or stepchild. (1983, c. 304, s. 1; 1985, c. 759, ss. 5.1-5.5; 1991, c. 727, s. 6.3; 1993, c. 553, s. 67; 1995, c. 243, s. 1;

1999-455, s. 10; 2001-337, s. 3; 2002-159, s. 55(m); 2009-537, s. 5; 2013-381, s. 4.2.)

§ 163-230.2. Method of requesting absentee ballots.

(a) Valid Types of Written Requests. - A completed written request form for an absentee ballot as required by G.S. 163-230.1 is valid only if it is on a form created by the State Board and signed by the voter requesting absentee ballots or that voter's near relative or verifiable legal guardian. The State Board shall make the form available at its offices, online, and in each county board of elections office, and that form may be reproduced. A voter may make a request in person or by writing to the county board for the form to request an absentee ballot. The request form for an absentee ballot shall require at least the following information:

(1) The name and address of the residence of the voter.

(2) The name and address of the voter's near relative or verifiable legal guardian if that individual is making the request.

(3) The address of the voter to which the application and absentee ballots are to be mailed if different from the residence address of the voter.

(4) One or more of the following in the order of preference:

a. The number of the voter's North Carolina drivers license issued under Article 2 of Chapter 20 of the General Statutes, including a learner's permit or a provisional license.

b. The number of the voter's special identification card for nonoperators issued under G.S. 20-37.7.

c. The last four digits of the applicant's social security number.

(5) The voter's date of birth.

(6) The signature of the voter or of the voter's near relative or verifiable legal guardian if that individual is making the request.

(a1) A completed request form for an absentee ballot shall be deemed a request to update the official record of voter registration for that voter and shall be confirmed in writing in accordance with G.S. 163-82.14(d).

(a2) The completed request form for an absentee ballot shall be delivered to the county board of elections. If the voter does not include the information requested in subdivision (a)(4) of this section, a copy of a document listed in G.S. 163-166.12(a)(2) shall accompany the completed request form.

(a3) Upon receiving a completed request form for an absentee ballot, the county board shall confirm that voter's registration. If that voter is confirmed as a registered voter of the county, the absentee ballots and certification form shall be mailed to the voter, unless personally delivered in accordance with G.S. 163-230.1(a1). If the voter's official record of voter registration conflicts with the completed request form for an absentee ballot or cannot be confirmed, the voter shall be so notified. If the county board cannot resolve the differences, no application or absentee ballots shall be issued.

(b) Invalid Types of Written Requests. - A request is not valid if it does not comply with subsection (a) of this section. If a county board of elections receives a request for an absentee ballot that does not comply with subsection (a) of this section, the board shall not issue an application and ballot under G.S. 163-230.1.

(c) Rules by State Board. - The State Board of Elections shall adopt rules for the enforcement of this section. (2002-159, s. 57(a); 2013-381, s. 4.3.)

§ 163-231. Voting absentee ballots and transmitting them to the county board of elections.

(a) Procedure for Voting Absentee Ballots. - In the presence of two persons who are at least 18 years of age, and who are not disqualified by G.S. 163-226.3(a)(4) or G.S. 163-237(b1), the voter shall do all of the following:

(1) Mark the voter's ballots, or cause them to be marked by that person in the voter's presence according to the voter's instruction.

(2) Fold each ballot separately, or cause each of them to be folded in the voter's presence.

(3) Place the folded ballots in the container-return envelope and securely seal it, or have this done in the voter's presence.

(4) Make the application printed on the container-return envelope according to the provisions of G.S. 163-229(b) and make the certificate printed on the container-return envelope according to the provisions of G.S. 163-229(b).

(5) Require those two persons in whose presence the voter marked that voter's ballots to sign the application and certificate as witnesses and to indicate those persons' addresses.

Alternatively to the prior paragraph of this subsection, any requirement for two witnesses shall be satisfied if witnessed by one notary public, who shall comply with all the other requirements of that paragraph. The notary shall affix a valid notarial seal to the envelope, and include the word "Notary Public" below his or her signature.

The persons in whose presence the ballot is marked shall at all times respect the secrecy of the ballot and the privacy of the absentee voter, unless the voter requests assistance and that person is otherwise authorized by law to give assistance. When thus executed, the sealed container-return envelope, with the ballots enclosed, shall be transmitted in accordance with the provisions of subsection (b) of this section to the county board of elections which issued the ballots.

(a1) Repealed by Session Laws 1987, c. 583, s. 1.

(b) Transmitting Executed Absentee Ballots to County Board of Elections. - The sealed container-return envelope in which executed absentee ballots have been placed shall be transmitted to the county board of elections who issued those ballots as follows:

(1) All ballots issued under the provisions of this Article and Article 21A of this Chapter shall be transmitted by mail or by commercial courier service, at the voter's expense, or delivered in person, or by the voter's near relative or verifiable legal guardian and received by the county board not later than 5:00 p.m. on the day of the statewide primary or general election or county bond election. Ballots issued under the provisions of Article 21A of this Chapter may also be electronically transmitted.

(2) If ballots are received later than the hour stated in subdivision (1) of this subsection, those ballots shall not be accepted unless one of the following applies:

a. Federal law so requires.

b. The ballots issued under this Article are postmarked and that postmark is dated on or before the day of the statewide primary or general election or county bond election and are received by the county board of elections not later than three days after the election by 5:00 p.m.

c. The ballots issued under Article 21A of this Chapter are received by the county board of elections not later than the end of business on the business day before the canvass conducted by the county board of elections held pursuant to G.S. 163-182.5.

(c) For purposes of this section, "Delivered in person" includes delivering the ballot to an election official at a one-stop voting site under G.S. 163-227.2 during any time that site is open for voting. The ballots shall be kept securely and delivered by election officials at that site to the county board of elections office for processing. (1939, c. 159, ss. 2, 5; 1941, c. 248; 1943, c. 736; c. 751, s. 1; 1945, c. 758, s. 5; 1963, c. 457, ss. 2, 5; 1967, c. 775, s. 1; 1971, c. 1247, s. 3; 1973, c. 536, s. 1; 1977, c. 469, s. 1; 1979, c. 799, s. 5; 1985, c. 562, ss. 1, 2; 1987, c. 583, ss. 1, 2; 1989 (Reg. Sess., 1990), c. 991, s. 4; 1999-455, s. 11; 2009-537, ss. 6, 8(a); 2011-182, s. 5; 2013-381, s. 4.4.)

§ 163-232. Certified list of executed absentee ballots; distribution of list.

The county board of elections shall prepare, or cause to be prepared, a list in at least quadruplicate, of all absentee ballots returned to the county board of elections to be counted, which have been approved by the county board of elections, and which have been received as of 5:00 p.m. on the day before the election. At the end of the list, the chairman shall execute the following certificate under oath:

"State of North Carolina

County of _____

I, _____, chairman of the _____ County board of elections, do hereby certify that the foregoing is a list of all executed absentee ballots to be voted in the election to be conducted on the _____ day of _____, _____, which have been approved by the county board of elections and which have been returned no later than 5:00 p.m. on the day before the election. I certify that the chairman, member, officer, or employee of the board of elections has not delivered ballots for absentee voting to any person other than the voter, by mail or by commercial courier service or in person, except as provided by law, and have not mailed or delivered ballots when the request for the ballot was received after the deadline provided by law.

This the _____ day of _____, _____

_____

(Signature of chairman of

county board of elections)

Sworn to and subscribed before me this _____ day of _____, _____.

Witness my hand and official seal.

_____

(Signature of officer

administering oath)

_____

(Title of officer)"

No later than 10:00 a.m. on election day, the county board of elections shall cause one copy of the list of executed absentee ballots, which may be a continuing countywide list or a separate list for each precinct, to be immediately deposited as "first-class" mail to the State Board of Elections. The board shall retain one copy in the board office for public inspection and the board shall cause two copies of the appropriate precinct list to be delivered to the chief judge of each precinct in the county. The county board of elections shall be authorized to call upon the sheriff of the county to distribute the list to the precincts. In addition the county board of elections shall, upon request, provide a copy of the complete list to the chairman of each political party, recognized under the provisions of G.S. 163-96, represented in the county.

The chief judge shall post one copy of the list immediately in a conspicuous location in the voting place and retain one copy until all challenges of absentee ballots have been heard by the county board of elections. Challenges shall be made to absentee ballots as provided in G.S. 163-89.

After receipt of the list of absentee voters required by this section the chief judge shall call the name of each person recorded on the list and enter an "A" in the appropriate voting square on the voter's permanent registration record, or a similar entry on the computer list used at the polls. If such person is already recorded as having voted in that election, the chief judge shall enter a challenge which shall be presented to the county board of elections for resolution by the board of elections prior to certification of results by the board.

All lists required by this section shall be retained by the county board of elections for a period of 22 months after which they may then be destroyed. (1939, c. 159, s. 6; 1943, c. 751, s. 3; 1963, c. 457, s. 6; 1967, c. 775, s. 1; 1973, c. 536, s. 1; 1977, c. 469, s. 1; 1981, c. 155, s. 1; c. 305, s. 4; 1985, c. 600, s. 7; 1993 (Reg. Sess., 1994), c. 762, s. 54; 1999-455, s. 12; 1999-456, s. 59.)

§ 163-232.1. Certified list of executed absentee ballots received on or after election day; publication of list.

(a) The county board of elections shall prepare, or cause to be prepared, a list in at least triplicate, of all absentee ballots issued under Article 20 of this Chapter returned to the county board of elections to be counted, which have been approved by the county board of elections, have not been included on the certified list prepared pursuant to G.S. 163-232, and which have been postmarked by the day of the statewide primary or general election or county bond election and received by the county board of elections not later than three days after the election by 5:00 p.m. The list shall be supplemented with new information each business day following the day of the election until the deadline for receipt of such absentee ballots. At the end of the list, the chairman shall execute the following certificate under oath:

"State of North Carolina

County of _____

I,_____, chair of the _____ County Board of Elections, do hereby certify that the foregoing is a list of all executed absentee ballots to be voted in the election to be conducted on the _____ day of _____, _____, which have been approved by the county board of elections and which have been postmarked by the day of the statewide primary or general election or county bond election and received by the county board of elections not later than three days after the election by 5:00 p.m. I certify that the chairman, member, officer, or employee of the board of elections has not delivered ballots for absentee voting to any person other than the voter, by mail or by commercial courier service or in person, except as provided by law, and have not mailed or delivered ballots when the request for the ballot was received after the deadline provided by law.

This the _____ day of _____, ____

_____

(Signature of chairman of

county board of elections)

Sworn to and subscribed before me this _____ day of _____, _____.

Witness my hand and official seal.

_____

(Signature of officer

administering oath)

_____

(Title of officer)"

(b)   The county board of elections shall prepare, or cause to be prepared, a list in at least triplicate, of all military-overseas ballots issued under Article 21A of this Chapter and returned to the county board of elections to be counted, which have been approved by the county board of elections, have not been included on the certified list prepared pursuant to G.S. 163-232, and which have been received by the county board of elections not later than three days after the election by 5:00 p.m. The list shall be supplemented with new information each business day following the day of the election until the deadline for receipt of such absentee ballots. At the end of the list, the chair shall execute the following certificate under oath:

"State of North Carolina

County of _____

I, _____, chair of the _____ County Board of Elections, do hereby certify that the foregoing is a list of all executed military-overseas ballots to be voted in the election to be conducted on the ____ day of _____, _____, which have been approved by the county board of elections, and which have been postmarked by the day of the statewide primary or general election or county bond election and received by the county board of elections not later than three days after the election by 5:00 p.m. I further certify that I have issued ballots to no other persons than those listed herein and further that I have not delivered military-overseas ballots to persons other than those listed herein; that this list constitutes the only precinct registration of covered voters whose names have not heretofore been entered on the regular registration of the appropriate precinct.

This the _____ day of _____, ____

_____

(Signature of chair of

county board of elections)

Sworn to and subscribed before me this _____ day of _____, _____.

Witness my hand and official seal.

_____

(Signature of officer

administering oath)

_____

(Title of officer)"

(c) The board shall post one copy of the most current version of each list in the board office in a conspicuous location for public inspection and shall retain one copy until all challenges of absentee ballots have been heard by the county board of elections. The county board of elections shall cause one copy of each of the final lists of executed absentee ballots required under subsection (a) and subsection (b) of this section to be deposited as "first-class" mail to the State Board of Elections no later than 10:00 a.m. of the next business day following the deadline for receipt of such absentee ballots. Challenges shall be made to absentee ballots as provided in G.S. 163-89. In addition the county board of elections shall, upon request, provide a copy of each of the lists to the chairman of each political party, recognized under the provisions of G.S. 163-96, represented in the county.

(d) All lists required by this section shall be retained by the county board of elections for a period of 22 months after which they may then be destroyed. (2009-537, s. 8(b); 2011-182, s. 6.)

§ 163-233. Applications for absentee ballots; how retained.

The county board of elections shall retain, in a safe place, the original of all applications made for absentee ballots and shall make them available to inspection by the State Board of Elections or to any person upon the directive of the State Board of Elections.

All applications for absentee ballots shall be retained by the county board of elections for a period of one year after which they may be destroyed. (1939, c. 159, s. 7; 1943, c. 751, s. 4; 1963, c. 457, s. 7; 1967, c. 775, s. 1; 1973, c. 536, s. 1; c. 1075, s. 5; 1977, c. 469, s. 1; 1999-455, s. 13.)

§ 163-233.1. Withdrawal of absentee ballots not allowed.

No person shall be permitted to withdraw an absentee ballot after such ballot has been mailed to or returned to the county board of elections. (1973, c. 536, s. 1; 1977, c. 469, s. 1.)

§ 163-234. Counting absentee ballots by county board of elections.

All absentee ballots returned to the county board of elections in the container-return envelopes shall be retained by the board to be counted by the county board of elections as herein provided.

(1) Only those absentee ballots returned to the county board of elections no later than 5:00 p.m. on the day before election day in a properly executed container-return envelope or absentee ballots received pursuant to G.S. 163-231(b)(ii) or (iii) shall be counted, except to the extent federal law requires otherwise.

(2) The county board of elections shall meet at 5:00 p.m. on election day in the board office or other public location in the county courthouse for the purpose of counting all absentee ballots except those which have been challenged before 5:00 p.m. on election day and those received pursuant to G.S. 163-231(b)(ii) or (iii). Any elector of the county shall be permitted to attend the meeting and allowed to observe the counting process, provided the elector shall not in any manner interfere with the election officials in the discharge of their duties.

Provided, that the county board of elections is authorized to begin counting absentee ballots issued under Article 21A of this Chapter between the hours of 9:00 A.M. and 5:00 P.M. and to begin counting all absentee ballots between the hours of 2:00 p.m. and 5:00 p.m. upon the adoption of a resolution at least two weeks prior to the election wherein the hour and place of counting absentee ballots shall be stated. Such resolution also may provide for an additional meeting following the day of the election and prior to the day of canvass to count absentee ballots received pursuant to G.S. 163-231(b)(ii) or (iii) as provided in subdivision (10) of this section. A copy of the resolutions shall be published once a week for two weeks prior to the election, in a newspaper having general circulation in the county. Notice may additionally be made on a radio or television station or both, but such notice shall be in addition to the newspaper and other required notice. The count shall be continuous until completed and the members shall not separate or leave the counting place except for unavoidable necessity, except that if the count has been completed prior to the time the polls close, it shall be suspended until that time pending receipt of any additional ballots. Nothing in this section shall prohibit a county board of elections from taking preparatory steps for the count earlier than the times specified in this section, as long as the preparatory steps do not reveal to any individual not engaged in the actual count election results before the times specified in this subdivision for the count to begin. By way of illustration and not limitation, a preparatory step for the count would be the entry of tally cards from direct record electronic voting units into a computer for processing. The board shall not announce the result of the count before 7:30 p.m.

(2a) Notwithstanding the provisions of subdivision (2) of this section, a county board of elections may, at each meeting at which it approves absentee ballot applications pursuant to G.S. 163-230.1(c) and (c1), remove those ballots from their envelopes and have them read by an optical scanning machine, without printing the totals on the scanner. The board shall complete the counting of these ballots at the times provided in subdivision (2) of this section. The State Board of Elections shall provide instructions to county boards of elections for executing this procedure, and the instructions shall be designed to ensure the accuracy of the count, the participation of board members of both parties, and the secrecy of the results before election day. This subdivision applies only in counties that use optical scan devices to count absentee ballots.

(3) The counting of absentee ballots shall not commence until a majority and at least one board member of each political party represented on the board is present and that fact is publicly declared and entered in the official minutes of the county board.

(4) The county board of elections may employ such assistants as deemed necessary to count the absentee ballots, but each board member present shall be responsible for and observe and supervise the opening and tallying of the ballots.

(5) As each ballot envelope is opened, the board shall cause to be entered into a pollbook designated "Pollbook of Absentee Voters" the name of the absentee voter, or if the pollbook is computer-generated, the board shall check off the name. Preserving secrecy, the ballots shall be placed in the appropriate ballot boxes, at least one of which shall be provided for each type of ballot. The "Pollbook of Absentee Voters" shall also contain the names of all persons who voted under G.S. 163-227.2, but those names may be printed by computer for inclusion in the pollbook.

After all ballots have been placed in the boxes, the counting process shall begin.

If one-stop ballots under G.S. 163-227.2 are counted electronically, that count shall commence at the time the polls close. If one-stop ballots are paper ballots counted manually, that count shall commence at the same time as other absentee ballots are counted.

If a challenge transmitted to the board on canvass day by a chief judge is sustained, the ballots challenged and sustained shall be withdrawn from the appropriate boxes, as provided in G.S. 163-89(e).

As soon as the absentee ballots have been counted and the names of the absentee voters entered in the pollbook as required herein, the board members and assistants employed to count the absentee ballots shall each sign the pollbook immediately beneath the last absentee voter's name entered therein. The county board of elections shall be responsible for the safekeeping of the pollbook of absentee voters.

(6)   Upon completion of the counting process the board members shall cause the results of the tally to be entered on the absentee abstract prescribed by the State Board of Elections. The abstract shall be signed by the members of the board in attendance and the original mailed immediately to the State Board of Elections. The county board of elections may have a separate count on the abstract for one-stop absentee ballots under G.S. 163-227.2.

(7)   One copy of the absentee abstract shall be retained by the county board of elections and the totals appearing thereon shall be added to the final totals of all votes cast in the county for each office as determined on the official canvass.

(8)   In the event a political party does not have a member of the county board of elections present at the meeting to count absentee ballots due to illness or other cause of the member, the counting shall not commence until the county party chairman of said absent member, or a member of the party's county executive committee, is in attendance. Such person shall act as an official witness to the counting and shall sign the absentee ballot abstract as an "observer."

(9)   The county board of elections shall retain all container-return envelopes and absentee ballots, in a safe place, for at least four months, and longer if any contest is pending concerning the validity of any ballot.

(10) The county board of elections shall meet after election day and prior to the date of canvass to determine where the container-return envelopes for absentee ballots received pursuant to G.S. 163-231(b)(ii) or (iii) has been properly executed. The county board of elections shall comply with the requirements of G.S. 163-230.1 for approval of applications. Any absentee ballots received pursuant to G.S. 163-231(b)(ii) or (iii) shall be counted by the county board of elections on the day of canvass. The county board of elections is also authorized to meet following the day of the election and prior to the day of canvass to count absentee ballots received pursuant to G.S. 163-231(b)(ii) or (iii) upon the adoption of a resolution pursuant to subdivision (2) of this section. The county board of elections shall comply with all other requirements of this section for the counting of such absentee ballots. (1939, c. 159, ss. 8, 9; 1945, c. 758, s. 8; 1953, c. 1114; 1963, c. 547, s. 8; 1967, c. 775, s. 1; c. 851, s. 2; 1973, c. 536, s. 1; 1975, c. 798, s. 3; 1977, c. 469, s. 1; c. 626, s. 1; 1989, c. 93, s. 7; 1993 (Reg. Sess., 1994), c. 762, s. 55; 1995, c. 243, s. 1; 1999-455, s. 14; 2005-159, s. 1; 2006-262, s. 1; 2009-537, s. 8(d); 2011-182, s. 7.)

§ 163-235. Repealed by Session Laws 1973, c. 536, s. 5.

§ 163-236. Violations by county board of elections.

The county board of elections shall be sole custodian of blank applications for absentee ballots, official ballots, and container-return envelopes for absentee ballots. The board shall issue and deliver blank applications for absentee ballots in strict accordance with the provisions of G.S. 163-230.1. The issuance of ballots to persons whose requests for absentee ballots have been received by the county board of elections under the provisions of G.S. 163-230.1 is the responsibility and duty of the county board of elections.

It shall be the duty of the county board of elections to keep current all records required by this Article and to make promptly all reports required by this Article. If that duty has been assigned to the chair, member, officer, or employee of the board of elections, that person shall carry out the duty.

The willful violation of this section shall constitute a Class 2 misdemeanor. (1939, c. 159, s. 14; 1963, c. 457, s. 10; 1967, c. 775, s. 1; 1977, c. 469, s. 1; 1987, c. 565, s. 9; 1993, c. 539, s. 1105; 1994, Ex. Sess., c. 24, s. 14(c); 1999-455, s. 15.)

§ 163-237. Certain violations of absentee ballot law made criminal offenses.

(a) False Statements under Oath Made Class 2 Misdemeanor. - If any person shall willfully and falsely make any affidavit or statement, under oath, which affidavit or statement under oath, is required to be made by the provisions of this Article, he shall be guilty of a Class 2 misdemeanor.

(b) False Statements Not under Oath Made Class 2 Misdemeanor. - Except as provided by G.S. 163-275(16), if any person, for the purpose of obtaining or voting any official ballot under the provisions of this Article, shall willfully sign any printed or written false statement which does not purport to be under oath, or which, if it purports to be under oath, was not duly sworn to, he shall be guilty of a Class 2 misdemeanor.

(b1) Candidate Witnessing Absentee Ballots of Nonrelative Made Class 2 Misdemeanor. - A person is guilty of a Class 2 misdemeanor if that person acts as a witness under G.S. 163-231(a) or G.S. 163-250(a) in any primary or election in which the person is a candidate for nomination or election, unless the voter is the candidate's near relative as defined in G.S. 163-230.1(f).

(c) Fraud in Connection with Absentee Vote; Forgery. - Any person attempting to aid and abet fraud in connection with any absentee vote cast or to be cast, under the provisions of this Article, shall be guilty of a misdemeanor. Attempting to vote by fraudulently signing the name of a regularly qualified voter is a Class I felony.

(d) Violations Not Otherwise Provided for Made Class 2 Misdemeanors. - If any person shall willfully violate any of the provisions of this Article, or willfully fail to comply with any of the provisions thereof, for which no other punishment is herein provided, he shall be guilty of a Class 2 misdemeanor. (1929, c. 164, s. 40; 1939, c. 159, ss. 12, 13, 15; 1967, c. 775, s. 1; 1977, c. 469, s. 1, 1985, c. 562, s. 6; 1987, c. 565, s. 8; 1993, c. 539, ss. 1106, 1324; 1994, Ex. Sess., c. 24, s. 14(c); 1999-455, s. 22.)

§ 163-238. Reports of violations to district attorneys.

It shall be the duty of the State Board of Elections to report to the district attorney of the appropriate prosecutorial district, any violation of this Article, or the failure of any person charged with a duty under its provisions to comply with and perform that duty, and it shall be the duty of the district attorney to cause such a person to be prosecuted therefor. (1939, c. 159, s. 16; 1967, c. 775, s. 1; 1977, c. 469, s. 1.)

§ 163-239. Article 21A relating to absentee voting by military and overseas voters not applicable.

Except as otherwise provided therein, Article 21A of this Chapter shall not apply to or modify the provisions of this Article. (1963, c. 457, s. 11; 1967, c. 775, s. 1; 1977, c. 469, s. 1; 2011-182, s. 8.)

§§ 163-240 to 163-240.5. Expired July 1, 1972.

§§ 163-241 through 163-244. Reserved for future codification purposes.

Article 21.

Military Absentee Registration and Voting in Primary and General Elections.

§ 163-245: Repealed by Session Laws 2011-182, s. 2, effective January 1, 2012.

§ 163-246: Repealed by Session Laws 2011-182, s. 2, effective January 1, 2012.

§ 163-247: Repealed by Session Laws 2011-182, s. 2, effective January 1, 2012.

§ 163-248: Repealed by Session Laws 2011-182, s. 2, effective January 1, 2012.

§ 163-249: Repealed by Session Laws 2011-182, s. 2, effective January 1, 2012.

§ 163-250: Repealed by Session Laws 2011-182, s. 2, effective January 1, 2012.

§ 163-251: Recodified as G.S. 163-258.26.

§ 163-252: Repealed by Session Laws 1973, c. 536, s. 5.

§§ 163-253 through 163-256: Recodified as G.S. 163-258.27 through 163-258.30, respectively.

§ 163-257: Repealed by Session Laws 2011-182, s. 2, effective January 1, 2012.

§ 163-258: Recodified as G.S. 163-258.31.

Article 21A.

Uniform Military and Overseas Voters Act.

Part 1. Uniform Military and Overseas Voters Act.

§ 163-258.1. Short title.

This Article may be cited as the Uniform Military and Overseas Voters Act. (2011-182, s. 1.)

§ 163-258.2. Definitions.

As used in this Article:

(1) "Covered voter" means any of the following:

a. A uniformed-service voter or an overseas voter who is registered to vote in this State.

b. A uniformed-service voter defined in subdivision (7) of this section whose voting residence is in this State and who otherwise satisfies this State's voter eligibility requirements.

c. An overseas voter who, before leaving the United States, was last eligible to vote in this State and, except for a State residency requirement, otherwise satisfies this State's voter eligibility requirements.

d. An overseas voter who, before leaving the United States, would have been last eligible to vote in this State had the voter then been of voting age and, except for a State residency requirement, otherwise satisfies this State's voter eligibility requirements.

e. An overseas voter who was born outside the United States, is not described in sub-subdivision c. or d. of this subdivision, and, except for a State residency requirement, otherwise satisfies this State's voter eligibility requirements, if:

1. The last place where a parent or legal guardian of the voter was, or under this Article would have been, eligible to vote before leaving the United States is within this State; and

2. The voter has not previously registered to vote in any other state.

(2) "Dependent" means an individual recognized as a dependent by a uniformed service.

(3) "Military-overseas ballot" means any of the following:

a. A federal write-in absentee ballot described in the Uniformed and Overseas Citizens Absentee Voting Act, section 103, 42 U.S.C. § 1973ff-2.

b. A ballot specifically prepared or distributed for use by a covered voter in accordance with this Article.

c. A ballot cast by a covered voter in accordance with this Article.

(4) "Overseas voter" means a United States citizen who is outside the United States.

(5) "State" means a state of the United States, the District of Columbia, Puerto Rico, the United States Virgin Islands, or any territory or insular possession subject to the jurisdiction of the United States.

(6) "Uniformed service" means any of the following:

a. Active and reserve components of the Army, Navy, Air Force, Marine Corps, and Coast Guard of the United States.

b. The Merchant Marine, the commissioned corps of the Public Health Service, and the commissioned corps of the National Oceanic and Atmospheric Administration of the United States.

c. The National Guard and state militia units.

(7) "Uniformed-service voter" means an individual who is qualified to vote and is one of the following:

a. A member of the active or reserve components of the Army, Navy, Air Force, Marine Corps, or Coast Guard of the United States who is on active duty.

b. A member of the Merchant Marine, the commissioned corps of the Public Health Service, or the commissioned corps of the National Oceanic and Atmospheric Administration of the United States.

c. A member of the National Guard or State militia unit who is on activated status.

d. A spouse or dependent of a member referred to in this subdivision.

(8) "United States," used in the territorial sense, means the several states, the District of Columbia, Puerto Rico, the United States Virgin Islands, and any territory or insular possession subject to the jurisdiction of the United States. (2011-182, s. 1.)

§ 163-258.3. Elections covered.

The voting procedures in this Article apply to all of the following:

(1) A primary, general, or special election for federal or State office.

(2) A State ballot measure.

(3) A primary, general, special, or runoff election for local government office or a local ballot measure if absentee balloting is allowed under Article 20 of this Chapter. (2011-182, s. 1.)

§ 163-258.4. Role of State Board of Elections.

(a) The State Board of Elections is the State official responsible for implementing this Article and the State's responsibilities under the Uniformed and Overseas Citizens Absentee Voting Act, 42 U.S.C. § 1973ff, et seq.

(b) The State Board of Elections shall make available to covered voters information regarding voter registration procedures for covered voters and procedures for casting military-overseas ballots. The State Board of Elections may delegate the responsibility under this subsection only to the State office designated in compliance with the Uniformed and Overseas Citizens Absentee Voting Act, section 102(b)(1), 42 U.S.C. § 1973ff-1(b)(1).

(c) The State Board of Elections shall establish an electronic transmission system through which covered voters may apply for and receive voter registration materials, military-overseas ballots, and other information under this Article.

(d) The State Board of Elections shall develop standardized absentee-voting materials, including privacy and transmission envelopes and their electronic equivalents, authentication materials, and voting instructions, to be used with the military-overseas ballot of a voter authorized to vote in any jurisdiction in this State, and, to the extent reasonably possible, shall do so in coordination with other states.

(e) The State Board of Elections shall prescribe the form and content of a declaration for use by a covered voter to swear or affirm specific representations pertaining to the voter's identity, eligibility to vote, status as a covered voter, and timely and proper completion of an overseas military ballot. The declaration shall be based on the declaration prescribed to accompany a federal write-in absentee ballot under the Uniformed and Overseas Citizens Absentee Voting Act, section 103, 42 U.S.C. § 1973ff-2, as modified to be consistent with this Article. The State Board of Elections shall ensure that a form for the execution of the declaration, including an indication of the date of execution of the declaration, is a prominent part of all balloting materials for which the declaration is required. (2011-182, s. 1.)

§ 163-258.5. Overseas voter's registration address.

In registering to vote, an overseas voter who is eligible to vote in this State shall use and shall be assigned to the precinct of the address of the last place of residence of the voter in this State, or, in the case of a voter described by G.S. 163-258.2(1)e., the address of the last place of residence in this State of the parent or legal guardian of the voter. If that address is no longer a recognized residential address, the voter shall be assigned an address for voting purposes. (2011-182, s. 1.)

§ 163-258.6. Methods of registering to vote.

(a) In addition to any other approved method for registering to vote, a covered voter may use a federal postcard application, as prescribed under the Uniformed and Overseas Citizens Absentee Voting Act, section 101(b)(2), 42 U.S.C. § 1973ff(b)(2), or the application's electronic equivalent, to apply to register to vote.

(b) A covered voter may use the declaration accompanying the federal write-in absentee ballot, as prescribed under the Uniformed and Overseas Citizens Absentee Voting Act, section 103, 42 U.S.C. § 1973ff-2, to apply to register to vote simultaneously with the submission of the federal write-in absentee ballot.

(c) The State Board of Elections shall ensure that the electronic transmission system described in G.S. 163-258.4(c) is capable of accepting both a federal postcard application and any other approved electronic registration application sent to the appropriate election official. The voter may use the electronic transmission system or any other approved method to register to vote.

(d) A covered voter's registration to vote by any method authorized by this section may be received at any time prior to the primary or election, but no later than 5:00 P.M. on the day before the primary or election. (2011-182, s. 1.)

§ 163-258.7. Methods of applying for military-overseas ballot.

(a) A covered voter who is registered to vote in this State may apply for a military-overseas ballot using either the regular application provided by Article 20 of this Chapter or the federal postcard application, as prescribed under the

Uniformed and Overseas Citizens Absentee Voting Act, section 101(b)(2), 42 U.S.C. § 1973ff(b)(2), or the application's electronic equivalent.

(b) A covered voter who is not registered to vote in this State may use the federal postcard application or the application's electronic equivalent simultaneously to apply to register to vote under G.S. 163-258.6 and to apply for a military-overseas ballot.

(c) The State Board of Elections shall ensure that the electronic transmission system described in G.S. 163-258.4(c) is capable of accepting the submission of both a federal postcard application and any other approved electronic military-overseas ballot application sent to the appropriate election official. The voter may use the electronic transmission system or any other approved method to apply for a military-overseas ballot.

(d) A covered voter may use the declaration accompanying the federal write-in absentee ballot, as prescribed under the Uniformed and Overseas Citizens Absentee Voting Act, section 103, 42 U.S.C. § 1973ff-2, as an application for a military-overseas ballot simultaneously with the submission of the federal write-in absentee ballot, if the declaration is received by the appropriate election official no later than 5:00 P.M. on the day before the election.

(e) To receive the benefits of this Article, a covered voter shall inform the appropriate election official that the voter is a covered voter. Methods of informing the appropriate election official that a voter is a covered voter include any of the following:

(1) The use of a federal postcard application or federal write-in absentee ballot.

(2) The use of an overseas address on an approved voter registration application or ballot application.

(3) The inclusion on an approved voter registration application or ballot application of other information sufficient to identify the voter as a covered voter.

(f) This Article does not preclude a covered voter from voting an absentee ballot under Article 20 of this Chapter. (2011-182, s. 1.)
§ 163-258.8. Timeliness and scope of application for military-overseas ballot.

An application for a military-overseas ballot is timely if received by the appropriate election official by 5:00 P.M. of the day before the election or primary. An application from a covered voter for a military-overseas ballot shall be considered a valid absentee ballot request for any election covered under G.S. 163-258.3 held during the calendar year in which the application was received. (2011-182, s. 1.)

§ 163-258.9. Transmission of unvoted ballots.

(a) Not later than 60 days before the statewide general election in even-numbered years and not later than 50 days before any other election, the county board of elections shall transmit a ballot and balloting materials to all covered voters who by that date submit a valid military-overseas ballot application, except for a second primary. Provided, in a presidential election year, the board of elections shall provide general election ballots no later than three days after nomination of the presidential and vice presidential candidates if that nomination occurs later than 63 days prior to the statewide general election and makes compliance with the 60-day deadline impossible. However, in the case of municipal elections, absentee ballots shall be made available no later than 30 days before an election. For a second primary which includes a candidate for federal office, the county board of elections shall transmit a ballot and balloting material to all covered voters who by that date submit a valid military-overseas ballot application no later than 45 days before the second primary. For a second primary which does not include a candidate for federal office, the transmission of the ballot and ballot materials shall be as soon as practicable and shall be transmitted electronically no later than three business days and by mail no later than 15 days from the date the appropriate board of elections orders that the second primary be held pursuant to G.S. 163-111. If additional offices are added to the ballot to fill a vacancy occurring after the deadline provided by this subsection, those ballots shall be transmitted as soon as practicable.

(b) A covered voter who requests that a ballot and balloting materials be sent to the voter by electronic transmission may choose facsimile transmission or electronic mail delivery, or, if offered by the voter's jurisdiction, Internet delivery. The election official in each jurisdiction charged with distributing a ballot and balloting materials shall transmit the ballot and balloting materials to the voter using the means of transmission chosen by the voter.

(c) If a ballot application from a covered voter arrives after the jurisdiction begins transmitting ballots and balloting materials to voters, the official charged with distributing a ballot and balloting materials shall transmit them to the voter not later than two business days after the application arrives. (2011-182, s. 1; 2013-381, s. 17(b).)

§ 163-258.10. Timely casting of ballot.

To be valid, a military-overseas ballot shall either be received by the appropriate county board of elections no later than the close of the polls, or the covered voter shall submit the ballot for mailing, electronic transmission, or other authorized means of delivery not later than 12:01 A.M., at the place where the voter completes the ballot, on the date of the election. (2011-182, s. 1.)

§ 163-258.11. Federal write-in absentee ballot.

A covered voter may use the federal write-in absentee ballot, in accordance with the Uniformed and Overseas Citizens Absentee Voting Act, section 103, 42 U.S.C. § 1973ff-2, to vote for all offices and ballot measures in a covered election. (2011-182, s. 1.)

§ 163-258.12. Receipt of voted ballot.

(a) A valid military-overseas ballot cast in accordance with G.S. 163-258.10 shall be counted if it is delivered to the address that the appropriate State or local election office has specified by the end of business on the business day before the canvass conducted by the county board of elections held pursuant to G.S. 163-182.5 to determine the final official results.

(b) If the ballot is timely received, it may not be rejected on the basis that it has a late postmark, an unreadable postmark, or no postmark. (2011-182, s. 1.)

§ 163-258.13. Declaration.

Each military-overseas ballot shall include or be accompanied by a declaration signed by the voter declaring that a material misstatement of fact in completing the document may be grounds for a conviction of perjury under the laws of the United States or this State. (2011-182, s. 1.)

§ 163-258.14. Confirmation of receipt of application and voted ballot.

The State Board of Elections, in coordination with local election officials, shall implement an electronic free access system by which a covered voter may determine by telephone, electronic mail, or Internet whether:

(1) The voter's federal postcard application or other registration or military-overseas ballot application has been received and accepted; and

(2) The voter's military-overseas ballot has been received and the current status of the ballot. (2011-182, s. 1.)

§ 163-258.15. Use of voter's electronic mail address.

(a) The county board of elections shall request an electronic mail address from each covered voter who registers to vote after January 1, 2012. An electronic mail address provided by a covered voter is not a public record under Chapter 132 of the General Statutes. The address may be used only for official communication with the voter about the voting process, including transmitting military-overseas ballots and election materials if the voter has requested electronic transmission, and verifying the voter's mailing address and physical location, as needed. The request for an electronic mail address shall describe the purposes for which the electronic mail address may be used and include a statement that any other use or disclosure of the electronic mail address is prohibited.

(b) A covered voter who provides an electronic mail address may request that the voter's application for a military-overseas ballot be considered a standing request for electronic delivery of a ballot for all elections held through December 31 of the year following the calendar year of the date of the application or another shorter period the voter specifies, including for any runoff elections that occur as a result of such elections. An election official shall provide a military-overseas ballot to a voter who makes a request for each election to which the request is applicable. A covered voter entitled to receive a military-overseas ballot for a primary election under this subsection is also entitled to receive a military-overseas ballot for the general election. (2011-182, s. 1.)

§ 163-258.16. Publication of election notice.

(a) Not later than 100 days before a regularly scheduled election to which this Article applies, and as soon as practicable in the case of an election or vacancy election not regularly scheduled, each county board of elections shall prepare an election notice for that jurisdiction to be used in conjunction with the federal write-in absentee ballot described in G.S. 163-258.11. For a second primary required by G.S. 163-111, the county board of elections shall prepare, no later than the day following the date the appropriate board of elections orders that a second primary be held, an election notice for that jurisdiction to be used in conjunction with the federal write-in absentee ballot. The election notice shall contain a list of all of the ballot measures and federal, State, and local offices that, as of that date, the official expects to be on the ballot on the date of the election. The notice also shall contain specific instructions for how a voter is to indicate on the federal write-in absentee ballot the voter's choice for each office to be filled and for each ballot measure to be contested.

(b) A covered voter may request a copy of an election notice. The official charged with preparing the election notice shall send the notice to the voter by facsimile, electronic mail, or regular mail, as the voter requests.

(c) As soon as ballot styles are printed, the county board of elections shall update the notice with the certified candidates for each office and ballot measure questions and make the updated notice publicly available.

(d) A county board of elections that maintains an Internet Web site shall make updated versions of its election notices regularly available on the Web site. (2011-182, s. 1.)

§ 163-258.17. Prohibition of nonessential requirements.

(a) If a voter's mistake or omission in the completion of a document under this Article does not prevent determining whether a covered voter is eligible to vote, the mistake or omission does not invalidate the document. Failure to satisfy a nonessential requirement, such as using paper or envelopes of a specified size or weight, does not invalidate a document submitted under this Article. In any write-in ballot authorized by this Article or in any vote for a write-in candidate on a regular ballot, if the intention of the voter is discernable under this State's uniform definition of what constitutes a vote, as required by the Help America Vote Act, 42 U.S.C. § 15481(a)(6), an abbreviation, misspelling, or other minor variation in the form of the name of a candidate or a political party shall be accepted as a valid vote.

(b) An authentication, other than the declaration specified in G.S. 163-258.13 or the declaration on the federal postcard application and federal write-in absentee ballot, is not required for execution of a document under this Article. The declaration and any information in the declaration may be compared against information on file to ascertain the validity of the document. (2011-182, s. 1.)

§ 163-258.18. Issuance of injunction or other equitable relief.

A court may issue an injunction or grant other equitable relief appropriate to ensure substantial compliance with, or enforce, this Article on application by:

(1) A covered voter alleging a grievance under this Article; or

(2) An election official in this State. (2011-182, s. 1.)

§ 163-258.19. Uniformity of application and construction.

In applying and construing this uniform act, consideration shall be given to the need to promote uniformity of the law with respect to its subject matter among states that enact it. (2011-182, s. 1.)

§ 163-258.20. Relation to Electronic Signatures in Global and National Commerce Act.

This Article modifies, limits, and supersedes the federal Electronic Signatures in Global and National Commerce Act, 15 U.S.C. § 7001, et seq., but does not modify, limit, or supersede section 101(c) of that act, 15 U.S.C. § 7001(c), or authorize electronic delivery of any of the notices described in section 103(b) of that act, 15 U.S.C. § 7003(b). (2011-182, s. 1.)

§ 163-258.21: Reserved for future codification purposes.

§ 163-258.22: Reserved for future codification purposes.

§ 163-258.23: Reserved for future codification purposes.

§ 163-258.24: Reserved for future codification purposes.

§ 163-258.25: Reserved for future codification purposes.

Part 2. Other Military and Overseas Voters Absentee Provisions.

§ 163-258.26. Certified list of approved military-overseas ballot applications; record of ballots received; disposition of list; list constitutes registration.

(a)   Preparation of List. - The chair of the county board of elections shall prepare, or cause to be prepared, a list in quadruplicate of all military-overseas ballots returned to the county board of elections under this Article to be counted which have been approved by the county board of elections. At the end of the list the chair shall execute the following certificate under oath:

"State of North Carolina

County of _____

I, _____, Chair of the _____ County Board of Elections, do hereby certify that the foregoing is a list of all executed military-overseas ballots to be voted in the election to be conducted on the _____ day of _____, ____, which have been approved by the County Board of Elections. I further certify that I have issued ballots to no other persons than those listed herein and further that I have not delivered military-overseas ballots to persons other than those listed herein; that this list constitutes the only precinct registration of covered voters whose names have not heretofore been entered on the regular registration of the appropriate precinct.

This the _____ day of _____, ____.

_____

(Signature of Chair of County Board of Elections)

Sworn to and subscribed before me this _____ day of _____, ____

_____

(Signature of Officer administering oath)

_____

(Title of officer)"

(b) Distribution of List. - No earlier than 3:00 P.M. on the day before the election and no later than 10:00 A.M. on election day, the chair shall cause one copy of the list of executed military-overseas ballots, which may be a continuing countywide list or a separate list for each precinct, to be immediately deposited as first-class mail to the State Board of Elections. The chair shall retain one copy in the board office for public inspection and shall cause two copies of the appropriate precinct list to be delivered to the chief judge of each precinct in the county. The chief judge shall post one copy in the voting place and retain one copy until all challenges of absentee ballots have been heard by the county board of elections. Challenges shall be made as provided in G.S. 163-89.

After receipt of the list of absentee voters required by this section the chief judge shall call the name of each person recorded on the list and enter an "A" in the appropriate voting square on the voter's permanent registration record, if any, or a similar entry on the computer list used at the polls. If such person is already recorded as having voted in that election, the chief judge shall enter a challenge which shall be presented to the chair of the county board of elections for resolution by the board of elections prior to certification of results by the board.

(c) List Constitutes Registration. - The "List of Applicants for Military-Overseas Ballots to Whom Ballots Have Been Issued" prescribed by this section, when delivered to the chief judges of the various precincts, shall constitute the only precinct registration of the covered voters listed thereon whose names are not already entered in the registration records of the appropriate precinct. Chief judges shall not add the names of persons listed on the covered voters list to the regular registration books of their precincts.

(d) Counting Ballots, Hearing Challenges. - The county board of elections shall count military-overseas ballots as provided for civilian absentee ballots in G.S. 163-234, and shall hear challenges as provided in G.S. 163-89. (1941, c. 346, ss. 7-10, 12, 13; 1943, c. 503, ss. 4, 5; 1963, c. 457, s. 15; 1967, c. 775, s. 1; 1973, c. 536, s. 2; 1977, c. 265, s. 17; 1979, c. 797, s. 3; 1981, c. 155, s. 2; c. 308, s. 3; 1983, c. 331, s. 4; 1993 (Reg. Sess., 1994), c. 762, ss. 56, 57; 1999-456, s. 59; 2011-182, s. 2.)

§ 163-258.27. Article inapplicable to persons after change of status; reregistration not required.

An individual who no longer qualifies as a covered voter under the provisions of this Article shall not be entitled subsequently to vote by military-overseas ballot under this Article, but if the covered voter was registered under the provisions of this Article that voter's registration shall remain valid for the remainder of the calendar year that voter registered, and that voter shall be entitled to vote in any primary or election for the remainder of the calendar year without having to reregister. If requested by election officials, the voter shall present proof of military status at the time of registration. This section does not entitle a person to vote in North Carolina if that person has become disqualified because of change of permanent residence to another State or because of conviction of a felony. (1943, c. 503, s. 12; 1967, c. 775, s. 1; 1999-424, s. 7(k); 2001-466, s. 4(e); 2011-182, s. 2.)

§ 163-258.28. Registration and voting on primary or election day.

Notwithstanding any other provisions of this Chapter, an individual shall be permitted to register in person at any time the office of the board of elections or the voting place is open, including the day of a primary or election if that individual was absent on the day the registration records close for an election, but returns to that individual's county of residence in North Carolina thereafter, and if the absence is due to uniformed service as defined by G.S. 163-258.2.

If an individual so absent on the day registration closes shall appear in person at the voting place on election day and is otherwise eligible to vote, that individual shall be entitled to register and vote at the voting place that day, regardless of whether the person's uniformed service status has changed since the close of registration. (1977, c. 93; 1999-424, s. 7(l); 2001-353, s. 3; 2009-281, s. 1; 2011-182, s. 2.)

§ 163-258.29. Absentee voting at office of board of elections.

Notwithstanding any other provisions of this Chapter, any covered voter under this Article shall be permitted to vote an absentee ballot pursuant to G.S. 163-227.2 if the covered voter has not already voted an absentee ballot which has been returned to the board of elections, and if the covered voter will not be in the county on the day of the primary or election.

In the event an absentee application or ballot has already been mailed to the covered voter applying to vote pursuant to G.S. 163-227.2, the board of elections shall void the application and ballot unless the voted absentee ballot has been received by the board of elections. The covered voter shall be eligible to vote pursuant to G.S. 163-227.2 no later than 5:00 P.M. on the day next preceding the primary, second primary or election. (1977, c. 93; 1979, c. 797, s. 4; 2011-182, s. 2.)

§ 163-258.30. Regulations of State Board of Elections.

(a) The State Board of Elections shall adopt rules and regulations to carry out the intent and purpose of G.S. 163-258.28 and G.S. 163-258.29 and to ensure that a proper list of persons voting under said sections shall be maintained by the boards of elections, and to ensure proper registration records, and such rules and regulations shall not be subject to the provisions of Article 2A of Chapter 150B of the General Statutes.

(b) The State Board of Elections shall be the single office responsible for providing information concerning voter registration and absentee voting procedures to be used by covered voters as to all elections and procedures relating to the use of federal write-in absentee ballots. Unless otherwise required by law, the State Board of Elections shall be responsible for maintaining contact and cooperation with the Federal Voting Assistance Program, the United States Department of Defense, and other federal entities that deal with military and overseas voting. The State Board of Elections shall, as needed, make recommendations concerning military and overseas citizen voting to the General Assembly, the Governor, and other State officials. (1977, c. 93; 1987, c. 827, s. 1; 2003-226, s. 18; 2011-182, s. 2; 2012-194, s. 37.)

§ 163-258.31. Emergency powers.

If an international, national, or local emergency or other situation arises that makes substantial compliance with this Article or the Uniformed and Overseas Citizens Absentee Voting Act impossible or unreasonable, the State Board of Elections may prescribe, by emergency rule, such special procedures or requirements as may be necessary to facilitate absentee voting by those absent uniformed services voters or overseas voters directly affected who are eligible to vote in this State. The rule shall become effective when filed with the Codifier of Rules. (2009-537, s. 9; 2011-182, s. 2.)

SUBCHAPTER VIII. REGULATION OF ELECTION CAMPAIGNS.

Article 22.

Corrupt Practices and Other Offenses against the Elective Franchise.

§§ 163-259 through 163-268. Repealed by Session Laws 1975, c. 565, s. 8.

§§ 163-269 through 163-270. Repealed by Session Laws 1999-31, s. 5(b).

§ 163-271. Intimidation of voters by officers made misdemeanor.

It shall be unlawful for any person holding any office, position, or employment in the State government, or under and with any department, institution, bureau, board, commission, or other State agency, or under and with any county, city, town, district, or other political subdivision, directly or indirectly, to discharge, threaten to discharge, or cause to be discharged, or otherwise intimidate or oppress any other person in such employment on account of any vote such voter or any member of his family may cast, or consider or intend to cast, or not to cast, or which he may have failed to cast, or to seek or undertake to control any vote which any subordinate of such person may cast, or consider or intend to cast, or not to cast, by threat, intimidation, or declaration that the position, salary, or any part of the salary of such subordinate depends in any manner whatsoever, directly or indirectly, upon the way in which subordinate or any member of his family casts, or considers or intends to cast, or not to cast his vote, at any primary or election. A violation of this section is a Class 2 misdemeanor. (1933, c. 165, s. 25; 1967, c. 775, s. 1; 1987, c. 565, s. 11; 1993, c. 539, s. 1109; 1994, Ex. Sess., c. 24, s. 14(c).)

§ 163-272. Repealed by Session Laws 1971, c. 872, s. 3.

§ 163-272.1. Penalties for violation of this Chapter.

Whenever in this Chapter it is provided that a crime is a misdemeanor, the punishment shall be for a Class 2 misdemeanor. (1987, c. 565, s. 1; 1993, c. 539, s. 1110; 1994, Ex. Sess., c. 24, s. 14(c).)

§ 163-273. Offenses of voters; interference with voters; penalty.

(a) Any person who shall, in connection with any primary or election in this State, do any of the acts and things declared in this section to be unlawful, shall be guilty of a Class 2 misdemeanor. It shall be unlawful:

(1) For a voter, except as otherwise provided in this Chapter, to allow his ballot to be seen by any person.

(2) For a voter to take or remove, or attempt to take or remove, any ballot from the voting enclosure.

(3) For any person to interfere with, or attempt to interfere with, any voter when inside the voting enclosure.

(4) For any person to interfere with, or attempt to interfere with, any voter when marking his ballots.

(5) For any voter to remain longer than the specified time allowed by this Chapter in a voting booth, after being notified that his time has expired.

(6) For any person to endeavor to induce any voter, while within the voting enclosure, before depositing his ballots, to show how he marks or has marked his ballots.

(7) For any person to aid, or attempt to aid, any voter by means of any mechanical device, or any other means whatever, while within the voting enclosure, in marking his ballots.

(b) Election officers shall cause any person committing any of the offenses set forth in subsection (a) of this section to be arrested and shall cause charges to be preferred against the person so offending in a court of competent jurisdiction. (1929, c. 164, s. 29; 1967, c. 775, s. 1; 1987, c. 565, s. 12; 1993, c. 539, s. 1111; 1994, Ex. Sess., c. 24, s. 14(c).)

§ 163-274. Certain acts declared misdemeanors.

(a) Class 2 Misdemeanors. - Any person who shall, in connection with any primary or election in this State, do any of the acts and things declared in this subsection to be unlawful, shall be guilty of a Class 2 misdemeanor. It shall be unlawful:

(1) For any person to fail, as an officer or as a judge or chief judge of a primary or election, or as a member of any board of elections, to prepare the books, ballots, and return blanks which it is his duty under the law to prepare, or to distribute the same as required by law, or to perform any other duty imposed upon him within the time and in the manner required by law;

(1a) For any member, director, or employee of a board of elections to alter a voter registration application or other voter registration record without either the written authorization of the applicant or voter or the written authorization of the State Board of Elections;

(2) For any person to continue or attempt to act as a judge or chief judge of a primary or election, or as a member of any board of elections, after having been legally removed from such position and after having been given notice of such removal;

(3) For any person to break up or by force or violence to stay or interfere with the holding of any primary or election, to interfere with the possession of any ballot box, election book, ballot, or return sheet by those entitled to possession of the same under the law, or to interfere in any manner with the performance of any duty imposed by law upon any election officer or member of any board of elections;

(4) For any person to be guilty of any boisterous conduct so as to disturb any member of any election board or any chief judge or judge of election in the performance of his duties as imposed by law;

(5) For any person to bet or wager any money or other thing of value on any election;

(5a) Repealed by Session Laws 1999-455, s. 21, applicable to elections held on or after January 1, 2000.

(6) For any person, directly or indirectly, to discharge or threaten to discharge from employment, or otherwise intimidate or oppose any legally qualified voter on account of any vote such voter may cast or consider or intend to cast, or not to cast, or which he may have failed to cast;

(7) For any person to publish in a newspaper or pamphlet or otherwise, any charge derogatory to any candidate or calculated to affect the candidate's chances of nomination or election, unless such publication be signed by the party giving publicity to and being responsible for such charge;

(8) For any person to publish or cause to be circulated derogatory reports with reference to any candidate in any primary or election, knowing such report to be false or in reckless disregard of its truth or falsity, when such report is calculated or intended to affect the chances of such candidate for nomination or election;

(9) For any person to give or promise, in return for political support or influence, any political appointment or support for political office;

(10) For any chairman of a county board of elections or other returning officer to fail or neglect, willfully or of malice, to perform any duty, act, matter or thing required or directed in the time, manner and form in which said duty, matter or thing is required to be performed in relation to any primary, general or special election and the returns thereof;

(11) For any clerk of the superior court to refuse to make and give to any person applying in writing for the same a duly certified copy of the returns of any primary or election or of a tabulated statement to a primary or election, the returns of which are by law deposited in his office, upon the tender of the fees therefor;

(12) For any person willfully and knowingly to impose upon any blind or illiterate voter a ballot in any primary or election contrary to the wish or desire of such voter, by falsely representing to such voter that the ballot proposed to him is such as he desires; or

(13) Except as authorized by G.S. 163-82.15, for any person to provide false information, or sign the name of any other person, to a written report under G.S. 163-82.15.

(14) For any person to be compensated based on the number of forms submitted for assisting persons in registering to vote.

(b) Class 1 Misdemeanor. - Any person who shall, in connection with any primary or election in this State, do any of the acts and things declared in this subsection to be unlawful shall be guilty of a Class 1 misdemeanor. It shall be unlawful for any person who has access to an official voted ballot or record to knowingly disclose in violation of G.S. 163-165.1(e) how an individual has voted that ballot. (1931, c. 348, s. 9; 1951, c. 983, s. 1; 1967, c. 775, s. 1; 1979, c. 135, s. 3; 1987, c. 565, s. 13; c. 583, s. 9; 1993, c. 539, s. 1112; 1994, Ex. Sess., c. 24, s. 14(c); 1993 (Reg. Sess., 1994), c. 762, s. 58(a)-(c); 1999-424, s. 7(h); 1999-426, s. 2(a); 1999-455, s. 21; 2007-391, ss. 9(b), 16(b); 2013-381, s. 14.1.)

§ 163-275. Certain acts declared felonies.

Any person who shall, in connection with any primary, general or special election held in this State, do any of the acts or things declared in this section to be unlawful, shall be guilty of a Class I felony. It shall be unlawful:

(1) For any person fraudulently to cause his name to be placed upon the registration books of more than one election precinct or fraudulently to cause or procure his name or that of any other person to be placed upon the registration books in any precinct when such registration in that precinct does not qualify such person to vote legally therein, or to impersonate falsely another registered voter for the purpose of voting in the stead of such other voter;

(2) For any person to give or promise or request or accept at any time, before or after any such primary or election, any money, property or other thing of value whatsoever in return for the vote of any elector;

(3) For any person who is an election officer, a member of an election board or other officer charged with any duty with respect to any primary or election, knowingly to make any false or fraudulent entry on any election book or any false or fraudulent returns, or knowingly to make or cause to be made any false statement on any ballot, or to do any fraudulent act or knowingly and

fraudulently omit to do any act or make any report legally required of such person;

(4)   For any person knowingly to swear falsely with respect to any matter pertaining to any primary or election;

(5)   For any person convicted of a crime which excludes him from the right of suffrage, to vote at any primary or election without having been restored to the right of citizenship in due course and by the method provided by law;

(6)   For any person to take corruptly the oath prescribed for voters;

(7)   For any person with intent to commit a fraud to register or vote at more than one precinct or more than one time, or to induce another to do so, in the same primary or election, or to vote illegally at any primary or election;

(8)   For any chief judge or any clerk or copyist to make any entry or copy with intent to commit a fraud;

(9)   For any election official or other officer or person to make, certify, deliver or transmit any false returns of any primary or election, or to make any erasure, alteration, or conceal or destroy any election ballot, book, record, return or process with intent to commit a fraud;

(10)   For any person to assault any chief judge, judge of election or other election officer while in the discharge of his duty in the registration of voters or in conducting any primary or election;

(11)   For any person, by threats, menaces or in any other manner, to intimidate or attempt to intimidate any chief judge, judge of election or other election officer in the discharge of his duties in the registration of voters or in conducting any primary or election;

(12)   For any chief judge, judge of election, member of a board of elections, assistant, marker, or other election official, directly or indirectly, to seek, receive or accept money or the promise of money, the promise of office, or other reward or compensation from a candidate in any primary or election or from any source other than such compensation as may be provided by law for his services;

(13)   For any person falsely to make or present any certificate or other paper to qualify any person fraudulently as a voter, or to attempt thereby to secure to

any person the privilege of voting, including declarations made under this Chapter, G.S. 20-37.7(d)(5), 20-37.7(d)(6), 130A-93.1(c), and 161-10(a)(8);

(14) For any officer to register voters and any other individual to knowingly and willfully receive, complete, or sign an application to register from any voter contrary to the provisions of G.S. 163-82.4; or

(15) Reserved for future codification purposes.

(16) For any person falsely to make the certificate provided by G.S. 163-229(b)(2) or G.S. 163-250(a).

(17) For any person, directly or indirectly, to misrepresent the law to the public through mass mailing or any other means of communication where the intent and the effect is to intimidate or discourage potential voters from exercising their lawful right to vote.

(18) For any person, knowing that a person is not a citizen of the United States, to instruct or coerce that person to register to vote or to vote. (1901, c. 89, s. 13; Rev., s. 3401; 1913, c. 164, s. 2; C.S., s. 4186; 1931, c. 348, s. 10; 1943, c. 543; 1965, c. 899; 1967, c. 775, s. 1; 1979, c. 539, s. 4; 1979, 2nd Sess., c. 1316, ss. 27, 28; 1981, cc. 63, 179; 1985, c. 562, s. 5; 1987, c. 565, s. 14; c. 583, s. 7; 1989, c. 770, s. 38; 1991, c. 727, s. 1; 1993, c. 553, s. 68; 1993 (Reg. Sess., 1994), c. 762, s. 58(d)-(g); 1999-424, s. 7(i); 2007-391, s. 17(a); 2013-381, s. 3.4.)

§ 163-276. Convicted officials; removal from office.

Any public official who shall be convicted of violating any provision of Article 14A or 22 of this Chapter, in addition to the punishment provided by law, shall be removed from office by the judge presiding, and, if the conviction is for a felony, shall be disqualified from voting until his citizenship is restored as provided by law. (1949, c. 504; 1967, c. 775, s. 1; 1985, c. 563, s. 11.3; 2002-159, s. 21(c).)

§ 163-277. Compelling self-incriminating testimony; person so testifying excused from prosecution.

No person shall be excused from attending or testifying or producing any books, papers or other documents before any court or magistrate upon any investigation, proceeding or trial for the violation of any of the provisions of this Article, upon the ground or for the reason that the testimony or evidence, documentary or otherwise, required of him may tend to incriminate or degrade him, but such person may be subpoenaed and required to testify by and for the State relative to any offense arising under the provisions of this Article; but such person shall not be prosecuted or subjected to any penalty or forfeiture for or on account of any transaction, matter or thing concerning which he may so testify or produce evidence, documentary or otherwise, and no testimony so given or produced shall be used against him upon any criminal investigation or proceeding, but such person so compelled to testify with respect to any acts of his own shall be immune from prosecution on account thereof, and shall be pardoned for any violation of law about which such person shall be so required to testify. (1931, c. 348, s. 11; 1967, c. 775, s. 1.)

§ 163-278. Duty of investigating and prosecuting violations of this Article.

It shall be the duty of the State Board of Elections and the district attorneys to investigate any violations of this Article, and the Board and district attorneys are authorized and empowered to subpoena and compel the attendance of any person before them for the purpose of making such investigation. The State Board of Elections and the district attorneys are authorized to call upon the Attorney General to furnish assistance by the State Bureau of Investigation in making the investigations of such violations. The State Board of Elections shall furnish the district attorney a copy of its investigation. The district attorney shall initiate prosecution and prosecute any violations of this Article. The provisions of G.S. 163-278.28 shall be applicable to violations of this Article. (1931, c. 348, s. 12; 1967, c. 775, s. 1; 1975, c. 565, s. 7.)

§§ 116-278.1 through 116-278.4. Reserved for future codification purposes.

Article 22A.

Regulating Contributions and Expenditures in Political Campaigns.

Part 1. In General.

§ 163-278.5. Scope of Article; severability.

The provisions of this Article apply to primaries and elections for North Carolina offices and to North Carolina referenda and do not apply to primaries and elections for federal offices or offices in other States or to non-North Carolina referenda. Any provision in this Article that regulates a non-North Carolina entity does so only to the extent that the entity's actions affect elections for North Carolina offices or North Carolina referenda.

The provisions of this Article are severable. If any provision is held invalid by a court of competent jurisdiction, the invalidity does not affect other provisions of the Article that can be given effect without the invalid provision.

This section applies to Articles and [Article] 22M of the General Statutes to the same extent that it applies to this Article. (1999-31, s. 6(a); 2000-140, s. 82; 2005-430, s. 7; 2007-349, s. 5; 2009-534, s. 6; 2013-360, s. 21.1(d); 2013-381, ss. 38.1(g), 48.2.)

§ 163-278.6. Definitions.

When used in this Article:

(1) The term "board" means the State Board of Elections with respect to all candidates for State, legislative, and judicial offices and the county board of elections with respect to all candidates for county and municipal offices. The term means the State Board of Elections with respect to all statewide referenda and the county board of elections conducting all local referenda.

(2) The term "broadcasting station" means any commercial radio or television station or community antenna radio or television station. Special definitions of "radio" and "television" that apply only in Part 1A of this Article are set forth in G.S. 163-278.38Z.

(3) The term "business entity" means any partnership, joint venture, joint-stock company, company, firm, or any commercial or industrial establishment or enterprise.

(4) The term "candidate" means any individual who, with respect to a public office listed in G.S. 163-278.6(18), has taken positive action for the purpose of bringing about that individual's nomination or election to public office. Examples of positive action include:

a. Filing a notice of candidacy or a petition requesting to be a candidate,

b. Being certified as a nominee of a political party for a vacancy,

c. Otherwise qualifying as a candidate in a manner authorized by law,

d. Making a public announcement of a definite intent to run for public office in a particular election, or

e. Receiving funds or making payments or giving the consent for anyone else to receive funds or transfer anything of value for the purpose of bringing about that individual's nomination or election to office. Transferring anything of value includes incurring an obligation to transfer anything of value.

Status as a candidate for the purpose of this Article continues if the individual is receiving contributions to repay loans or cover a deficit or is making expenditures to satisfy obligations from an election already held. Special definitions of "candidate" and "candidate campaign committee" that apply only in Part 1A of this Article are set forth in G.S. 163-278.38Z.

(5) The term "communications media" or "media" means broadcasting stations, carrier current stations, newspapers, magazines, periodicals, outdoor advertising facilities, billboards, newspaper inserts, and any person or individual whose business is polling public opinion, analyzing or predicting voter behavior or voter preferences. Special definitions of "print media," "radio," and "television" that apply only in Part 1A of this Article are set forth in G.S. 163-278.38Z.

(6) The terms "contribute" or "contribution" mean any advance, conveyance, deposit, distribution, transfer of funds, loan, payment, gift, pledge or subscription of money or anything of value whatsoever, made to, or in coordination with, a candidate to support or oppose the nomination or election of one or more clearly identified candidates, to a political committee, to a political party, or to a referendum committee, whether or not made in an election year, and any contract, agreement, or other obligation to make a contribution. An expenditure forgiven by a person or entity to whom it is owed shall be reported as a contribution from that person or entity. These terms include, without limitation, such contributions as labor or personal services, postage, publication of campaign literature or materials, in-kind transfers, loans or use of any supplies, office machinery, vehicles, aircraft, office space, or similar or related services, goods, or personal or real property. These terms also include, without limitation, the proceeds of sale of services, campaign literature and materials, wearing

apparel, tickets or admission prices to campaign events such as rallies or dinners, and the proceeds of sale of any campaign-related services or goods. Notwithstanding the foregoing meanings of "contribution," the word shall not be construed to include services provided without compensation by individuals volunteering a portion or all of their time on behalf of a candidate, political committee, or referendum committee. The term "contribution" does not include an "independent expenditure." If:

a. Any individual, person, committee, association, or any other organization or group of individuals, including but not limited to, a political organization (as defined in section 527(e)(1) of the Internal Revenue Code of 1986) makes, or contracts to make, any disbursement for any electioneering communication, as defined in this section; and

b. That disbursement is coordinated with a candidate, an authorized political committee of that candidate, a State or local political party or committee of that party, or an agent or official of any such candidate, party, or committee

that disbursement or contracting shall be treated as a contribution to the candidate supported by the electioneering communication or that candidate's party and as an expenditure by that candidate or that candidate's party.

(6a) (6f) [Reserved.]

(6g) The term "coordinated expenditure" means an expenditure that is made in concert or cooperation with, or at the request or suggestion of, a candidate, a candidate campaign committee as defined in G.S. 163-278.38Z(3), the agent of the candidate, or the agent of the candidate campaign committee. An expenditure for the distribution of information relating to a candidate's campaign, positions, or policies, that is obtained through publicly available resources, including a candidate campaign committee, is not a coordinated expenditure if it is not made in concert or cooperation with, or at the request or suggestion of, a candidate, the candidate campaign committee, the agent of the candidate, or the agent of the candidate campaign committee.

(6h) The term "coordination" means in concert or cooperation with, or at the request or suggestion of.

(7) The term "corporation" means any corporation established under either domestic or foreign charter, and includes a corporate subsidiary and any business entity in which a corporation participates or is a stockholder, a partner

or a joint venturer. The term applies regardless of whether the corporation does business in the State of North Carolina.

(7a) The term "costs of collection" means monies spent by the State Board of Elections in the collection of the penalties levied under this Article to the extent the costs do not constitute more than fifty percent (50%) of the civil penalty. The costs are presumed to be ten percent (10%) of the civil penalty unless otherwise determined by the State Board of Elections based on the records of expenses incurred by the State Board of Elections for its collection procedures.

(7b) The term "day" means calendar day.

(7c) The term "election cycle" means the period of time from January 1 after an election for an office through December 31 after the election for the next term of the same office. Where the term is applied in the context of several offices with different terms, "election cycle" means the period from January 1 of an odd-numbered year through December 31 of the next even-numbered year.

(8) The term "election" means any general or special election, a first or second primary, a run-off election, or an election to fill a vacancy. The term "election" shall not include any local or statewide referendum.

(8a) Recodified as (8p).

(8b) (8i) [Reserved.]

(8j) The term "electioneering communication" means any broadcast, cable, or satellite communication, or mass mailing, or telephone bank that has all the following characteristics:

a. Refers to a clearly identified candidate for elected office.

b. In the case of the general election in November of the even-numbered year is aired or transmitted after September 7 of that year, and in the case of any other election is aired or transmitted within 60 days of the time set for absentee voting to begin pursuant to G.S. 163-227.2 in an election for that office.

c. May be received by either:

1. 50,000 or more individuals in the State in an election for statewide office or 7,500 or more individuals in any other election if in the form of broadcast, cable, or satellite communication.

2. 20,000 or more households, cumulative per election, in a statewide election or 2,500 households, cumulative per election, in any other election if in the form of mass mailing or telephone bank.

(8k) The term "electioneering communication" does not include any of the following:

a. A communication appearing in a news story, commentary, or editorial distributed through the facilities of any broadcasting station, unless those facilities are owned or controlled by any political party, political committee, or candidate.

b. A communication that constitutes an expenditure or independent expenditure under this Article.

c. A communication that constitutes a candidate debate or forum conducted pursuant to rules adopted by the Board or that solely promotes that debate or forum and is made by or on behalf of the person sponsoring the debate or forum.

d. A communication made while the General Assembly is in session which, incidental to advocacy for or against a specific piece of legislation pending before the General Assembly, urges the audience to communicate with a member or members of the General Assembly concerning that piece of legislation or a solicitation of others as defined in G.S. 120C-100(a)(13) properly reported under Chapter 120C of the General Statutes.

e. A communication that meets all of the following criteria:

1. Does not mention any election, candidacy, political party, opposing candidate, or voting by the general public.

2. Does not take a position on the candidate's character or qualifications and fitness for office.

3. Proposes a commercial transaction.

f. A public opinion poll conducted by a news medium, as defined in G.S. 8-53.11(a)(3), conducted by an organization whose primary purpose is to conduct or publish public opinion polls, or contracted for by a person to be conducted by an organization whose primary purpose is to conduct or publish public opinion polls. This sub-subdivision shall not apply to a push poll. For the purpose of this sub-subdivision, "push poll" shall mean the political campaign technique in which an individual or organization attempts to influence or alter the view of respondents under the guise of conducting a public opinion poll.

g. A communication made by a news medium, as defined in G.S. 8-53.11(a)(3), if the communication is in print.

(8l) (8o) [Reserved.]

(8p) The term "enforcement costs" means salaries, overhead, and other monies spent by the State Board of Elections in the enforcement of the penalties provisions of this Article, including the costs of investigators, attorneys, travel costs for State Board employees and its attorneys, to the extent the costs do not constitute more than fifty percent (50%) of the sum levied for the enforcement costs and civil late penalty.

(9) The terms "expend" or "expenditure" mean any purchase, advance, conveyance, deposit, distribution, transfer of funds, loan, payment, gift, pledge or subscription of money or anything of value whatsoever, whether or not made in an election year, and any contract, agreement, or other obligation to make an expenditure, to support or oppose the nomination, election, or passage of one or more clearly identified candidates, or ballot measure. An expenditure forgiven by a person or entity to whom it is owed shall be reported as a contribution from that person or entity. Supporting or opposing the election of clearly identified candidates includes supporting or opposing the candidates of a clearly identified political party. The term "expenditure" also includes any payment or other transfer made by a candidate, political committee, or referendum committee.

(9a) The term "independently expend" or "independent expenditure" means an expenditure to support or oppose the nomination or election of one or more clearly identified candidates that is not a coordinated expenditure. Supporting or opposing the election of clearly identified candidates includes supporting or opposing the candidates of a clearly identified political party. A contribution is not an independent expenditure. As applied to referenda, the term "independent expenditure" applies if consultation or coordination does not take place with a referendum committee that supports a ballot measure the expenditure supports, or a referendum committee that opposes the ballot measure the expenditure opposes.

(10) The term "individual" means a single individual or more than one individual.

(11) The term "insurance company" means any person whose business is making or underwriting contracts of insurance, and includes mutual insurance companies, stock insurance companies, and fraternal beneficiary associations.

(12) The term "labor union" means any union, organization, combination or association of employees or workmen formed for the purposes of securing by united action favorable wages, improved labor conditions, better hours of labor or work-related benefits, or for handling, processing or righting grievances by employees against their employers, or for representing employees collectively or individually in dealings with their employers. The term includes any unions to which Article 10, Chapter 95 applies.

(12a) (12j) [Reserved.]

(12k) The term "mass mailing" means any mailing by United States mail or facsimile to 20,000 or more households, cumulative per election, in a statewide election or 2,500 households, cumulative per election, in any other election.

(13) The term "person" means any business entity, corporation, insurance company, labor union, or professional association.

(14) The term "political committee" means a combination of two or more individuals, such as any person, committee, association, organization, or other entity that makes, or accepts anything of value to make, contributions or expenditures and has one or more of the following characteristics:

a. Is controlled by a candidate;

b. Is a political party or executive committee of a political party or is controlled by a political party or executive committee of a political party;

c. Is created by a corporation, business entity, insurance company, labor union, or professional association pursuant to G.S. 163-278.19(b); or

d. Has the major purpose to support or oppose the nomination or election of one or more clearly identified candidates.

Supporting or opposing the election of clearly identified candidates includes supporting or opposing the candidates of a clearly identified political party. If the entity qualifies as a "political committee" under sub-subdivision a., b., c., or d. of this subdivision, it continues to be a political committee if it receives contributions or makes expenditures or maintains assets or liabilities. A political committee ceases to exist when it winds up its operations, disposes of its assets, and files its final report.

The term "political committee" includes the campaign of a candidate who serves as his or her own treasurer.

Special definitions of "political action committee" and "candidate campaign committee" that apply only in Part 1A of this Article are set forth in G.S. 163-278.38Z.

(15) The term "political party" means any political party organized or operating in this State, whether or not that party is recognized under the provisions of G.S. 163-96. A special definition of "political party organization" that applies only in Part 1A of this Article is set forth in G.S. 163-278.38Z.

(16) Repealed by Session Laws 1999-31, s. 4.

(17) The term "professional association" means any trade association, group, organization, association, or collection of persons or individuals formed for the purposes of advancing, representing, improving, furthering or preserving the interests of persons or individuals having a common vocation, profession, calling, occupation, employment, or training.

(18) The term "public office" means any office filled by election by the people on a statewide, county, municipal or district basis, and this Article shall be applicable to such elective offices whether the election therefor is partisan or nonpartisan.

(18a) The term "referendum" means any question, issue, or act referred to a vote of the people of the entire State by the General Assembly, a unit of local government, or by the people under any applicable local act and includes constitutional amendments and State bond issues. The term "referendum" includes any type of municipal, county, or special district referendum and any initiative or referendum authorized by a municipal charter or local act. A recall election shall not be considered a referendum within the meaning of this Article.

(18b) The term "referendum committee" means a combination of two or more individuals such as a committee, association, organization, or other entity or a combination of two or more business entities, corporations, insurance companies, labor unions, or professional associations such as a committee, association, organization, or other entity the primary purpose of which is to support or oppose the passage of any referendum on the ballot. If the entity qualifies as a "referendum committee" under this subdivision, it continues to be a referendum committee if it receives contributions or makes expenditures or maintains assets or liabilities. A referendum committee ceases to exist when it winds up its operations, disposes of its assets, and files its final report.

(18c) (18j) [Reserved.]

(18k) The term "telephone bank" means telephone calls that are targeted to the relevant electorate, except when those telephone calls are made by volunteer workers, whether or not the design of the telephone bank system, development of calling instructions, or training of volunteers was done by paid professionals.

(19) The term "treasurer" means an individual appointed by a candidate, political committee, or referendum committee as provided in G.S. 163-278.7 or G.S. 163-278.40A. (1973, c. 1272, s. 1; 1975, c. 798, ss. 5, 6; 1979, c. 500, s. 1; c. 1073, ss. 1-3, 19, 20; 1981, c. 837, s. 1; 1983, c. 331, s. 6; 1985, c. 352, ss. 1-3; 1997-515, ss. 4(a)-(c), 7(b)-(d); 1999-31, ss. 1(a), (b), 2(a)-(c), 3, 4(a); 1999-424, s. 6(a), (b); 2002-159, s. 55(n); 2003-278, s. 5; 2004-125, s. 3; 2004-127, s. 15; 2004-203, s. 12(b); 2005-430, s. 10; 2006-264, s. 23; 2007-391, s. 3; 2008-150, s. 6(a); 2008-187, s. 33(a); 2009-534, ss. 1, 3(a), (b); 2010-170, s. 1; 2011-31, s. 20; 2013-381, s. 50.1.)

§ 163-278.7. Appointment of political treasurers.

(a) Each candidate, political committee, and referendum committee shall appoint a treasurer and, under verification, report the name and address of the treasurer to the Board. Only an individual who resides in North Carolina shall be appointed as a treasurer. A candidate may appoint himself or any other individual, including any relative except his spouse, as his treasurer, and, upon failure to file report designating a treasurer, the candidate shall be concluded to have appointed himself as treasurer and shall be required to personally fulfill the duties and responsibilities imposed upon the appointed treasurer and subject to the penalties and sanctions hereinafter provided.

(b) Each appointed treasurer shall file with the Board at the time required by G.S. 163-278.9(a)(1) a statement of organization that includes:

(1) The Name, Address and Purpose of the Candidate, Political Committee, or Referendum Committee. - When the political committee or referendum committee is created pursuant to G.S. 163-278.19(b), the name shall be or include the name of the corporation, insurance company, business entity, labor union or professional association whose officials, employees, or members established the committee. When the political committee or referendum committee is not created pursuant to G.S. 163-278.19(b), the name shall be or include the economic interest, if identifiable, principally represented by the committee's organizers or intended to be advanced by use of the committee's receipts.

(2) The names, addresses, and relationships of affiliated or connected candidates, political committees, referendum committees, political parties, or similar organizations;

(3) The territorial area, scope, or jurisdiction of the candidate, political committee, or referendum committee;

(4) The name, address, and position with the candidate or political committee of the custodian of books and accounts;

(5) The name and party affiliation of the candidate(s) whom the committee is supporting or opposing, and the office(s) involved;

(5a) The name of the referendum(s) which the referendum committee is supporting or opposing, and whether the committee is supporting or opposing the referendum;

(6) The name of the political committee or political party being supported or opposed if the committee is supporting the ticket of a particular political or political party;

(7) A listing of all banks, safety deposit boxes, or other depositories used, including the names and numbers of all accounts maintained and the numbers

of all such safety deposit boxes used, provided that the Board shall keep any account number included in any report filed after March 1, 2003, and required by this Article confidential except as necessary to conduct an audit or investigation, except as required by a court of competent jurisdiction, or unless confidentiality is waived by the treasurer. Disclosure of an account number in violation of this subdivision shall not give rise to a civil cause of action. This limitation of liability does not apply to the disclosure of account numbers in violation of this subdivision as a result of gross negligence, wanton conduct, or intentional wrongdoing that would otherwise be actionable.

(8)   The name or names and address or addresses of any assistant treasurers appointed by the treasurer. Such assistant treasurers shall be authorized to act in the name of the candidate, political committee, or referendum committee and shall be fully responsible for any act or acts committed by the assistant treasurer. The treasurer shall be fully liable for any violation of this Article committed by any assistant treasurer; and

(9)   Any other information which might be requested by the Board that deals with the campaign organization of the candidate or referendum committee.

(c)   Any change in information previously submitted in a statement of organization shall be reported to the Board within a 10-day period following the change.

(d)   A candidate, political committee or referendum committee may remove his or its treasurer. In case of the death, resignation or removal of his or its treasurer before compliance with all obligations of a treasurer under this Article, such candidate, political committee or referendum committee shall appoint a successor within 10 days of the vacancy of such office, and certify the name and address of the successor in the manner provided in the case of an original appointment.

(e)   Every treasurer of a referendum committee shall receive, prior to every election in which the referendum committee is involved, training from the State Board of Elections as to the duties of the office, including the requirements of G.S. 163-278.13(e1), provided that the treasurer may designate an employee or volunteer of the committee to receive the training.

(f)   Every treasurer of a political committee shall participate in training as to the duties of the office within three months of appointment and at least once every four years thereafter. The State Board of Elections shall provide the training as to the duties of the office in person, through regional seminars, and through interactive electronic means. The treasurer may designate an assistant treasurer to participate in the training, if one is named under subdivision (b)(8) of this section. The treasurer may choose to participate in training prior to each election in which the political committee is involved. All such training shall be free of charge to the treasurer and assistant treasurer. (1973, c. 1272, s. 1; 1979, c. 500, s. 2; c. 1073, ss. 4, 5, 16, 18, 20; 1987, c. 113, s. 1; 1995, c. 315, s. 1; 2002-159, s. 57.1(a); 2004-203, s. 59(a); 2005-430, s. 10.1; 2006-195, s. 7; 2009-534, s. 4.)

§ 163-278.7A. Gifts from federal political committees.

It shall be permissible for a federal political committee, as defined by the Federal Election Campaign Act and regulations adopted pursuant thereto, to make contributions to a North Carolina candidate or political committee registered under this Article with the State Board of Elections or a county board of elections, provided that the contributing committee does all the following:

(1) Is registered with the State Board of Elections consistent with the provisions of this Article.

(2) Complies with reporting requirements specified by the State Board of Elections. Those requirements shall not be more stringent than those required of North Carolina political committees registered under this Article, unless the federal political committee makes any contribution to a North Carolina candidate or political committee in any election in excess of four thousand dollars ($4,000) for that election. "Election" shall be as defined in G.S. 163-278.13(d).

(3) Makes its contributions within the limits specified in this Article.

(4) Appoints an assistant or deputy treasurer who is a resident of North Carolina and stipulates to the State Board of Elections that the designated in-State resident assistant or deputy treasurer shall be authorized to produce whatever records reflecting political activity in North Carolina the State Board of Elections deems necessary. (1995 (Reg. Sess., 1996), c. 593, s. 1; 2003-274, s. 1.)

§ 163-278.8. Detailed accounts to be kept by political treasurers.

(a) The treasurer of each candidate, political committee, and referendum committee shall keep detailed accounts, current within not more than seven days after the date of receiving a contribution or making an expenditure, of all contributions received and all expenditures made by or on behalf of the candidate, political committee, or referendum committee. The accounts shall include the information required by the State Board of Elections on its forms.

(b) Accounts kept by the treasurer of a candidate, political committee, or referendum committee or the accounts of a treasurer or political committee at any bank or other depository listed under G.S. 163-278.7(b)(7), may be inspected, before or after the election to which the accounts refer, by a member, designee, agent, attorney or employee of the Board who is making an investigation pursuant to G.S. 163-278.22.

(c) Repealed by Session Laws 2004-125, s. 5(a), effective July 20, 2004, and applicable to contributions made on or after January 1, 2003.

(d) Repealed by Session Laws 2006-195, s. 4, effective January 1, 2007, and applicable to all contributions made and accepted on or after that date.

(e) All expenditures for media expenses shall be made by a verifiable form of payment. The State Board of Elections shall prescribe methods to ensure an audit trail for every expenditure so that the identity of each payee can be determined. All media expenditures in any amount shall be accounted for and reported individually and separately with specific descriptions to provide a reasonable understanding of the expenditure.

(f) All expenditures for nonmedia expenses (except postage) of more than fifty dollars ($50.00) shall be made by a verifiable form of payment. The State Board of Elections shall prescribe methods to ensure an audit trail for every expenditure so that the identity of each payee can be determined. All expenditures for nonmedia expenses of fifty dollars ($50.00) or less may be made by check or by cash payment. All nonmedia expenditures of more than fifty dollars ($50.00) shall be accounted for and reported individually and separately with a specific description to provide a reasonable understanding of the expenditure, but expenditures of fifty dollars ($50.00) or less may be accounted for and reported in an aggregated amount, but in that case the treasurer shall account for and report that the treasurer made expenditures of fifty dollars ($50.00) or less each, the amounts, dates, and the purposes for which made. In the case of a nonmedia expenditure required to be accounted for individually and separately with a specific description to provide a reasonable understanding of the expenditure by this subsection, if the expenditure was to an individual, the report shall list the name and address of the individual.

(g) All proceeds from loans shall be recorded separately with a detailed analysis reflecting the amount of the loan, the source, the period, the rate of interest, and the security pledged, if any, and all makers and endorsers.

(h) The treasurer shall maintain all moneys of the political committee in a bank account or bank accounts used exclusively by the political committee and shall not commingle those funds with any other moneys. (1973, c. 1272, s. 1; 1977, c. 635, s. 1; 1979, c. 1073, ss. 16, 20; 1981, c. 814, s. 1; 1985, c. 353, ss. 1, 2; 1993 (Reg. Sess., 1994), c. 744, s. 1; 1999-424, s. 7(m); 2004-125, s. 5(a); 2005-430, ss. 2, 3; 2006-161, ss. 2, 3; 2006-195, s. 4; 2008-150, s. 10(a).)

§ 163-278.8A. (For effective date and applicability, see Editor's note) Campaign sales by political party executive committees.

(a) Exempt Purchase Price Not Treated as "Contribution." - Notwithstanding the provisions of G.S. 163-278.6(6), the purchase price of goods or services sold by a political party executive committee as provided in subsection (b) of this section shall not be treated as a "contribution" for purposes of account-keeping under G.S. 163-278.8, for purposes of the reporting of contributions under G.S. 163-278.11, or for the purpose of the limit on contributions under G.S. 163-278.13. The treasurer is not required to obtain, maintain, or report the name or other identifying information of the purchaser of the goods or services, as long as the requirements of subsection (b) of this section are satisfied. However, the proceeds from the sales of those goods and services shall be treated as contributions for other purposes, and expenditures of those proceeds shall be reported as expenditures under this Article.

(b) Exempt Purchase Price. - A purchase price for goods or services sold by a political party executive committee qualifies for the exemption provided in subsection (a) of this section as long as the sale of the goods or services adheres to a plan that the treasurer has submitted to and that has been approved in writing by the Executive Director of the State Board of Elections. The Executive Director shall approve the treasurer's plan upon and only upon finding that all the following requirements are satisfied:

(1) That the price to be charged for the goods or services is reasonably close to the market price for the goods or services.

(2) That the total amount to be raised from sales under all plans by the committee does not exceed ten thousand dollars ($10,000) per election cycle.

(3) That no purchaser makes total purchases under the plan that exceed fifty dollars ($50.00).

(4) That the treasurer include in the report under G.S. 163-278.11, covering the relevant time period, all of the following:

a. A description of the plan.

b. The amount raised from sales under the plan.

c. The number of purchases made.

(5) That the treasurer shall include in the appropriate report under G.S. 163-278.11 any in-kind contribution made to the political party executive committee in providing the goods or services sold under the plan and that no in-kind contribution accepted as part of the plan violates any provision of this Article.

The Executive Director may require a format for submission of a plan, but that format shall not place undue paperwork burdens upon the treasurer. As used in this subdivision, the term "election cycle" has the same meaning as in G.S. 163-278.6(7c). (2008-150, s. 8(a).)

§ 163-278.9. Statements filed with Board.

(a) Except as provided in G.S. 163-278.10A, the treasurer of each candidate and of each political committee shall file with the Board under certification of the treasurer as true and correct to the best of the knowledge of that officer the following reports:

(1) Organizational Report. - The appointment of the treasurer as required by G.S. 163-278.7(a), the statement of organization required by G.S. 163-278.7(b), and a report of all contributions and expenditures not previously reported shall be filed with the Board no later than the tenth day following the day the candidate files notice of candidacy or the tenth day following the organization of the political committee, whichever occurs first. Any candidate whose campaign is being conducted by a political committee which is handling all contributions and expenditures for his campaign shall file a statement with the Board stating

such fact at the time required herein for the organizational report. Thereafter, the candidate's political committee shall be responsible for filing all reports required by law.

(2)   Repealed by Session Laws 1999-31, s. 7(a), effective January 1, 2000.

(3)   Postprimary Report(s). - Repealed by Session Laws 1997-515, s. 1.

(4)   Preelection Report. - Repealed by Session Laws 1997-515, s. 1.

(4a)   48-Hour Report. - A political committee or political party that receives a contribution or transfer of funds shall disclose within 48 hours of receipt a contribution or transfer of one thousand dollars ($1,000) or more received before an election but after the period covered by the last report due before that election. The disclosure shall be by report to the State Board of Elections identifying the source and amount of the funds. The State Board of Elections shall specify the form and manner of making the report, including the reporting of in-kind contributions.

(5)   Repealed by Session Laws 1985, c. 164, s. 1.

(5a)   Quarterly Reports. - During even-numbered years during which there is an election for that candidate or in which the campaign committee is supporting or opposing a candidate, the treasurer shall file a report by mailing or otherwise delivering it to the Board no later than seven working days after the end of each calendar quarter covering the prior calendar quarter, except that:

a.   The report for the first quarter shall also cover the period in April through the seventeenth day before the primary, the first quarter report shall be due seven days after that date, and the second quarter report shall not include that period if a first quarter report was required to be filed; and

b.   The report for the third quarter shall also cover the period in October through the seventeenth day before the election, the third quarter report shall be due seven days after that date, and the fourth quarter report shall not include that period if a third quarter report was required to be filed.

(6)   Semiannual Reports. - If contributions are received or expenditures made for which no reports are otherwise required by this Article, any and all such contributions and expenditures shall be reported by the last Friday in July,

covering the period through the last day of June, and shall be reported by the last Friday in January, covering the period through the last day of December.

(b)   Except as otherwise provided in this Article, each report shall be current within seven days prior to the date the report is due and shall list all contributions received and expenditures made which have not been previously reported.

(c)   Repealed by Session Laws 1985, c. 164, s. 6.1.

(d)   Candidates and committees for municipal offices are not subject to subsections (a), (b) and (c) of this section, unless they make contributions or expenditures concerning elections covered by this Part. Reports for those candidates and committees are covered by Part 2 of this Article.

(e)   Notwithstanding subsections (a) through (c) of this section, any political party (including a State, district, county, or precinct committee thereof) which is required to file reports under those subsections and under the Federal Election Campaign Act of 1971, as amended (2 U.S.C. 434), shall instead of filing the reports required by those subsections, file with the State Board of Elections:

(1)   The organizational report required by subsection (a)(1) of this section, and

(2)   A copy of each report required to be filed under 2 U.S.C. 434, such copy to be filed on the same day as the federal report is required to be filed.

(f)   Any report filed under subsection (e) of this section may include matter required by the federal law but not required by this Article.

(g)   Any report filed under subsection (e) of this section must contain all the information required by G.S. 163-278.11, notwithstanding that the federal law may set a higher reporting threshold.

(h)   Any report filed under subsection (e) of this section may reflect the cumulative totals required by G.S. 163-278.11 in an attachment, if the federal law does not permit such information in the body of the report.

(i)   Any report or attachment filed under subsection (e) of this section must be certified.

(j) Treasurers for the following entities shall electronically file each report required by this section that shows a cumulative total for the election cycle in excess of five thousand dollars ($5,000) in contributions, in expenditures, or in loans, according to rules adopted by the State Board of Elections:

(1) A candidate for statewide office;

(2) A State, district, county, or precinct executive committee of a political party, if the committee makes contributions or independent expenditures in excess of five thousand dollars ($5,000) that affect contests for statewide office;

(3) A political committee that makes contributions in excess of five thousand dollars ($5,000) to candidates for statewide office or makes independent expenditures in excess of five thousand dollars ($5,000) that affect contests for statewide office.

The State Board of Elections shall provide the software necessary to file an electronic report to a treasurer required to file an electronic report at no cost to the treasurer.

(k) All reports under this section must be filed by a treasurer or assistant treasurer who has completed all training as to the duties of the office required by G.S. 163-278.7(f). (1973, c. 1272, s. 1; 1975, c. 565, s. 1; 1979, c. 500, ss. 3, 16; c. 730; 1981, c. 837, s. 2; 1985, c. 164, ss. 1, 6-6.2; 1987 (Reg. Sess., 1988), c. 1028, s. 6; 1991 (Reg. Sess., 1992), c. 1032, s. 10A; 1997-515, ss. 1(a), 4(d1), 5(a), 12(a); 1999-31, s. 7(a), (b); 2001-235, s. 2; 2001-419, s. 7; 2001-487, s. 97(b); 2002-159, s. 21(d); 2006-195, ss. 5.1, 8; 2008-150, ss. 9(c), (d), 11(a).)

§ 163-278.9A. Statements filed by referendum committees.

(a) The treasurer of each referendum committee shall file under verification with the Board the following reports:

(1) Organizational Report. - The appointment of the treasurer as required by G.S. 163-278.7(a), the statement of organization required by G.S. 163-278.7(b), and a report of all contributions and expenditures shall be filed with the Board no later than the tenth day following the organization of the referendum committee.

(2) Pre-Referendum Report. - The treasurer shall file a report with the Board no later than the tenth day preceding the referendum.

(2a) 48-Hour Report. - A referendum committee that receives a contribution or transfer of funds shall disclose within 48 hours of receipt a contribution or transfer of one thousand dollars ($1,000) or more received before a referendum but after the period covered by the last report due before that referendum. The disclosure shall be by report to the State Board of Elections identifying the source and amount of such funds. The State Board of Elections shall specify the form and manner of making the report, including the reporting of in-kind contributions.

(3) Final Report. - The treasurer shall file a final report no later than the tenth day after the referendum. If the final report fails to disclose a final accounting of all contributions and expenditures, a supplemental final report shall be filed no later than January 7, after the referendum, and shall be current through December 31 after the referendum.

(4) Annual Reports. - If contributions are received or expenditures made during a calendar year for which no reports are otherwise required by this Article, any and all such contributions and expenditures shall be reported by January 7 of the following year.

(b) Except as otherwise provided in this Article, each report shall be current within seven days prior to the date the report is due and shall list all contributions received and expenditures made which have not been previously reported. (1979, c. 1073, s. 6; 1997-515, s. 12(b); 2002-159, s. 21(e); 2008-150, s. 11(b).)

§ 163-278.10. Procedure for inactive candidate or committee.

If no contribution is received or expenditure made by or on behalf of a candidate, political committee, or referendum committee during a period described in G.S. 163-278.9, the treasurer shall file with the Board, at the time required by G.S. 163-278.9, a statement to that effect and it shall not be required that any inactive candidate or committee so filing a report of inactivity file any additional reports required by G.S. 163-278.9 so long as the candidate or committee remains inactive. (1973, c. 1272, s. 1; 1979, c. 1073, s. 20.)

§ 163-278.10A. Threshold of $1,000 for financial reports for certain candidates.

(a) Notwithstanding any other provision of this Chapter, a candidate for a county office, municipal office, local school board office, soil and water conservation district board of supervisors, or sanitary district board shall be exempted from the reports of contributions, loans, and expenditures required in G.S. 163-278.9(a), 163-278.40B, 163-278.40C, 163-278.40D, and 163-278.40E if to further the candidate's campaign that candidate:

(1) Does not receive more than one thousand dollars ($1,000) in contributions, and

(2) Does not receive more than one thousand dollars ($1,000) in loans, and

(3) Does not spend more than one thousand dollars ($1,000).

To qualify for the exemption from those reports, the candidate's treasurer shall file a certification that the candidate does not intend to receive in contributions or loans or expend more than one thousand dollars ($1,000) to further the candidate's campaign. The certification shall be filed with the Board at the same time the candidate files the candidate's Organizational Report as required in G.S. 163-278.7, G.S. 163-278.9, and G.S. 163-278.40A. If the candidate's campaign is being conducted by a political committee which is handling all contributions, loans, and expenditures for the candidate's campaign, the treasurer of the political committee shall file a certification of intent to stay within the threshold amount. If the intent to stay within the threshold changes, or if the one-thousand-dollar ($1,000) threshold is exceeded, the treasurer shall immediately notify the Board and shall be responsible for filing all reports required in G.S. 163-278.9 and 163-278.40B, 163-278.40C, 163-278.40D, and 163-278.40E; provided that any contribution, loan, or expenditure which would have been required to be reported on an earlier report but for this section shall be included on the next report required after the intent changes or the threshold is exceeded.

(b) The exemption from reporting in subsection (a) of this section applies to political party committees under the same terms as for candidates, except that the term "to further the candidate's campaign" does not relate to a political party committee's exemption, and all contributions, expenditures, and loans during an election shall be counted against the political party committee's threshold amount. (1987 (Reg. Sess., 1988), c. 1028, s. 2; c. 1081, s. 3; 1989, c. 449; c. 770, s. 53; 1997-515, s. 4(e); 2001-235, s. 3; 2009-534, s. 5.)

§ 163-278.11. Contents of treasurer's statement of receipts and expenditures.

(a) Statements filed pursuant to provisions of this Article shall set forth the following:

(1) Contributions. - Except as provided in subsection (a1) of this section, a list of all contributions received by or on behalf of a candidate, political committee, or referendum committee. The statement shall list the name and complete mailing address of each contributor, the amount contributed, the principal occupation of the contributor, and the date such contribution was received. The total sum of all contributions to date shall be plainly exhibited. Forms for required reports shall be prescribed by the Board. As used in this section, "principal occupation of the contributor" means the contributor's:

a. Job title or profession; and

b. Employer's name or employer's specific field of business activity.

The State Board of Elections shall prepare a schedule of specific fields of business activity, adapting or modifying as it deems suitable the business activity classifications of the Internal Revenue Code or other relevant classification schedules. In reporting a contributor's specific field of business activity, the treasurer shall use the classification schedule prepared by the State Board.

(2) Expenditures. - A list of all expenditures required under G.S. 163-278.8 made by or on behalf of a candidate, political committee, or referendum committee. The statement shall list the name and complete mailing address of each payee, the amount paid, the purpose, and the date such payment was made. The total sum of all expenditures to date shall be plainly exhibited. Forms for required reports shall be prescribed by the Board. In accounting for all expenditures in accordance with G.S. 163-278.8(e) and G.S. 163-278.8(f), the payee shall be the individual or person to whom the candidate, political committee, or referendum committee is obligated to make the expenditure. If the expenditure is to a financial institution for revolving credit or a reimbursement for a payment to a financial institution for revolving credit, the statement shall also include a specific itemization of the goods and services purchased with the revolving credit. If the obligation is for more than one good or service, the statement shall include a specific itemization of the obligation so as to provide a reasonable understanding of the obligation.

(3) Loans. - Every candidate and treasurer shall attach to the campaign transmittal submitted with each report an addendum listing all proceeds derived from loans for funds used or to be used in this campaign. The addendum shall be in the form as prescribed by the State Board of Elections and shall list the amount of the loan, the source, the period, the rate of interest, and the security pledged, if any, and all makers and endorsers.

(a1) Threshold for Reporting Identity of Contributor. - A treasurer shall not be required to report the name, address, or principal occupation of any individual who contributes fifty dollars ($50.00) or less to the treasurer's committee during an election as defined in G.S. 163-278.13. The State Board of Elections shall provide on its reporting forms for the reporting of contributions below that threshold. On those reporting forms, the State Board may require date and amount of contributions below the threshold, but may treat differently for reporting purposes contributions below the threshold that are made in different modes and in different settings.

(b) Statements shall reflect anything of value paid for or contributed by any person or individual, both as a contribution and expenditure. A political party executive committee that makes an expenditure that benefits a candidate or group of candidates shall report the expenditure, including the date, amount, and purpose of the expenditure and the name of and office sought by the candidate or candidates on whose behalf the expenditure was made. A candidate who benefits from the expenditure shall report the expenditure or the proportionate share of the expenditure from which the candidate benefitted as an in-kind contribution if the candidate or the candidate's committee has coordinated with the political party executive committee concerning the expenditure.

(c) Best Efforts. - When a treasurer shows that best efforts have been used to obtain, maintain, and submit the information required by this Article for the candidate or political committee, any report of that candidate or committee shall be considered in compliance with this Article and shall not be the basis for criminal prosecution or the imposition of civil penalties, other than forfeiture of a contribution improperly accepted under this Article. The State Board of Elections shall promulgate rules that specify what are "best efforts" for purposes of this Article, adapting as it deems suitable the provisions of 11 C.F.R. § 104.7. The rules shall include a provision that if the treasurer, after complying with this Article and the rules, does not know the occupation of the contributor, it shall suffice for the treasurer to report "unable to obtain". (1973, c. 1272, s. 1; 1977,

c. 635, s. 2; 1979, c. 1073, s. 20; 1997-515, ss. 2(a), (b), 3(a); 2006-161, s. 4; 2006-195, s. 5; 2007-391, s. 35(a); 2008-187, s. 33(a).)

§ 163-278.12. Special reporting of contributions and independent expenditures.

(a) Subject to G.S. 163-278.39 and G.S. 163-278.14, individuals and other entities not otherwise prohibited from doing so may make independent expenditures. In the event an individual, person, or other entity making independent expenditures but not otherwise required to report them makes independent expenditures in excess of one hundred dollars ($100.00), that individual, person, or entity shall file a statement of such independent expenditure with the appropriate board of elections in the manner prescribed by the State Board of Elections.

(b) Any person or entity other than an individual that is permitted to make contributions but is not otherwise required to report them shall report each contribution in excess of one hundred dollars ($100.00) with the appropriate board of elections in the manner prescribed by the State Board of Elections.

(c) In assuring compliance with subsections (a) and (b) of this section, the State Board of Elections shall require the identification of each person or entity making a donation of more than one hundred dollars ($100.00) to the entity filing the report if the donation was made to further the reported independent expenditure or contribution. If the donor is an individual, the statement shall also contain the principal occupation of the donor. The "principal occupation of the donor" shall mean the same as the "principal occupation of the contributor" in G.S. 163-278.11.

(d) Contributions or independent expenditures required to be reported under this section shall be reported within 30 days after they exceed one hundred dollars ($100.00) or 10 days before an election the contributions or independent expenditures affect, whichever occurs earlier.

(e) The State Board of Elections shall require subsequent reporting of independent expenditures according to the same schedule required of political committees under G.S. 163-278.9(a). An individual or person that makes an independent expenditure shall disclose by report to the State Board of Elections within 48 hours of incurring an expense of five thousand dollars ($5,000) or more or receiving a donation of one thousand dollars ($1,000) or more for making an independent expenditure before an election but after the period covered by the last report due before that election.

(f) For the purposes of subsection (c) of this section, a donation to the person or entity making the independent expenditure is deemed to have been donated to further the independent expenditure if any of subdivisions (1) through (4) of this subsection apply. For purposes of this subsection, the "filer" is the person or entity making the independent expenditure and responsible for filing the report, or an agent of that person or entity. For purposes of this subsection, the "donor" is the person or entity donating to the filer the funds or other thing of value, or an agent of that person or entity.

(1) The donor designates, requests, or suggests that the donation be used for an independent expenditure or for multiple independent expenditures, and the filer agrees to use the donation for an independent expenditure.

(2) The filer expressly solicited the donor for a donation for making or paying for an independent expenditure.

(3) The donor and the filer engaged in substantial written or oral discussion regarding the donor's making, donating, or paying for an independent expenditure.

(4) The donor or the filer knew or had reason to know of the filer's intent to make independent expenditures with the donation.

A donation shall not be deemed to be made to further an independent expenditure if the donation was a commercial transaction occurring in the ordinary course of business between the donor and the filer unless there is affirmative evidence that the amounts were donated to further an independent expenditure. In determining the amount of a donation that was made to further any particular independent expenditure, there shall be excluded any amount that was designated by the donor with respect to a different election than the election that is the subject of the independent expenditure covered by the report.

Subdivisions (1) through (4) of this subsection shall also apply to reports made under subsection (c) of this section concerning contributions. However, nothing in this section shall be interpreted to limit the effect of the prohibition on making contributions in the name of another in G.S. 163-278.14.

(g)   All reports required by this section shall be filed according to rules adopted by the State Board of Elections. If the expense incurred is greater than five thousand dollars ($5,000), the report shall be filed electronically. The State Board of Elections shall provide the software necessary to file the electronic report to any individual or person required to file an electronic report at no cost to that individual or person. (1973, c. 1272, s. 1; 1979, c. 107, s. 15; c. 1073, s. 20; 1999-31, s. 2(d); 2004-127, s. 16; 2010-170, s. 2.)

§ 163-278.12A: Repealed by Session Laws 2004-125, s. 4, effective July 20, 2004.

§ 163-278.12B: Reserved for future codification purposes.

§ 163-278.12C. Special reporting of electioneering communications.

(a)   Every individual or person that incurs an expense for the direct costs of producing or airing electioneering communications aggregating in excess of five thousand dollars ($5,000) shall file the following reports with the appropriate board of elections in the manner prescribed by the State Board of Elections:

(1)   The identification of the individual or person incurring the expense, of any individual or person sharing or exercising direction or control over the activities of that individual or person, and of the custodian of the books and accounts of the individual or person incurring the expense.

(2)   The principal place of business of the person incurring the expense, if not an individual.

(3)   The amount of each expense incurred during the period covered by the statement and the identification of the individual or person to whom the expense was incurred.

(4)   The elections to which the electioneering communications pertain, if any, and the names, if known, of the candidates identified or to be identified.

(5)   The names and addresses of all entities that donated, to further an electioneering communication or electioneering communications, funds or anything of value whatsoever in an aggregate amount of more than one thousand dollars ($1,000) during the reporting period. If the donor is an

individual, the statement shall also contain the principal occupation of the donor. The "principal occupation of the donor" shall mean the same as the "principal occupation of the contributor" in G.S. 163-278.11.

(b) The initial report shall be filed with the State Board no later than the 10th day following the day the individual or person incurs an expense for the direct costs of producing or airing an electioneering communication. The State Board shall require subsequent reporting according to the same schedule required of political committees under G.S. 163-278.9(a). An individual or person that produces or airs an electioneering communication shall disclose by report to the State Board within 48 hours of incurring an expense of five thousand dollars ($5,000) or more or receiving a donation of one thousand dollars ($1,000) or more for making an electioneering communication before an election but after the period covered by the last report due before that election.

(c) For the purposes of subdivision (a)(5) of this section, a donation to the person or entity making the electioneering communication is deemed to have been donated to further the electioneering communication if any of subdivisions (1) through (4) of this subsection apply. For purposes of this subsection, the "filer" is the person or entity making the electioneering communication and responsible for filing the report, or an agent of that person or entity. For purposes of this subsection, the "donor" is the person or entity donating to the filer the funds or other thing of value, or an agent of that person or entity.

(1) The donor designates, requests, or suggests that the donation be used for an electioneering communication or electioneering communications, and the filer agrees to use the donation for that purpose.

(2) The filer expressly solicited the donor for a donation for making or paying for an electioneering communication.

(3) The donor and the filer engaged in substantial written or oral discussion regarding the donor's making, donating, or paying for an electioneering communication.

(4) The donor or the filer knew or had reason to know of the filer's intent to make electioneering communication with the donation.

A donation shall not be deemed to be made to further an electioneering communication if the donation was a commercial transaction occurring in the ordinary course of business between the donor and the filer unless there is affirmative evidence that the amounts were donated to further an electioneering communication. In determining the amount of a donation that was made to further any particular electioneering communication, there shall be excluded any amount that was designated by the donor with respect to a different election than the election that is the subject of the electioneering communication covered by the report.

(d) All reports required by this section shall be filed according to rules adopted by the State Board. If the expense incurred is greater than five thousand dollars ($5,000), the report shall be filed electronically. The State Board shall provide the software necessary to file the electronic report to any individual or person required to file an electronic report at no cost to that individual or person. (2010-170, s. 3.)

§ 163-278.13. Limitation on contributions.

(a) No individual, political committee, or other entity shall contribute to any candidate or other political committee any money or make any other contribution in any election in excess of five thousand dollars ($5,000) for that election.

(a1) Effective for each odd-numbered calendar year beginning in 2015, the dollar amount of the contribution limitation established by subsections (a), (b), and (c) of this subsection shall be increased as provided in this subsection. On July 1 of each even-numbered year, the State Board of Elections shall calculate from data from the Bureau of Labor Statistics of the United States Department of Labor Register the percent difference between the price index for the July 1 of the previous even-numbered year. That percentage increase shall be multiplied by the previous dollar amount contribution limit, that number added to the previous dollar amount contribution limit, and the total shall become effective with respect to contributions made or accepted on or after January 1 of the next odd-numbered year. If the amount after adjustment is not a multiple of one hundred dollars ($100.00), the total shall be rounded to the nearest multiple of one hundred dollars ($100.00). As used in this subsection the term "price index" means the average over a calendar year of the Consumer Price Index (all items - United States city average) published monthly by the Bureau of Labor Statistics. The revised amount of the dollar limit of contributions shall remain in effect for two calendar years until the next adjustment is made. The State Board of Elections shall publish the revised amount in the North Carolina Register and shall notify the Reviser of Statutes who shall adjust the dollar amounts in subsections (a), (b), and (c) of this section.

(b) No candidate or political committee shall accept or solicit any contribution from any individual, other political committee, or other entity of any money or any other contribution in any election in excess of five thousand dollars ($5,000) for that election.

(c) Notwithstanding the provisions of subsections (a) and (b) of this section, it shall be lawful for a candidate or a candidate's spouse to make a contribution to the candidate or to the candidate's treasurer of any amount of money or to make any other contribution in any election in excess of five thousand dollars ($5,000) for that election.

(d) For the purposes of this section, the term "an election" means the period of time from January 1 of an odd-numbered year through the day of the primary, the day after the primary through the day of the second primary, or the day after the primary through December 31 of the next even-numbered year, without regard to whether the candidate is opposed or unopposed in the election, except that where a candidate is not on the ballot in a second primary, that second primary is not "an election" with respect to that candidate.

(d1) Notwithstanding subsections (a) and (b) of this section, a candidate or political committee may accept a contribution knowing that the contribution is to be reimbursed to the entity making the contribution and knowing the candidate or political committee has funds sufficient to reimburse the entity making the contribution if all of the following conditions are met:

(1) The entity submits sufficient information of the contribution to the candidate or political committee for reimbursement within 45 days of the contribution.

(2) The candidate or political committee makes a reimbursement to the entity making the contribution within seven days of submission of sufficient information.

(3) The candidate or political committee indicates on its report under G.S. 163-278.11 that the good, service, or other item resulting in the reimbursement is an expenditure of the candidate or political committee, and notes if the contribution was by credit card.

(4) The contribution does not exceed one thousand dollars ($1,000.00).

(d2) Any contribution, or portion thereof, made under subsection (d1) of this section that is not submitted for reimbursement in accordance with subsection (d1) of this section shall be treated as a contribution for purposes of this section. Any contribution, or portion thereof, made under subsection (d1) of this section that is not reimbursed in accordance with subsection (d1) of this section shall be treated as a contribution for purposes of this section.

(e) This section shall not apply to any national, State, district or county executive committee of any political party. For the purposes of this section only, the term "political party" means only those political parties officially recognized under G.S. 163-96.

(e1) No referendum committee which received any contribution from a corporation, labor union, insurance company, business entity, or professional association may make any contribution to another referendum committee, to a candidate or to a political committee.

(e2) Repealed by Session Laws 2013-360, s. 21.1(f) and Session Laws 2013-381, s 38.1(i), effective July 1, 2013.

(e3) Repealed by Session Laws 2013-381, s. 42.3, effective January 1, 2014.

(e4) Repealed by Session Laws 2013-381, s. 38.1(j), effective July 1, 2013.

(e5) The contribution limits of subsections (a) and (b) of this section do not apply to contributions made to an independent expenditure political committee. For purposes of this section, an "independent expenditure political committee" is a political committee whose treasurer makes and abides by a certification to the State Board of Elections that the political committee does not and will not make contributions, directly or indirectly, to candidates or to political committees that make contributions to candidates. The State Board of Elections shall provide forms for implementation of this subsection. This subsection shall not apply to a candidate or a political committee controlled by a candidate. The exception of this subsection is in addition to any other exception provided by law.

(f) Repealed by Session Laws 2013-360, s. 21.1(f), effective July 1, 2013. (1973, c. 1272, s. 1; 1979, c. 1073, ss. 8, 20; 1981, c. 225; 1987, c. 565, s. 15; 1993, c. 539, s. 1113; 1994, Ex. Sess., c. 24, s. 14(c); 1997-515, s. 8(a); 1999-31, s. 5(c); 2002-158, s. 2; 2006-192, ss. 15, 16, 17; 2007-391, s. 36; 2007-484, s. 43.8(c); 2007-510, s. 1(c); 2007-540, ss. 2, 3; 2008-150, ss. 6(c), 7(a); 2008-

187, s. 33(a); 2013-360, s. 21.1(e), (f); 2013-381, ss. 38.1(h), (i), (j), 42.1, 42.2, 42.3, 53.1(a).)

§ 163-278.13A: Repealed by Session Laws 1997-515, s. 9.

§ 163-278.13B. Limitation on fund-raising during legislative session.

(a)   Definitions. - For purposes of this section:

(1)   "Limited contributor" means a lobbyist registered under Chapter 120C of the General Statutes, that lobbyist's agent, that lobbyist's principal as defined in G.S. 120C-100(11) or a political committee that employs or contracts with or whose parent entity employs or contracts with a lobbyist registered under Chapter 120C of the General Statutes.

(2)   "Limited contributee" means a member of or candidate for the Council of State, a member of or candidate for the General Assembly.

(3)   The General Assembly is in "regular session" from the date set by law or resolution that the General Assembly convenes until the General Assembly either adjourns sine die or recesses or adjourns for more than 10 days.

(4)   A contribution is "made" during regular session if the check or other instrument is dated during the session, or if the check or other instrument is delivered to the limited contributee during session, or if the limited contributor pledges during the session to deliver the check or other instrument at a later time.

(5)   A contribution is "accepted" during regular session if the check or other instrument is dated during the session, or if the limited contributee receives the check or other instrument during session and does not return it within 10 days, or agrees during session to receive the check or other instrument at a later time.

(b)   Prohibited Solicitations. - While the General Assembly is in regular session, no limited contributee or the real or purported agent of a limited contributee shall:

(1)   Solicit a contribution from a limited contributor to be made to that limited contributee or to be made to any other candidate, officeholder, or political committee; or

(2)   Solicit a third party, requesting or directing that the third party directly or indirectly solicit a contribution from a limited contributor or relay to the limited contributor the limited contributee's solicitation of a contribution.

It shall not be deemed a violation of this section for a limited contributee to serve on a board or committee of an organization that makes a solicitation of a limited contributor as long as that limited contributee does not directly participate in the solicitation and that limited contributee does not directly benefit from the solicitation.

(c)   Prohibited Contributions. - While the General Assembly is in regular session:

(1)   No limited contributor shall make or offer to make a contribution to a limited contributee.

(2)   No limited contributor shall make a contribution to any candidate, officeholder, or political committee, directing or requesting that the contribution be made in turn to a limited contributee.

(3)   No limited contributor shall transfer any amount of money or anything of value to any entity, directing or requesting that the entity use what was transferred to contribute to a limited contributee.

(4)   No limited contributee or the real or purported agent of a limited contributee prohibited from solicitation by subsection (b) of this section shall accept a contribution from a limited contributor.

(5)   No limited contributor shall solicit a contribution from any individual or political committee on behalf of a limited contributee. This subdivision does not apply to a limited contributor soliciting a contribution on behalf of a political party executive committee if the solicitation is solely for a separate segregated fund kept by the political party limited to use for activities that are not candidate-specific, including generic voter registration and get-out-the-vote efforts, pollings, mailings, and other general activities and advertising that do not refer to a specific individual candidate.

(d)   Exception. - The provisions of this section do not apply with regard to a limited contributee during the three weeks prior to the day of a second primary if that limited contributee is a candidate who will be on the ballot in that second primary.

(e) Prosecution. - A violation of this section is a Class 2 misdemeanor. (1997-515, s. 9(b); 1999-31, s. 5(d); 1999-453, s. 6(a); 2000-136, s. 1; 2006-201, s. 21.)

§ 163-278.13C. Campaign contributions prohibition.

(a) No lobbyist may make a contribution as defined in G.S. 163-278.6 to a candidate or candidate campaign committee as defined in G.S. 163-278.38Z when that candidate meets any of the following criteria:

(1) Is a legislator as defined in G.S. 120C-100.

(2) Is a public servant as defined in G.S. 138A-3(30)a. and G.S. 120C-104.

(b) No lobbyist may do any of the following with respect to a candidate or candidate campaign committee described in subdivisions (a)(1) and (a)(2) of this section:

(1) Collect a contribution or multiple contributions from one or more contributors intended for that candidate or candidate campaign committee.

(2) Take possession of a contribution or multiple contributions intended for that candidate or candidate campaign committee.

(3) Transfer or deliver a collected contribution or multiple contributions to the intended candidate or candidate campaign committee.

(c) This section shall not apply to a lobbyist, who has filed a notice of candidacy for office under G.S. 163-106 or Article 11 of Chapter 163 of the General Statutes or has been nominated under G.S. 163-114 or G.S. 163-98, making a contribution to that lobbyist's candidate campaign committee.

(d) For purposes of this section, the term "lobbyist" shall mean an individual registered as a lobbyist under Chapter 120C of the General Statutes. (2006-201, s. 18; 2007-347, s. 5(a), (b); 2008-213, s. 86; 2013-381, s. 47.1(a).)

§ 163-278.14. No contributions in names of others; no anonymous contributions; contributions in excess of fifty dollars; no contribution without specific designation of contributor.

(a) No individual, political committee, or other entity shall make any contribution anonymously or in the name of another. No candidate, political committee, referendum committee, political party, or treasurer shall knowingly accept any contribution made by any individual or person in the name of another individual or person or made anonymously. If a candidate, political committee, referendum committee, political party, or treasurer receives anonymous contributions or contributions determined to have been made in the name of another, he shall pay the money over to the Board, by check, and all such moneys received by the Board shall be deposited in the Civil Penalty and Forfeiture Fund of the State of North Carolina. This subsection shall not apply to any contribution by an individual with the lawful authority to act on behalf of another individual, whether through power of attorney, trustee, or other lawful authority.

(b) No entity shall make, and no candidate, committee or treasurer shall accept, any monetary contribution in excess of fifty dollars ($50.00) unless such contribution is in the form of a check, draft, money order, credit card charge, debit, or other noncash method that can be subject to written verification. No contribution in the form of check, draft, money order, credit card charge, debits, or other noncash method may be made or accepted unless it contains a specific designation of the intended contributee chosen by the contributor. The State Board of Elections may prescribe guidelines as to the reporting and verification of any method of contribution payment allowed under this Article. For contributions by money order, the State Board shall prescribe methods to ensure an audit trail for every contribution so that the identity of the contributor can be determined. For a contribution made by credit card, the credit card account number of a contributor is not a public record.

(c) No political committee or referendum committee shall make any contribution unless in doing so it reports to the recipient the contributor's name as required in G.S. 163-278.7(b)(1). (1973, c. 1272, s. 1; 1979, c. 1073, s. 19; 1987, c. 113, s. 2; 1999-453, s. 4(a); 2001-319, s. 10(a); 2002-159, s. 55(k); 2004-125, s. 5(b); 2005-430, s. 1; 2006-195, ss. 1, 5.2; 2007-484, s. 23; 2010-169, s. 6(b).)

§ 163-278.14A. Evidence that communications are "to support or oppose the nomination or election of one or more clearly identified candidates."

(a) The following shall be means of proving that an individual or other entity acted "to support or oppose the nomination or election of one or more clearly identified candidates": presenting evidence of financial sponsorship of communications to the general public that use phrases such as "vote for", "reelect", "support", "cast your ballot for", "(name of candidate) for (name of office)", "(name of candidate) in (year)", "vote against", "defeat", "reject", "vote pro-(policy position)" or "vote anti-(policy position)" accompanied by a list of candidates clearly labeled "pro-(policy position)" or "anti-(policy position)", or communications of campaign words or slogans, such as posters, bumper stickers, advertisements, etc., which say "(name of candidate)'s the One", "(name of candidate) '98", "(name of candidate)!", or the names of two candidates joined by a hyphen or slash.

(b) Notwithstanding the provisions of subsection (a) of this section, a communication shall not be subject to regulation as a contribution or expenditure under this Article if it:

(1) Appears in a news story, commentary, or editorial distributed through the facilities of any broadcasting station, newspaper, or magazine, unless those facilities are owned or controlled by any political party, or political committee;

(2) Is distributed by a corporation solely to its stockholders and employees; or

(3) Is distributed by any organization, association, or labor union solely to its members or to subscribers or recipients of its regular publications, or is made available to individuals in response to their request, including through the Internet. (1999-453, s. 3(a); 2008-150, s. 6(b).)

§ 163-278.15. No acceptance of contributions made by corporations, foreign and domestic, or other prohibited sources.

(a) No candidate, political committee, political party, or treasurer shall accept any contribution made by any corporation, foreign or domestic, regardless of whether such corporation does business in the State of North Carolina, or made by any business entity, labor union, professional association, or insurance company. This section does not apply with regard to entities permitted to make contributions by G.S. 163-278.19(f).

(b) A candidate or political committee may accept a contribution knowing that the contribution is the proceeds of a loan made in the ordinary course of business by a financial institution if all of the following conditions are met:

(1) The full amount of the loan is secured by collateral placed, or by guaranties given, by one or more individuals or entities who are not prohibited by this Article from making contributions to the candidate or political committee. The value of the collateral posted by each individual or entity, or the amount of each guaranty, may not exceed the contribution limitations applicable under this Article to each individual or entity. The value of collateral posted may exceed the contribution limitations applicable under this Article in cases where the amount of the loan secured by that collateral does not exceed the contribution limitations applicable to the individual or entity.

(2) During the time that any loan remains outstanding and unpaid, then the value of any collateral posted, or the amount of each guaranty, for that loan shall be considered to be a contribution by the individual or entity securing the loan. If the loan, or any portion of the loan, is repaid to the financial institution by the candidate or political committee to whom the loan was made during the contribution limitation period for the same "election" as defined in G.S. 163-278.13(d) in which the loan was made, the individual or entity securing the loan shall be eligible to further contribute to that candidate or political committee up to the amount of the repayment. If multiple individuals or entities secured the loan that is repaid to the financial institution by the candidate or political committee, then the amount repaid shall be prorated amongst the multiple individuals or entities.

(3) If the loan is to the candidate or political committee, only the candidate, the candidate's spouse, or the political committee to whom the loan was made may repay the loan.

The State Board of Elections shall develop forms for reporting the proceeds of loans in a full and accurate manner. (1973, c. 1272, s. 1; 1999-31, s. 5(e); 2006-195, s. 6; 2006-262, s. 4.1(c).)

§ 163-278.16. Regulations regarding timing of contributions and expenditures.

(a) Except as provided in G.S. 163-278.6(14) and G.S. 163-278.12, no contribution may be received or expenditure made by or on behalf of a candidate, political committee, or referendum committee:

(1) Until the candidate, political committee, or referendum committee appoints a treasurer and certifies the name and address of the treasurer to the Board; and

(2) Unless the contribution is received or the expenditure made by or through the treasurer of the candidate, political committee, or referendum committee.

(b) through (e) Repealed by Session Laws 1975, c. 565, s. 2.

(f), (g) Repealed by Session Laws 1999-453, s. 2(b). (1973, c. 1272, s. 1; 1975, c. 565, s. 2; 1979, c. 500, s. 4; c. 1073, ss. 19, 20; 1987, c. 652; 1997-515, s. 13.1(a); 1999-31, ss. 1(d), 4(b); 1999-453, s. 2(b).)

§ 163-278.16A. Restriction on use of State funds by declared candidate for Council of State for advertising or public service announcements using their names, pictures, or voices.

After December 31 prior to a general election in which a Council of State office will be on the ballot, no declared candidate for that Council of State office shall use or permit the use of State funds for any advertisement or public service announcement in a newspaper, on radio, or on television that contains that declared candidate's name, picture, or voice, except in case of State or national emergency and only if the announcement is reasonably necessary to that candidate's official function. For purposes of this section, "declared candidate" means someone who has publicly announced an intention to run. (1997-515, s. 13(a).)

§ 163-278.16B. Use of contributions for certain purposes.

(a) A candidate or candidate campaign committee may use contributions only for the following purposes:

(1) Expenditures resulting from the campaign for public office by the candidate or candidate's campaign committee.

(2) Expenditures resulting from holding public office.

(3) Donations to an organization described in section 170(c) of the Internal Revenue Code of 1986 (26 U.S.C. § 170(c)), provided that the candidate or the candidate's spouse, children, parents, brothers, or sisters are not employed by the organization.

(4) Contributions to a national, State, or district or county committee of a political party or a caucus of the political party.

(5) Contributions to another candidate or candidate's campaign committee.

(6) To return all or a portion of a contribution to the contributor.

(7) Payment of any penalties against the candidate or candidate's campaign committee for violation of this Article imposed by a board of elections or a court of competent jurisdiction.

(8) Payment to the Escheat Fund established by Chapter 116B of the General Statutes.

(9) Legal expense donation not in excess of four thousand dollars ($4,000) per calendar year to a legal expense fund established pursuant to Article 22M of Chapter 163 of the General Statutes.

(b) As used in this section, the term "candidate campaign committee" means the same as in G.S. 163-278.38Z(3).

(c) Contributions made to a candidate or candidate campaign committee do not become a part of the personal estate of the individual candidate. The candidate may file with the board a written designation of those funds that directs to which of the permitted uses in subsection (a) of this section those funds shall be paid in the event of the death or incapacity of the candidate. If the candidate fails to file the written designation before death, the personal representative of the estate may file the written designation within 90 days of the date of death, and may only direct those funds to donations under subdivision (a)(3) of this section. After the payment of permitted outstanding debts of the account, the candidate's filed written designation shall control. If the candidate files no such written designation, the funds after payment of permitted outstanding debts shall be distributed in accordance with subdivision (a)(8) of this section. (2006-161, s. 1; 2007-391, s. 30; 2008-187, s. 33(a); 2008-213, s. 87; 2009-534, s. 2(h); 2010-100, s. 1.)

§ 163-278.17. Statements of media outlets regarding political advertising.

(a) Repealed by Session Laws 1985, c. 183, s. 1.

(b) Each media outlet shall require written authority for each expenditure from each candidate, treasurer or individual making or authorizing an expenditure. A candidate may authorize advertisement paid for by a treasurer appointed by the candidate. All written authorizations of expenditures signed by a candidate, treasurer or individual shall be deemed public records and copies of those written authorizations shall be available for inspection during normal business hours at the office(s) of the media outlet making the publication or broadcast nearest to the place(s) of publication or broadcast.

(c) Repealed by Session Laws 1985, c. 183, s. 2.

(d) Each media outlet shall require written authority for each independent expenditure or electioneering communication from each individual, person, or entity making or authorizing an independent expenditure or electioneering communication. All written authorizations of independent expenditures or electioneering communications shall be deemed public records, and copies of those written authorizations shall be available for inspection during normal business hours at the office(s) of the media outlet making the publication or broadcast nearest to the place(s) of publication or broadcast. The written authorization shall include all of the following:

(1) The name and address of the individual, person, or entity making the independent expenditure or electioneering communication.

(2) The information required by G.S. 163-278.39(a), provided however that the provisions of G.S. 163-278.39(a)(7) and (a)(8) shall not apply to radio or television advertising. (1973, c. 1272, s. 1; 1975, c. 565, s. 3; 1979, c. 500, ss. 5, 6; c. 1073, s. 9; 1985, c. 183, ss. 1, 2; 2010-170, s. 4.)

§ 163-278.18. Normal commercial charges for political advertising.

(a) No media and no supplier of materials or services shall charge or require a candidate, treasurer, political party, or individual to pay a charge for advertising, materials, space, or services purchased for or in support of or in opposition to any candidate, political committee, or political party that is higher than the normal charge it requires other customers to pay for comparable advertising, materials, space, or services purchased for other purposes.

(b) A newspaper, magazine, or other advertising medium shall not charge any candidate, treasurer, political committee, political party, or individual for any advertising for or in support of or in opposition to any candidate, political committee or political party at a rate higher than the comparable rate charged to other persons for advertising of comparable frequency and volume; and every candidate, treasurer, political party or individual, with respect to political advertising, shall be entitled to the same discounts afforded by the advertising medium to other advertisers under comparable conditions and circumstances. (1973, c. 1272, s. 1; 1977, c. 856.)

§ 163-278.19. Violations by corporations, business entities, labor unions, professional associations and insurance companies.

(a) Except as provided in subsections (a2), (b), (d), (e), (f), and (g) of this section it shall be unlawful for any corporation, business entity, labor union, professional association or insurance company directly or indirectly do any of the following:

(1) To make any contribution to a candidate or political committee.

(2) To pay or use or offer, consent or agree to pay or use any of its money or property for any contribution to a candidate or political committee.

(3) To compensate, reimburse, or indemnify any person or individual for money or property so used or for any contribution or expenditure so made.

It shall also be unlawful for any officer, director, stockholder, attorney, agent or member of any corporation, business entity, labor union, professional association or insurance company to aid, abet, advise or consent to any such contribution, or for any person or individual to solicit or knowingly receive any such contribution. Supporting or opposing the election of clearly identified candidates includes supporting or opposing the candidates of a clearly identified political party. Any officer, director, stockholder, attorney, agent or member of any corporation, business entity, labor union, professional association or insurance company aiding or abetting in any contribution made in violation of this section shall be guilty of a Class 2 misdemeanor, and shall in addition be liable to such corporation, business entity, labor union, professional association or insurance company for the amount of such contribution and the same may be recovered of him upon suit by any stockholder or member thereof.

(a1) A transfer of funds shall be deemed to have been a contribution made indirectly if it is made to any committee or political party account, whether inside or outside this State, with the intent or purpose of being exchanged in whole or in part for any other funds to be contributed or expended in an election for North Carolina office or to offset any other funds contributed or expended in an election for North Carolina office.

(a2) Proceeds of loans made in the ordinary course of business by financial institutions may be used for contributions made in compliance with this Chapter. Financial institutions may also grant revolving credit to political committees and referendum committees in the ordinary course of business.

(b) It shall, however, be lawful for any corporation, business entity, labor union, professional association or insurance company to communicate with its employees, stockholders or members and their families on any subject; to conduct nonpartisan registration and get-out-the-vote campaigns aimed at their employees, stockholders, or members and their families; or for officials and employees of any corporation, insurance company or business entity or the officials and members of any labor union or professional association to establish, administer, contribute to, and to receive and solicit contributions to a separate segregated fund to be utilized for political purposes, and those individuals shall be deemed to become and be a political committee as that term is defined in G.S. 163-278.6(14) or a referendum committee as defined in G.S. 163-278.6(18b); provided, however, that it shall be unlawful for any such fund to make a contribution or expenditure by utilizing contributions secured by physical force, job discrimination, financial reprisals or the threat of force, job discrimination or financial reprisals, or by dues, fees, or other moneys required as a condition of membership or employment or as a requirement with respect to any terms or conditions of employment, including, without limitation, hiring, firing, transferring, promoting, demoting, or granting seniority or employment-related benefits of any kind, or by moneys obtained in any commercial transaction whatsoever.

(c) A violation of this section is a Class 2 misdemeanor. In addition, the acceptance of any contribution, reimbursement, or indemnification under subsection (a) shall be a Class 2 misdemeanor.

(d) Whenever a candidate or treasurer is an officer, director, stockholder, attorney, agent, or employee of any corporation, business entity, labor union, professional association or insurance company, and by virtue of his position therewith uses office space and communication facilities of the corporation, business entity, labor union, professional association or insurance company in the normal and usual scope of his employment, the fact that the candidate or treasurer receives telephone calls, mail, or visits in such office which relates to activities prohibited by this Article shall not be considered a violation under this section.

(e) Notwithstanding the prohibitions specified in this Article and Article 22 of this Chapter, a political committee organized under provisions of this Article shall be entitled to receive and the corporation, business entity, labor union, professional association, or insurance company designated on the committee's organizational report as the parent entity of the employees or members who organized the committee is authorized to give reasonable administrative support that shall include record keeping, computer services, billings, mailings to members of the committee, membership development, fund-raising activities, office supplies, office space, and such other support as is reasonably necessary for the administration of the committee.

The approximate cost of any reasonable administrative support shall be submitted to the committee, in writing, and the committee shall include that cost on the report required by G.S. 163-278.9(a)(6). Also included in the report shall be the approximate allocable portion of the compensation of any officer or employee of the corporation, business entity, labor union, professional association, or insurance company who has devoted more than thirty-five percent (35%) of his time during normal business hours of the corporation, business entity, labor union, professional association, or insurance company during the period covered by the required report. The approximate cost submitted by the parent corporation, business entity, labor union, professional association, or insurance company shall be entered on the committee's report as the final entry on its list of "contributions" and a copy of the written approximate cost received by it shall be attached.

The reasonable administrative support given by a corporation, business entity, labor union, professional association, or insurance company shall be designated on the books of the corporation, business entity, labor union, professional association, or insurance company as such and may not be treated by it as a business deduction for State income tax purposes.

(f)   This section does not prohibit a contribution by an [a] person or entity that:

(1)   Has as an express purpose promoting social, educational, or political ideas and not to generate business income;

(2)   Does not have shareholders or other persons which have an economic interest in its assets and earnings; and

(3)   Was not established by a business corporation, by an insurance company, by a business entity, including, but not limited to, those chartered under Chapter 55, Chapter 55A, Chapter 55B, or Chapter 58 of the General Statutes, by a professional association, or by a labor union and does not receive substantial revenue from such entities. Substantial revenue is rebuttably presumed to be more than ten percent (10%) of total revenues in a calendar year.

(g)   If a political committee has as its only purpose accepting contributions and making expenditures to influence elections, and that political committee incorporates as a nonprofit corporation to shield its participants from liability created outside this Chapter, that political committee is not considered to be a corporation for purposes of this section. Incorporation of a political committee does not relieve any individual, person, or other entity of any liability, duty, or obligation created pursuant to any provision of this Chapter. To obtain the benefits of this subsection, an incorporating political committee must state exactly the following language as the only purpose for which the corporation can be organized: "to accept contributions and make expenditures to influence elections as a political committee pursuant to G.S. 163-278.6(14) only." No political committee shall do business as a political committee after incorporation unless it has been certified by the State Board of Elections as being in compliance with this subsection. (1973, c. 1272, s. 1; 1975, c. 565, s. 6; 1979, c. 517, ss. 1, 2; 1985, c. 354; 1987, c. 113, s. 3; c. 565, s. 16; 1993, c. 539, ss. 1115, 1116; c. 553, s. 69; 1994, Ex. Sess., c. 24, s. 14(c); 1999-31, ss. 4(d), 5(a), 6(b); 2001-487, s. 97(a); 2002-159, s. 57.3(a), (b); 2006-195, s. 3; 2006-262, ss. 4.1(a), (b), 4.3; 2010-170, s. 5.)

§ 163-278.19A. Contributions allowed.

Notwithstanding any other provision of this Chapter, it is lawful for any person as defined in G.S. 163-278.6(13) to contribute to a referendum committee. (1979, c. 1073, s. 7.)

§ 163-278.19B. Political party headquarters building funds.

Notwithstanding the provisions of G.S. 163-278.19, a person prohibited by that section from making a contribution may donate to political parties and political parties may accept from such a person money and other things of value donated to a political party headquarters building fund. Donations to the political party headquarters building fund shall be subject to all the following rules:

(1)   The donations solicited and accepted are designated to the political party headquarters building fund.

(2)   Potential donors to that fund are advised that all donations will be exclusively for the political party headquarters building fund.

(3)   The political party establishes a separate segregated bank account into which shall be deposited only donations for the political party headquarters building fund from persons prohibited by G.S. 163-278.19 from making contributions.

(4)   The donations deposited in the separate segregated bank account for the political party headquarters building fund will be spent only to purchase a principal headquarters building, to construct a principal headquarters building, to renovate a principal headquarters building, to pay a mortgage on a principal headquarters building, to repay donors if a principal headquarters building is not purchased, constructed, or renovated, or to pay building rent or monthly or bimonthly utility expenses incurred to operate the principal headquarters building. Donations deposited into that account shall be used solely for the purposes set forth in the preceding sentence, and specifically shall not be used for headquarters equipment other than fixtures, personnel compensation, or travel or fundraising expenses or requirements of any kind. Notwithstanding the above, personnel compensation and in-kind benefits may be paid to no more than three personnel whose functions are primarily administrative in nature, such as providing accounting, payroll, or campaign finance reporting services,

for the party and whose job functions require no more than ten percent (10%) of work time to be spent on political advocacy each calendar year

(5) The political party executive committee shall report donations to and spending by a political party headquarters building fund on every report required to be made by G.S. 163-278.9. If a committee is excused from making general campaign finance reports under G.S. 163-278.10A, that committee shall nonetheless report donations in any amount to and spending in any amount by the political party headquarters building fund at the times required for reports in G.S. 163-278.9.

If all the criteria set forth in subdivisions (1) through (5) of this section are complied with, then donations to and spending by a political party headquarters building fund do not constitute contributions or expenditures as defined in G.S. 163-278.6. If those criteria are complied with, then donations may be made to a political party headquarters building fund. (1999-426, s. 9(a); 2013-381, s. 43.1.)

§ 163-278.20: Repealed by Session Laws 2006-195, s. 2, effective January 1, 2007, and applicable to all contributions made and accepted on and after that date.

§ 163-278.21. Promulgation of policy and administration through State Board of Elections.

The State Board of Elections shall have responsibility, adequate staff, equipment and facilities, for promulgating all regulations necessary for the enforcement and administration of this Article and to prevent the circumvention of the provisions of this Article. The State Board of Elections shall empower the Executive Director with the responsibility for the administrative operations required to administer this Article and may delegate or assign to him such other duties from time to time by regulations or orders of the State Board of Elections. (1973, c. 1272, s. 1; 1975, c. 798, s. 7; 1999-453, s. 5(c); 2001-319, s. 11.)

§ 163-278.22. Duties of State Board.

It shall be the duty and power of the State Board:

(1)   To prescribe forms of statements and other information required to be filed by this Article, to furnish such forms to the county boards of elections and individuals, media or others required to file such statements and information, and to prepare, publish and distribute or cause to be distributed to all candidates at the time they file notices of candidacy a manual setting forth the provisions of this Article and a prescribed uniform system for accounts required to file statements by this Article.

(2)   To accept and file any information voluntarily supplied that exceeds the requirements of this Article.

(3)   To develop a filing, coding, and cross-indexing system consonant with the purposes of this Article.

(4)   To make statements and other information filed with it available to the public at a charge not to exceed actual cost of copying.

(5)   To preserve reports and statements filed under this Article. Such reports and statements, after a period of two years following the election year, may be transferred to the Department of Cultural Resources, Office of Archives and History, and shall be preserved for a period of 10 years.

(6)   To prepare and publish such reports as it may deem appropriate.

(7)   To make investigations to the extent the Board deems necessary with respect to statements filed under the provisions of this Article and with respect to alleged failures to file any statement required under the provisions of this Article or Article 22M of the General Statutes and, upon complaint under oath by any registered voter, with respect to alleged violations of any part of this Article or Article 22M of the General Statutes.

(8)   After investigation, to report apparent violations by candidates, political committees, referendum committees, legal expense funds, individuals or persons to the proper district attorney as provided in G.S. 163-278.27.

(9)   To prescribe and furnish forms of statements and other material to the county boards of elections for distribution to candidates and committees required to be filed with the county boards.

(10) To instruct the chairman and director of elections of each county board as to their respective duties and responsibilities relative to the administration of this Article.

(11) To require appropriate certification of delinquent or late filings from the county boards of elections and to execute the same responsibilities relative to such reports as provided in G.S. 163-278.27.

(12) To assist county boards of elections in resolving questions arising from the administration of this Article.

(13) To require county boards of elections to hold such hearings, make such investigations, and make reports to the State Board as the State Board deems necessary in the administration of this Article.

(14) To calculate, assess, and collect civil penalties pursuant to this Article.

(15) To establish a process for determination as to whether communication is an expenditure, independent expenditure, or electioneering communication prior to the airing or distribution of that communication when so requested by an individual or person producing a communication. The responsibility for the determination may be delegated to the Executive Director. If the responsibility is delegated to the Executive Director, the process established by the State Board shall require a written determination by the Executive Director to include stated findings and an opportunity for immediate appeal to the State Board of the determination by the Executive Director. (1973, c. 1272, s. 1; 1975, c. 798, s. 8; 1977, c. 626, s. 1; 1979, c. 500, ss. 9, 12, 13; c. 1073, s. 18; 1995, c. 243, s. 1; 1997-515, s. 7(e); 2002-159, s. 35(n); 2007-349, ss. 2, 3; 2010-170, s. 6.)

§ 163-278.23. Duties of Executive Director of Board.

The Executive Director of the Board shall inspect or cause to be inspected each statement filed with the Board under this Article within 30 days after the date it is filed. The Executive Director shall advise, or cause to be advised, no more than 30 days and at least five days before each report is due, each candidate or treasurer whose organizational report has been filed, of the specific date each report is due. He shall immediately notify any individual, candidate, treasurer, political committee, referendum committee, media, or other entity that may be required to file a statement under this Article if:

(1) It appears that the individual, candidate, treasurer, political committee, referendum committee, media, or other entity has failed to file a statement as required by law or that a statement filed does not conform to this Article; or

(2) A written complaint is filed under oath with the Board by any registered voter of this State alleging that a statement filed with the Board does not conform to this Article or to the truth or that an individual, candidate, treasurer, political committee, referendum committee, media, or other entity has failed to file a statement required by this Article.

The entity that is the subject of the complaint will be given an opportunity to respond to the complaint before any action is taken requiring compliance.

The Executive Director of the Board of Elections shall issue written opinions to candidates, the communications media, political committees, referendum committees, or other entities upon request, regarding filing procedures and compliance with this Article. Any such opinion so issued shall specifically refer to this paragraph. If the candidate, communications media, political committees, referendum committees, or other entities rely on and comply with the opinion of the Executive Director of the Board of Elections, then prosecution or civil action on account of the procedure followed pursuant thereto and prosecution for failure to comply with the statute inconsistent with the written ruling of the Executive Director of the Board of Elections issued to the candidate or committee involved shall be barred. Nothing in this paragraph shall be construed to prohibit or delay the regular and timely filing of reports. The Executive Director shall file all opinions issued pursuant to this section with the Codifier of Rules to be published unedited in the North Carolina Register and the North Carolina Administrative Code.

This section applies to Articles and [Article] 22M of the General Statutes to the same extent that it applies to this Article. (1973, c. 1272, s. 1; 1975, c. 334; c. 565, s. 4; 1979, c. 500, s. 7; c. 1073, ss. 12, 13, 17; 1985, c. 759, s. 6.1; 1999-424, s. 6(c); 1999-453, s. 5(b); 1999-456, s. 63; 2001-319, s. 11; 2005-430, s. 8; 2007-349, s. 6; 2013-360, s. 21.1; 2013-381, ss. 43.1, 47.1, 48.3.)

§ 163-278.24. Statements examined within four months.

Within four months after the date of each election or referendum, the Executive Director shall examine or cause to be examined each statement filed with the Board under this Article, and, referring to the election or referendum, determine whether the statement conforms to law and to the truth. (1973, c. 1272, s. 1; 1979, c. 500, s. 8; c. 1073, s. 14; 1985, c. 183, s. 3; 2001-319, s. 11.)

§ 163-278.25. Issuance of declaration of nomination or certificate of election.

No declaration of nomination and no certificate of election shall be granted to any candidate until the candidate or his treasurer has filed the statements referring to the election he is required to file under this Article. Within 24 hours after reaching a decision that a declaration of nomination or certificate of election should not be granted, the Board shall give written notice of that decision, by telegraph or certified mail, to the candidate and the candidate's treasurer. Failure to grant certification shall not affect a successful candidate's title to an office to which he has been otherwise duly elected. (1973, c. 1272, s. 1.)

§ 163-278.26. Appeals from State Board of Elections; early docketing.

Any candidate for nomination or election who is denied a declaration of nomination or certificate of election, pursuant to G.S. 163-278.25, may, within five days after the action of the Board under that section, appeal to the Superior Court of Wake County for a final determination of any questions of law or fact which may be involved in the Board's action. The cause shall be entitled "In the Matter of the Candidacy of _____." It shall be placed on the civil docket of that court and shall have precedence over all other civil actions. In the event of an appeal, the chairman of the Board shall certify the record to the clerk of that court within five days after the appeal is noted.

The record on appeal shall consist of all reports filed by the candidate or his treasurer with the Board pursuant to this Article, and a memorandum of the Board setting forth with particularity the reasons for its action in denying the candidate a declaration of nomination or certificate of election. Written notice of the appeal shall be given to the Board by the candidate or his attorney, and may be effected by mail or personal delivery. On appeal, the cause shall be heard de novo. (1973, c. 1272, s. 1.)

§ 163-278.27. Criminal penalties; duty to report and prosecute.

(a) Any individual, candidate, political committee, referendum committee, treasurer, person or media who intentionally violates the applicable provisions of G.S. 163-278.7, 163-278.8, 163-278.9, 163-278.10, 163-278.11, 163-278.12, 163-278.13, 163-278.13B, 163-278.14, 163-278.16, 163-278.16B, 163-278.17, 163-278.18, 163-278.19, 163-278.20, 163-278.39, 163-278.40A, 163-278.40B, 163-278.40C, 163-278.40D, 163-278.40E, or 163-278.40J is guilty of a Class 2 misdemeanor. The statute of limitations as stated in G.S. 15-1 shall run from the day the last report is due to be filed with the appropriate board of elections for the election cycle for which the violation occurred.

(a1) A violation of G.S. 163-278.32 by making a certification knowing the information to be untrue is a Class I felony.

(a2) A person or individual who intentionally violates G.S. 163-278.14(a) or G.S. 163-278.19(a) and the unlawful contributions total more than ten thousand dollars ($10,000) per election is guilty of a Class I felony.

(b) Whenever the Board has knowledge of or has reason to believe there has been a violation of any section of this Article, it shall report that fact, together with accompanying details, to the following prosecuting authorities:

(1) In the case of a candidate for nomination or election to the State Senate or State House of Representatives: report to the district attorney of the prosecutorial district in which the candidate for nomination or election resides;

(2) In the case of a candidate for nomination or election to the office of Governor, Lieutenant Governor, Secretary of State, State Auditor, State Treasurer, State Superintendent of Public Instruction, State Attorney General, State Commissioner of Agriculture, State Commissioner of Labor, State Commissioner of Insurance, and all other State elective offices, Justice of the Supreme Court, Judge of the Court of Appeals, judge of a superior court, judge of a district court, and district attorney of the superior court: report to the district attorney of the prosecutorial district in which Wake County is located;

(3) In the case of an individual other than a candidate, including, without limitation, violations by members of political committees, referendum committees or treasurers: report to the district attorney of the prosecutorial district in which the individual resides; and

(4) In the case of a person or any group of individuals: report to the district attorney or district attorneys of the prosecutorial district or districts in which any

of the officers, directors, agents, employees or members of the person or group reside.

(c)   Upon receipt of such a report from the Board, the appropriate district attorney shall prosecute the individual or persons alleged to have violated a section or sections of this Article.

(d)   As a condition of probation, a sentencing judge may order that the costs incurred by the State Board of Elections in investigating and aiding the prosecution of a case be paid to the State Board of Elections by the defendant on such terms and conditions as set by the judge. (1973, c. 1272, s. 1; 1979, c. 500, s. 10; c. 1073, ss. 15, 19; 1981, c. 837, s. 4; 1987, c. 565, s. 17; 1993, c. 539, s. 1118; 1994, Ex. Sess., c. 24, s. 14(c); 1999-453, s. 2(c); 2001-419, s. 2; 2006-161, s. 5; 2007-391, s. 1(b); 2008-150, s. 9(b); 2008-187, s. 29; 2010-169, s. 6(a).)

§ 163-278.28. Issuance of injunctions; special prosecutors named.

(a)   The superior courts of this State shall have jurisdiction to issue injunctions or grant any other equitable relief appropriate to enforce the provisions of this Article upon application by any registered voter of the State.

(b)   If the Board makes a report to a district attorney under G.S. 163-278.27 and no prosecution is initiated within 45 days after the report is made, any registered voter of the prosecutorial district to whose district attorney a report has been made, or any board of elections in that district, may, by verified affidavit, petition the superior court for that district for the appointment of a special prosecutor to prosecute the individuals or persons who have or who are believed to have violated any section of this Article. Upon receipt of a petition for the appointment of a special prosecutor, the superior court shall issue an order to show cause, directed at the individuals or persons alleged in the petition to be in violation of this Article, why a special prosecutor should not be appointed. If there is no answer to the order, the court shall appoint a special prosecutor. If there is an answer, the court shall hold a hearing on the order, at which both the petitioning and answering parties may be heard, to determine whether a prima facie case of a violation and failure to prosecute exists. If there is such a prima facie case, the court shall so find and shall thereupon appoint a special prosecutor to prosecute the alleged violators. The special prosecutor shall take the oath required of assistant district attorneys by G.S. 7A-63, shall serve as an assistant district attorney pro tem of the appropriate district, and shall prosecute the alleged violators. (1973, c. 1272, s. 1; 1979, c. 500, s. 11.)

§ 163-278.29. Compelling self-incriminating testimony; individual so testifying excused from prosecution.

No individual shall be excused from attending or testifying or producing any books, papers, or other documents before any court upon any proceeding or trial of another for the violation of any of the provisions of this Article, upon the ground or for the reason that the testimony or evidence, documentary or otherwise, required of him may tend to incriminate him, but such individual may be subpoenaed and required to testify by and for the State relative to any offense arising under the provisions of this Article; but such individual shall not be prosecuted or subjected to any penalty or forfeiture for or on account of any transaction, matter or thing concerning which he may be compelled to testify or produce evidence, documentary or otherwise, and no compelled testimony so given or produced shall be used against him upon any criminal proceeding, but such individual so compelled to testify with respect to any acts of his own shall be immune from prosecution on account thereof. (1973, c. 1272, s. 1.)

§ 163-278.30. Candidates for federal offices to file information reports.

Candidates for nomination in a party primary or for election in a general or special election to the offices of United States Senator, member of the United States House of Representatives, President or Vice-President of the United States shall file with the Board all reports they or political committee treasurers or other agents acting for them are required to file under the Federal Election Campaign Act of 1971, P.L. 92-225, as amended (T. 2, U.S.C. section 439). Those reports shall be filed with the Board at the times required by that act. The Board shall, with respect to those reports, have the following duties only:

(1) To receive and maintain in an orderly manner all reports and statements required to be filed with it;

(2) To preserve reports and statements filed under the Federal Election Campaign Act. Such reports and statements, after a period of two years following the election year, may be transferred to the Department of Cultural Resources, Division of Archives and History, and shall be preserved for a period of 10 years or for such period as may be required by federal law.

(3) To make the reports and statements filed with it available for public inspection and copying during regular office hours, commencing as soon as practicable but not later than the end of the day during which they were received, and to permit copying of any such report or statement by hand or by duplicating machine, requested by any individual, at the expense of such individual; and

(4) To compile and maintain a current list of all statements or parts of statements pertaining to each candidate.

Any duty of a candidate to file and the State Board to receive and make available under this section may be met by an agreement between the State Board and the Federal Election Commission, the effect of which is for the Federal Election Commission to provide promptly to the State Board the information required by this section. (1973, c. 1272, s. 1; 1979, c. 500, s. 14; 2002-159, s. 55(l).)

§ 163-278.31: Repealed by Session Laws 1985, c. 183, s. 4.

§ 163-278.32. Statements under oath.

Any statement required to be filed under this Article shall be signed and certified as true and correct by the individual, media, candidate, treasurer or others required to file it, and shall be certified as true and correct to the best of the knowledge of the individual, media, candidate, treasurer or others filing the statement; provided further that the candidate shall certify as true and correct to the best of his knowledge the organizational report and appointment of treasurer filed for the candidate or the candidate's principal campaign committee. A certification under this Article shall be treated as under oath, and any person making a certification under this Article knowing the information to be untrue is guilty of a Class I felony. (1973, c. 1272, s. 1; 1999-426, s. 10(a); 2001-235, s. 1; 2007-391, s. 1(a).)

§ 163-278.33. Applicability of Article 22.

Sections 163-271 through 163-278 shall be applicable to the offices covered by this Article and G.S. 163-271 through 163-278 shall be applicable to all elective offices not covered by this Article. (1973, c. 1272, s. 3; 1975, c. 50; c. 565, s. 10; 2002-159, s. 21(f).)

§ 163-278.34. Civil penalties.

(a) Civil Penalties for Late Filing. - Except as provided in G.S. 163-278.9 and G.S. 163-278.9A, all reports, statements or other documents required by this Article to be filed with the Board shall be filed either by manual delivery to or by mail addressed to the Board. Timely filing shall be complete if postmarked on the day the reports, statements or other documents are to be delivered to the Board. If a report, statement or other document is not filed within the time required by this Article, then the individual, person, media, candidate, political committee, referendum committee or treasurer responsible for filing shall pay to the State Board of Elections election enforcement costs and a civil late penalty as follows:

(1) Two hundred fifty dollars ($250.00) per day for each day the filing is late for a report that affects statewide elections, not to exceed a total of ten thousand dollars ($10,000); and

(2) Fifty dollars ($50.00) per day for each day the filing is late for a report that affects only nonstatewide elections, not to exceed a total of five hundred dollars ($500.00).

If the form is filed by mail, no civil late penalty shall be assessed for any day after the date of postmark. No civil late penalty shall be assessed for any day when the Board office at which the report is due is closed. The State Board shall immediately notify, or cause to be notified, late filers, from which reports are apparently due, by mail, of the penalties under this section. The State Board of Elections may waive a late penalty if it determines there is good cause for the waiver.

If the Board determines by clear and convincing evidence that the late filing constitutes a willful attempt to conceal contributions or expenditures, the Board may assess a civil penalty in an amount to be determined by that Board, plus the costs of investigation, assessment, and collection. The civil penalty shall not exceed three times the amount of the contributions and expenditures willfully attempted to be concealed.

(b) Civil Penalties for Illegal Contributions and Expenditures. - If an individual, person, political committee, referendum committee, candidate, or other entity intentionally makes or accepts a contribution or makes an unlawful expenditure in violation of this Article, then that entity shall pay to the State Board of Elections, in an amount to be determined by that Board, a civil penalty and the costs of investigation, assessment, and collection. The civil penalty shall not exceed three times the amount of the unlawful contribution or expenditure involved in the violation. The State Board of Elections may, in addition to the civil penalty, order that the amount unlawfully received be paid to the State Board by check, and any money so received by the State Board shall be deposited in the Civil Penalty and Forfeiture Fund of North Carolina.

(c) Civil Remedies Other Than Penalties. - The State Board of Elections, in lieu of or in addition to imposing a civil penalty under subsection (a) or (b) of this section, may take one or more of the following actions with respect to a violation for which a civil penalty could be imposed:

(1) Issue an order requiring the violator to cease and desist from the violation found.

(2) Issue an order to cease receiving contributions and making expenditures until a delinquent report has been filed and any civil penalty satisfied.

(3) Issue an order requiring the violator to take any remedial action deemed appropriate by the Board.

(4) Issue an order requiring the violator to file any report, statement, or other information as required by this Article or the rules adopted by the Board.

(5) Publicly reprimand the violator for the violation.

(d) Facts in Mitigation. - An individual or other entity notified that a penalty has been assessed against it may submit an affidavit to the State Board of Elections stating the facts in mitigation. The State Board of Elections may waive a civil penalty in whole or in part if it determines there is good cause for the waiver.

(e) Calculation and Assessment. - The State Board shall calculate and assess the amount of the civil penalty due under subsection (a) or (b) of this section and shall notify the person who is assessed the civil penalty of the amount. The notice of assessment shall be served by any means authorized under G.S. 1A-1, Rule 4, and shall direct the violator either to pay the assessment or to contest the assessment within 30 days by filing a petition for a contested case under Article 3 of Chapter 150B of the General Statutes. If a violator does not pay a civil penalty assessed by the Board within 30 days after it is due, the Board shall request the Attorney General to institute a civil action to recover the amount of the assessment. The civil action may be brought in the superior court of any county where the report was due to be filed or any county where the violator resides or maintains an office. A civil action must be filed within three years of the date the assessment was due. An assessment that is not contested is due when the violator is served with a notice of assessment. An assessment that is contested is due at the conclusion of the administrative and judicial review of the assessment. The State Board of Elections shall pay the clear proceeds of civil penalties collected under this section to the Civil Penalty and Forfeiture Fund pursuant to G.S. 115C-457.2. The State Board of Elections shall reduce the monies collected by the enforcement costs and the collection costs to determine the clear proceeds payable to the Civil Penalty and Forfeiture Fund. Monies set aside for the costs of enforcement and the costs of collection shall be credited to accounts of the State Board of Elections.

(f)   Notifying and Consulting With District Attorney. - Before assessing a civil penalty under subsection (b) of this section or imposing a civil remedy under subsection (c) of this section, the State Board of Elections shall notify and consult with the district attorney who would be responsible under G.S. 163-278.27 for bringing a criminal prosecution concerning the violation. (1973, c. 1272, s. 1; 1975, c. 565, s. 5; 1979, c. 1073, s. 19; 1997-515, s. 7(a); 2001-353, s. 10; 2001-419, s. 1; 2007-391, ss. 2(a), 37; 2008-187, s. 33(a).)

§ 163-278.34A. Presumptions.

In any proceeding brought pursuant to this Article in which a presumption arises from the proof of certain facts, the defendant may offer some evidence to rebut the presumption, but the State bears the ultimate burden of proving the essential elements of its case. (1999-31, s. 1(c); 1999-453, s. 3.1(a).)

§ 163-278.35. Preservation of records.

All reports, records and accounts required by this Article to be made, kept, filed, or maintained by any individual, media, candidate or treasurer shall be preserved and retained by the individual, media, candidate or treasurer for at least two years counting from the date of the election to which such reports, records and accounts refer. (1973, c. 1272, s. 1.)

§ 163-278.36: Repealed by Session Laws 2007-349, s. 4, effective January 1, 2008.

§ 163-278.37. County boards of elections to preserve reports.

The county boards of elections shall preserve all reports and statements filed with them pursuant to this Article for such period of time as directed by the State Board of Elections. (1979, c. 500, s. 15.)

§ 163-278.38. Effect of failure to comply.

The failure to comply with the provisions of this Article shall not invalidate the results of any referendum. (1979, c. 1073, s. 11.)

§§ 163-278.38A through 163-278.38Y. Reserved for future codification purposes.

Part 1A. Disclosure Requirements for Media Advertisements.

§ 163-278.38Z. Definitions.

As used in this Part:

(1) "Advertisement" means any message appearing in the print media, on television, or on radio that constitutes a contribution or expenditure under this Article.

(2) "Candidate" means any individual who, with respect to a public office listed in G.S. 163-278.6(18), has filed a notice of candidacy or a petition requesting to be a candidate, or has been certified as a nominee of a political party for a vacancy, or has otherwise qualified as a candidate in a manner authorized by law, or has filed a statement of organization under G.S. 163-278.7

and is required to file periodic financial disclosure statements under G.S. 163-278.9.

(3) "Candidate campaign committee" means any political committee organized by or under the direction of a candidate.

(4) "Full-screen" means the only picture appearing on the television screen during the oral disclosure statement contains the disclosing person, that the picture occupies all visible space on the television screen, and that the image of the disclosing person occupies at least fifty percent (50%) of the vertical height of the television screen.

(5) "Political action committee" has the same meaning as "political committee" in G.S. 163-278.6(14), except that "political action committee" does not include any political party or political party organization.

(6) "Political party organization" means any political party executive committee or any political committee that operates under the direction of a political party executive committee or political party chair.

(7) "Print media" means billboards, cards, newspapers, newspaper inserts, magazines, mass mailings, pamphlets, fliers, periodicals, and outdoor advertising facilities.

(8) "Radio" means any radio broadcast station that is subject to the provisions of 47 U.S.C. §§ 315 and 317.

(9) "Scan line" means a standard term of measurement used in the electronic media industry calculating a certain area in a television advertisement.

(10) "Sponsor" means a candidate, candidate committee, political party organization, political action committee, referendum committee, individual, or other entity that purchases an advertisement.

(11) "Television" means any television broadcast station, cable television system, wireless-cable multipoint distribution system, satellite company, or telephone company transmitting video programming that is subject to the provisions of 47 U.S.C. §§ 315 and 317.

(12) "Unobscured" means the only printed material that may appear on the television screen is a visual disclosure statement required by law, and nothing is blocking the view of the disclosing person's face. (1999-453, s. 2(a); 2004-203, s. 12(a); 2010-170, s. 7.)

§ 163-278.39. Basic disclosure requirements for all political advertisements.

(a) Basic Requirements. - It shall be unlawful for any sponsor to sponsor an advertisement in the print media or on radio or television that constitutes an expenditure, independent expenditure, electioneering communication, or contribution required to be disclosed under this Article unless all the following conditions are met:

(1) It bears the legend or includes the statement: "Paid for by ___ [Name of candidate, candidate campaign committee, political party organization, political action committee, referendum committee, individual, or other sponsor]." In television advertisements, this disclosure shall be made by visual legend.

(2) The name used in the labeling required in subdivision (1) of this subsection is the name that appears on the statement of organization as required in G.S. 163-278.7(b)(1) or G.S. 163-278.12C(a).

(3) Repealed by Session Laws 2001-353, s. 5, effective August 10, 2001.

(4) Repealed by Session Laws 2013-381, s. 56.1, effective January 1, 2014.

(5) In a print media advertisement supporting or opposing the nomination or election of one or more clearly identified candidates, the sponsor states whether it is authorized by a candidate. The visual legend in the advertisement shall state either "Authorized by [name of candidate], candidate for [name of office]" or "Not authorized by a candidate." This subdivision does not apply if the sponsor of the advertisement is the candidate the advertisement supports or that candidate's campaign committee.

(6) In a print media advertisement that identifies a candidate the sponsor is opposing, the sponsor discloses in the advertisement the name of the candidate who is intended to benefit from the advertisement. This subdivision applies only when the sponsor coordinates or consults about the advertisement or the expenditure for it with the candidate who is intended to benefit.

(7), (8) Repealed by Session Laws 2013-381, s. 56.1, effective January 1, 2014.

If an advertisement described in this section is jointly sponsored, the disclosure statement shall name all the sponsors.

(b) Size Requirements. - In a print media advertisement covered by subsection (a) of this section, the height of all disclosure statements required by that subsection shall constitute at least five percent (5%) of the height of the printed space of the advertisement, provided that the type shall in no event be less than 12 points in size. In an advertisement in a newspaper or a newspaper insert, the total height of the disclosure statement need not constitute five percent of the printed space of the advertisement if the type of the disclosure statement is at least 28 points in size. If a single advertisement consists of multiple pages, folds, or faces, the disclosure requirement of this section applies only to one page, fold, or face. In a television advertisement covered by subsection (a) of this section, the visual disclosure legend shall constitute four percent (4%) of vertical picture height in size, and where the television advertisement that appears is paid for by a candidate or candidate campaign committee, the visual disclosure legend shall appear simultaneously with an easily identifiable photograph of the candidate for at least two seconds. In a radio advertisement covered by subsection (a) of this section, the disclosure statement shall last at least two seconds, provided the statement is spoken so that its contents may be easily understood.

(c) Misrepresentation of Authorization. - Notwithstanding G.S. 163-278.27(a), any candidate, candidate campaign committee, political party organization, political action committee, referendum committee, individual, or other sponsor making an advertisement in the print media or on radio or television bearing any legend required by subsection (a) of this section that misrepresents the sponsorship or authorization of the advertisement is guilty of a Class 1 misdemeanor. (1999-453, s. 2(a); 2001-317, s. 1; 2001-353, s. 5; 2010-170, s. 8; 2013-381, ss. 44.2, 56.1.)

§ 163-278.39A: Repealed by Session Laws 2013-381, s. 44.1, effective January 1, 2014.

§ 163-278.39B: Recodified as G.S. 163-278.38Z by Session Laws 2004-203, s. 12(a), effective August 17, 2004.

§ 163-278.39C. Scope of disclosure requirements.

The disclosure requirements of this Part apply to any sponsor of an advertisement in the print media or on radio or television the cost or value of which constitutes an expenditure or contribution required to be disclosed under this Article, except that the disclosure requirements of this Part:

(1)   Do not apply to an individual who makes uncoordinated independent expenditures aggregating less than one thousand dollars ($1,000) in a political campaign; and

(2)   Do not apply to an individual who incurs expenses with respect to a referendum.

The disclosure requirements of this Part do not apply to any advertisement the expenditure for which is required to be disclosed by G.S. 163-278.12A alone and by no other law. (1999-453, s. 2(a).)

Part 2. Municipal Campaign Reporting.

§ 163-278.40. Definitions.

When used in this Part, words and phrases have the same meaning as in G.S. 163-278.6, except that:

(1)   The term "board" means the county board of elections;

(2)   The term "city" means any incorporated city, town, or village. (1981, c. 837, s. 3; 1997-515, s. 4(d).)

§ 163-278.40A. Organizational report.

(a)   Each candidate and political committee in a city election shall appoint a treasurer and, under verification, report the name and address of the treasurer to the board. A candidate may appoint himself or any other individual, including any relative except his spouse, as his treasurer. If the candidate fails to designate a treasurer, the candidate shall be deemed to have appointed himself as treasurer. A candidate or political committee may remove his or its treasurer.

(b) The organizational report shall state the bank account and number of such campaign fund. Each report required by this Part shall reflect all contributions, expenditures and loans made in behalf of a candidate. The organizational report shall be filed with the county board of elections within 10 days after the candidate files a notice of candidacy with the county board of elections, or within 10 days following the organization of the political committee, whichever occurs first. (1981, c. 837, s. 3.)

§ 163-278.40B. Campaign report; partisan election.

In any city election conducted on a partisan basis in accordance with G.S. 163-279(a)(2) and 163-291, the following reports shall be filed in addition to the organizational report:

(1) Thirty-five-day Report. - The treasurer shall file a report with the board 35 days before the primary.

(1a) Pre-primary Report. - The treasurer shall file a report with the board no later than the tenth day preceding each primary election.

(2) Pre-election Report. - The treasurer shall file a report 10 days before the election, unless a second primary is held and the candidate appeared on the ballot in the second primary, in which case the report shall be filed 10 days before the second primary.

(3) Repealed by Session Laws 1985, c. 164, s. 2.

(4) Semiannual Reports. - If contributions are received or expenditures made during any part of a calendar year, for which no reports are otherwise required by this section, any and all those contributions and expenditures shall be reported on semiannual reports due on the last Friday in July, covering the period through June 30, and due on the last Friday in January, covering the period through December 31 of the previous year. (1981, c. 837, s. 3; 1985, c. 164, s. 2; 1987 (Reg. Sess., 1988), c. 1028, s. 7; 2001-419, s. 3.)

§ 163-278.40C. Campaign report; nonpartisan election and runoff.

If any city election conducted under the nonpartisan election and runoff basis in accordance with G.S. 163-279(a) (4) and 163-293, the following reports shall be filed in addition to the organizational report:

(1)   Thirty-five-day Report. - The treasurer shall file a report with the board 35 days before the election.

(1a)   Pre-election Report. - The treasurer shall file a report with the board 10 days before the election.

(1b)   Pre-runoff Report. - The treasurer shall file a report with the board 10 days before the runoff if the candidate is in a runoff.

(2)   Repealed by Session Laws 1985, c. 164, s. 3.

(3)   Semiannual Reports. - If contributions are received or expenditures made during any part of a calendar year, for which no reports are otherwise required by this section, any and all those contributions and expenditures shall be reported on semiannual reports due on the last Friday in July, covering the period through June 30, and due on the last Friday in January, covering the period through December 31 of the previous year. (1981, c. 837, s. 3; 1985, c. 164, s. 3; 1987 (Reg. Sess., 1988), c. 1028, s. 8; 2001-419, s. 4.)

§ 163-278.40D. Campaign report; nonpartisan primary and elections.

In any city election conducted under the nonpartisan primary method in accordance with G.S. 163-279(a)(3) and 163-294, the following reports shall be filed in addition to the organizational report:

(1)   Thirty-five-day Report. - The treasurer shall file a report with the board 35 days before the primary if the candidate is in a primary or the same length of time before the election if the candidate is not in a primary.

(1a)   Pre-primary and Pre-election Reports. - The treasurer shall file a report 10 days before the primary if the candidate is in a primary and 10 days before the election.

(2)   Repealed by Session laws 1985, c. 164, s. 4.

(3) Semiannual Reports. - If contributions are received or expenditures made during any part of a calendar year, for which no reports are otherwise required by this section, any and all those contributions and expenditures shall be reported on semiannual reports due on the last Friday in July, covering the period through June 30, and due on the last Friday in January, covering the period through December 31 of the previous year. (1981, c. 837, s. 3; 1985, c. 164, s. 4; 1987 (Reg. Sess., 1988), c. 1028, s. 9; 2001-419, s. 5.)

§ 163-278.40E. Campaign report; nonpartisan plurality.

In any city election conducted under the nonpartisan plurality method under G.S. 163-279(a)(1) and 163-292, the following reports shall be filed in addition to the organizational report:

(1) Thirty-five-day Report. - The treasurer shall file a report with the board 35 days before the election.

(1a) Pre-election Report. - The treasurer shall file a report 10 days before the election.

(2) Repealed by Session Laws 1985, c. 164, s. 5.

(3) Semiannual Reports. - If contributions are received or expenditures made during any part of a calendar year, for which no reports are otherwise required by this section, any and all those contributions and expenditures shall be reported on semiannual reports due on the last Friday in July, covering the period through June 30, and due on the last Friday in January, covering the period through December 31 of the previous year. (1981, c. 837, s. 3; 1985, c. 164, s. 5; 1987 (Reg. Sess., 1988), c. 1028, s. 10; 2001-419, s. 6.)

§ 163-278.40F. Form of report.

Forms of reports under this Part shall be prescribed by the board. (1981, c. 837, s. 3.)

§ 163-278.40G. Content.

Except as otherwise provided in this Part, each report shall be current within seven days prior to the date the report is due and shall list all contributions received and expenditures made which have not been previously reported. (1981, c. 837, s. 3.)

§ 163-278.40H. Notice of reports due.

The director of the board shall advise, or cause to be advised, no less than five days nor more than 15 days before each report is due each candidate or treasurer whose organizational report has been filed under G.S. 163-278.40A of the specific date each report is due. He shall immediately notify any individual, candidate, treasurer, or political committee, to file a statement under this Part if:

(1) It appears that the individual, candidate, treasurer, or political committee has failed to file a statement as required by law or that a statement filed does not conform to this Part; or

(2) A written complaint is filed under oath with the board by any registered voter of this State alleging that a statement filed with the board does not conform to this Part or to the truth or that an individual, candidate, treasurer, or political committee has failed to file a statement required by this Part. (1981, c. 837, s. 3; 1995, c. 243, s. 1.)

§ 163-278.40I. Part 1 to apply.

(a) Except as provided in this Part or in G.S. 163-278.9(d), the provisions of Part 1 shall apply to municipal elections covered by this Part.

(b) G.S. 163-278.7, 163-278.9(a), (b) and (c), 163-278.22(1) and (9), the first paragraph of 163-278.23, 163-278.24, 163-278.25, and 163-278.26 shall not apply to this Part. (1981, c. 837, s. 3.)

§ 163-278.40J. Other committees report by municipal schedule.

A candidate or political committee that appoints a treasurer under G.S. 163-278.7 shall make reports according to the schedule under this Part if it makes contributions or expenditures concerning municipal elections. (2008-150, s. 9(a).)

Article 22B.

Appropriations from the North Carolina Political Parties Financing Fund.

§§ 163-278.41 through 163-278.45: Repealed by Session Laws 2013-381, s. 38.1(c), effective July 1, 2013.

Article 22C.

Appropriations from the North Carolina Candidates Financing Fund.

§ 163-278.46: Repealed by Session Laws 2002-158, s. 5, effective January 1, 2003.

§ 163-278.47: Repealed by Session Laws 2002-158, s. 5, effective January 1, 2003.

§ 163-278.48: Repealed by Session Laws 2002-158, s. 5, effective January 1, 2003.

§ 163-278.49: Repealed by Session Laws 2002-158, s. 5, effective January 1, 2003.

§ 163-278.50: Repealed by Session Laws 2002-158, s. 5, effective January 1, 2003.

§ 163-278.51: Repealed by Session Laws 2002-158, s. 5, effective January 1, 2003.

§ 163-278.52: Repealed by Session Laws 2002-158, s. 5, effective January 1, 2003.

§ 163-278.53: Repealed by Session Laws 2002-158, s. 5, effective January 1, 2003.

§ 163-278.54: Repealed by Session Laws 2002-158, s. 5, effective January 1, 2003.

§ 163-278.55: Repealed by Session Laws 2002-158, s. 5, effective January 1, 2003.

§ 163-278.56: Repealed by Session Laws 2002-158, s. 5, effective January 1, 2003.

§ 163-278.57: Repealed by Session Laws 2002-158, s. 5, effective January 1, 2003.

§§ 163-278.58 through 163-278.60. Reserved for future codification purposes.

Article 22D.

The North Carolina Public Campaign Fund.

§§ 163-278.61 through 163-278.67: Repealed by Session Laws 2013-360, s. 21.1(a) and Session Laws 2013-381, s. 38.1(a), effective July 1, 2013.

§ 163-278.68: Repealed by Session Laws 2011-266, s. 1.2(a), effective July 1, 2011.

§ 163-278.69. (See Editor's note for contingent repeal) Voter education.

(a) Judicial Voter Guide. - The Board shall publish a Judicial Voter Guide that explains the functions of the appellate courts and the laws concerning the election of appellate judges, the purpose and function of the Public Campaign Fund, and the laws concerning voter registration. The Board shall distribute the Guide to as many voting-age individuals in the State as practical, through a mailing to all residences or other means it deems effective. The distribution shall occur no more than 28 days nor fewer than seven days before the one-stop voting period provided in G.S. 163-227.2 for the primary and no more than 28 days nor fewer than seven days before the one-stop voting period provided in G.S. 163-227.2 for the general election.

(b) Candidate Information. - The Judicial Voter Guide shall include information concerning all candidates for the Supreme Court and the Court of Appeals, as provided by those candidates according to a format provided to the candidates by the Board. The Board shall request information for the Guide from each candidate according to the following format:

(1) Place of residence.

(2) Education.

(3) Occupation.

(4) Employer.

(5) Date admitted to the bar.

(6) Legal/judicial experience.

(7) Candidate statement. Concerning that statement, the Board shall send to the candidates instructions as follows: "Your statement may include information such as your qualifications, your endorsements, your ratings, why you are seeking judicial office, why you would make a good judge, what distinguishes you from your opponent(s), your acceptance of spending and fund-raising limits to qualify to receive funds from the Public Campaign Fund, and any other information relevant to your candidacy. The State Board of Elections will reject any portion of any statement which it determines contains obscene, profane, or defamatory language. The candidate shall have three days to resubmit the candidate statement if the Board rejects a portion of the statement.

The entire entry for a candidate shall be limited to 250 words.

(c) Disclaimer. - The Judicial Voter Guide shall contain the following statement: "Statements by candidates do not express or reflect the opinions of the State Board of Elections." (2002-158, s. 1; 2005-276, s. 23A.1(d); 2005-430, s. 6; 2006-192, s. 14; 2007-391, s. 4(a); 2008-187, s. 33(a); 2009-543, s. 6.)

§ 163-278.70: Repealed by Session Laws 2013-360, s. 21.1(a) and Session Laws 2013-381, s. 38.1(a), effective July 1, 2013.

§§ 163-278.71 through 163-278.79: Reserved for future codification purposes.

Article 22E.

Electioneering Communications.

§ 163-278.80: Repealed by Session Laws 2010-170, s. 10, effective September 23, 2010.

§ 163-278.81: Repealed by Session Laws 2010-170, s. 10, effective September 23, 2010.

§ 163-278.82: Repealed by Session Laws 2010-170, s. 10, effective September 23, 2010.

§ 163-278.83: Repealed by Session Laws 2010-170, s. 10, effective September 23, 2010.

§ 163-278.84: Repealed by Session Laws 2010-170, s. 10, effective September 23, 2010.

§ 163-278.85: Repealed by Session Laws 2010-170, s. 10, effective September 23, 2010.

§ 163-278.86: Repealed by Session Laws 2010-170, s. 10, effective September 23, 2010.

§ 163-278.87: Repealed by Session Laws 2010-170, s. 10, effective September 23, 2010.

§ 163-278.88: Repealed by Session Laws 2010-170, s. 10, effective September 23, 2010.

§ 163-278.89: Repealed by Session Laws 2010-170, s. 10, effective September 23, 2010.

Article 22F.

Mass Mailings and Telephone Banks: Electioneering Communications.

§ 163-278.90: Repealed by Session Laws 2010-170, s. 11, effective September 23, 2010.

§ 163-278.91: Repealed by Session Laws 2010-170, s. 11, effective September 23, 2010.

§ 163-278.92: Repealed by Session Laws 2010-170, s. 11, effective September 23, 2010.

§ 163-278.93: Repealed by Session Laws 2010-170, s. 11, effective September 23, 2010.

§ 163-278.94: Repealed by Session Laws 2010-170, s. 11, effective September 23, 2010.

Article 22J.

The Voter-Owned Elections Act.

§§ 163-278.95 through 163-278.99D: Repealed by Session Laws 2013-381, s. 38.1(b), effective July 1, 2013.

§ 163-278.99E. Voter education.

(a)   Voter Guide. - The Board shall publish a Voter Guide that explains the functions of office as defined in G.S. 163-278.96(12) and the laws concerning the election of the Council of State, the purpose and function of the Fund, and the laws concerning voter registration. The Board shall distribute the Guide to as many voting-age individuals in the State as practical, through a mailing to all residences or other means it deems effective. The State Board of Elections shall maintain a list of the addresses from which mailed Voter Guides are returned as undeliverable. That list shall be available for public inspection. The distribution shall occur no more than 28 days nor fewer than seven days before the one-stop voting period provided in G.S. 163-227.2 for the primary and no more than 28 days nor fewer than seven days before the one-stop voting period provided in G.S. 163-227.2 for the general election.

(b)   Candidate Information. - The Voter Guide shall include information concerning all candidates for office as defined in G.S. 163-278.96(12), as provided by those candidates according to a format provided to the candidates by the Board. The Board shall request information for the Guide from each candidate according to the following format:

(1) Place of residence.

(2) Education.

(3) Occupation.

(4) Employer.

(5) Previous elective offices held.

(6) Endorsements, limited to 50 words. Concerning endorsements, the Board shall send to the candidates instructions as follows: "In order to have an endorsement published, you must provide written confirmation to the Board from the endorsing person or organization that you received that person's or organization's endorsement."

(7) Candidate statement, limited to 150 words. Concerning that statement, the Board shall send to the candidates instructions as follows: "Your statement may include information such as your qualifications, your endorsements, why you would make a good elected official, what distinguishes you from your opponent(s), and any other information relevant to your candidacy. The State Board of Elections will reject any portion of any statement which it determines contains obscene, profane, or defamatory language. The candidate shall have three days to resubmit the candidate statement if the Board rejects a portion of the statement."

(c) Disclaimer. - The Voter Guide shall contain the following statement: "Statements by candidates do not express or reflect the opinions of the State Board of Elections."

(d) (See Editor's note for contingent repeal) Relationship to the Judicial Voter Guide. - The Board may publish the Voter Guide in conjunction with the Judicial Voter Guide described in G.S. 163-278.69. (2007-391, s. 4(b); 2007-484, s. 43.8(c); 2007-540, s. 1; 2008-187, s. 33(a); 2013-360, s. 21.1(i); 2013-381, s. 38.1(l).)

Article 22G.

Candidate-Specific Communications.

§§ 163-278.100 through 163-278.103: Repealed by Session Laws 2013-381, s. 48.1, effective January 1, 2013.

§ 163-278.104: Reserved for future codification purposes.

§ 163-278.105: Reserved for future codification purposes.

§ 163-278.106: Reserved for future codification purposes.

§ 163-278.107: Reserved for future codification purposes.

§ 163-278.108: Reserved for future codification purposes.

§ 163-278.109: Reserved for future codification purposes.

Article 22H.

Mass Mailings and Telephone Banks: Candidate-Specific Communications.

§§ 163-278.110 through 163-278.113: Repealed by Session Laws 2013-381, s. 48.4, effective January 1, 2014.

Article 22I.

Reserved for future codification purposes.

§§ 163-278.114 through 163-278.299: Reserved for future codification purposes.

Article 22M.

Legal Expense Funds.

§ 163-278.300. Definitions.

As used in this Article, the following terms mean:

(1) Board. - The State Board of Elections.

(2) Renumbered.

(3) Elected officer. - Any individual serving in or seeking a public office. An individual is seeking a public office when that individual has filed any notice, petition, or other document required by law or local act as a condition of election to public office. An individual continues to be an elected officer for purposes of this Article as long as a legal action commenced while the individual was an elected officer continues. If a legal action is commenced after an individual ceases to serve in or seek public office but the legal action concerns subject matter in the individual's official capacity as an elected officer, for purposes of this Article, that individual is an elected officer as long as that legal action continues.

(4) Expenditure. - An expenditure means any purchase, advance, conveyance, deposit, distribution, transfer of funds, loan, payment, gift, pledge, subscription of money, anything of value whatsoever, and any contract, agreement, promise, or other obligation to make an expenditure, by a legal defense fund for a permitted use as provided in G.S. 163-278.320. An expenditure forgiven by a person or entity to whom it is owed shall be reported as a legal expense donation.

(5) Legal action. - A formal dispute in a judicial, legislative, or administrative forum, including but not limited to, a civil or criminal action filed in a court, a complaint or protest filed with a board of elections, an election contest filed under Article 3 of Chapter 120 of the General Statutes or G.S. 163-182.13A, or a complaint filed with the State Ethics Commission or Legislative Ethics Committee. The term "legal action" also includes investigations made or conducted before the commencement of any formal proceedings. The term "legal action" does not include the election itself or the campaign for election.

(5a) Legal expense donation. - A legal expense donation means any advance, conveyance, deposit, distribution, transfer of funds, loan, payment, gift, subscription of money, or anything of value whatsoever, and any contract, agreement, or other obligation to make a contribution to a legal expense fund for a permitted use as provided in G.S. 163-278.320. The term "legal expense donation" does not include either of the following:

a. The provision of legal services to an elected officer by the State or any of its political subdivisions when those services are authorized or required by law, or

b. The provision of free or pro bono legal advice or legal services, provided that any costs incurred or expenses advanced for which clients are liable under other provisions of law shall be deemed legal expense donations.

(6) Legal expense fund. - Any collection of money for the purpose of funding a legal action, or a potential legal action, taken by or against an elected officer in that elected officer's official capacity.

(7) Official capacity. - Related to or resulting from the campaign for public office or related to or resulting from holding public office. "Official capacity" is not limited to "scope and course of employment" as used in G.S. 143-300.3.

(8) Public office. - As defined in G.S. 163-278.6.

(9) Treasurer. - An individual appointed by an elected officer or other individual or group of individuals collecting money for a legal expense fund. (2007-349, s. 1; 2009-534, s. 2(a).)

§ 163-278.301. Creation of legal expense funds.

(a) An elected officer, or another individual or group of individuals on the elected officer's behalf, shall create a legal expense fund if given a legal expense donation, other than from that elected officer's self, spouse, parents, brothers, or sisters, for any of the following purposes:

(1) To fund an existing legal action taken by or against the elected officer in that elected officer's official capacity.

(2) To fund a potential legal action taken by or against an elected officer in that elected officer's official capacity.

(b) This section shall not apply to any payment to the State or any of its political subdivisions.

(c) The legal expense fund shall comply with all provisions of this Article.

(d)   If an elected officer funds legal actions entirely from that elected officer's own legal expense donations or those of the elected officer's spouse, parents, brothers, or sisters, that elected officer is not required to create a legal expense fund. If a legal expense fund accepts legal expense donations as described in subsection (a) of this section, that legal expense fund shall report the elected officer's own legal expense donations and those of those family members along with the other legal expense donations in accordance with G.S. 163-278.310.

(e)   No more than one legal expense fund shall be created by or for an elected officer for the same legal action. Legal actions arising out of the same set of transactions and occurrences are deemed the same legal action for purposes of this subsection. A legal expense fund created for one legal action or potential legal action may be kept open by or on behalf of the elected officer for subsequent legal actions or potential legal actions.

(f)   Contractual arrangements, including liability insurance, or commercial relationships or arrangements made in the normal course of business if not made for the purpose of lobbying, are not "legal expense donations" for purposes of this Article. Use of such contractual arrangements to fund legal actions does not by itself require the elected officer to create a legal expense fund. If a legal expense fund has been created pursuant to subsection (a) of this section, such contractual arrangements shall be reported as expenditures.

(g)   A violation of this Article shall be punishable as a Class 1 misdemeanor. (2007-349, s. 1; 2009-534, s. 2(b).)

§ 163-278.302: Reserved for future codification purposes.

§ 163-278.303: Reserved for future codification purposes.

§ 163-278.304: Reserved for future codification purposes.

§ 163-278.305: Reserved for future codification purposes.

§ 163-278.306. Treasurer.

(a)   Each legal expense fund shall appoint a treasurer and, under verification, report the name and address of the treasurer to the Board.

(b) A legal expense fund may remove its treasurer. In case of the death, resignation, or removal of its treasurer, the legal expense fund shall appoint a successor within 10 calendar days of the vacancy and certify the name and address of the successor in the same manner provided in the case of an original appointment.

(c) Every treasurer of a legal expense fund shall receive training from the Board as to the duties of the office within three months of appointment and at least once every four years thereafter. (2007-349, s. 1.)

§ 163-278.307. Detailed accounts to be kept by treasurer.

(a) The treasurer of each legal expense fund shall keep detailed accounts, current within seven calendar days after the date of receiving a legal expense donation or making an expenditure, of all legal expense donations received and all expenditures made by or on behalf of the legal expense fund.

(b) Accounts kept by the treasurer of a legal expense fund or the accounts of a treasurer or legal expense fund at any bank or other depository may be inspected by a member, designee, agent, attorney, or employee of the Board who is making an investigation pursuant to G.S. 163-278.22.

(c) For purposes of this section, "detailed accounts" shall mean at least all information required to be included in the quarterly report required under this Article.

(d) When a treasurer shows that best efforts have been used to obtain, maintain, and submit the information required by this Article, any report of the legal expense shall be considered in compliance with this Article and shall not be the basis for criminal prosecution or the imposition of civil penalties. The State Board of Elections shall adopt rules to implement this subsection. (2007-349, s. 1; 2009-534, s. 2(c).)

§ 163-278.308. Reports filed with Board.

(a) The treasurer of each legal expense fund shall file with the Board the following reports:

(1) Organizational report. - The report required under G.S. 163-278.309.

(2) Quarterly report. - The report required under G.S. 163-278.310.

(b) Any report or attachment required by this Article must be filed under certification of the treasurer as true and correct to the best of the knowledge of that officer.

(c) The organizational report shall be filed within 10 calendar days of the creation of the legal expense fund. All quarterly reports shall be filed with the Board no later than 10 business days after the end of each calendar quarter.

(d) Treasurers shall electronically file each report required by this section that shows a cumulative total for the quarter in excess of five thousand dollars ($5,000) in legal expense donations or expenditures, according to rules adopted by the Board. The Board shall provide the software necessary to the treasurer to file the required electronic report at no cost to the legal expense fund.

(e) Any statement required to be filed under this Article shall be signed and certified as true and correct by the treasurer and shall be certified as true and correct to the best of the treasurer's knowledge. The elected officer creating the legal expense fund, or the other individual or group of individuals creating the legal expense fund on the elected officer's behalf, shall certify as true and correct to the best of their knowledge the organizational report and appointment of the treasurer. A certification under this Article shall be treated as under oath, and any individual making a certification under this Article knowing the information to be untrue is guilty of a Class I felony. (2007-349, s. 1; 2009-534, s. 2(d).)

§ 163-278.309. Organizational report.

(a) Each appointed treasurer shall file with the Board a statement of organization that includes all of the following:

(1) The name, address, and purpose of the legal expense fund.

(2) The names, addresses, and relationships of affiliated or connected elected officers, candidates, political committees, referendum committees, political parties, or similar organizations.

(3) The name, address, and position with the legal expense fund of the custodian of books and accounts.

(4) A listing of all banks, safety deposit boxes, or other depositories used, including the names and numbers of all accounts maintained and the numbers of all such safety deposit boxes used. The Board shall keep any account number required by this Article confidential except as necessary to conduct an audit or investigation, except as required by a court of competent jurisdiction, or except as confidentiality is waived by the treasurer. Disclosure of an account number in violation of this subdivision shall not give rise to a civil cause of action. This limitation of liability does not apply to the disclosure of account numbers in violation of this subdivision as a result of gross negligence, wanton conduct, or intentional wrongdoing that would otherwise be actionable.

(5) The name or names and address or addresses of any assistant treasurers appointed by the treasurer. Such assistant treasurers shall be authorized to act in the name of the treasurer, who shall be fully responsible for any act or acts committed by an assistant treasurer, and the treasurer shall be fully liable for any violation of this Article committed by any assistant treasurer.

(6) Any other information which might be requested by the Board that deals with the legal expense fund organization.

(b) Any change in information previously submitted in a statement of organization shall be reported to the Board within 10 calendar days following the change. (2007-349, s. 1.)

§ 163-278.310. Quarterly report.

The treasurer of each legal expense fund shall be required to file a quarterly report with the Board containing all of the following:

(1) Legal expense donations. - The name and complete mailing address of each donor, the amount of the legal expense donation, the principal occupation of the donor, and the date the legal expense donation was received. The total sum of all legal expense donations to date shall also be plainly exhibited. The treasurer is not required to report the name of any donor making a total legal expense donation of fifty dollars ($50.00) or less in a calendar quarter, but shall instead report the fact that the treasurer has received a total legal expense

donation of fifty dollars ($50.00) or less, the amount of the legal expense donation, and the date of receipt.

(2) Expenditures. - A list of all expenditures made by or on behalf of the legal expense fund. The report shall list the name and complete mailing address of each payee, the amount paid, the purpose, and the date such payment was made. The total sum of all expenditures to date shall also be plainly exhibited. The payee shall be the entity to whom the legal expense fund is obligated to make the expenditure. If the expenditure is to a financial institution for revolving credit or a reimbursement for a payment to a financial institution for revolving credit, the statement shall also include a specific itemization of the goods and services purchased with the revolving credit. If the obligation is for more than one good or service, the statement shall include a specific itemization of the obligation so as to provide a reasonable understanding of the obligation.

(3) Loans. - All proceeds from loans shall be recorded separately with a detailed analysis reflecting the amount of the loan, the source, the period, the rate of interest, and the security pledged, if any, and all makers and endorsers. (2007-349, s. 1; 2009-534, s. 2(e).)

§ 163-278.311: Reserved for future codification purposes.

§ 163-278.312: Reserved for future codification purposes.

§ 163-278.313: Reserved for future codification purposes.

§ 163-278.314: Reserved for future codification purposes.

§ 163-278.315: Reserved for future codification purposes.

§ 163-278.316. Limitations on legal expense donations.

(a) No entity shall make, and no treasurer shall accept, any monetary legal expense donation in excess of fifty dollars ($50.00) unless such legal expense donation is in the form of a check, draft, money order, credit card charge, debit, or other noncash method that can be subject to written verification. No legal expense donation in the form of check, draft, money order, credit card charge, debit, or other noncash method may be made or accepted unless it contains a specific designation of the intended donee chosen by the donor.

(b) The State Board of Elections may adopt rules as to the reporting and verification of any method of legal expense donation payment allowed under this Article. For legal expense donations by money order, the State Board shall adopt rules to ensure an audit trail for every legal expense donation so that the identity of the donor can be determined.

(c) For any legal expense donation made by credit card, the credit card account number of a donor is not a public record.

(d) No legal expense fund shall accept legal expense donations from a corporation, labor union, insurance company, professional association, or business entity in excess of four thousand dollars ($4,000) per calendar year. No legal expense fund shall accept legal expense donations from a corporation which when totaled with legal expense donations to the same legal expense fund for the same calendar year from any affiliated corporation exceed the per calendar year legal expense donation limits for that legal expense fund. No legal expense fund shall accept legal expense donations from a labor union which when totaled with legal expense donations to the same legal expense fund for the same calendar year from any affiliated labor union exceed the per calendar year legal expense donation limits for that legal expense fund. No legal expense fund shall accept legal expense donations from an insurance company which when totaled with legal expense donations to the same legal expense fund for the same calendar year from any affiliated insurance company exceed the per calendar year legal expense donation limits for that legal expense fund. No legal expense fund shall accept legal expense donations from a professional association which when totaled with legal expense donations to the same legal expense fund for the same calendar year from any affiliated professional association exceed the per calendar year legal expense donation limits for that legal expense fund. No legal expense fund shall accept legal expense donations from a business entity which when totaled with legal expense donations to the same legal expense fund for the same calendar year from any affiliated business entity exceed the per calendar year legal expense donation limits for that legal expense fund. The definitions of corporation, labor union, insurance company, professional association, and business entity are the same as those in G.S. 163-278.6. This subsection does not apply to political committees created pursuant to G.S. 163-278.19(b), except that no legal expense fund shall accept a legal expense donation which would be a violation of G.S. 163-278.13B if accepted by a candidate or political committee. This subsection does not apply to corporations permitted to make contributions in G.S. 163-278.19(f).

(e) No entity shall make a legal expense donation to a legal expense fund that the legal expense fund could not accept under subsection (d) of this section. (2007-349, s. 1; 2009-534, s. 2(f).)

§ 163-278.317: Reserved for future codification purposes.

§ 163-278.318: Reserved for future codification purposes.

§ 163-278.319: Reserved for future codification purposes.

§ 163-278.320. Permitted uses of legal expense funds.

(a) A legal expense fund may be used for reasonable expenses actually incurred by the elected officer in relation to a legal action or potential legal action brought by or against the elected officer in that elected officer's official capacity. The elected officer's campaign itself shall not be funded from a legal expense fund.

(b) Upon closing a legal expense account, the treasurer shall distribute the remaining monies in the legal expense fund to any of the following:

(1) The Indigent Persons' Attorney Fee Fund under Article 36 of Chapter 7A of the General Statutes.

(2) The North Carolina State Bar for the provision of civil legal services for indigents.

(3) Payments to an organization described in section 170(c) of the Internal Revenue Code of 1986 (26 U.S.C. § 170(c)), provided that the candidate or the candidate's spouse, children, parents, brothers, or sisters are not employed by the organization.

(4) To return all or a portion of a legal expense donation to the donor.

(5) Payment to the Escheat Fund established by Chapter 116B of the General Statutes. (2007-349, s. 1; 2009-534, s. 2(g).)

§ 163-278.321: Reserved for future codification purposes.

§ 163-278.322: Reserved for future codification purposes.

§ 163-278.323: Reserved for future codification purposes.

§ 163-278.324: Reserved for future codification purposes.

§ 163-278.325: Reserved for future codification purposes.

§ 163-278.326: Reserved for future codification purposes.

§ 163-278.327: Reserved for future codification purposes.

§ 163-278.328: Reserved for future codification purposes.

§ 163-278.329: Reserved for future codification purposes.

Subchapter IX. Municipal Elections.

Article 23.

Municipal Election Procedure.

§ 163-279. Time of municipal primaries and elections.

(a) Primaries and elections for offices filled by election of the people in cities, towns, incorporated villages, and special districts shall be held in 1973 and every two or four years thereafter as provided by municipal charter on the following days:

(1) If the election is nonpartisan and decided by simple plurality, the election shall be held on Tuesday after the first Monday in November.

(2) If the election is partisan, the election shall be held on Tuesday after the first Monday in November, the first primary shall be held on the second Tuesday after Labor Day, and the second primary, if required, shall be held on the fourth Tuesday before the election.

(3) If the election is nonpartisan and the nonpartisan primary method of election is used, the election shall be held on Tuesday after the first Monday in

November and the nonpartisan primary shall be held on the fourth Tuesday before the election.

(4)   If the election is nonpartisan and the election and runoff election method of election is used, the election shall be held on the fourth Tuesday before the Tuesday after the first Monday in November, and the runoff election, if required, shall be held on Tuesday after the first Monday in November.

(b)   Repealed by Session Laws 2011-141, s. 1(a), effective July 1, 2011.

(c)   Officers of sanitary districts elected in 1970 shall hold office until the first Monday in December, 1973, notwithstanding G.S. 130-126. Beginning in 1973, sanitary district elections shall be held at the times provided in this section or in G.S. 130A-50(b1). (1971, c. 835, s. 1; 1973, c. 1115; 1987, c. 22, s. 2; 2006-192, s. 3; 2011-141, s. 1(a).)

§ 163-280: Repealed by Session Laws 2011-31, ss. 1-3, effective April 7, 2011.

§ 163-280.1: Repealed by Session Laws 2011-31, ss. 1-3, effective April 7, 2011.

§ 163-281: Repealed by Session Laws 2011-31, ss. 1-3, effective April 7, 2011.

§ 163-282. Residency defined for voting in municipal elections.

The rules for determining residency within a municipality shall be the same as prescribed in G.S. 163-57 for determining county residency. No person shall be entitled to reside in more than one city or town at the same time. (1971, c. 835, s. 1.)

§ 163-283. Right to participate or vote in party primary.

No person shall be entitled to vote or otherwise participate in the primary election of any political party unless that person complies with all of the following:

(1)   Is a registered voter.

(2) Has declared and has had recorded on the registration book or record the fact that the voter affiliates with the political party in whose primary the voter proposes to vote or participate.

(3) Is in good faith a member of that party.

Notwithstanding the previous paragraph, any unaffiliated voter who is authorized under G.S. 163-119 may also vote in the primary if the voter is otherwise eligible to vote in that primary except for subdivisions (2) and (3) of the previous paragraph.

Any person who will become qualified by age to register and vote in the general election for which the primary is held, even though not so qualified by the date of the primary election, shall be entitled to register while the registration books are open during the regular registration period prior to the primary and then to vote in the primary after being registered, provided however, under full-time and permanent registration, such an individual may register not earlier than 60 days nor later than the last day for making application to register under G.S. 163-82.6(c) prior to the primary. In addition, persons who will become qualified by age to register and vote in the general election for which the primary is held, who do not register during the special period may register to vote after such period as if they were qualified on the basis of age, but until they are qualified by age to vote, they may vote only in primary elections. (1971, c. 835, s. 1; 1983, c. 331, s. 5; 1987, c. 408, s. 5; c. 457, s. 2; 1991 (Reg. Sess., 1992), c. 1032, s. 8; 1993 (Reg. Sess., 1994), c. 762, s. 62; 2008-150, s. 5(c); 2009-541, s. 24; 2013-381, s. 16.6.)

§ 163-283.1. Voting in nonpartisan primary.

Any person who will become qualified by age to register and vote in the general election for which a nonpartisan primary is held, even though not so qualified by the date of the primary, shall be entitled to register for the primary and general election prior to the primary and then to vote in the primary after being registered. Such a person may register not earlier than 60 days nor later than the last day for making application to register under G.S. 163-82.6(c) prior to the primary. (2009-541, s. 25; 2013-381, s. 16.7.)

§ 163-284. Mandatory administration by county boards of elections.

(a) Repealed by Session Laws 2011-31, s. 4, effective April 7, 2011.

(b) The registration of voters and the conduct of all elections in municipalities and special districts shall be under the authority of the county board of elections. Any contested election or allegations of irregularities shall be made to the county board of elections and appeals from such rulings may be made to the State Board of Elections under existing statutory provisions and rules or regulations adopted by the State Board of Elections.

Each municipality and special district shall reimburse the county board of elections for the actual cost involved in the administration required under this section. (1971, c. 835, s. 1; 1973, c. 793, s. 84; 2011-31, s. 4.)

§ 163-284.1. Special district elections conducted by county.

All elections held in and for a sanitary district, fire district or other special district, including school administrative units, shall be conducted by the county board of elections notwithstanding the fact that the taxes of the special district may be levied by a city. (1971, c. 835, s. 1.)

§ 163-285: Repealed by Session Laws 2011-31, s. 5, effective April 7, 2011.

§ 163-286. Conduct of municipal and special district elections; application of Chapter 163.

(a) To the extent that the laws, rules and procedures applicable to the conduct of primary, general and special elections by county boards of elections under Articles 3, 4, 5, 6, 7A, 8, 9, 10, 11, 12, 13, 14, 15, 19 and 22 of this Chapter are not inconsistent with provisions of this Article, those laws, rules and procedures shall apply to municipal and special district elections and their conduct by the board of elections conducting those elections. The State Board of Elections shall have the same authority over all such elections as it has over county and State elections under those Articles.

(b) Repealed by Session Laws 2011-31, s. 6, effective April 7, 2011. (1971, c. 835, s. 1; 1973, c. 793, s. 85; 1993 (Reg. Sess., 1994), c. 762, s. 64; 2011-31, s. 6.)

§ 163-287. Special elections; procedure for calling.

(a) Any county, municipality, or any special district shall have authority to call special elections as permitted by law. Prior to calling a special election, the governing body of the county, municipality, or special district shall adopt a resolution specifying the details of the election, and forthwith deliver the resolution to the local board of elections. The resolution shall call on the local board of elections to conduct the election described in the resolution and shall state the date on which the special election is to be conducted. The special election may be held only at the same time as any other State, county or municipal general election or at the same time as the primary election in any even-numbered year.

(b) Legal notice of the special election shall be published no less than 45 days prior to the special election. The local board of elections shall be responsible for publishing the legal notice. The notice shall state the date and time of the special election, the issue to be submitted to the voters, and the precincts in which the election will be held. This subsection shall not apply to bond elections.

(c) The last sentence of subsection (a) of this section shall not apply to any special election related to the public health or safety, including a vacancy in the office of sheriff or a bond referendum for financing of health and sanitation systems, if the governing body adopts a resolution stating the need for the special election at a time different from any other State, county, or municipal general election or the primary in any even-numbered year.

(d) The last sentence of subsection (a) of this section shall not apply to municipal incorporation or recall elections pursuant to local act of the General Assembly.

(e) The last sentence of subsection (a) of this section shall not apply to municipal elections to fill vacancies in office pursuant to local act of the General Assembly where more than six months remain in the term of office, and if less than six months remain in the office, the governing board may fill the vacancy for the remainder of the unexpired term notwithstanding any provision of a local act of the General Assembly.

(f) This section shall not impact the authority of the courts or the State Board to order a new election at a time set by the courts or State Board under this Chapter. (1971, c. 835, s. 1; 1973, c. 793, s. 86; 1993 (Reg. Sess., 1994), c. 762, s. 65; 2011-31, s. 7; 2013-381, s. 10.1.)

§ 163-288. Registration for city elections; county and municipal boards of elections.

The registration record of the county board of elections shall be the official registration record for voters to vote in all elections, city, district, county, State or national. (1971, c. 835, s. 1; 1973, c. 793, s. 87; 1981, c. 33, s. 5; 1991 (Reg. Sess., 1992), c. 1032, s. 7; 1993 (Reg. Sess., 1994), c. 762, s. 66; 2011-31, s. 8.)

§ 163-288.1. Activating voters for newly annexed or incorporated areas.

(a) Whenever any new city or special district is incorporated or whenever an existing city or district annexes any territory, the city or special district shall cause a map of the corporate or district limits to be prepared from the boundary descriptions in the act, charter or other document creating the city or district or authorizing or implementing the annexation. The map shall be delivered to the county board of elections conducting the elections for the city or special district. The board of elections shall then activate for city or district elections each voter eligible to vote in the city or district who is registered to vote in the county to the extent that residence addresses shown on the county registration certificates can be identified as within the limits of the city or special district. Each voter whose registration is thus activated for city or special district elections shall be so notified by mail. The cost of preparing the map of the newly incorporated city or special district or of the newly annexed area, and of activating voters eligible to vote therein, shall be paid by the city or special district. In lieu of the procedures set forth in this section, the county board of elections may use either of the methods of registration of voters set out in G.S. 163-288.2 when activating voters pursuant to the incorporation of a new city or election of city officials or both under authority of an act of the General Assembly or when activating voters after an annexation of new territory by a city or special district under Chapter 160A, Article 4A, or other general or local law.

(b) Each voter whose registration is changed by the county or municipal board of elections in any manner pursuant to any annexation or expunction under this subsection shall be so notified by mail.

(c) The State Board of Elections shall have authority to adopt regulations for the more detailed administration of this section. (1971, c. 835, s. 1; 1973, c. 793, s. 88; 1977, c. 752, s. 1; 2011-31, s. 9.)

§ 163-288.1A. Activating voters when charter revised.

Whenever a city has not held the most recent two elections required by its charter or this Chapter, and the General Assembly amends the charter of that city and provides that the county board of elections shall conduct the elections of that city, voters shall be activated for the elections of that city in accordance with G.S. 163-288.1 or G.S. 163-288.2. In such a case, the county shall prepare the map required by G.S. 163-288.1(a). (1985, c. 350.)

§ 163-288.2. Registration in area proposed for incorporation or annexed.

(a) Whenever the General Assembly incorporates a new city and provides in the act of incorporation for a referendum on the question of incorporation or for a special election for town officials or for both, or whenever an existing city or special district annexes new territory under the provisions of Chapter 160A, Article 4A, or other general or local law, the board of elections of the county in which the proposed city is located or in which the newly annexed territory is located shall determine those individuals eligible to vote in the referendum or special election or in the city or special district elections. In determining the eligible voters the board may, in its discretion, use either of the following methods:

METHOD A. - The board of elections shall prepare a list of those registered voters residing within the proposed city or newly annexed territory. The board shall make this list available for public inspection in its office for a two-week period ending on the twenty-fifth day before the day of the referendum or special election, or the next scheduled city or special district election. During this period, any voter resident within the proposed city or newly annexed territory and not included on the list may cause his name to be added to the list. At least one week and no more than two weeks before the day the period of public inspection is to begin, the board shall cause notice of the list's availability to be posted in at least two prominent places within the proposed city or newly annexed territory and may cause the notice to be published in a newspaper of general circulation within the county. The notice shall state that the list has been prepared, that only those persons listed may vote in the referendum or special election, that the list will be available for public inspection in the board's office, that any qualified voter not included on the list may cause his name to be added to the list during the two-week period of public inspection, and that persons in newly annexed territory should present themselves so their registration records may be activated for voting in city or special district elections in the newly annexed territory. Notice may additionally be made on a radio or television station or both, but such notice shall be in addition to the newspaper and other required notice.

METHOD B. - The board of elections shall conduct a special registration of eligible persons desiring to vote in the referendum or special election or in the newly annexed territory. The registration records shall be open for a two-week period (except Sundays) ending on the twenty-fifth day before the day of the referendum or special election or the next scheduled city or special district election. On the two Saturdays during that two-week period, the records shall be located at the voting place for the referendum or special election or the next scheduled city or special district election; on the other days it may, in the discretion of the board, be kept at the voting place, at the office of the board, or at the place of business of a person designated by the board to conduct the special registration. At least one week and no more than two weeks before the day the period of special registration is to begin, the board shall cause notice of the registration to be posted in at least two prominent places within the proposed city or newly annexed territory and may cause the notice to be published in a newspaper of general circulation within the county. The notice shall state the purpose and times of the special registration, the location of the registration records, that only those persons registered in the special registration may vote in the referendum or special election, and that persons in newly annexed territory should present themselves so their registration records may be activated for voting in city or special district elections in the newly annexed territory. Notice may additionally be made on a radio or television station or both, but such notice shall be in addition to the newspaper and other required notice.

(b) Only those persons registered pursuant to this section may vote in the referendum or special election, provided, however, that in cases where voters are activated under either Method A or B to vote in a city or special district that annexes territory, the city or special district shall permit them to vote in the city or special district's election and shall, as well, permit other voters to vote in such elections who did not register under the provisions of this section if they are otherwise registered, qualified and eligible to vote in the same. (1973, c. 551; 1977, c. 752, s. 2; 1981, c. 33, s. 6; 1989, c. 93, s. 9; 1991 (Reg. Sess., 1992), c. 1032, s. 9; 1993 (Reg. Sess., 1994), c. 762, s. 67.)

§ 163-288.3. Payment of cost of elections on question of formation of a new municipality or special district.

Whenever a referendum or election is held on the question of incorporation of a new municipality or the formation of a special district, the cost of the election shall be paid by the new municipality or special district in the event the voters approve of incorporation or creation and the new municipality or special district is established. If the voters disapprove and the new municipality or special district is not established, the cost of the election shall be paid by the county. The cost of the election shall be advanced by the county, which shall be reimbursed within 18 months of the date of election, by the municipality or special district if it is established. (1981, c. 786, s. 1.)

§ 163-289. Right to challenge; challenge procedure.

(a) The rules governing challenges in municipal elections shall be the same as are now applicable to challenges made in a county election, provided however, any voter who challenges another voter's right to vote in any municipal or special district election must reside in such municipality or special district.

(b) Whenever a challenge is made pursuant to this section, the appropriate board of elections shall process such challenge in accordance with the provisions of Article 8 of Chapter 163 of the General Statutes as such Article is applicable.

(c) Repealed by Session Laws 2011-31, s. 10, effective April 7, 2011. (1971, c. 835, s. 1; 1973, c. 793, s. 89; 2011-31, s. 10.)

§ 163-290. Alternative methods of determining the results of municipal elections.

(a) Each city, town, village, and special district in this State shall operate under one of the following alternative methods of nominating candidates for and determining the results of its elections:

(1) The partisan primary and election method set out in G.S. 163-291.

(2) The nonpartisan primary and election method set out in G.S. 163-294.

(3) The nonpartisan plurality method set out in G.S. 163-292.

(4) The nonpartisan election and runoff election method set out in G.S. 163-293.

(b) Each city whose charter provides for partisan municipal elections as of January 1, 1972, shall operate under the partisan primary and election method until such time as its charter is amended to provide for nonpartisan elections. Each city, town, village, and special district whose elections are by charter or general law nonpartisan may select the nonpartisan primary and election method, the nonpartisan plurality method, or the nonpartisan election and runoff election method by resolution of the municipal governing board adopted and filed with the State Board of Elections not later than 5:00 P.M. Monday, January 31, 1972, except that a city whose charter provides for a nonpartisan primary as of January 1, 1972, may not select the plurality method unless its charter is so amended. If the municipal governing board does not exercise its option to select another choice before that time, the municipality shall operate under the method specified in the following table:

Cities, towns and villages of

    less than 5,000   Plurality

Cities, towns and villages of

    5,000 or more   Election and Runoff Election

Special districts   Plurality

After January 31, 1972, each city, town and village may change its method of election from one to another of the methods set out in subsection (a) by act of the General Assembly or in the manner provided by law for amendment of its charter. (1971, c. 835, s. 1.)
Article 24.

Conduct of Municipal Elections.

§ 163-291. Partisan primaries and elections.

The nomination of candidates for office in cities, towns, villages, and special districts whose elections are conducted on a partisan basis shall be governed by the provisions of this Chapter applicable to the nomination of county officers, and the terms "county board of elections," "chairman of the county board of elections," "county officers," and similar terms shall be construed with respect to municipal elections to mean the appropriate municipal officers and candidates, except that:

(1)   The dates of primary and election shall be as provided in G.S. 163-279.

(2)   A candidate seeking party nomination for municipal or district office shall file notice of candidacy with the board of elections no earlier than 12:00 noon on the first Friday in July and no later than 12:00 noon on the third Friday in July preceding the election, except:

a.   In the year following a federal decennial census, a candidate seeking party nomination for municipal or district office in any city which elects members of its governing board on a district basis, or requires that candidates reside in a district in order to run, shall file his notice of candidacy with the board of elections no earlier than 12:00 noon on the fourth Monday in July and no later than 12:00 noon on the second Friday in August preceding the election; and

b.   In the second year following a federal decennial census, if the election is held then under G.S. 160A-23.1, a candidate seeking party nomination for municipal or district office shall file his notice of candidacy with the board of elections at the same time as notices of candidacy for county officers are required to be filed under G.S. 163-106.

No person may file a notice of candidacy for more than one municipal office at the same election. If a person has filed a notice of candidacy for one office with the county board of elections under this section, then a notice of candidacy may not later be filed for any other municipal office for that election unless the notice of candidacy for the first office is withdrawn first.

(3)   The filing fee for municipal and district primaries shall be fixed by the governing board not later than the day before candidates are permitted to begin filing notices of candidacy. There shall be a minimum filing fee of five dollars ($5.00). The governing board shall have the authority to set the filing fee at not less than five dollars ($5.00) nor more than one percent (1%) of the annual salary of the office sought unless one percent (1%) of the annual salary of the office sought is less than five dollars ($5.00), in which case the minimum filing fee of five dollars ($5.00) will be charged. The fee shall be paid to the board of elections at the time notice of candidacy is filed.

(4)   The municipal ballot may not be combined with any other ballot.

(5) The canvass of the primary and second primary shall be held on the seventh day following the primary or second primary. In accepting the filing of complaints concerning the conduct of an election, a board of elections shall be subject to the rules concerning Sundays and holidays set forth in G.S. 103-5.

(6) Candidates having the right to demand a second primary shall do so not later than 12:00 noon on the Thursday following the canvass of the first primary. (1971, c. 835, s. 1; 1973, c. 870, s. 1; 1975, c. 370, s. 2; 1983, c. 330, s. 2; 1985, c. 599, ss. 2, 3; 1989 (Reg. Sess., 1990), c. 1012, s. 3; 1995 (Reg. Sess., 1996), c. 553, s. 2; 1999-227, s. 5; 2003-278, s. 10(e), (f); 2006-192, s. 4; 2009-414, s. 2.)

§ 163-292. Determination of election results in cities using the plurality method.

In conducting nonpartisan elections and using the plurality method, elections shall be determined in accordance with the following rules:

(1) When more than one person is seeking election to a single office, the candidate who receives the highest number of votes shall be declared elected.

(2) When more persons are seeking election to two or more offices (constituting a group) than there are offices to be filled, those candidates receiving the highest number of votes, equal in number to the number of offices to be filled, shall be declared elected.

(3) If two or more candidates receiving the highest number of votes each receive the same number of votes, the board of elections shall determine the winner by lot. (1971, c. 835, s. 1.)
§ 163-293. Determination of election results in cities using the election and runoff election method.

(a) Except as otherwise provided in this section, nonpartisan municipal elections in cities using the election and runoff election method shall be determined by a majority of the votes cast. A majority within the meaning of this section shall be determined as follows:

(1) When more than one person is seeking election to a single office, the majority shall be ascertained by dividing the total vote cast for all candidates by

two. Any excess of the sum so ascertained shall be a majority, and the candidate who obtains a majority shall be declared elected.

(2) When more persons are seeking election to two or more offices (constituting a group) than there are offices to be filled, the majority shall be ascertained by dividing the total vote cast for all candidates by the number of offices to be filled, and by dividing the result by two. Any excess of the sum so ascertained shall be a majority, and the candidates who obtain a majority shall be declared elected. If more candidates obtain a majority than there are offices to be filled, those having the highest vote (equal to the number of offices to be filled) shall be declared elected.

(b) If no candidate for a single office receives a majority of the votes cast, or if an insufficient number of candidates receives a majority of the votes cast for a group of offices, a runoff election shall be held as herein provided:

(1) If no candidate for a single office receives a majority of the votes cast, the candidate receiving the highest number of votes shall be declared elected unless the candidate receiving the second highest number of votes requests a runoff election in accordance with subsection (c) of this section. In the runoff election only the names of the two candidates who received the highest and next highest number of votes shall be printed on the ballot. No space for write-in votes shall be included on the ballot for the runoff election.

(2) If candidates for two or more offices (constituting a group) are to be selected and aspirants for some or all of the positions within the group do not receive a majority of the votes, those candidates equal in number to the positions remaining to be filled and having the highest number of votes shall be declared elected unless some one or all of the candidates equal in number to the positions remaining to be filled and having the second highest number of votes shall request a runoff election in accordance with subsection (c) of this section. In the runoff election to elect candidates for the positions in the group remaining to be filled, the names of all those candidates receiving the highest number of votes and demanding a runoff election shall be printed on the ballot. No space for write-in votes shall be included on the ballot for the runoff election.

(c) The canvass of the first election shall be held on the seventh day after the election. A candidate entitled to a runoff election may do so by filing a written request for a runoff election with the board of elections no later than 12:00 noon on the Thursday after the result of the first election has been officially declared. In accepting the filing of complaints concerning the conduct of an election, a board of elections shall be subject to the rules concerning Sundays and holidays set forth in G.S. 103-5.

(d) Tie votes; how determined:

(1) If there is a tie for the highest number of votes in a first election, the board of elections shall conduct a recount and declare the results. If the recount shows a tie vote, a runoff election between the two shall be held unless one of the candidates, within three days after the result of the recount has been officially declared, files a written notice of withdrawal with the board of elections. Should that be done, the remaining candidate shall be declared elected.

(2) If one candidate receives the highest number of votes cast in a first election, but short of a majority, and there is a tie between two or more of the other candidates receiving the second highest number of votes, the board of elections shall declare the candidate having the highest number of votes to be elected, unless all but one of the tied candidates give written notice of withdrawal to the board of elections within three days after the result of the first election has been officially declared. If all but one of the tied candidates withdraw within the prescribed three-day period, and the remaining candidate demands a runoff election in accordance with subsection (c) of this section, a runoff election shall be held between the candidate who received the highest vote and the remaining candidate who received the second highest vote.

(e) Runoff elections shall be held on the date fixed in G.S. 163-279(a)(4). Persons whose registrations become valid between the date of the first election and the runoff election shall be entitled to vote in the runoff election, but in all other respects the runoff election shall be held under the laws, rules, and regulations provided for the first election.

(f) A second runoff election shall not be held. The candidates receiving the highest number of votes in a runoff election shall be elected. If in a runoff election there is a tie for the highest number of votes between two candidates, the board of elections shall determine the winner by lot. (1971, c. 835, s. 1; 1973, c. 793, s. 90; 1995 (Reg. Sess., 1996), c. 553, s. 3; 2003-278, s. 10(g); 2010-170, s. 15.5(a).)

§ 163-294. Determination of election results in cities using nonpartisan primaries.

(a) In cities whose elections are nonpartisan and who use the nonpartisan primary and election method, there shall be a primary to narrow the field of candidates to two candidates for each position to be filled if, when the filing period closes, there are more than two candidates for a single office or the number of candidates for a group of offices exceeds twice the number of positions to be filled. If only one or two candidates file for a single office, no primary shall be held for that office and the candidates shall be declared nominated. If the number of candidates for a group of offices does not exceed twice the number of positions to be filled, no primary shall be held for those offices and the candidates shall be declared nominated.

(b) In the primary, the two candidates for a single office receiving the highest number of votes, and those candidates for a group of offices receiving the highest number of votes, equal to twice the number of positions to be filled, shall be declared nominated. In both the primary and election, a voter should not mark more names for any office than there are positions to be filled by election. If two or more candidates receiving the highest number of votes each received the same number of votes, the board of elections shall determine their relative ranking by lot, and shall declare the nominees accordingly. The canvass of the primary shall be held on the seventh day following the primary. In accepting the filing of complaints concerning the conduct of an election, a board of elections shall be subject to the rules concerning Sundays and holidays set forth in G.S. 103-5.

(c) In the election, the names of those candidates declared nominated without a primary and those candidates nominated in the primary shall be placed on the ballot. The candidate for a single office receiving the highest number of votes shall be elected. Those candidates for a group of offices receiving the highest number of votes, equal in number to the number of positions to be filled, shall be elected. If two candidates receiving the highest number of votes each received the same number of votes, the board of elections shall determine the winner by lot. (1971, c. 835, s. 1; 1991, c. 341, s. 1; 1995 (Reg. Sess., 1996), c. 553, s. 4; 2001-460, s. 6; 2003-278, s. 10(h).)

§ 163-294.1. Death of candidates or elected officers.

(a) This section shall apply only to municipal and special district elections.

(b) If a candidate for political party nomination for office dies, becomes disqualified, or withdraws before the primary but after the ballots have been printed, the provisions of G.S. 163-112 shall govern.

If a candidate for nomination in a nonpartisan municipal primary dies, becomes disqualified, or withdraws before the primary but after the ballots have been printed, the board of elections shall determine whether or not there is time to reprint the ballots. If the board determines that there is not enough time to reprint the ballots, the deceased or disqualified candidate's name shall remain on the ballots. If he receives enough votes for nomination, such votes shall be disregarded and the candidate receiving the next highest number of votes below the number necessary for nomination shall be declared nominated. If the death or disqualification of the candidate leaves only two candidates for each office to be filled, the nonpartisan primary shall not be held and all candidates shall be declared nominees.

If a nominee for political party nomination dies, becomes disqualified, or withdraws after the primary and before election day, the provisions of G.S. 163-114 shall govern.

If a candidate in a nonpartisan election dies, becomes disqualified, or withdraws before election day and after the ballots have been printed, the board of elections shall determine whether there is enough time to reprint the ballots. If there is not enough time to reprint the ballots, and should the deceased or disqualified candidate receive enough votes to be elected, the board of elections shall declare the office vacant, and it shall be filled as provided by law.

(c) If a person elected to any city office dies, becomes disqualified, or resigns on or after election day and before he has qualified by taking the oath of office, the office shall be deemed vacant, and shall be filled as provided by law.

(d) A vacancy that occurs in a municipal or special district elective office shall be filled by the governing body as provided in G.S. 160A-63. In the case of a special district, the words "city council" as used in G.S. 160A-63, shall mean the governing body of the special district. (1971, c. 835, s. 1; 1985, c. 619.)

§ 163-294.2. Notice of candidacy and filing fee in nonpartisan municipal elections.

(a) Each person offering himself as a candidate for election to any municipal office in municipalities whose elections are nonpartisan shall do so by filing a notice of candidacy with the board of elections in the following form, inserting the words in parentheses when appropriate:

"Date _____;

I hereby file notice that I am a candidate for election to the office of _____ (at large) (for the _____ Ward) in the regular municipal election to be held in _____ on ____, ____

(municipality)

Signed _____

(Name of Candidate)

Witness: _____

For the Board of Elections"

The notice of candidacy shall be either signed in the presence of the chairman or secretary of the board of elections or the director of elections of that county, or signed and acknowledged before an officer authorized to take acknowledgments who shall certify the notice under seal. An acknowledged and certified notice may be mailed to the board of elections. The candidate shall sign the notice of candidacy with his legal name and, in his discretion, any nickname by which he is commonly known, in the form that he wishes it to appear upon the ballot but substantially as follows: "Richard D. (Dick) Roc." A candidate may also, in lieu of his legal first name and legal middle initial or middle name (if any) sign his nickname, provided that he appends to the notice of candidacy an affidavit that he has been commonly known by that nickname for at least five years prior to the date of making the affidavit, and notwithstanding the previous sentence, if the candidate has used his nickname in lieu of first and middle names as permitted by this sentence, unless another candidate for the same office who files a notice of candidacy has the same last name, the nickname shall be printed on the ballot immediately before the candidate's surname but shall not be enclosed by parentheses. If another candidate for the same office who filed a notice of candidacy has the same last name, then the candidate's name shall be printed on the ballot in accordance with the next sentence of this subsection. The candidate shall also include with the affidavit the way his name (as permitted by law) should be listed on the ballot if another candidate with the same last name files a notice of candidacy for that office.

(b) Only persons who are registered to vote in the municipality shall be permitted to file notice of candidacy for election to municipal office. The board of elections shall inspect the voter registration lists immediately upon receipt of the notice of candidacy and shall cancel the notice of candidacy of any candidate who is not eligible to vote in the election. The board shall give notice of cancellation to any candidate whose notice of candidacy has been cancelled under this subsection by mail or by having the notice served on him by the county sheriff.

(c) Candidates seeking municipal office shall file their notices of candidacy with the board of elections no earlier than 12:00 noon on the first Friday in July and no later than 12:00 noon on the third Friday in July preceding the election, except:

(1) In the year following a federal decennial census, candidates seeking municipal office in any city which elects members of its governing board on a district basis, or requires that candidates reside in a district in order to run, shall file their notices of candidacy with the board of elections no earlier than 12:00 noon on the fourth Monday in July and no later than 12:00 noon on the second Friday in August preceding the election; and

(2) In the second year following a federal decennial census, if the election is held then under G.S. 160A-23.1, candidates seeking municipal office shall file their notices of candidacy with the board of elections at the same time as notices of candidacy for county officers are required to be filed under G.S. 163-106.

Notices of candidacy which are mailed must be received by the board of elections before the filing deadline regardless of the time they were deposited in the mails.

(d) Any person may withdraw his notice of candidacy at any time prior to the close of business on the third business day prior to the filing deadline prescribed in subsection (c), and shall be entitled to a refund of his filing fee if he does so.

(e) The filing fee for the primary or election shall be fixed by the governing board not later than the day before candidates are permitted to begin filing notices of candidacy. There shall be a minimum filing fee of five dollars ($5.00).

The governing board shall have the authority to set the filing fee at not less than five dollars ($5.00) nor more than one percent (1%) of the annual salary of the office sought unless one percent (1%) of the annual salary of the office sought is less than five dollars ($5.00), in which case the minimum filing fee of five dollars ($5.00) will be charged. The fee shall be paid to the board of elections at the time notice of candidacy is filed.

(f) No person may file a notice of candidacy for more than one municipal office at the same election. If a person has filed a notice of candidacy for one office with the board of elections under this section, then a notice of candidacy may not later be filed for any other municipal office for the election unless the notice of candidacy for the first office is withdrawn first. (1971, c. 835, s. 1; 1973, c. 870, s. 2; 1975, c. 370, s. 2; 1977, c. 265, s. 18; 1981, c. 32, s. 3; 1983, c. 330, s. 3; c. 644, ss. 1, 2; 1985, c. 472, s. 5; c. 558, s. 3; c. 599, s. 1; 1989 (Reg. Sess., 1990), c. 1012, s. 4; 1995, c. 243, s. 1; 1999-227, s. 6; 1999-456, s. 59; 2006-192, s. 5; 2009-414, s. 3; 2013-381, s. 21.2.)

§ 163-294.3. Sole candidates to be voted upon in nonpartisan municipal elections.

Each candidate for municipal office in nonpartisan municipal elections shall be voted upon, even though only one candidate has filed or has been nominated for a given office, in order that the voters may have the opportunity to cast write-in votes under the general election laws. (1971, c. 835, s. 1.)

§ 163-294.4. Failure of candidates to file; death of a candidate before election.

(a) If in a nonpartisan municipal election, when the filing period expires, candidates have not filed for all offices to be filled, the board of elections may extend the filing period for five days.

(b) If at the time the filing period closes only two persons have filed notice of candidacy for election to a single office or only as many persons have filed notices of candidacy for group offices as there are offices to be filled, and thereafter one of the candidates dies before the election and before the ballots are printed, the board of elections shall, upon notification of the death, immediately reopen the filing period for an additional five days during which time additional candidates shall be permitted to file for election. If the ballots have been printed at the time the board of elections receives notice of the candidate's death, the board shall determine whether there will be sufficient time to reprint them before the election if the filing period is reopened for three days. If the board determines that there will be sufficient time to reprint the ballots, it shall reopen the filing period for three days to allow other candidates to file for election.

(c) If the ballots have been printed at the time the board of elections receives notice of a candidate's death, and if the board determines that there is not enough time to reprint the ballots before the election if the filing period is reopened for three days, then, regardless of the number of candidates remaining for the office, the ballots shall not be reprinted and the name of the deceased candidate shall remain on the ballots. If a deceased candidate should poll the highest number of votes in the election, even though short of a majority the board of elections shall declare the office vacant and it shall be filled in the manner provided by law. If no candidate in an election receives a majority of the votes cast and the second highest vote is cast for a deceased candidate, no runoff election shall be held, but the board of elections shall declare the candidate receiving the highest vote to be elected. (1971, c. 835, s. 1.)

§ 163-295. Municipal and special district elections; application of Chapter 163.

To the extent that the laws, rules and procedures applicable to the conduct of primary, general or special elections by county boards of elections under Articles 3, 4, 5, 6, 7A, 8, 9, 10, 11, 11B, 12, 13, 14, 15, 19 and 22 of this Chapter are not inconsistent with the provisions of this Article, those laws, rules and procedures shall apply to municipal and special district elections and their conduct by the board of elections conducting those elections. The State Board of Elections shall have the same authority over all such elections as it has over county and State elections under those Articles. (1971, c. 835, s. 1; 1973, c. 793, s. 91; 1993 (Reg. Sess., 1994), c. 762, s. 68; 2006-155, s. 5.)

§ 163-296. Nomination by petition.

In cities conducting partisan elections, any qualified voter who seeks to have his name printed on the regular municipal election ballot as an unaffiliated candidate may do so in the manner provided in G.S. 163-122, except that the petitions and affidavits shall be filed not later than 12:00 noon on the Friday preceding the seventh Saturday before the election, and the petitions shall be signed by a number of qualified voters of the municipality equal to at least four percent (4%) of the whole number of voters qualified to vote in the municipal election according to the voter registration records of the State Board of Elections as of January 1 of the year in which the general municipal election is held. A person whose name appeared on the ballot in a primary election is not eligible to have his name placed on the regular municipal election ballot as an unaffiliated candidate for the same office in that year. The Board of Elections shall examine and verify the signatures on the petition, and shall certify only the names of signers who are found to be qualified registered voters in the municipality. Provided that in the case where a qualified voter seeks to have his name printed on the regular municipal election ballot as an unaffiliated candidate for election from an election district within the municipality, the petition shall be signed by four percent (4%) of the voters qualified to vote for that office. (1971, c. 835, s. 1; 1979, c. 23, ss. 2, 4, 5; c. 534, ss. 3, 4; 1989, c. 402; 1991, c. 297, s. 2; 2004-127, s. 8(b); 2006-264, s. 21.)

§ 163-297. Structure at voting place; marking off limits of voting place.

Precincts in which municipal primaries and elections are conducted shall conform, in all regards, to the requirements stipulated in G.S. 163-129 and all other provisions contained in Chapter 163 relating to county and State elections. (1971, c. 835, s. 1.)

§ 163-298. Municipal primaries and elections.

The phrases "county board of elections," and "chairman of the board of elections" as used in this Article, with respect to all municipal primaries and elections, shall mean the county board of elections and its chairman in all municipalities. The words "general election," as used in this Article, shall include regular municipal elections, runoff elections, and nonpartisan primaries, except where specific provision is made for municipal elections and nonpartisan primaries. (1971, c. 835, s. 1; 2011-31, s. 21.)

§ 163-299. Ballots; municipal primaries and elections.

(a)   The ballots printed for use in general and special elections under the provisions of this Article shall contain:

(1) The names of all candidates who have been put in nomination in accordance with the provisions of this Chapter by any political party recognized in this State, or, in nonpartisan municipal elections, the names of all candidates who have filed notices of candidacy or who have been nominated in a nonpartisan primary.

(2) The names of all persons who have qualified as unaffiliated candidates under the provisions of G.S. 163-296.

(3) All questions, issues and propositions to be voted on by the people.

(b) The form of municipal ballots to be used in partisan municipal elections shall be the same as the form prescribed in this Chapter for the county ballot.

(c) The names of candidates for nomination or election in municipal primaries or elections shall be placed on the ballot in strict alphabetical order, unless the municipal governing body has adopted a resolution no later than 60 days prior to a primary or election requesting that candidates' names be rotated on ballots. In the event such a resolution has been adopted, then the board of elections responsible for printing the ballots shall have them printed so that the name of each candidate shall, as far as practicable, occupy alternate positions on the ballot; to that end the name of each candidate shall occupy with reference to the name of every other candidate for the same office, first position, second position and every other position, if any, upon an equal number of ballots, and the ballots shall be distributed among the precinct voting places impartially and without discrimination.

(d) The provisions of Articles 14A and 15A of this Chapter shall apply to ballots used in municipal primaries and elections in the same manner as it is applied to county ballots.

(e) The rules contained in G.S. 163-182.1 and G.S. 163-182.2 for counting primary ballots shall be followed in counting ballots in municipal primaries and nonpartisan primaries.

(f) The requirements contained in G.S. 163-182.2(b) shall apply to all municipal elections.

(g) The county board of elections shall, in addition to the requirements contained in G.S. 163-182.5 canvass the results in a nonpartisan municipal primary, election or runoff election, and in a special district election, the number of legal votes cast in each precinct for each candidate, the name of each person voted for, and the total number of votes cast in the municipality or special district for each person for each different office. (1971, c. 835, s. 1; 1979, c. 534, s. 4; c. 806; 2001-398, ss. 10 - 12; 2001-460, ss. 7, 8; 2004-127, s. 5; 2011-31, s. 22.)

§ 163-300. Disposition of duplicate abstracts in municipal elections.

Within nine days after a primary or election is held in any municipality, the chairman of the county board of elections shall mail to the chairman of the State Board of Elections, the duplicate abstract prepared in accordance with G.S. 163-182.6. One copy shall be retained by the county board of elections as a permanent record and one copy shall be filed with the city clerk. (1971, c. 835, s. 1; 2001-398, s. 13; 2003-278, s. 10(i); 2011-31, s. 23.)

§ 163-301. Chairman of election board to furnish certificate of elections.

Not earlier than five days nor later than 10 days after the results of any municipal election have been officially determined and published in accordance with G.S. 163-182.5, the chairman of the county board of elections shall issue certificates of election, under the hand and seal of the chairman, to all municipal and special district officers. In issuing such certificates of election the chairman shall be restricted by the provisions of G.S. 163-182.14. (1971, c. 835, s. 1; 2001-398, s. 14; 2011-31, s. 24.)

§ 163-302. Absentee voting.

(a) In any municipal election, including a primary or general election or referendum, conducted by the county board of elections, absentee voting may, upon resolution of the municipal governing body, be permitted. Such resolution must be adopted no later than 60 days prior to an election in order to be effective for that election. Any such resolution shall remain effective for all future elections unless repealed no later than 60 days before an election. A copy of all resolutions adopted under this section shall be filed with the State Board of Elections and the county board of elections conducting the election within 10 days of passage in order to be effective. Absentee voting shall not be permitted in any municipal election unless such election is conducted by the county board of elections. In addition, absentee voting shall be allowed in any referendum on incorporation of a municipality.

(b) The provisions of Articles 20 and 21 of this Chapter shall apply to absentee voting in municipal elections, special district elections, and other elections for an area less than an entire county other than elections for the General Assembly, except that the earliest date by which absentee ballots shall be required to be available for absentee voting in such elections shall be 30 days prior to the primary or election or as quickly following the filing deadline specified in G.S. 163-291(2) or G.S. 163-294.2(c) as the county board of elections is able to secure the official ballots. In elections on incorporation of a municipality not held at the same time as another election in the same area, the county board of elections shall adopt a special schedule of meetings of the county board of elections to approve absentee ballot applications so as to reduce the cost of the process, and to further implement the last paragraph of G.S. 163-230(2)a. If no application has been received since the last meeting, no meeting shall be held of the county board of elections under such schedule unless the meeting is scheduled for another purpose. If another election is being held in the same area on the same day, or elsewhere in the county, the cost of per diem for meetings of the county board of elections to approve absentee ballots shall not be considered a cost of the election to be billed to the municipality being created. (1971, c. 835, s. 1; 1975, c. 370, s. 1; c. 836; 1977, c. 475, s. 1; 1983, c. 324, s. 6; 1991 (Reg. Sess., 1992), c. 933, s. 1.)

§ 163-303. Repealed by Session Laws 1977, c. 265, s. 19.

§ 163-304. State Board of Elections to have jurisdiction over municipal elections, and to advise; emergency and ongoing administration by county board.

(a) Authority and Duty of State Board. - The State Board of Elections shall have the same authority over municipal elections as it has over county and State elections. The State Board of Elections shall advise and assist cities, towns, incorporated villages and special districts, their members and legal officers on the conduct and administration of their elections and registration procedure.

The county boards of elections shall be governed by the same rules for settling controversies with respect to counting ballots or certification of the returns of the vote in any municipal or special district election as are in effect for settling such controversies in county and State elections.

(b) through (e) Repealed by Session Laws 2011-31, s. 25, effective April 7, 2011. (1971, c. 835, s. 1; 1973, c. 793, s. 92; 1999-426, s. 6(a); 2001-319, s. 11; 2001-374, s. 3; 2011-31, s. 25; 2012-194, s. 22(b).)

§ 163-305. Validation of elections.

All elections, and the results thereof, previously held in and for any municipality, special district, or school administrative unit pursuant to Subchapter IX, Chapter 163, are hereby validated. (1973, c. 492, s. 1.)

§ 163-306. Assumption of office by mayors and councilmen.

Newly elected mayors and councilmen (members of the governing body) shall take office as prescribed by G.S. 160A-68. (1973, c. 866.)

§§ 163-307 through 163-320. Reserved for future codification purposes.

SUBCHAPTER X. ELECTION OF APPELLATE, SUPERIOR, AND DISTRICT COURT JUDGES.

Article 25.

Nomination and Election of Appellate, Superior, and District Court Judges.

§ 163-321. Applicability.

The nomination and election of justices of the Supreme Court, judges of the Court of Appeals, and superior and district court judges of the General Court of Justice shall be as provided by this Article. (1996, 2nd Ex. Sess., c. 9, s. 7; 2001-403, s. 1; 2002-158, s. 7.)

§ 163-322. Nonpartisan primary election method.

(a) General. - Except as provided in G.S. 163-329, there shall be a primary to narrow the field of candidates to two candidates for each position to be filled if, when the filing period closes, there are more than two candidates for a single office or the number of candidates for a group of offices exceeds twice the number of positions to be filled. If only one or two candidates file for a single office, no primary shall be held for that office and the candidates shall be declared nominated. If the number of candidates for a group of offices does not exceed twice the number of positions to be filled, no primary shall be held for those offices and the candidates shall be declared nominated.

(b) Determination of Nominees. - In the primary, the two candidates for a single office receiving the highest number of votes, and those candidates for a group of offices receiving the highest number of votes, equal to twice the number of positions to be filled, shall be declared nominated. If two or more candidates receiving the highest number of votes each receive the same number of votes, the State Board of Elections shall determine their relative ranking by lot, and shall declare the nominees accordingly. The canvass of the primary shall be held on the same date as the primary canvass fixed under G.S. 163-182.5. The canvass shall be conducted in accordance with Article 15A of this Chapter.

(c) Determination of Election Winners. - In the election, the names of those candidates declared nominated without a primary and those candidates nominated in the primary shall be placed on the ballot. The candidate for a single office receiving the highest number of votes shall be elected. Those candidates for a group of offices receiving the highest number of votes, equal in number to the number of positions to be filled, shall be elected. If two candidates receiving the highest number of votes each received the same number of votes, the State Board of Elections shall determine the winner by lot. (1996, 2nd Ex. Sess., c. 9, s. 7; 2003-278, s. 10(j).)

§ 163-323. Notice of candidacy.

(a) Form of Notice. - Each person offering to be a candidate for election shall do so by filing a notice of candidacy with the State Board of Elections in the following form, inserting the words in parentheses when appropriate:

Date _____

I hereby file notice that I am a candidate for election to the office of _____ in the regular election to be held _____, _____.

Signed _____

                                                            (Name of Candidate)

Witness:

_____
_

The notice of candidacy shall be either signed in the presence of the chairman or secretary of the State Board of Elections, or signed and acknowledged before an officer authorized to take acknowledgments who shall certify the notice under seal. An acknowledged and certified notice may be mailed to the State Board of Elections. In signing a notice of candidacy, the candidate shall use only the candidate's legal name and, in his discretion, any nickname by which commonly known. A candidate may also, in lieu of that candidate's first name and legal middle initial or middle name, if any, sign that candidate's nickname, provided the candidate appends to the notice of candidacy an affidavit that the candidate has been commonly known by that nickname for at least five years prior to the date of making the affidavit. The candidate shall also include with the affidavit the way the candidate's name (as permitted by law) should be listed on the ballot if another candidate with the same last name files a notice of candidacy for that office.

A notice of candidacy signed by an agent or any person other than the candidate himself shall be invalid.

(b)   Time for Filing Notice of Candidacy. - Candidates seeking election to the following offices shall file their notice of candidacy with the State Board of Elections no earlier than 12:00 noon on the second Monday in February and no later than 12:00 noon on the last business day in February preceding the election:

Justices of the Supreme Court.

Judges of the Court of Appeals.

Judges of the superior courts.

Judges of the district courts.

(c) Withdrawal of Notice of Candidacy. - Any person who has filed a notice of candidacy for an office shall have the right to withdraw it at any time prior to the close of business on the third business day prior to the date on which the right to file for that office expires under the terms of subsection (b) of this section.

(d) Certificate That Candidate Is Registered Voter. - Candidates shall file along with their notice a certificate signed by the chairman of the board of elections or the director of elections of the county in which they are registered to vote, stating that the person is registered to vote in that county, and if the candidacy is for superior court judge and the county contains more than one superior court district, stating the superior court district of which the person is a resident. In issuing such certificate, the chairman or director shall check the registration records of the county to verify such information. During the period commencing 36 hours immediately preceding the filing deadline, the State Board of Elections shall accept, on a conditional basis, the notice of candidacy of a candidate who has failed to secure the verification ordered herein subject to receipt of verification no later than three days following the filing deadline. The State Board of Elections shall prescribe the form for such certificate, and distribute it to each county board of elections no later than the last Monday in December of each odd-numbered year.

(e) Candidacy for More Than One Office Prohibited. - No person may file a notice of candidacy for more than one office or group of offices described in subsection (b) of this section, or for an office or group of offices described in subsection (b) of this section and an office described in G.S. 163-106(c), for any one election. If a person has filed a notice of candidacy with a board of elections under this section or under G.S. 163-106(c) for one office or group of offices, then a notice of candidacy may not later be filed for any other office or group of offices under this section when the election is on the same date unless the notice of candidacy for the first office is withdrawn under subsection (c) of this section.

(f) Notice of Candidacy for Certain Offices to Indicate Vacancy. - In any election in which there are two or more vacancies for the office of justice of the Supreme Court, judge of the Court of Appeals, or district court judge to be filled by nominations, each candidate shall, at the time of filing notice of candidacy, file with the State Board of Elections a written statement designating the vacancy to which the candidate seeks election. Votes cast for a candidate shall be effective only for election to the vacancy for which the candidate has given notice of candidacy as provided in this subsection.

A person seeking election for a specialized district judgeship established under G.S. 7A-147 shall, at the time of filing notice of candidacy, file with the State Board of Elections a written statement designating the specialized judgeship to which the person seeks nomination.

(g) No person may file a notice of candidacy for superior court judge unless that person is at the time of filing the notice of candidacy a resident of the judicial district as it will exist at the time the person would take office if elected. No person may be nominated as a superior court judge under G.S. 163-114 unless that person is at the time of nomination a resident of the judicial district as it will exist at the time the person would take office if elected. This subsection implements Article IV, Section 9(1) of the North Carolina Constitution which requires regular Superior Court Judges to reside in the district for which elected. (1996, 2nd Ex. Sess., c. 9, s. 7; 1998-217, s. 36(a); 2001-403, s. 1; 2001-466, s. 5.1(b); 2002-158, s. 7; 2002-159, s. 21(g); 2013-381, s. 21.3.)

§ 163-324. Filing fees required of candidates; refunds.

(a) Fee Schedule. - At the time of filing a notice of candidacy under this Article, each candidate shall pay to the State Board of Elections a filing fee for the office he seeks in the amount of one percent (1%) of the annual salary of the office sought.

(b) Refund of Fees. - If any person who has filed a notice of candidacy and paid the filing fee prescribed in subsection (a) of this section withdraws his notice of candidacy within the period prescribed in G.S. 163-323(c), he shall be entitled to have the fee he paid refunded. The chairman of the State Board of Elections shall cause a warrant to be drawn on the State Treasurer for the refund payment.

If any person who has filed a notice of candidacy and paid the filing fee prescribed in subsection (a) of this section dies prior to the date of the election, the personal representative of the estate shall be entitled to have the fee refunded if application is made to the board of elections to which the fee was paid no later than one year after the date of death, and refund shall be made in the same manner as in withdrawal of notice of candidacy. (1996, 2nd Ex. Sess., c. 9, s. 7.)

§ 163-325. Petition in lieu of payment of filing fee.

(a)   General. - Any qualified voter who seeks election under this Article may, in lieu of payment of any filing fee required for the office he seeks, file a written petition requesting him to be a candidate for a specified office with the State Board of Elections.

(b)   Requirements of Petition; Deadline for Filing. - If the candidate is seeking the office of justice of the Supreme Court, judge of the Court of Appeals, or superior or district court judge, that individual shall file a written petition with the State Board of Elections no later than 12:00 noon on Monday preceding the filing deadline before the primary. If the office is justice of the Supreme Court or judge of the Court of Appeals, the petition shall be signed by 8,000 registered voters in the State. If the office is superior court or district court judge, the petition shall be signed by five percent (5%) of the registered voters of the election area in which the office will be voted for. The board of elections shall verify the names on the petition, and if the petition and notice of candidacy are found to be sufficient, the candidate's name shall be printed on the appropriate ballot. Petitions must be presented to the county board of elections for verification at least 15 days before the petition is due to be filed with the State Board of Elections. The State Board of Elections may adopt rules to implement this section and to provide standard petition forms. (1996, 2nd Ex. Sess., c. 9, s. 7; 2001-403, s. 1; 2002-158, s. 7; 2013-381, s. 22.2.)

§ 163-326. Certification of notices of candidacy.

(a)   Names of Candidates Sent to Secretary of State. - Within three days after the time for filing notices of candidacy with the State Board of Elections under the provisions of G.S. 163-323(b) has expired, the chairman or secretary of that Board shall certify to the Secretary of State the name and address of each person who has filed with the State Board of Elections, indicating in each instance the office sought.

(b)   Notification of Local Boards. - No later than 10 days after the time for filing notices of candidacy under the provisions of G.S. 163-323(b) has expired, the chairman of the State Board of Elections shall certify to the chairman of the county board of elections in each county in the appropriate district the names of candidates for nomination to the offices of justice of the Supreme Court, judge of the Court of Appeals, and superior and district court judge who have filed the required notice and paid the required filing fee or presented the required petition to the State Board of Elections, so that their names may be printed on the official judicial ballot for justice of the Supreme Court, judge of the Court of Appeals, and superior and district court.

(c) Receipt of Notification by County Board. - Within two days after receipt of each of the letters of certification from the chairman of the State Board of Elections required by subsection (b) of this section, each county elections board chairman shall acknowledge receipt by letter addressed to the chairman of the State Board of Elections. (1996, 2nd Ex. Sess., c. 9, s. 7; 2001-403, s. 1; 2002-158, s. 7.)

§ 163-327: Repealed by Session Laws 2006-192, s. 9(a), effective August 3, 2006, and applicable to vacancies occurring on or after August 3, 2006.

§ 163-327.1. Rules when vacancies for superior court judge are to be voted on.

If a vacancy occurs in a judicial district for any offices of superior court judge, and on account of the occurrence of such vacancy, there is to be an election for one or more terms in that district to fill the vacancy or vacancies, at that same election in accordance with G.S. 163-9 and Article IV, Section 19 of the North Carolina Constitution, the nomination and election shall be determined by the following special rules in addition to any other provisions of law:

(1) If the vacancy occurs prior to the opening of the filing period under G.S. 163-323(b), nominations shall be made by primary election as provided by this Article, without designation as to the vacancy.

(2) If the vacancy occurs beginning on opening of the filing period under G.S. 163-323(b), and ending on the sixtieth day before the general election, candidate filing shall be as provided by G.S. 163-329 without designation as to the vacancy.

(3) The general election ballot shall contain, without designation as to vacancy, spaces for the election to fill the vacancy where nominations were made or candidates filed under subdivision (1) or (2) of this section. Except as

provided in G.S. 163-329, the persons receiving the highest numbers of votes equal to the term or terms to be filled shall be elected to the term or terms. (2001-460, s. 10; 2006-192, s. 8(b).)

§ 163-328. Failure of candidates to file; death or other disqualification of a candidate; no withdrawal from candidacy.

(a) Insufficient Number of Candidates. - If when the filing period expires, candidates have not filed for an office to be filled under this Article, the State Board of Elections shall extend the filing period for five days for any such offices.

(a1) Death or Disqualification of Candidate Before Primary. - If a candidate for nomination in a primary dies or becomes disqualified before the primary but after the ballots have been printed, the State Board of Elections shall determine whether or not there is time to reprint the ballots. If the Board determines that there is not enough time to reprint the ballots, the deceased or disqualified candidate's name shall remain on the ballots. If that candidate receives enough votes for nomination, such votes shall be disregarded and the candidate receiving the next highest number of votes below the number necessary for nomination shall be declared nominated. If the death or disqualification of the candidate leaves only two candidates for each office to be filled, the nonpartisan primary shall not be held and all candidates shall be declared nominees.

(b) Earlier Non-Primary Vacancies; Reopening Filing. - If there is no primary because only one or two candidates have filed for a single office, or the number of candidates filed for a group of offices does not exceed twice the number of positions to be filled, or if a primary has occurred and eliminated candidates, and thereafter a remaining candidate dies or otherwise becomes disqualified before the election and before the ballots are printed, the State Board of Elections shall, upon notification of the death or other disqualification, immediately reopen the filing period for an additional five days during which time additional candidates shall be permitted to file for election. If the ballots have been printed at the time the State Board of Elections receives notice of the candidate's death or other disqualification, the Board shall determine whether there will be sufficient time to reprint them before the election if the filing period is reopened for three days. If the Board determines that there will be sufficient time to reprint the ballots, it shall reopen the filing period for three days to allow other candidates to file for election, and that election shall be conducted as provided in G.S. 163-329(b1).

(c) Later Vacancies; Ballots Not Reprinted. - If the ballots have been printed at the time the State Board of Elections receives notice of a candidate's death or other disqualification, and if the Board determines that there is not enough time to reprint the ballots before the election if the filing period is reopened for three days, then regardless of the number of candidates remaining for the office or group of offices, the ballots shall not be reprinted and the name of the vacated candidate shall remain on the ballots. If a vacated candidate should poll the highest number of votes in the election for a single office or enough votes to be elected to one of a group of offices, the State Board of Elections shall declare the office vacant and it shall be filled in the manner provided by law.

(d) No Withdrawal Permitted of Living, Qualified Candidate After Close of Filing. - After the close of the candidate filing period, a candidate who has filed a notice of candidacy for the office, who has not withdrawn notice before the close of filing as permitted by G.S. 163-323(b), who remains alive, and has not become disqualified for the office may not withdraw his or her candidacy. That candidate's name shall remain on the ballot, any votes cast for the candidacy shall be counted in primary or election, and if the candidate wins, the candidate may fail to qualify by refusing to take the oath of office.

(e) Death, Disqualification, or Failure to Qualify After Election. - If a person elected to the office of justice of the Supreme Court, judge of the Court of Appeals, or superior or district court judge dies or becomes disqualified on or after election day and before he has qualified by taking the oath of office, or fails to qualify by refusing to take the oath of office, the office shall be deemed vacant and shall be filled as provided by law. (1996, 2nd Ex. Sess., c. 9, s. 7; 1999-424, s. 4(b); 2006-192, s. 9(b).)

§ 163-329. Elections to fill vacancy in office created after primary filing period opens.

(a) General. - If a vacancy is created in the office of justice of the Supreme Court, judge of the Court of Appeals, or judge of superior court after the filing period for the primary opens but more than 60 days before the general election, and under the Constitution of North Carolina an election is to be held for that position, such that the office shall be filled in the general election as provided in G.S. 163-9, the election to fill the office for the remainder of the term shall be conducted without a primary using the method provided in subsection (b1) of this section. If a vacancy is created in the office of justice of the Supreme Court, judge of the Court of Appeals, or judge of superior court before the filing period for the primary opens, and under the Constitution of North Carolina an election is to be held for that position, such that the office shall be filled in the general election as provided in G.S. 163-9, the election to fill the office for the remainder of the term shall be conducted in accordance with G.S. 163-322.

(b)   Repealed by Session Laws 2006-192, s. 8(a), effective August 3, 2006, and applicable to vacancies occurring on or after that date.

(b1)   Method for Vacancy Election. - If a vacancy for the office of justice of the Supreme Court, judge of the Court of Appeals, or judge of the superior court occurs more than 60 days before the general election and after the opening of the filing period for the primary, then the State Board of Elections shall designate a special filing period of one week for candidates for the office. If more than two candidates file and qualify for the office in accordance with G.S. 163-323, then the Board shall conduct the election for the office as follows:

(1)   When the vacancy described in this section occurs more than 63 days before the date of the second primary for members of the General Assembly, a special primary shall be held on the same day as the second primary. The two candidates with the most votes in the special primary shall have their names placed on the ballot for the general election held on the same day as the general election for members of the General Assembly.

(2)   When the vacancy described in this section occurs less than 64 days before the date of the second primary, a general election for all the candidates shall be held on the same day as the general election for members of the General Assembly and the results shall be determined on a plurality basis as provided by G.S. 163-292.

(3)   Repealed by Session Laws 2013-381, s. 51.1, effective January 1, 2014.

(c)   Applicable Provisions. - Except as provided in this section, the provisions of this Article apply to elections conducted under this section.

(d)   Rules. - The State Board of Elections shall adopt rules for the implementation of this section. The rules are not subject to Article 2A of Chapter 150B of the General Statutes. The rules shall include the following:

(1) If after the first-choice candidate is eliminated, a ballot does not indicate one of the uneliminated candidates as an alternative choice, the ballot is exhausted and shall not be counted after the initial round.

(2) The fact that the voter does not designate a second or third choice does not invalidate the voter's higher choice or choices.

(3) The fact that the voter gives more than one ranking to the same candidate shall not invalidate the vote. The highest ranking given a particular candidate shall count as long as the candidate is not eliminated.

(4) In case of a tie between candidates such that two or more candidates have an equal number of first choices and more than two candidates qualify for the second round, instant runoff voting shall be used to determine which two candidates shall advance to the second round. (1996, 2nd Ex. Sess., c. 9, s. 7; 2001-403, s. 12.1; 2002-158, s. 7; 2006-192, s. 8(a); 2013-381, s. 51.1.)

§ 163-330. Voting in primary.

Any person who will become qualified by age to register and vote in the general election for which the primary is held, even though not so qualified by the date of the primary, shall be entitled to register for the primary and general election prior to the primary and then to vote in the primary after being registered. Such person may register not earlier than 60 days nor later than the last day for making application to register under G.S. 163-82.6(c) prior to the primary. (1996, 2nd Ex. Sess., c. 9, s. 7; 2009-541, s. 26; 2013-381, s. 16.8.)

§ 163-331. Date of primary.

The primary shall be held on the same date as established for primary elections under G.S. 163-1(b). (1996, 2nd Ex. Sess., c. 9, s. 7.)

§ 163-332. Ballots.

(a) General. - In elections there shall be official ballots. The ballots shall be printed to conform to the requirement of G.S. 163-165.6(c) and to show the name of each person who has filed notice of candidacy, and the office for which each aspirant is a candidate.

Only those who have filed the required notice of candidacy with the proper board of elections, and who have paid the required filing fee or qualified by petition, shall have their names printed on the official primary ballots. Only those candidates properly nominated shall have their names appear on the official general election ballots.

(b) Ballots to Be Furnished by County Board of Elections. - It shall be the duty of the county board of elections to print official ballots for the following offices to be voted for in the primary:

Justice of the Supreme Court.

Judge of the Court of Appeals.

Superior court judge.

District court judge.

In printing ballots, the county board of elections shall be governed by instructions of the State Board of Elections with regard to width, color, kind of paper, form, and size of type.

Three days before the election, the chairman of the county board of elections shall distribute official ballots to the chief judge of each precinct in his county, and the chief judge shall give a receipt for the ballots received. On the day of the primary, it shall be the chief judge's duty to have all the ballots so delivered available for use at the precinct voting place. (1996, 2nd Ex. Sess., c. 9, s. 7; 2001-403, s. 1; 2001-460, s. 9; 2002-158, s. 7.)

§ 163-333: Repealed by Session Laws 2001-398, s. 15.

§ 163-334. Counting of ballots.

Counting of ballots in primaries and elections held under this Article shall be under the same rules as for counting of ballots in nonpartisan municipal elections under Article 24 of this Chapter. (1996, 2nd Ex. Sess., c. 9, s. 7.)

§ 163-335. Other rules.

Except as provided by this Article, the conduct of elections shall be governed by Subchapter VI of this Chapter. (1996, 2nd Ex. Sess., c. 9, s. 7.)

Vision Books Order Form

Fax Orders:	1-980-299-5965
Phone Orders:	1-704-898-0770
E-mail Orders:	www.visionbooks.org
Mail Orders:	Vision Books, LLC P.O. Box 42406 Charlotte, NC 28215

Shipp To:
Name_____
Address_____
City_____State_____Zip_____
Phone_____Fax_____
Email_____@_____

Bill To: We can bill a third party on your behalf.
Name_____
Address_____
City_____State_____Zip_____
Phone____(_____)_____Fax_____
Email_____@_____

Pamphlet Number ($15.00 Each)	Qty	Total Cost
_____	_____	_____
_____	_____	_____
_____	_____	_____
_____	_____	_____
_____	_____	_____
_____	_____	_____
_____	_____	_____
<u>Full Volume Set 1-92</u>	<u>92 Pamphlets</u>	<u>1,380.00</u>

Free Shipping & Handling on Full Volume Orders
Add $1.00 Shipping & Handling Per Pamphlet $_____

Total Cost $_____

Thank you for your support. Management!

DID YOU ENJOY THIS BOOK?

Vision Books, LLC would like to hear from you! If you or someone you know has been fasely imprisoned, we would like to hear your story. If the 'North Carolina Criminal Law and Procedure' has had an effect in your life or if you have suggestions, we would like to hear from you. Send your letters to:

Vision Books, LLC
Attn: Staff Writers
P.O. Box 42406
Charlotte, NC 28215
Email: staff@visionbooks.org

Order Additional Copies:

Fax Orders:	1-980-299-5965
Phone Orders:	1-704-898-0770
E-mail Orders:	www.visionbooks.org
Mail Orders:	Vision Books, LLC P.O. Box 42406 Charlotte, NC 28215

www.ingramcontent.com/pod-product-compliance
Lightning Source LLC
Chambersburg PA
CBHW051624170526
45167CB00001B/57